The Life of the Author: D. H. Lawrence

THE LIFE OF THE AUTHOR

This new series aims to transform literary biography from its status as a resource for facts and details to that of a dynamic, innovative aspect of teaching, criticism and research. Outside universities lives of writers are by far the most popular genre of books about literature, but within them they are neglected as a focus for interpretation and as frameworks for advanced research. *The Life of the Author* will reverse this imbalance by exploring new questions on how and why our conception of the author frames our evaluation and understanding of their work.

New books in this series

The Life of the Author: D. H. Lawrence
The Life of the Author: Jane Austen
The Life of the Author: Charles Dickens
The Life of the Author: John Milton
The Life of the Author: Maya Angelou
The Life of the Author: William Shakespeare
The Life of the Author: Nathaniel Hawthorne

The Life of the Author: D. H. Lawrence

Andrew Harrison

WILEY Blackwell

This edition first published 2024

Registered Office(s)
John Wiley & Sons, Inc., 111 River Street, Hoboken, NJ 07030, USA
John Wiley & Sons Ltd, The Atrium, Southern Gate, Chichester, West Sussex, PO19 8SQ, UK

For details of our global editorial offices, customer services, and more information about Wiley products, visit us at www.wiley.com.

Wiley also publishes its books in a variety of electronic formats and by print-on-demand. Some content that appears in standard print versions of this book may not be available in other formats.

Library of Congress Cataloging-in-Publication Data Applied for
Paperback ISBN: 9781119669531

Cover Design: Wiley
Cover Image: D. H. Lawrence in Chapala, Mexico, 1923. University of Nottingham, Manuscripts and Special Collections, La Wb 1/9.

Set in 9.5/12.5pt STIXTwoText by Straive, Pondicherry, India
Printed and bound by CPI Group (UK) Ltd, Croydon, CR0 4YY

C9781119669531_150324

For my father, Albert Edward Harrison (1932–1973).

Contents

List of Illustrations

Preface

This book does not follow the traditional biographical model of providing a detailed linear narrative of the life of D. H. Lawrence from birth to death. There are many scholarly and popular biographies of the author that offer more or less comprehensive accounts of his life; readers can find these listed in the Bibliography.[1] I address here some of the ways in which Lawrence's life can illuminate his writing (and vice versa). The book is organised chronologically, focusing on nine important subjects in the author's life and writing. Chapters 1–3 cover Lawrence's early life up to his completion of the first version of *Women in Love* in November 1916, while Chapters 6–9 deal with his writings from the spring of 1917 to the end of his life; Chapters 4 and 5 offer a reflective interlude, considering subjects which became particularly pressing for Lawrence during the war years, but which occupy a central position across his career, namely his treatment of taboo topics, his conflicted relationship to the literary marketplace and the censorship of his work, and his attitudes to sex, sexuality and sexual identity. In each chapter, details from the biographical record are drawn upon to provide interpretive contexts for the close analyses of texts. The coverage of texts is necessarily selective, but I have tried to offer fresh readings of Lawrence's work in different genres. Although seven of the nine chapters are strictly chronological, the issues addressed are clearly relevant to more than one period in the author's life, and I hope readers will be stimulated to extend my approach and find resonances of their own as they read (or re-read) Lawrence's writing.

Students and general readers encountering Lawrence's work for the first time could be forgiven for being intimidated by the sheer volume of his writing, and by the extensive biographical and critical industries that have grown up around the man and his work. Although Lawrence died at the age of 44, he was a prodigiously industrious author. During his lifetime, he published eleven novels, eight volumes of poetry plus *Collected Poems*, six volumes of short stories and novellas, three plays, three books of travel writings, a school history textbook, two books on psychology, a volume of critical essays on American literature, a volume of reflective philosophical essays, a volume of his paintings and four books of translations from Italian into English. He also helped his friend S. S. Koteliansky to complete translations of two works from Russian into English. A simple list of this kind is, however, misleading, since Lawrence also published extensively in magazines, journals and newspapers, a good number of his writings were not published during his lifetime, and some works were very close to completion or in production at the time of his death. In addition, he wrote reviews plus several introductions to the books of friends and contacts. The Cambridge University Press Edition of Lawrence's works runs to 40 volumes (1980–2018). These include his unfinished and abandoned novel *Mr Noon* and early versions of four of his published novels. The Cambridge University Press Edition of his letters comprises eight volumes (1979–2000), containing over 5500 letters, and further correspondence which has come to light since 2000 is being published on an annual basis in the *Journal of D. H. Lawrence Studies* (2006–present).

In his novel *Dubin's Lives* (1979), Bernard Malamud describes the feeling of trepidation which his central character, the biographer William Dubin, feels as he contemplates beginning a book about Lawrence, and thinks of how many writings by and about his subject he will need to assimilate: 'Sometimes he felt like an ant about to eat an oak tree' (Malamud 1979: 20). Dubin is intensely aware of all the published biographies of Lawrence and volumes of criticism about him: he reflects that Lawrence is 'so vastly written about – someone had said second to Shakespeare; or if not second, third, Samuel Johnson intervening' (Malamud 1979: 19). It is sobering to think that Malamud's novel was published in the same year as the first volume of the Cambridge Edition. How much more cause for trepidation might Dubin have had if he was contemplating the task in the wake of that Edition, and with the added weight of the criticism and scholarship that has appeared since 1979?

Fortunately, the Cambridge Edition has revivified Lawrence studies. The renewed attention it has brought to Lawrence's life and work, and the different perspectives and approaches it has opened up, have made him at once a more accessible and appealing author. In the 1970s, Lawrence's reputation was at a low point. F. R. Leavis's earlier championing of him as a normative moralist in the 'Great Tradition' of English fiction had been challenged by scholars in Britain and the United States who emphasised the nihilistic qualities in his writing, and complications in his moral outlook.[2] Kate Millett's feminist attack on Lawrence in her influential 1970 book *Sexual Politics* had cast a shadow over his reputation inside and outside academia. The Cambridge Edition of his works moved the emphasis away from Lawrence as a moralist, propagandist and prophetic figure to focus instead on his painstaking methods of composition and his earnest and enterprising engagements with the publishing industry. As each new volume of the letters appeared, people began to see in detail the extent of his involvement with contemporary literary culture and the literary marketplace. Lawrence went from being viewed exclusively as a tortured genius at odds with his contemporary society, or a troubled soul with psychological hang-ups, to being appreciated as a fully modern author just as committed to his craft as contemporaries like James Joyce and Virginia Woolf.

This transformation in our way of understanding Lawrence has generated revisionary interpretations of his writing. Critics have reassessed his response to a whole range of subjects, from women, his contemporaries, and creativity, to psychoanalysis, translation, science, philosophy, and travel and cultural difference. Various helpful introductory guides and volumes of essays have been published on his relationship to contemporary aesthetic and social or cultural contexts.[3] Where second-wave feminism created an atmosphere of hostility to Lawrence as a cultural icon and spokesperson on sex, the recent intensification of concern for the environment and the experience of the global Coronavirus pandemic have created renewed interest in Lawrence and ecology, and Lawrence and mental health.[4]

Scholarly biographies written in the wake of the Cambridge Edition have offered much fuller and more detailed accounts of Lawrence's writing life, reflecting the sheer energy and courage he put into supporting himself and his wife as a professional author who was never popular, and who dared to challenge attitudes to the body, sex and censorship.[5] They have also sought to correct some powerful misconceptions. The story of the working-class man who eloped with an aristocrat has been subjected to necessary revision. John Worthen has stressed the complexity of Lawrence's relationship to Eastwood and to the working class.[6] He has also established that Lawrence and Frieda's departure together to Germany in May 1912 was 'very far from being an elopement' (Worthen 1991: 393), and he has comprehensively dismantled any suggestion that the Frieda Weekley whom Lawrence met in March 1912 was an aristocrat.[7] Another enduring misconception about Lawrence is that he was in denial about the diagnosis of tuberculosis with which he was confronted in Mexico City in March 1925. David Ellis has shown just how blunt a term 'denial' is to describe the reactions of a man whose only hope was remission, and who faced not only 'the moral stigma attached to the disease' (Ellis 2008: 24) but limitations on his freedom to travel from openly admitting that he had tuberculosis.[8] Ellis has even emphasised the difficulty involved in clearly establishing the cause of Lawrence's death, since tuberculosis, recurrent bouts of bronchitis and pleurisy were all implicated in his final illness.

Despite these efforts to revise myths and misconceptions, they continue to be reproduced in literary criticism. This book aims to foreground several areas of complication and contention in the biographical record, showing how they can generate a fresh understanding of Lawrence's writing. A careful, inclusive and questioning approach to biographical sources is necessary in order to avoid condemning Lawrence as a traitor to the working class and as unequivocally sexist, racist and fascistic, or conversely making him over into a fourth-wave feminist, an environmental activist or a mental health specialist *avant la lettre*. Acknowledging the complexity of Lawrence's relationship to the working class, his attitude to suffragism, his responsiveness to the natural world and wavering relation to discourses of otherness and race, and his concern not with conventional medical cures for physical ailments but with wholeness of being and the healing of psychic wounds, opens up his writing to discussion and renewed engagement rather than closing it down in the rush to damn the author as reactionary or praise him as prescient and forward-thinking. The approach adopted here is to move from a considered engagement with biographical detail to an alert and questioning reading of Lawrence's writing.

The use of biography to inform critical readings of Lawrence's works is so entrenched within Lawrence studies that it seems strange to reflect on or attempt to justify the method. Life and writing seem so intermingled in Lawrence's case that one naturally moves between the two. Several of the leading Lawrence scholars since F. R. Leavis have written biographies of Lawrence in the course of their careers as Lawrence critics and/or editors of his works and letters. Lawrence is a writer who engaged explicitly and energetically with pressing issues in his contemporary world, and he used his writing to gain a purchase on these issues. His vocation as an author was premised upon challenging the views of readers and in the process undermining what he saw as the unthinking attitudes of the Establishment. In reading Lawrence's work, we enter a world which is clearly informed by his multifaceted perspectives. One does not need to know very much about Lawrence to be aware that what one is reading is presented through the prism of a distinctive consciousness. Richard Aldington once described Lawrence as 'the most personal of writers', suggesting that his 'books become more intelligible, more vivid, even than they are without such help, if they are related to what is known of his personality and his life history'.[9] When I first taught a module on Lawrence in 1998 at the University of East Anglia, one disconcerted student told me how much she was struggling to read Lawrence's novels because she sensed that there was a key to understanding them which she did not possess. I now see this as a very perceptive response to the way in which Lawrence's worldview is subtly embedded in the texture of his fiction. Engaging with that worldview offers keys with which to unlock his work.

Lawrence realised and worked through his responses to contemporary issues in his writing. Writing, for him, was a means of understanding his experiences, and of externalising and transforming feelings of self-division, powerlessness, disgust and rage. This is surely what Lawrence meant when he said that his motto was 'Art for my sake' (*1L* 491). Writing was also, of course, a means of adopting different voices, perspectives and personae. It offered Lawrence a way of escaping from, or critiquing, his own views and modes of life, and of considering alternative paths he might have taken or could take in the future. The characters in Lawrence's fiction who seem most autobiographical (from Cyril Beardsall to Paul Morel, Rupert Birkin, Rawdon Lilly, Richard Lovatt Somers, Clifford Chatterley and Oliver Mellors) are often satirised or subjected to irony or harsh criticism. The speakers in his poetry must be approached as provisional voices offering particular windows onto the world, even where (as in some of the late verse) they express views in a disarmingly frank and apparently unironic manner which we might be tempted to see as unproblematically authorial.

James Joyce is said to have told his French translator that in *Ulysses* he had 'put in so many enigmas and puzzles that it will keep the professors busy for centuries arguing over what I meant, and that's the only way of insuring one's immortality' (Ellmann 1982: 521). Lawrence might have said the same about the teasing manner in which he combined fiction and autobiography. Jessie Chambers (the closest friend of Lawrence's youth, his sometime partner, and the person with whom he shared his early reading and writing) records how, as a young man, Lawrence spoke with her about George Borrow: 'He said that Borrow had mingled autobiography and fiction so inextricably in *Lavengro* that the most astute critics could not be sure where the one ended and the other began. From his subtle smile I felt he was wondering whether he might not do something in the same fashion himself' (Chambers 1935: 110). In his writing, Lawrence often drew very closely on his own life and the lives of others. Events in his fiction frequently map onto events in his life, or in the lives of family, friends and contacts; he used the names of people and places he knew, sometimes literally, sometimes in a disguised or composite form, and he modelled some of his most memorable characters on real-life individuals. His wife Frieda liked to feel that she was a powerful presence in some of his texts and welcomed being fictionalised as (for example) Ursula Brangwen in *The Rainbow* and *Women in Love*, Johanna Keighley in *Mr Noon*, Tanny Lilly in *Aaron's Rod* and Harriett Somers in *Kangaroo*. The Armenian author Dikran Kouyoumdjian (better known under his pen name Michael Arlen) is said to have been happy to serve as the model for the Irish playwright Michaelis in *Lady Chatterley's Lover*.[10] Others were deeply hurt and angry when they recognised themselves in his work, including Jessie Chambers (depicted as Miriam Leivers in *Sons and Lovers*), Philip Heseltine (depicted as Julius Halliday in *Women in Love*), Lady Ottoline Morrell (depicted as Hermione Roddice in the same novel) and Compton Mackenzie (depicted as Cameron Gee in 'Two Blue Birds' and Cathcart in 'The Man Who Loved Islands'). Lawrence was unapologetic about drawing in his fiction on his own life and the lives of his contacts. The only piece of writing we know he had scruples about publishing because of its potentially hurtful fictionalised depiction of real-life individuals was his novella *The Virgin and the Gipsy*, which contains a cruel portrayal of Frieda's first husband, Ernest Weekley, and his family, and Lawrence apparently chose not to publish this because of the problems it might create for Frieda's daughters by Weekley rather than the impact it might have on Weekley himself.[11]

Lawrence's unflattering depiction in his fiction of people he knew, especially those who had offered him emotional and practical and/or financial support, still has the power to incite strong criticism of him on moral grounds. There are two points which we should consider, however, before rushing to judgement of him. Firstly, as I have noted, he frequently depicted himself in a strongly critical and satirical manner, and he upheld the right of others to depict him in any way they wished in their own creative work. Secondly, with the significant exception of *Sons and Lovers*, truthfulness to life was not a value by which he measured his art. In the process of writing *Sons and Lovers*, he asked Jessie Chambers to provide him with her own account of events in their early life together, and the notes she provided informed his revision of his novel. It is understandable, then, that she should have seen the published text as an act of betrayal. In this case, however, we might say that in the process of re-shaping his novel Lawrence moved beyond an attempt to be faithful to the past and looked instead to reflect on the ways in which his own early experiences, and those of his central protagonist, revealed the damaging nature and consequences of excessive spiritual love between mothers and sons. From this point on, Lawrence's interest would lie in exploring through his writing the important contemporary resonances of his own experiences, and of the experiences of others.

The nearest Lawrence came to drawing literally on his life in his fiction was in the second part of *Mr Noon*. This text was arguably abandoned because he failed to find in it the broader significance of his experiences, so it lacked the necessary thread or idea which would enable it to cohere as a work of art. In his published works, autobiographical elements and details drawn from life are incorporated and transformed in a manner which allows him to address themes which he considered central to his contemporary world, whether it was the restlessness and rebellion of the modern woman in *The Rainbow*, the war spirit in *Women in Love*, the need for post-war political reform in *Kangaroo*, or the need to re-connect with our bodies and sex as an antidote to the abstracting qualities of modernity and the mass media in *Lady Chatterley's Lover*.

Writing was never, then, a simple matter of self-expression for Lawrence. By drawing on and embellishing in his writing the experiences and viewpoints of both himself and others, Lawrence sought to create the shifting patterns and relative significance which he came to see as central constituents of fully-realised art. In his essay 'Morality and the Novel' (1925), he declares that it is immoral for the artist to use art to project specific moral values. Art, like life, should be about realising ever-changing relationships in the moment.[12] Whether or not Lawrence always succeeds in avoiding using fiction to advance his own values is an open question, of course, but generations of students have discovered sufficient grounds in *Sons and Lovers* for sympathising with Miriam Leivers and criticising Paul Morel, or found Rupert Birkin in *Women in Love* verbose and absurd, and gravitated towards Gerald Crich as its compelling tragic hero, or found themselves identifying at times with Clifford Chatterley and recoiling at others from the snobbishness of Constance Chatterley or the abrasive bitterness and sexual brutality of Oliver Mellors. Great art opens out onto complexity, causing us to question the grounds for our moral judgements.

Lawrence's sense of the irreducible complexity of art informed his strong reaction against literary criticism which claimed to 'explain' his writing or to paraphrase its meaning or significance. As he famously declared: 'If you try to nail anything down, in the novel, either it kills the novel, or the novel gets up and walks away with the nail' (*STH* 172). He told a friend that he 'hated' a lengthy Freudian appreciation of *Sons and Lovers* by the American psychoanalyst and critic Alfred Booth Kuttner: 'My poor book: it was, as art, a fairly complete truth: so they carve a half lie out of it, and say "Voilà". Swine!' (*2L* 655). In *Mr Noon*, the novel with an equal claim to being autobiographical, he anticipated the attentions of the psychoanalysing critic and directly addressed his reader in a combative fashion, telling her: 'you can't sniff out any specific why or any specific wherefore, with your carrion-smelling psycho-analysing nose, because there *is* no why and wherefore' (*MN* 205). This shows Lawrence's keen awareness, by early 1921, of the intrusive presumption of critics who would scan his more autobiographical fiction for symptoms of the author's psychological ailments and hang-ups, and of the prurience of censors on the lookout for salacious details with which to confirm their preconceptions about the obscenity of his mind and his work. By directly addressing his readers in this fashion, he was attempting to undermine their interpretive complacency and challenging them to discover *any* strand of meaning or logic in his text. In the case of *Mr Noon*, one could argue that the extent of his self-awareness was harmful to the text, since his determination to resist his readers' discovery of any 'why' or 'wherefore' prevented him too from discovering any central threads of significance in his use of autobiographical material.

Lawrence was not usually inclined to explain his prose fiction, unless it was to defend the form and structure of his early work to friends and literary advisors. The published and unpublished forewords and introductions he wrote to accompany his fiction, poetry and paintings draw attention to some strands of meaning in the texts and art, and to the contexts in which we can understand them, but never in a reductive or prescriptive way. Again, however, there is a significant exception to the rule. The furore caused by *Lady Chatterley's Lover*, and the action of pirate publishers in profiteering from it, drove Lawrence to articulate his motives in writing the novel. In 'My Skirmish with Jolly Roger', first published as a foreword to the Paris Popular Edition of the novel, and then in the revised and greatly extended version known as *A Propos of 'Lady Chatterley's Lover'*, he underscored the ambition of the novel, emphasising (for example) his desire to reclaim the four-letter words as healthy descriptive terms for the body and sex, and the urgent need to think clearly and wholesomely about sex as a means of addressing the counterfeit emotions of cinema, journalism and popular fiction. Perhaps Lawrence's sense of the author's moral responsibility to avoid using art as propaganda was offset in this case by the perceived urgency of these issues. He finally decided not to publish the extended essay, and it did not appear in print until late June 1930, over three months after his death.[13] Any attentive reader attempting to use the essay to nail down the novel will certainly find it getting up and walking away with the nail.

Lawrence was the first to admit to his own inconsistency.[14] Here, as elsewhere in Lawrence, we are confronted with complexity, contradiction and paradox. It is these qualities in the man and his writing that make him such an unsettling, provocative and enlivening subject for biography and criticism. The following chapters seek to foreground the complexities of key issues in Lawrence biography, using them to open up the writing to new perspectives and approaches, recognising contradictions and paradoxes as critical elements both in the author's identity and in the nature of his texts as fully-realised works of art.

Notes

1 The most detailed and reliable account of Lawrence's life is still that provided in the three-volume Cambridge biography (Worthen 1991; Kinkead-Weekes 1996; Ellis 1998).
2 See Spilka (1964). Widmer (1962), for example, emphasised the nihilism in Lawrence's writing, while Clarke (1969) focused on complications and paradoxes.
3 See, for example, Poplawski (1996), Becket (2002), Harrison (2018a), Brown and Reid (2020) and Grice (2024).
4 See, for example, Gifford (2023) and Feigel (2022).
5 In addition to the Cambridge biography, see Worthen (1989), Worthen (2005) and Harrison (2016).
6 See Worthen (1986) and Worthen (1991).
7 See Worthen (1995).
8 Ellis notes that shortly before Lawrence left Mexico for the United States following his diagnosis, the US 'government had . . . passed legislation aimed at preventing anyone with tuberculosis from coming into the country' (Ellis 2008: 25). Lawrence used rouge to mask the pallor of his cheeks, but he was still subjected to medical inspection at the border and only admitted back into the country on a six-month visa.

9 Transcription from 'Son and Lover: A Portrait of D. H. Lawrence', The Third Programme, BBC Radio, 8 May 1955. La Av 3/2/2 (University of Nottingham).

10 Edward Titus to D. H. Lawrence (9 September 1929): 'Mike is a tremendous admirer of you and he feels greatly elated at having served you as one of the characters in Lady Chatterly [*sic*]' (*7L* 475–476 fn. 6).

11 See *VG* xxiii.

12 See *STH* 175: 'It is the *relation itself* which is the quick and the central clue to life, not the man, nor the woman, nor the children that result from the relationship, as a contingency'.

13 See *7L* 633 (30 January 1930).

14 See Frieda Lawrence (1934: 61): 'He'd have quick changes of mood and thought. This puzzled me. "But Lawrence, last week you said exactly the opposite of what you are saying now". / "And why shouldn't I? Last week I felt like that, now like this. Why shouldn't I?"

Acknowledgements

I am grateful to Katy Loffman and Lesley Pollinger of Paper Lion Ltd, acting on behalf of the Estate of Frieda Lawrence Ravagli, for permission to quote from the letters and works of D. H. Lawrence. I would like to thank the School of English at the University of Nottingham for granting me a semester of research leave to work on this book, and the Faculty of Arts for awarding me an Arts Research Fellowship which gave me a further semester to complete it. Special thanks to James Moran, Máire ní Fhlathúin and Adam Rounce for their warm collegiality. I extend thanks to the Series Editor, Richard Bradford, for his kind support and unfailing encouragement, to Nicole Allen, Pascal Raj Francois and Liz Wingett at Wiley-Blackwell for all their help, and to Sivasri Chandrasekaran for her diligent copy-editing. My sincerest gratitude to Hayley Cotterill and all the staff in Manuscripts and Special Collections at the University of Nottingham for their support of my research, and especially to Amy Bowler, Mark Bentley and Catherine Martin for their help with the images. I have benefited greatly from the support and camaraderie offered to me by the D. H. Lawrence Societies of Great Britain and North America, and by Carolyn Melbourne and the staff at the D. H. Lawrence Birthplace Museum. I gratefully acknowledge the assistance of the three anonymous readers who provided astute and helpful feedback on the penultimate draft of the book. My thanks also go to my mother for her constant love and guidance, to John Worthen for his continued support of my work on Lawrence, and to Annalise Grice for discussing with me the materials and arguments developed in the book. I take sole responsibility for all shortcomings in the finished volume.

List of Abbreviations

Quotations from the letters and works of D. H. Lawrence in the main text and notes refer readers to the Cambridge Edition of the author's works using the short forms listed below.

Letters of D. H. Lawrence

1L — *The Letters of D. H. Lawrence Volume I: September 1901–May 1913*, ed. James T. Boulton. Cambridge: Cambridge UP, 1979.

2L — *The Letters of D. H. Lawrence Volume II: June 1913–October 1916*, ed. George J. Zytaruk and James T. Boulton. Cambridge: Cambridge UP, 1981.

3L — *The Letters of D. H. Lawrence Volume III: October 1916–June 1921*, ed. James T. Boulton and Andrew Robertson. Cambridge: Cambridge UP, 1984.

4L — *The Letters of D. H. Lawrence Volume IV: June 1921–March 1924*, ed. Warren Roberts, James T. Boulton and Elizabeth Mansfield. Cambridge: Cambridge UP, 1987.

5L — *The Letters of D. H. Lawrence Volume V: March 1924–March 1927*, ed. James T. Boulton and Lindeth Vasey. Cambridge: Cambridge UP, 1989.

6L — *The Letters of D. H. Lawrence Volume VI: March 1927–November 1928*, ed. James T. Boulton and Margaret H. Boulton with Gerald M. Lacy. Cambridge: Cambridge UP, 1991.

7L — *The Letters of D. H. Lawrence Volume VII: November 1928–February 1930*, ed. Keith Sagar and James T. Boulton. Cambridge: Cambridge UP, 1993.

8L — *The Letters of D. H. Lawrence Volume VIII: Previously Uncollected Letters and General Index*, ed. James T. Boulton. Cambridge: Cambridge UP, 2000.

Works of D. H. Lawrence

A	*Apocalypse and the Writings on Revelation*, ed. Mara Kalnins. Cambridge: Cambridge UP, 1980.
AR	*Aaron's Rod*, ed. Mara Kalnins. Cambridge: Cambridge UP, 1988.
BB	*The Boy in the Bush*, with M. L. Skinner, ed. Paul Eggert. Cambridge: Cambridge UP, 1990.
EmyE	*England, My England and Other Stories*, ed. Bruce Steele. Cambridge: Cambridge UP, 1990.
FLC	*The First and Second Lady Chatterley Novels*, ed. Dieter Mehl and Christa Jansohn. Cambridge: Cambridge UP, 1999.
Fox	*The Fox, The Captain's Doll, The Ladybird*, ed. Dieter Mehl. Cambridge: Cambridge UP, 1992.
FWL	*The First 'Women in Love'*, ed. John Worthen and Lindeth Vasey. Cambridge: Cambridge UP, 1998.
IR	*Introductions and Reviews*, ed. N. H. Reeve and John Worthen. Cambridge: Cambridge UP, 2005.
K	*Kangaroo*, ed. Bruce Steele. Cambridge: Cambridge UP, 1994.
LAH	*Love Among the Haystacks and Other Stories*, ed. John Worthen. Cambridge: Cambridge UP, 1987.
LCL	*Lady Chatterley's Lover and A Propos of 'Lady Chatterley's Lover'*, ed. Michael Squires. Cambridge: Cambridge UP, 1993.
LEA	*Late Essays and Articles*, ed. James T. Boulton. Cambridge: Cambridge UP, 2004.
LG	*The Lost Girl*, ed. John Worthen. Cambridge: Cambridge UP, 1981.
MEH	*Movements in European History*, ed. Philip Crumpton. Cambridge: Cambridge UP, 1989.
MM	*Mornings in Mexico and Other Essays*, ed. Virginia Crosswhite Hyde. Cambridge: Cambridge UP, 2009.
MN	*Mr Noon*, ed. Lindeth Vasey. Cambridge: Cambridge UP, 1984.
Paintings	*The Paintings of D. H. Lawrence*. London: Mandrake Press, 1929.
PFU	*Psychoanalysis and the Unconscious and Fantasia of the Unconscious*, ed. Bruce Steele. Cambridge: Cambridge UP, 2004.
Plays	*The Plays*, ed. Hans-Wilhelm Schwarze and John Worthen. Cambridge: Cambridge UP, 1999.
PM	*Paul Morel*, ed. Helen Baron. Cambridge: Cambridge UP, 2003.
PO	*The Prussian Officer and Other Stories*, ed. John Worthen. Cambridge: Cambridge UP, 1983.
Poems	*The Poems*. 3 Vols., ed. Christopher Pollnitz. Cambridge: Cambridge UP, 2013, 2018.
PS	*The Plumed Serpent*, ed. L. D. Clark. Cambridge: Cambridge UP, 1987.

Q	*Quetzalcoatl*, ed. N. H. Reeve. Cambridge: Cambridge UP, 2011.
R	*The Rainbow*, ed. Mark Kinkead-Weekes. Cambridge: Cambridge UP, 1989.
RDP	*Reflections on the Death of a Porcupine and Other Essays*, ed. Michael Herbert. Cambridge: Cambridge UP, 1988.
SCAL	*Studies in Classic American Literature*, ed. Ezra Greenspan, Lindeth Vasey and John Worthen. Cambridge: Cambridge UP, 2003.
SEP	*Sketches of Etruscan Places and Other Italian Essays*, ed. Simonetta de Filippis. Cambridge: Cambridge UP, 1992.
SL	*Sons and Lovers*, ed. Helen Baron and Carl Baron. Cambridge: Cambridge UP, 1992.
SM	*St. Mawr and Other Stories*, ed. Brian Finney. Cambridge: Cambridge UP, 1983.
SS	*Sea and Sardinia*, ed. Mara Kalnins. Cambridge: Cambridge UP, 1997.
STH	*Study of Thomas Hardy and Other Essays*, ed. Bruce Steele. Cambridge: Cambridge UP, 1985.
T	*The Trespasser*, ed. Elizabeth Mansfield. Cambridge: Cambridge UP, 1981.
TI	*Twilight in Italy and Other Essays*, ed. Paul Eggert. Cambridge: Cambridge UP, 1994.
VG	*The Virgin and the Gipsy and Other Stories*, ed. Michael Herbert, Bethan Jones and Lindeth Vasey. Cambridge: Cambridge UP, 2006.
VicG	*The Vicar's Garden and Other Stories*, ed. N. H. Reeve. Cambridge: Cambridge UP, 2009.
WL	*Women in Love*, ed. David Farmer, Lindeth Vasey and John Worthen. Cambridge: Cambridge UP, 1987.
WP	*The White Peacock*, ed. Andrew Robertson. Cambridge: Cambridge UP, 1983.
WWRA	*The Woman Who Rode Away and Other Stories*, ed. Dieter Mehl and Christa Jansohn. Cambridge: Cambridge UP, 1995.

1

Lawrence, Eastwood and Working-Class Experience

The story of D. H. Lawrence's first meeting with Ford Madox Hueffer[1] in September 1909, and of how Hueffer accepted Lawrence's work for publication in the journal he was then editing, the *English Review*, and became Lawrence's mentor, has often been told. This was one of two truly transformational events in Lawrence's early life, the other being his meeting with Frieda Weekley in early March 1912. They were pivotal moments in Lawrence's development as a person and an author, and as such they feature centrally in the biographies.

For their accounts of the context to Lawrence's meeting with Hueffer, biographers have had to rely on Jessie Chambers's memoir, *D. H. Lawrence: A Personal Record* (1935), while the only source which deals with the meeting itself is Hueffer's essay on Lawrence in his *Portraits from Life* (1937). Jessie recalls how Lawrence introduced the *English Review* to her family when he returned to Eastwood, the mining town on the Nottinghamshire-Derbyshire border where he was born, to spend Christmas with his family at the end of his first term as an elementary school teacher at Davidson Road School in Croydon, south-east London. This would have been sometime between 23 December 1908 and 10 January 1909. He must have shown them the first number of the journal, of December 1908, which contained contributions from (among others) Thomas Hardy, Henry James, Joseph Conrad, John Galsworthy and H. G. Wells. Jessie notes that they were 'delighted' with the *English Review*, and with her father's backing they decided to subscribe to it. She 'soon noticed that the Editor was prepared to welcome new talent' (Chambers 1935: 156) and she 'begged' Lawrence to submit some of his work, 'but he refused absolutely', stating that he was not anxious to 'get into print', and in any case the journal would 'never take it'. He agreed, however, to let her submit on his behalf any of his work she chose, so long as she gave him a *nom de plume*, since he said he did not want 'folk in Croydon to know I write poetry'.

The Life of the Author: D. H. Lawrence, First Edition. Andrew Harrison.

Jessie picked out what she thought were the best poems Lawrence had sent to her since he left Eastwood to take up his teaching post in early October 1908. She copied them out 'one beautiful June morning' in 1909. She chose 'Discipline', 'Dreams Old and Nascent' and 'Baby-Movements', plus 'several other poems whose titles I don't remember'; she placed 'Discipline' first because she thought 'the unusual title might attract the Editor's attention' (Chambers 1935: 157). 'Discipline' and 'Dreams Old and Nascent' were poems dealing with Lawrence's early experiences as a teacher; 'Baby-Movements' was inspired by his affection for Hilda Mary Jones, the second daughter of John and Marie Jones (the couple in whose home he lodged in Croydon). In her cover letter, Jessie described Lawrence as 'a young man who had been writing for a number of years, and who would be very grateful for any recognition'; she gave his name 'but said that if any of the poems were printed they should appear under the *nom de plume* of Richard Greasley (Richards was an unacknowledged name of Lawrence's, and Greasley was his home parish)' (Chambers 1935: 158).[2]

Hueffer's reply arrived at some point between 1 and 14 August, while Lawrence was on holiday with his family on the Isle of Wight. Hueffer found the poems 'very interesting' and felt that the author had 'undoubted talent', but he injected a note of caution into his praise, commenting that 'nowadays luck played such a large part in a literary career'. He said that if Jessie would get Lawrence 'to come and see me some time when he is in London perhaps something might be done'. Jessie replied that when Lawrence was back from his holiday she was 'sure he would be glad to call on Mr Hueffer'. Soon after 14 August, she gave him Hueffer's letter. He murmured to her '*You* are my luck' and took it to show his mother. Jessie 'never saw it again' (Chambers 1935: 158–159).

Lawrence travelled back to Croydon on Sunday 29 August and began teaching the following day. Jessie states that Lawrence went to see Hueffer in September. If so, the meeting happened at some point between Wednesday 1 September and Saturday 11 September. Unfortunately, Hueffer's account of the meeting, which took place at 84 Holland Park Avenue, his flat above a fishmonger and poulterer's shop which doubled as the offices of the *English Review*, is very brief and unreliable, for reasons which will soon become clear. He recalled that after Lawrence's arrival was announced by his secretary, Olive Thomas, his visitor stood in the doorway, like a fox 'going to make a raid on the hen-roost before him' (Ford 1937: 76). Hueffer records Lawrence saying 'This isn't my idea, Sir, of an editor's office'. When Hueffer defended his room, describing the 'feeling of thankfulness and satisfaction' he got from coming to it from outdoors, Lawrence is said to have replied: 'That's all very well. But it doesn't look like a place in which one would make money ... The room may be all right for your private tastes ... which aren't mine, though that does not matter. But it isn't one to inspire confidence in creditors. Or contributors' (Ford 1937: 77–78).

What else passed between them, he does not say. Surviving letters suggest, however, that Hueffer was encouraging and supportive. On his twenty-fourth birthday, 11 September, Lawrence reported to Louie Burrows, a friend whose family lived in the village of Cossall, around six miles south-east of Eastwood: 'It is supposed to be a secret, but I guess I shall have to tell you. The editor of the *English Review* has accepted some of my Verses, and wants to put them into the *English Review*, the November issue ... The editor, Ford Madox Hueffer, says he will be glad to read any of the work I like to send him – which is a great relief, is it not?' (*1L* 137–138). He told Jessie that Hueffer was 'fairish, fat, about forty, and the kindest man on earth', and he boasted about the invitations to dinner with 'celebrities' and 'two R.A.s' (Chambers 1935: 163) that accrued from Hueffer's support.

Hueffer stresses Lawrence's 'shynesses' (Ford 1937: 76) in their first meeting. It is quite plausible that Lawrence hid his nervousness about meeting Hueffer by adopting the kind of confident, assertive, even brash demeanour that Hueffer ascribes to him. However, the phrases he puts into Lawrence's mouth are transposed in a revised form from Jessie's account in her memoir of her visit to Croydon almost three months later, on the weekend of 27–28 November, when Lawrence took her to meet Hueffer at his flat before they all went together to have lunch with Hueffer's partner, Violet Hunt, at her home, 'South Lodge', 80 Campden Hill Road.[3] Most of the rest of Hueffer's essay is unreliable too. He states that he read 'The Fox' shortly before writing his essay, which accounts for the image he used for Lawrence's attitude as he stood in the doorway.[4] Hueffer weaves together details from his recent reading of Jessie's memoir and some of Lawrence's writing with vaguely recalled information about Lawrence's early life (perhaps drawing in part on *Sons and Lovers*); he even erroneously suggests that he once met Lawrence's father.[5]

Setting aside the inaccuracies and inventions, however, the main problem with the essay is Hueffer's determination to present the Lawrence he first met as a working-class writer. He takes issue with Jessie by stating that she first wrote to him to ask if he 'would care to see anything – and then should it be poetry or prose' (Ford 1937: 72); he says he requested both, so she sent him the poems together with 'Odour of Chrysanthemums', a story of mining life set in Eastwood which Lawrence actually began writing later in the year. Ford therefore describes his own trepidation on meeting Lawrence as being all to do with class: 'If he really was the son of a working coal-miner, how exactly was I to approach him in conversation?' (Ford 1937: 75). Jessie notes that at Violet Hunt's gathering, Ezra Pound asked Hueffer 'How would *you* speak to a working man?', and Hueffer replied 'I should speak to a working man in exactly the same way that I should speak to any other man, because I don't think there is any difference' (Chambers 1935: 174). Ford repeats the anecdote as a sign that he 'automatically regarded every human being as my equal' (Ford 1937: 75), but his essay is full of class consciousness and class condescension.

In fact, the only person who directly claims that Jessie divulged details of the occupation of Lawrence's father in her initial letter to Hueffer is Violet Hunt. In her memoir, *The Flurried Years* (1926), Hunt suggests that Jessie described Lawrence as 'the son of a miner, and not very strong', but the latter phrase is not one Jessie seems likely to have used, and the fact that Hunt also recalled Jessie saying that 'her sweetheart was schoolmaster in the same school' (Hunt 1926: 47) casts doubt on the accuracy of her memory. Two of the three poems we know Jessie sent to Hueffer allude to Lawrence's career as a teacher; they contain no mention at all of coal mining. Lawrence was taken up by Hueffer as a poet, on the basis of several distinctive, observant but whimsical verses, shot through with the kind of highly literary Pre-Raphaelite qualities which Lawrence would shortly discover in the work of another young *English Review* poet, Rachel Annand Taylor. Lawrence told Louie Burrows in the letter of 11 September that his poems were 'all in the rough, and want revising'; he said that he was 'very hard at work, slogging verse into form'. He added: 'I never thought of myself blossoming out as a poet – I had planted my beliefs in my prose' (*1L* 137–138).

It is important to pause the biographical narrative at this point in early September 1909 in order to reflect on how Lawrence and the writing he had produced up to that point had been shaped by his upbringing in Eastwood. In future years, Lawrence would express impatience with producing the short biographical notes required by publishers, in part because he knew they wished to emphasise his working-class roots in a Nottinghamshire mining town. While it was true that his father, Arthur, was a miner (albeit a 'butty', or mining contractor, in charge of a small team of men at Brinsley Colliery), and he was born in a small two-up two-down terraced house, his early life had been largely determined by the outlook and ambition of his mother. Lydia Lawrence (née Beardsall) had been born in Manchester and grew up in Sheerness in Kent as the daughter of an engineer. An injury which her father suffered at work reduced the family to poverty and forced them to move to Nottingham to be close to his relations. Her four sisters all married into the middle or lower-middle classes. Lydia's maternal uncle, John Newton, was married to Arthur's maternal aunt, Alvina Parsons. Lydia and Arthur met in 1874 at a Christmas party thrown by John and Alvina, and married a year later, on 27 December 1875. They lived together in Brinsley, New Cross, South Normanton and Old Radford before settling in Eastwood in 1883. Lawrence was the fourth of their five children (three boys and two girls), and their youngest son.

Lydia was determined that none of her sons should follow their father into the pit. Fundamental differences in the outlooks and values of Lydia and Arthur led to conflict and estrangement in their marriage. Through strict domestic economy, Lydia ensured that the family lived with a degree of dignity and distinction. She used the shop window in their first Eastwood home to sell lace in order to supplement the family's income. During Lawrence's time in Eastwood, up to October

1908, when he left for Croydon, his family had moved three times, each house improving on the last, from a terraced house with a shop window in Victoria Street, to an end terrace with an extra strip of garden in the Breach, to a house on Walker Street with a wide view down onto Brinsley Colliery and the surrounding countryside, and finally to a house on Lynn Croft situated at the top of a steep street with a bay window and a back garden looking out onto Lydia's beloved Congregational Chapel. In February 1896, Lydia bought ten shares at £1 each in the Ideal Brick Press Syndicate Ltd.[6] In August 1899, she purchased a second-hand pianette for £6, which she was able to pay for in full by 1 November.[7] Lawrence was the only one among his circle of friends to have paints bought for him, and the first to get a new bicycle.[8]

Lydia's drive to improve the family's circumstances strongly influenced the lives of her three sons. The eldest, George Arthur, who had the closest emotional ties with his father, seems to have rebelled against the pressure to 'get on'. He worked for a time at High Park Colliery before being apprenticed to a picture framer. At the age of 19, he impulsively took the King's Shilling while out with a friend in Ilkeston, signing on to serve for seven years with the King's Own Scottish Borderers; he soon regretted the act and was bought out by his mother 15 months later (perhaps with money she borrowed from one of her sisters). Shortly after his release he took up with a girl against his mother's wishes and was forced to marry her when she fell pregnant. He subsequently got a job as a turner and went to live in Nottingham. By September 1909, he and his wife Ada had three children (two sons and a daughter). The next eldest son, William Ernest (known as Ernest or 'Ern'), was his mother's favourite. He excelled at school, both academically and in sports. Like George, he had to leave school at age 14. He worked at first for the Co-op at Langley Mill before moving at the age of 18 to the Offices of the Shipley Colliery Company and then acting as a clerk for a bicycle company in Coventry. He taught shorthand and typing on a private basis, and at the British School in Eastwood. Finally, he landed a job as a clerk for a firm of solicitors, John Holman and Sons, in central London.[9] His death from erysipelas on 11 October 1901, at the age of 23, devastated the family.

Lawrence (known to friends as 'Bert') grew up in Ernest's shadow, but he achieved his own mark of distinction when he won a County Council Scholarship to Nottingham High School, which he attended between September 1898 (when he was 13) and July 1901. Afterwards, he was employed for a few months as a clerk for J. H. Haywood, a surgical appliances manufacturer in Nottingham, before a bout of pneumonia forced him to leave. Following his recovery, he worked as a pupil-teacher at the British School and received training at the Ilkeston Pupil-Teacher Centre. He then took the King's Scholarship examination in order to study at University College Nottingham. He was placed in the First Division of the First Class. He spent one year earning some money as a full-time pupil-teacher at the British School before beginning his studies at the College in September 1906. He left with a teacher's certificate in summer 1908. He secured the job in Croydon in late September of the same year.

Lawrence began writing in spring 1905, at the age of 19, and his first works were poems. 'Campions', 'Guelder Roses' and perhaps 'The Wild Common' date to this period. As their titles suggest, his impetus to write came not from the streets of Eastwood, but from the surrounding countryside. In the early summer of 1901, during his last term at the High School, he had gone with his mother to visit the Chambers family at their home, Haggs Farm, in nearby Underwood. Lydia had got to know Ann Chambers through their shared attendance at the Chapel, which – with its Sunday School and Literary Society – occupied a central place in the social life of the Lawrence family. Ann's husband, Edmund, used to have a milk round in Eastwood, but in 1898 he and his wife moved with their seven children (three daughters and four sons) two miles away and became tenant farmers. Haggs Farm was situated in beautiful open countryside, at the back of the large Moorgreen Reservoir and on the edge of Sherwood Forest, close to the Annesley hills. Lawrence immediately established a close bond with Edmund Chambers, then with May (the eldest daughter), and finally with the other children. It was with Jessie, however, that he found the closest ties. She was the most literary of the children, and the most brooding and reflective. She resented her brothers for their patronising treatment of her as a young woman and longed to improve her lot in life. Once her initial sense of reserve in front of the privileged scholarship boy fell away, she found an ally in Lawrence as a precocious young man with a similarly immersive appreciation of literature.

In the summer of 1902, while Lawrence was still convalescing from the bout of pneumonia which put an end to his job as a clerk, he visited Haggs Farm more and more frequently, helping out with farming jobs. Haggs Farm became a second home for him, away from the tensions in his own family. His imagination and love of literature flourished in this setting, and a more fun-loving and exuberant side to his nature found free expression. May Chambers noted how he could light up the room 'with a dancing light like a sunbeam' (Nehls 1959: 570). He and the members of the Chambers family 'would join together and sing songs, or sometimes we would dance, and sometimes read aloud in turn from a book we all wanted to read at once. It was a splendid time for all of us, and Bert was always the centre to whom we all looked as leader, a position he thoroughly enjoyed' (Nehls 1959: 589).

Lydia Lawrence naturally came to resent all the time her son was spending there. Lawrence would be forced to give her minute accounts of what took place, and in the small world of Eastwood news got around about their antics, coloured by the family's feeling that Bert was being stolen away from them. In time Lydia and her sisters would make Lawrence aware of the perceived impropriety of his spending so much time with Jessie. When May Chambers challenged Lawrence about these things, he said: 'To know all is to forgive all' (Nehls 1959: 602).

Lydia Lawrence valued books and literature as ways to escape the meanness of her surroundings in Eastwood. She was a keen reader, and her tastes straddled the popular and highbrow. Lawrence remembered her being impatient with George Meredith's *Diana of the Crossways* (1885) and 'terribly thrilled' (*LEA* 177) by Mrs Henry Wood's bestseller *East Lynne* (1861). His father, in contrast, was 'scarcely able to read or write' (*LEA* 112); the open (sometimes violent) animosity between Arthur and Lydia, caused by Arthur's sense of being marginalised, undervalued, and even despised, by his wife and children, was one of the mitigating factors to which Lawrence alluded in his remark to May. Lydia Lawrence nurtured and shared cultural aspirations first with Ernest, and then with Lawrence. Lawrence's youngest sister Ada noted how she loved to discuss religion and philosophy with the Scottish minister of the Congregational Chapel, the Reverend Robert Reid.[10] She joined the Co-Operative Women's Guild, whose members met to address social issues and the history of the co-operative movement.

Lydia's outlook can be perfectly gauged by the fact that on 19 July 1892, for her forty-first birthday, her 15-year-old son George presented her with a copy of George Eliot's *Scenes of Clerical Life* (1857), containing a careful inscription in his best handwriting wishing her 'many happy returns of the day, and a long, happy and prosperous life'.[11] Lawrence noted that his mother wrote with 'a fine Italian hand' (*LEA* 177) and she would have encouraged such refinement in her children. The summer before his death, Ernest had bought *The International Library of Famous Literature*, edited by Dr Richard Garnett, a twenty-volume set which Jessie noted was treated with 'reverence amounting to awe' (Chambers 1935: 92) in the Lawrence household. For Lydia, reading was linked to 'getting on'. In contrast, Lawrence discovered a rich imaginative freedom through his shared reading with Jessie at the Haggs. They would meet to borrow books from the Mechanics Institute Library in Eastwood, which was open for two hours on a Thursday evening. They recited poems together, discussing the lives of the authors. Lawrence oversaw re-enactments of scenes from the texts they loved best in the fields surrounding the farm. Jessie became 'the threshing floor on which he threshed out all his beliefs' (*SL* 265).

F. T. Palgrave's *Golden Treasury of Songs and Lyrics* became a 'kind of Bible' to Jessie and Lawrence around the time of her eighteenth birthday, in January 1905. Jessie says that they read poems by Shelley, Wordsworth and Keats, and she particularly records his fondness for poems by William Cowper, Robert Burns and Thomas De Quincey: 'He liked 'Fair Helen' [the traditional Scottish ballad] very much, and later he taught it to his boys in the Croydon school' (Chambers 1935: 100). She notes that Lawrence gave her 'a selection of Shelley and at other times

The Blessed Damozel and the *Rubáiyát of Omar Khayyám*, and I gave him Blake's *Songs of Innocence* and *Songs of Experience*' (Chambers 1935: 101).

It is little wonder that his own early poems are so intensely literary; 'Guelder Roses' even contains a reference to 'the thought-drenched eyes / Of some Pre-Raphaelite mystic queen / Who haunts me' (*Poems* 1397), revealing the influence on him of Dante Gabriel Rossetti. In summer 1908, he would read Walt Whitman, whose importance for him is clear in the free-verse form of his early poems about school and teaching (two of which Jessie sent to Hueffer). In the Easter of 1906 he began work on a novel, which he initially entitled 'Laetitia', a forerunner of *The White Peacock*. He based its plot on George Eliot, contrasting two relationships. The eponymous Lettie falls pregnant outside marriage by Leslie Tempest, the son of a colliery owner; to avoid social stigma she marries a farmer's son, George Worthington, and they emigrate together to Canada. The surviving fragment of the novel reveals Lawrence's indebtedness to literary romances like *Lorna Doone* (1869), whose key scenes Lawrence and Jessie had acted out together on the Annesley hills. As Lawrence worked on the novel by fits and starts over the following three and a half years it blended the original romance elements with tragic and French naturalist qualities, revealing the shifts in his reading and influences. He dispensed with the pregnancy plot and had Lettie marry Leslie Tempest, focusing on her rejection of the farmer's son (renamed George Saxton) and his fall into alcoholism. Lawrence said that his family considered his writing an 'affectation'. At some point, his mother read a chapter of the novel and said 'But my boy, how do you know it was like that? You don't know —' (*LEA* 112). In August 1907, when Lawrence was at College and the novel was still in an early state, Jessie asked Lydia what she thought of it, and perhaps in reference to Lettie's pregnancy, she replied 'To think that *my* son should have written such a story' (Chambers 1935: 117).

This response to her youngest son's writing reflected her dislike of the changes she would have detected in him by this date. Lawrence's questioning of religion and his loss of religious faith in 1906–1907, around the age of 21, was precipitated by his reading of T. H. Huxley, Darwin and Ernst Haeckel, and of books by Herbert Spencer, J. M. Robertson, Robert Blatchford and Philip Vivian. Ann Chambers was dismayed when Lawrence introduced such texts and ideas to her children, and she looked to protect her youngest from their influence. Lawrence could tone down his views in the company of his mother, and of Edmund and Ann Chambers, and he continued to attend Chapel for his mother's sake, but it became necessary for him to seek out the company of those with whom he could express his scepticism, and his increasingly scathing views on religion. He was particularly sustained by his friendship with William ('Willie') Hopkin, a shopkeeper in Eastwood who was a renowned atheist and socialist. Willie and his wife Sallie, a suffragette, involved Lawrence in the Eastwood Debating Society, which they set up to offset what they saw as the conservatism of the Chapel Literary Society. Lawrence made new friends through it, including Alice Dax, the wife of an Eastwood optician and another very outspoken suffragette, and her friend Blanche Jennings, who lived in Liverpool. He began to seriously question the values of his upbringing and his education. At College, Lawrence joined the 'Society for the Study of Social Questions'. When he delivered a paper to the Debating Society, on 19 March 1908 at the Hopkins' home on Devonshire Drive, he used the occasion to challenge the theories of education which he was being forced to assimilate, attacking Johann Friedrich Herbart's suggestion that aesthetic interest is aroused by a sense of harmony by invoking the pleasure derived from the honesty of the challenging, disreputable authors he was reading (Edgar Allan Poe, Émile Zola, Guy de Maupassant and Maxim Gorky) who 'express their deep, real feelings' (*STH* 226).[12]

Lawrence's critical questioning of social and aesthetic matters was inseparable from his questioning of religion and education. In the earliest stages, by Easter 1906, his views evolved in dialogue with his reading of works by Charles Lamb, Ralph Waldo Emerson, Henry David Thoreau and Thomas Carlyle. Carlyle was an especially important sounding post for him. As John Worthen has noted, 'At times, reading Carlyle, one can hear the swingeing certainties of Lawrence's prose': 'Lawrence took from Carlyle what he needed – and then transformed it into his own way of understanding and feeling' (Worthen 1991: 122). We can see this happening in Lawrence's annotations in his copy of *Past and Present* (1843). In Book III, Chapter XIII, Carlyle asserts his belief that 'in no time, since the beginnings of Society, was the lot of those same dumb millions of toilers so entirely unbearable as it is even in the days now passing over us'; 'Do we wonder', he writes, 'at French Revolutions, Chartisms, Revolts of Three Days?' Lawrence wrote in the margin 'Unemployed Processions'. In Book III, Chapter XV, when Carlyle declares 'But we will leave this of "Religion"; of which, to say truth, it is chiefly profitable in these unspeakable days to keep silence', Lawrence wrote 'Oh verily'. In Book IV, Chapter IV, when Carlyle emphasises the necessity for workers to form a 'veritable brotherhood' and notes that 'Chelsea Hospitals, pensions, promotions, rigorous lasting covenant on the one side and on the other, are indispensable even for a hired fighter', Lawrence wrote: 'It is true – why no such covenant of miners and teachers!'[13]

Lawrence's observations show him applying Carlyle's early Victorian insights to his own world, seeking out a kindred spirit in his questioning of religious authority and his development of an incipient political awareness. He once referred to himself during his College years as suffering from 'spiritual dyspepsia' (Nehls 1959: 609), tacitly acknowledging the influence of Carlyle, who was afflicted by the physical ailment throughout most of his adult life. Lawrence's marginal comment about the absence of any covenant between miners and teachers reveals his rather gauche desire to link his father's manual occupation with his own labours as a poorly-paid pupil-teacher. Although Lawrence grew up in a mining community with a collier as a father, his own world was one of desk jobs, scholarships, teaching, and the reading and writing he had begun with his mother's encouragement and developed through his contact with the Chambers family. In a conversation with Lawrence about the merits of realist writing, May Chambers once pointed out that he was different to most people, and he is said to have commented 'Oh, yes, the great unwashed ... But there are others, you know' (Nehls 1959: 610). Willie Hopkin's daughter, Enid Hilton, noted that in Eastwood 'you either belonged or you didn't': since as a scholarship boy Lawrence was 'no longer accepted by, or really belonging to' the town he became merely 'an observer and recorder of the mining world' (Hilton 1993: 15). There is just one account of the young Lawrence going down a mine. During his time working as a pupil-teacher, a newly-appointed teacher was keen to experience the world of the miners in Eastwood, and Lawrence joined a small party that gained permission to be taken down. May Chambers was in the group and she notes how Lawrence was the first to speak when they came to the surface: 'Didn't it blow hard coming up the shaft! Didn't it blow up your trousers!' (Nehls 1959: 587).

When, in December 1907, Lawrence wrote to the Reverend Robert Reid to discuss the cause of his loss of faith, he described being profoundly affected by witnessing the poverty in 'the lowest parts of Sneinton' and asked how it was possible 'that a God who speaks to all hearts can let Belgravia go laughing to a vicious luxury, and Whitechapel cursing to a filthy debauchery' (*1L* 40). The suffering of the working classes was something that he alluded to as happening in Nottingham and London, not in Eastwood. Indeed, when Lawrence started teaching in Croydon he was shocked by the signs of poverty he witnessed in the dress and appearance of some of his pupils; families in Eastwood would do anything to avoid sending their children out with dirty clothes or holes in their shoes. He was apparently very sceptical of Willie Hopkin's socialist views; Enid Hilton recalled him laughing at her father and telling him, 'You are wasting your time, Willie .... All this will come later, social change, why are you spending energy on it now?' (Hilton 1993: 8). After Alice Dax introduced Lawrence and Jessie Chambers to the journal *The New Age*, evidently trying to interest them in its socialist outlook, Lawrence subscribed to it, but Jessie reports that he 'liked it far more for its literature than its politics. He was never really interested in politics, and was quickly irritated and bored by the subject' (Chambers 1935: 120). Jessie remembered Hueffer saying to her in November 1909, 'You're a sort of Socialist, I suppose?' She noted: 'Not a single political idea had crossed my mind in those days' (Chambers 1935: 170). When Lawrence revised the paper he delivered to the Debating Society, he gave it the title 'Art and the Individual: A Paper for Socialists', addressing it to 'readers of the "New Age"', but (as Annalise Grice suggests) his intended readers were ideal rather than practical socialists.[14] In the opening paragraph, he wrote: 'we, who are not hungry and thirsty for material things, and who have not the tough spirit or the single purpose of a political fighter, we will stay at home, and in wicked sloth forget the din that rages round the platform, such time as in our own fields the lark is nigh' (*STH* 135). Lawrence refers to Carlyle in both the paper and its revised version,[15] and Carlyle's influence is obvious in the mannered style of his address to his implied readers.

D. H. Lawrence, *c.*12 December 1908. University of Nottingham, Manuscripts and Special Collections, La Phot 1/3/1.

If Lawrence's earliest poetry was inspired by the countryside surrounding Eastwood, so was his earliest prose fiction. His first novel was set around Moorgreen Reservoir; he even re-titled it 'Nethermere' (his fictional name for the Reservoir) in recognition of the importance of its country setting. 'A Page from the Annals of Gresleia' (later revised as 'Ruby-Glass' and then 'A Fragment of Stained Glass') was a tale which created an imaginary event in the history of the nearby ruins of Beauvale Priory and the lives of the Carthusian monks who once lived there. 'Goose Fair' was an historical tale of the lace trade in Nottingham, co-written with Louie Burrows. 'The Vicar's Garden' (an early version of 'The Shadow in the Rose Garden') is set in Robin Hood's Bay, where Lawrence holidayed with his family in the summer of 1907. 'A Prelude' (which won a Christmas story competition for the best story of an enjoyable Christmas and was published in the *Nottinghamshire Guardian* in December 1907) is a rural tale set around an imaginary Haggs Farm. In its earliest form, 'The White Stocking' was a slight tale based on an amusing anecdote from his mother's early life.

The only thing Lawrence had written by September 1909 which drew directly on his experience of working-class Eastwood was a dialect poem of January 1909 entitled 'Violets for the Dead'. Lawrence was fascinated by Eastwood speech patterns and the Eastwood dialect. May Chambers records his 'keen interest in words and phrases' (Nehls 1959: 600). 'Violets for the Dead' is presented in the form of a dialogue between a brother and sister, who reflect on the recent burial of their wayward sibling Ted. The brother tells of a mysterious and grief-stricken young female mourner who went up to his rain-sodden grave after the family had moved off and threw a handful of violets on his coffin. Lawrence used the Eastwood dialect word 'slive' (meaning 'creep') to describe the woman's surreptitious movements. The poem ends with the brother's question about the woman and her relationship with their brother: 'Dost think there was öwt between 'em? / Tha knows 'e'd a winsome way wi 'im, an' she / Was th' little, cuddlin sort, as 'as nöwt ter screen em' (*Poems* 1407). 'Violets for the Dead' faithfully reproduces the speech patterns Lawrence heard in his home town, but it is self-consciously literary too, reflecting his early love of Robert Burns; in 1913, he would start, but then abandon, a novel which transferred Burns's early life to his own Nottinghamshire-Derbyshire border country.[16]

Ford Madox Hueffer probably knew nothing about Lawrence's particular background when they first met, except that he was a teacher in Croydon and came from a small town in Nottinghamshire. Lawrence would almost certainly have mentioned Jessie Chambers to him, since she was the intermediary who had contacted Hueffer in the first place and facilitated the meeting, but whether he mentioned Eastwood we simply do not know. Hueffer learned more in the following weeks, however, as he introduced Lawrence to 'all the Swells' (*1L* 145). Hueffer evidently thought that he had discovered a genuinely working-class writer, but when he read the manuscript of 'Nethermere' he had a rude awakening. In the letter of support which he wrote about it, and which Lawrence copied out before Violet Hunt delivered the manuscript to Heinemann, he perceptively noted that it was of 'the school of Lorna Doone': he stated that 'the book, with its enormous prolixity of detail, sins against almost every canon of art as I conceive it', but he added that 'Properly handled ... it might have considerable success, and I don't think that in these matters I am at all a bad judge' (*8L* 2–3). The recommendation helped to secure Lawrence a contract with Heinemann.

In later years, Lawrence would comment that Hueffer was 'most kind and most friendly—Got Heinemann to accept the MS., a ragged and bulky mass, of *The White Peacock*—invited the schoolteacher to lunch—introduced him to Edward Garnett [the son of Dr Richard Garnett]—and Garnett became a generous and genuine friend. Hueffer and Garnett launched D. H. into the literary world' (*LEA* 113). Lydia Lawrence, to whom Lawrence proudly showed the contract for his novel, would also acknowledge Hueffer's kindness to her son, remarking on 8 February 1910, in a letter to her sister Ada Krenkow, that he had been 'such a friend to Bert, so kind & helpful'.[17]

Hueffer, however, sought to address Lawrence's prolixity by espousing the value of the Flaubertian impersonality and economy of expression which he so admired. One of the things he would have tried to rein in was the literariness of Lawrence's writing. Hueffer had 'never known any young man of his age so well read in all the dulnesses that spread between Milton and George Eliot' (Ford 1937: 82). He was 'inclined to prescribe to him a course of workingman novels', the idea of which Lawrence found 'oppressive' (Ford 1937: 83). In a section of the editorial to the first number of the *English Review*, Hueffer had described 'the poor' as 'breaking in on us everywhere': 'But of knowledge of the lives and aspirations of the poor man how little we have. We are barred off from him by the invisible barriers: we have no records of his views in literature. It is astonishing how little literature has to show of the life of the poor'.[18] He encouraged, or maybe instructed, Lawrence to write about Eastwood, recognising that his ability to describe a mining town and the life of miners as one who had grown up in such a place as the son of a miner would be his unique selling point as an author. As Worthen observes, 'it can hardly be a coincidence that, in the autumn of 1909, Lawrence wrote first his play *A Collier's Friday Night*, then his short story 'Odour of Chrysanthemums' and then, in December 1909, two sketches of school life in Croydon ['A Lesson on a Tortoise' and 'Lessford's Rabbits'] which can also be linked with Hueffer' (Worthen 1991: 217).

A Collier's Friday Night is closely autobiographical. The stage directions reproduce in minute detail things specific to the Lawrence household such as the books they have in the kitchen (including *The International Library of Famous Literature*), their crockery and kitchen utensils, and the piano music they play. In focusing on Friday night (which was market night in Eastwood, and the day for baking bread and courting), the play presents the fraught relationship between Lawrence's father (George Lambert in the play) and his mother (Mrs Lambert), and the hostility that both Lawrence (Ernest Lambert) and his sister Ada (Nellie Lambert) felt towards him. In its depiction of the close intellectual relationship between Ernest Lambert and Maggie Pearson, it also explores the complex bonds between Lawrence and Jessie Chambers, probing Lydia Lawrence's resentment of Jessie's intimacy with Lawrence and the cruelty of Ada's friends in tormenting Jessie and drawing attention to the awkwardness of her situation in the Lawrence household. The play also gestures in a frank and unflinching manner towards the examination of the intense mother–son bond that would occupy such a central position in *Sons and Lovers*. Stage directions refer to the '*abnormal emotions and proximity*' of Ernest Lambert and his mother, to the '*dangerous gentleness*' between them, and to the '*safe reserve of their souls*' being '*broken*' (*Plays* 57, 59).

However, if *A Collier's Friday Night* represents the first instance of Lawrence using his writing to work through his feelings about his mother, repeating and presenting his emotions 'to be master of them' (*2L* 90), it is also a carefully and very deliberately structured piece of writing. The artfulness of the play is emphasised by the way that Lawrence changes both the central character and the setting from their real-life originals. Lawrence gives Ernest Lambert his dead brother's name and makes him a student at a college in Derby rather than Nottingham; Ernest is in some ways the least developed and complex character in the play, and Lawrence seems at pains to prevent us from empathising too closely with him, underscoring his aloofness and priggishness. The layout of the miner's house described in the play combines aspects of the Lawrences' third and fourth houses in Eastwood (the houses in Walker Street and Lynn Croft). The play also brings together the basic situation in the Lawrence household in November 1906 with details relevant to the time of writing in November 1909.[19]

A Collier's Friday Night is constructed around certain basic contrasts and unresolved conflicts between the characters. The most obvious contrast is that between the father and Ernest. George Lambert's major complaint against his wife is that she has set their children against him, and while she spoils Ernest she holds things back from himself. This is confirmed during the play by Mrs Lambert's purchase of grapes and pine-nuts from the market, the former being bought because Ernest likes them and the latter to make a cake for Ernest. While Lambert comes home from the pit to a meal of meat, gravy and cabbage followed by rice pudding, Ernest returns from college and tells his mother that he has eaten an asparagus omelette in a vegetarian restaurant. Lambert has brought home the weekly wages to be divided among his team of daymen at the pit, while Ernest asks for money from his mother for a copy of 'Piers the Ploughman' and 'two books of Horace' (*Plays* 15). Ernest's effete language, with references to 'piffle', an 'Infernal shindy!', and 'foolery and flummery' (*Plays* 15, 23, 27), his boasting to his mother of Professor Staynes's view that he has an 'instinct for Latin' (*Plays* 15), his reading of French verse with Maggie, and his recourse to French and German words in his interactions with friends and family, form a stark contrast to the blunt, bad-tempered assertiveness of his father's regionally-inflected speech.

The other major contrast is between Maggie Pearson and Beatrice Wyld (a depiction of Alice Hall, a friend of the Cooper family who lived next door to the Lawrences in Lynn Croft. One of the Cooper girls, Gertrude or 'Gertie', appears in the play as Gertie Coomber). Beatrice's vivaciousness and cruelty serve to accentuate Maggie's brooding and spiritual nature. In a scene which Lawrence would draw upon again in the 'Strife in Love' chapter of *Sons and Lovers*, Mrs Lambert asks Ernest to keep an eye on the bread in the oven while she goes to market. Ernest's repartee with Beatrice distracts him, but when the bread burns Maggie is the scapegoat; she knows that Mrs Lambert will blame her, not Beatrice, for turning her son's head.

In April 1912, Lawrence added a note to the manuscript of *A Collier's Friday Night* describing it as 'most horribly green' (*Plays* xxviii). The play draws clear lines between the characters and shows Ernest, Nellie and their friends inhabiting a world of high culture quite oblivious to the life and ways of their father and his fellow miners, whom they scoff at behind their backs. At one point in Act III, the father hovers his fist so near Ernest's nose that '*he draws his head back, quivering with intense passion and loathing, and lifts his hands*', but, on hearing his wife's supplications to their son, Lambert '*withdraws*' in a '*movement of defeat*' (*Plays* 52). When Lambert threatens his wife with stopping supporting the family, telling her 'I'll stop it, I'll stop it—or they can go' (*Plays* 50), she retorts '*you* don't keep us' and tells him that the family is kept by herself and Nellie. In *Sons and Lovers*, which Lawrence was working on when he wrote the note, he would offer a more thorough analysis of the psychological impact of the father's alienation within the house on all of its members, and he would attend more fully to the mother's crippling financial dependence on her husband.

Lawrence's ability to adapt to his new social environment in Croydon, and to Hueffer's literary circles, proved disconcerting to both his family and Jessie. His mother and his closest sibling, Ada, were displeased with him, feeling that he was changing and breaking away from home, but Lawrence insisted that he 'had to change, and leave the old things' (Chambers 1935: 159). Jessie witnessed the full force of Lawrence's detachment first-hand when she visited him in Croydon for that memorable weekend in late November 1909. On the morning of Saturday 27 November, he met her at King's Cross Station and took her to see the 'big shops'. After having lunch at Selfridge's, they visited the National Gallery. Lawrence then took her to Waterloo Bridge, showing her 'the bridges at night, with the lights of the trams reflected' (Chambers 1935: 165). They went to see Alfred Sutro's play *Making a Gentleman* at the Garrick Theatre. Back at Lawrence's lodgings at 12 Colworth Road, Lawrence made a supper of macaroni and showed her his latest writings: 'There were poems, quite a number that I had not seen, and a play that was about his home on a Friday night. Sitting there in the tiny suburban room, it troubled me deeply to see his home put before me in his vivid phrases' (Chambers 1935: 166). Lawrence kept Jessie up until two o'clock talking about his writing and their different prospects in life. Jessie reported that she bent her head, 'and the tears ran down into my lap, because in my heart was no hope at all, but only fortitude' (Chambers 1935: 167).

The immediate context for Jessie's upset was her uncertain future, since (as Worthen has noted) 'four days later, Jessie gave a month's notice to her school authorities; she was moving from Underwood to the Musters Road School in Nottingham, and at least one of the reasons was the continued strain of living at home with her family at the Haggs' (Worthen 1991: 219). Yet her feelings would have been intensified by the experience of renewed intimacy with Lawrence in a situation which emphasised his movement outside the former life he had shared with her. In Selfridge's, he had written a postcard to his new love interest, Agnes Holt, arranging to take Jessie to meet her on Sunday morning before the visit to Hueffer. Reading Lawrence's play in the midst of such tumult would have underscored for Jessie his emotional detachment from Eastwood and from his family and friends. The degree of cool analysis he brought to his family life, and his relationship with his mother and with Jessie herself, must have shocked her. She remembered telling Lawrence on the Saturday night that the play was 'very true' (Chambers 1935: 166). Lawrence gave her the manuscript to read on the train journey home. The new poems he showed her may have been those he had recently entered into his second University College Nottingham notebook.[20] It opens with the poems which Jessie had sent to Hueffer and which had just been published in the *English Review* ('Discipline', 'A Still Afternoon/Dreams Old and Nascent' and 'Baby-Movements'); if Jessie was shown the notebook she would have seen that the poems, which she had copied out to send to Hueffer, had been neatly entered into the new book by Agnes Holt.

We can only imagine what Jessie made of *A Collier's Friday Night*. In Act III, Mrs Lambert openly expresses her resentment of Maggie Pearson, telling Ernest 'No, I *don't* like her—and I *can't* say I do'. Although Ernest initially defends Maggie and stands his ground, his mother's strong emotional appeals finally cause him to tell her: 'You know, Mater—I don't care for her—really—not half as I care for you' (*Plays* 55, 56). The hurt this must have caused Jessie was a portent of the greater pain she would subsequently feel at the depiction of the entire development of their relationship in *Sons and Lovers*. Writing for the first time about his upbringing, and thinking about how he might present it to a middle-class metropolitan audience or readership, necessitated a degree of objectivity, but it brought out in Lawrence an almost brutal capacity to depict in an analytical mode his most intimate experiences and feelings. He would later state: 'You have to have something vicious in you, to be a creative writer' (*IR* 324).

Hueffer's injunction to write about Eastwood caused Lawrence to turn for the first time to stories connected with his father's family. 'Odour of Chrysanthemums' fictionalises the death of his paternal uncle James in an accident at Brinsley Colliery in February 1880, five years before Lawrence was born, and it incorporates things which Lawrence heard his paternal grandmother (Louisa Lawrence) say about it when he was a child. He would use the same event slightly differently in his play *The Widowing of Mrs. Holroyd*. When Edward Garnett (Lawrence's second mentor, and an experienced reader for the publisher Duckworth) read 'Violets for the Dead' and encouraged him to write further dialect poems, one of the three he produced was 'A Collier's Wife', in which the eponymous wife and her rather timid son are surprised by a knock at the door from a miner informing them that their husband and father has been injured down the pit and is in hospital in

Nottingham. Lawrence could have been drawing here on several injuries which his father sustained at various points during his childhood (the most serious one being a compound fracture of his right leg in November 1903, which left him with a permanent limp).[21]

Lawrence's prolix style, and his commitment to romance, however, did not simply go away. Alongside these Eastwood writings, he produced fictions which drew on a new twist in his troubling relationship with Jessie, and on his interactions with, and attraction to, a fellow teacher he got to know in Croydon named Helen Corke. On Christmas Eve 1909, Lawrence visited Haggs Farm and proposed that he and Jessie should begin a sexual relationship. The experiment was not a success. In the short story 'A Modern Lover' (begun around December 1909), a young man returns to his Midlands home from 'all the South-Country which he had fled' (*LAH* 29) and seeks out his former love at the farm where she lives with her parents, only to find that she has taken another lover in his absence; in the course of their interactions, an old intimacy is reignited, but when he leaves they can only stand 'together, apart', since he is 'too spent to think of anything to say', while she is 'too overcome with grief and fear and a little resentment' (*LAH* 48). 'The Saga of Siegmund' (the first version of his second novel, *The Trespasser*, written between February and August 1910) fictionalises Helen Corke's affair with her married violin teacher, Herbert Macartney, who committed suicide on 7 August 1909 after spending a week with her on the Isle of Wight. When Lawrence showed Hueffer the manuscript of the novel his mentor said that it was 'a rotten work of genius, one fourth of which is the stuff of masterpiece'. Hueffer's sharp criticism of the novel rested on his earlier insistence to Lawrence that 'prose *must* be impersonal, like Turguenev or Flaubert' (*1L* 178). He would convince Lawrence that the combination of its eroticism and florid style meant that it was 'finally, pornographic' (*1L* 229); Hueffer advised Lawrence not to publish it for fear that it might damage his fledgling career. Lawrence only returned to it in January 1912, with Edward Garnett's encouragement and advice; following revision, it was published by Duckworth in May 1912.

Writing the great autobiographical novel of his life in Eastwood, the book which both Hueffer and Garnett hoped he might produce, proved a much more difficult, painful and protracted process. Sometime during the first half of 1910, he started but soon abandoned a novel based on his mother's pre-marital life, now known as 'Matilda'.[22] Then, in October 1910, he began a novel entitled 'Paul Morel'. Only a plan of it survives,[23] but this shows that Lawrence was now focusing – perhaps in response to his mother's recently-diagnosed abdominal cancer – on the unhappy marriage of his parents and its consequences for them, and for their children. He wrote one hundred manuscript pages, but his mother's death on 9 December put a halt to work on it. Shortly before her death, he became engaged to Louie Burrows. Work on his novel needed to resume if he was to make sufficient money from it to supplement his teacher's pay and enable them to marry. He wrote a wholly different 355-page draft between mid-March and mid-July 1911. This version has survived and been published as *Paul Morel.* It draws closely on Lawrence's experiences as a young boy in Eastwood, but it also incorporates events in the life of his wider family, including his paternal uncle Walter's accidental killing of his 15-year-old son, also called Walter, at their home in Ilkeston on 18 March 1900. Lawrence told Louie: 'I'm afraid it's heterogeneous' (*1L* 263).

His renewed contact with Jessie at this time led him to send the manuscript to her for comment. Jessie encouraged Lawrence to stay closer to the experiences of his nuclear family (including the death of his brother Ernest), and to 'keep it true to life' (Chambers 1935: 192). Lawrence worked on the third version between November 1911 and June 1912. This time his progress was interrupted by another serious bout of pneumonia shortly after a visit to Garnett at his home, the Cearne, near Edenbridge, Kent, on the weekend of 18–19 November. It ended his teaching career and precipitated the breaking of his engagement to Louie. He saw out the worst of his illness in Croydon before convalescing for a month in Bournemouth from 6 January to 3 February 1912, then (following a brief stay with Garnett) he moved back to Eastwood, living with his family in his elder sister Emily's house in Queens Square between 9 February and 3 May.

Before his illness, he had asked Jessie to send him her own memories of their 'early days' (Chambers 1935: 193), since he wished to incorporate these into his revision of the novel and his account of the relationship between Paul Morel and Miriam Leivers. He collected her notes on his return to Eastwood. Lawrence began working again on the novel, delivering pages to Jessie as he wrote. As Helen and Carl Baron note, in the new version 'Lawrence ... placed Miriam in the context of the Leivers family at the farm', so Jessie 'read it as history rather than fiction and took exception to a great deal of it, writing her objections freely over the pages of Lawrence's manuscript' (*SL* xxxiv).[24] She gave him four pages of criticisms. Lawrence took some account of her responses, but he ultimately insisted on analysing the failure of their relationship in fictional form on his own terms. Jessie came to see the novel as a betrayal of their friendship and intimacy.

If his time in Croydon and the period of illness and convalescence had caused him to view his relationship with Jessie in more detached and critical terms, it also deepened his detachment from working-class Eastwood. Lawrence's arrival back in his home town coincided with the first national miners' strike. On 2 February, the Miners' Federation proposed a new schedule of wages and when negotiations failed the miners came out on strike on 26 February; their action would last until 6 April. Lawrence wrote several short stories and sketches about the strike, thinking they might be topical and saleable: Garnett immediately placed 'The Miner at Home' with *The Nation*, but 'Her Turn', 'Strike-Pay' and 'A Sick Collier' would not be published until September 1913, the first two in the *Westminster Gazette* and the third in the *New Statesman*. These short pieces are more concerned with what Macdonald Daly terms the 'domestic repercussions' (Daly 1994a: 135) of the strike than the specific details of the industrial dispute; they offer insights into the contrasting attitudes to the strike of the miners and their wives, suggesting how interpersonal dynamics replicate 'in the household the structures of the public dispute being waged outside' (Daly 1994a: 138). Lawrence helped to deliver relief tickets in Eastwood and expressed sympathy for the plight of the working families,[25] but (as Daly observes) it would be 'an exaggeration' to describe his depiction of the striking workers in his letters and writing as revealing 'solidarity, far less commitment': his is 'the ambiguous voice of the suburban schoolmaster who regularly encountered manual workers and reacted variously with wondering admiration and cynical repugnance' (Daly 1994a: 145).

In a letter to Garnett, Lawrence now referred to 'Paul Morel' as his 'colliery novel' (*1L* 372). In March 1912, he met and fell in love with Frieda Weekley, and in May they travelled together to Germany. In late April, Lawrence showed Garnett the manuscript, and he began revising it with Garnett's advice. He wrote to Jessie, telling her that he was 'going through *Paul Morel*. I'm sorry it turned out as it has. You'll have to go on forgiving me' (Chambers 1935: 216). He sent the finished manuscript to Heinemann on 9 June 1912, but they swiftly rejected it because of its 'want of reticence' (*1L* 421 n. 4). As he had done with *The Trespasser*, he turned for support to Garnett, who gave him notes for revision. Lawrence revised the novel between early August and 18 November 1912. Garnett got the novel accepted by Duckworth, but he told Lawrence that significant cuts must be made to the manuscript. Garnett made these cuts himself, removing outspoken words, phrases and passages, and editing it down, removing ten per cent of the text to make it a suitable length for the circulating libraries.

The most striking aspects of *Sons and Lovers* are (in the first part) its wealth of social detail and its evocation of a whole social milieu and way of life, and (in the second) its remarkable psychological analysis of Paul Morel's failed relationships with Miriam (based on Jessie) and Clara Dawes (a composite figure, drawing on aspects of Louie Burrows, Alice Dax and Frieda Weekley), and the impasse in his emotional and erotic lives. The novel provides almost documentary insight into the daily lives of Paul's parents, Gertrude and Walter Morel, and their children. It shows us in great detail the layout of the miners' houses, with their exclusive front parlour rooms (where Gertrude invites the clergyman, Mr Heaton, to take tea), their warm and claustrophobic back kitchens (where people bake, eat, sit, and argue), their sculleries (where the crockery and kitchen utensils are kept, and where Morel bathes), the pantries for food storage, and the dreadful ash-pits (or open privies) and alleys running between the terraces, 'where the children played and the women gossiped and the men smoked' (*SL* 10). We are told that miners' hearths are 'sacred to the family' (*SL* 238). When Gertrude goes into labour with Paul, she strikes the back of the fire grate with a poker to alert Mrs Kirk, her neighbour, who climbs onto her washing 'copper' to scale the fence separating their houses: 'It was an understood thing that if one woman wanted her neighbour, she should put the poker in the fire and bang at the back of the fireplace, which, as the fires were back to back, would make a great noise in the adjoining house' (*SL* 40).

Here, as elsewhere in the novel, the narrator seems to be acting as a mediator between the working-class life he describes and his implied middle-class readership. There are a number of occasions early in the novel where some term, or some aspect of working-class behaviour, is glossed for the benefit of those unaccustomed to such things. In Chapter II, there is even a footnote to explain Barker's question to Walter Morel as they prepare to end their work shift down the pit: 'Shall ter finish, Sorry?' We are told that 'Sorry' is 'a common form of address. It is perhaps a corruption of "Sirrah"' (*SL* 41). An early instance of explanatory backtracking occurs in the description of daily rituals around the all-important kitchen fireplace: 'The fire was never let to go out. It was raked just at bed-time. That is, a great piece of coal, a raker, was placed so that it would be nearly burned through by morning' (*SL* 23). After a section of the first chapter describing Walter's unstable income as a 'butty' too ready to criticise the pit managers, an explanation is provided of what his job entails:

> A butty is a contractor. Two or three butties are given a certain length along a seam of coal, which they are to mine forward to a certain distance. They were paid something like 3/4 for every ton of coal they turned out. Out of this, they had to pay the men, holers and loaders, whom they hired by the day, and also for tools, powder, and so on. If their stall was a good one, and the pit was turning full time, then they got a hundred or two tons of coal out, and made good money. If their stall was a poor one, they might work just as hard, and earn very little. (*SL* 26)

Notice how Lawrence explains 'butty', but expects us to know what 'holers' and 'loaders' are. He is rather vague in his description of the amounts of coal mined from productive stalls. He seems a little uncertain of what his middle-class readership would know, and also unsure of some specific mining details.

The need to describe and explain this unfamiliar world to his middle-class readership is underscored when William's metropolitan girlfriend (based on Ernest's fiancée, Louisa Lily Western Dennis, who like her fictional counterpart was known as 'Gipsy') enters the Morel house at Christmastime and is unable to orientate herself when confronted by its host of strange customs and unwritten codes of conduct:

> She glanced round the kitchen. It was small and curious to her, with its glittering kissing-bunch, its evergreens behind the pictures, its wooden chairs and little deal table ... In such a household, in Streatham, Miss Western would have been a lady condescending to her inferiors. These people were, to her, certainly clownish—in short, the working classes. How was she to adjust herself? (*SL* 143–144)

The fictional 'Gyp' (whom Lawrence calls Louisa Lily Denys Western) is an unsympathetic character in the text: she is superficial and insensitive to her new surroundings, and she treats Annie (the character based on Ada) as a servant and misjudges Mrs Morel's need for the observance of certain standards, choosing the wrong photograph to send her and addressing William as 'Chubby' (*SL* 143) in front of his family. Compare her failure to understand the Morel household with the greater social ease and familiarity of Clara, who, in spite of her dubious status as a married woman estranged from her husband (Baxter Dawes), has the experience of working-class life necessary to put Gertrude at her ease.

However, the nature of the explanations of working-class language, occupations and behaviour in *Sons and Lovers* might cause us to question the narrator's own sympathies where certain features of working-class life are concerned. Walter Morel's manners are a point in question. His drinking and eating habits, and his slovenliness, are subjected to constant rebuke in the novel; the narrator tells us that 'He loathed a fork. It is a modern introduction which has scarcely reached the common people. What Morel preferred was a clasp knife' (*SL* 37–38). The tone here is difficult to grasp, since it seems at once to snigger slightly at the 'common people', but only in the context of narrating Walter's daily customs in a way actually likely to endear us to him. His outbursts of drunken violence and his menacing and provocative behaviour must be set against the wonderful description of him making the gunpowder fuses with William and Annie, and telling them stories about Taffy the pit-horse.[26]

As the central consciousness in the novel, Paul Morel exhibits a problematic and divided attitude to the working-class environment he inhabits. As a young man, he idolises 'Gyp', much to his mother's disgust, and he remains rather blind to his father's working and socialising life outside the home. When he goes to the pit bank to tell his father that William is dead we are shown Walter's silent despair and told that Paul overlooks it:

> Morel walked on a few strides, then leaned up against a truck side, his hand over his eyes. He was not crying. Paul stood looking round, waiting. On the weighing machine a truck trundled slowly. Paul saw everything, except his father leaning against the truck as if he were tired. (*SL* 167)

This is one of very few moments in the novel when we see Morel giving way to despair, and not transforming it into brutal outbursts and acts of violence or avoiding it by pretending it is not there or by leaving the house. Although elsewhere he is shown to be a bad sufferer, here he does *not* cry, or whimper, like Paul; he is 'manly' – a quality Gertrude admires in men.[27]

The blindness to Walter Morel's feelings in this instance is a failing in Paul, *not* in the novel itself, but some critics have suggested that Lawrence spends too little time exploring the pressures exerted on Walter by his physically demanding and dangerous work. Early in the novel we are given access to Gertrude's thoughts as she reflects on her despair at being trapped in Bestwood (the name given to Eastwood),[28] but only once (in Chapter II) is Walter's evening mood traced back to his dissatisfaction with his work.[29] We have no comparable access to *his* thoughts; he seems to lack any tragic potential because of his inability to contextualise the conditions of his life. Daly observes that 'Morel's sub-literacy and inarticulacy conveniently prevent his own voice from being heard', so 'there is no point in the novel where we are invited to see things in a larger perspective than the rather confined view of Mrs Morel and the children' (Worthen and Harrison 2005: 83–84). We are led to believe that his working life is easy and natural to him: 'It scarcely seemed hard to him, to leave the fresh, cool air of morning, and go down. He was so used to it, it came simply and naturally' (*SL* 38). This omniscient statement strikes a discordant note. In Chapter V, Walter has an accident; like Lawrence's father, he suffers a compound fracture of his leg as a result of a fall of rock in the mine shaft, which entails a great loss of blood.[30] Can his life underground really be so simple and natural to him, or does this reveal a failure of understanding in the narrator (and in the author) comparable to Paul's partial blindness?

The novel contains a self-reflexive awareness of the difficulty involved in offering a sympathetic insight into working-class life which is not simultaneously glib or patronising. In Chapter X, Paul discusses the issue of class with his mother:

> "You know," he said to his mother, "I don't want to belong to the well-to-do middle class. I like my common people best. I belong to the common people."

> "But if anyone else said so, my son, wouldn't you be in a tear. *You* know you consider yourself equal to any gentleman."
>
> "In myself," he answered, "not in my class or my education or my manners. But in myself, I am."
>
> "Very well then—then why talk about the common people."
>
> "Because—the difference between people isn't in their class, but in themselves.—Only from the middle classes, one gets ideas, and from the common people—life itself, warmth. You feel their hates and loves—"
>
> "It's all very well, my boy—but then why don't you go and talk to your father's pals?" (*SL* 298)

Mrs Morel clearly sees the problem inherent in Paul's idealisation of the working classes. As Daly notes, 'the common people' is 'hardly a phrase favoured by those who genuinely identify with the working class' (Worthen and Harrison 2005: 88). Elsewhere in the novel, Paul uses the word 'common' pejoratively: he describes Clara to his mother as 'nice ... And not a bit common!' (*SL* 359), and when he tells his mother about his experience of collecting his father's wages on a Friday afternoon, he refers to the colliers as 'hateful, and common, and hateful' (*SL* 97).

Although Paul treats class as a superficial aspect of identity separable from one's true self, the novel shows that the material circumstances of one's life are defining and inescapable. Paul acts on the belief that he can fashion his own identity, drawing strength from both the middle and working classes without suffering the displacement experienced by his brother William. However, in the manner of the great realist tradition which Lawrence's mentors had encouraged him to assimilate, and novels like *Middlemarch* (1871), *Madame Bovary* (1857) and *Anna Karenina* (1878), *Sons and Lovers* insists on setting the lives of its characters in a concrete social setting which exerts a powerful and tragic influence over them. The novel opens with a description not of the Morel family but of Bestwood and the development of the Nottinghamshire and Derbyshire coalfields from the time of Charles II in the seventeenth century. Even before Paul's birth, the lives of the Morels are shown to be shaped by industrial history and the financial motives of the colliery owners. The sons' individual movements outwards and upwards into a wider social world are troublingly mirrored in the family's rather circumscribed progression from one house to the next in Bestwood. They have the room to achieve some localised distinction (even acquiring the services of a maid, Minnie, in their last home),[31] but their efforts are contained within Bestwood, and they remain tethered to the incomes of the father and Paul.

It is Gertrude who believes in the power of men (not women) to escape such determinism, and to move up the social ladder through aspiration and industry:

'She frankly *wanted* [Paul] to climb into the middle classes, a thing not very difficult, she knew. And she wanted him in the end to marry a lady' (*SL* 299). One reading of the novel would see it as a critique of Mrs Morel's mistaken ideology of male self-improvement.[32] While she is content to see Annie married off in a modest way to a steady man, she encourages her first-born son, William, to take the initiative and drag himself into the middle classes. For a time it seems to work, as he moves among the families of the wealthier tradesmen in Bestwood and finally gets a job in London, where he uses all of his income to support his claim to a middle-class lifestyle, spending money extravagantly on food and Christmas presents, or wasting it on replacement gloves for his careless and snobbish fiancée. Yet, his social aspiration brings him no real happiness: he seems about to trap himself in a loveless marriage, but he dies before he gets the chance, suffering alone in his grim lodgings at Elmers End (the fictional equivalent of Ernest's lodgings in Catford).

It is education and reading that serve in the novel as the catalysts for progression up the social ladder, as they had done in the Lawrence home. Yet, her sons' propensities for reading and study are mixed blessings for Mrs Morel. William studies so hard that he becomes fretful and his mother has to urge him to lighten up for the sake of his health;[33] likewise, Paul's delight in reading is shared with Miriam Leivers, with whom he develops an intellectual kinship that threatens to alienate him from his family. His mother must 'sadly' (*SL* 251) admit that she has no interest in the things he reads and discusses with Miriam, and in one of the most quietly profound moments in the novel, Walter Morel tells Paul 'tha writes i' such a fashion, I canna ma'e it out' (*SL* 419). The novel explores the undesired consequences of Mrs Morel's drive to educate her sons to move up the social ladder: their mental alienation from the social world that nurtured them.

Repetitive patterns show that Paul is unconsciously tied to his family background and doomed to repeat the damaged lives of his parents and siblings. His brother Arthur wins a scholarship to the Grammar School but inherits the reckless impulsiveness of his father, getting into numerous scrapes before almost ruining himself by signing up to serve in the army. Paul seems to be assuming the role of the deceased William, not only by inheriting his brother's suit (which is too big for him)[34] and his mother's affections, but in other, less obvious ways. He replicates his brother's brutal impatience when teaching Miriam maths and French; his irritable gloominess 'reminded [Mrs Morel] of William. But Paul was worse' (*SL* 324). The novel contains numerous echoes which connect characters and events to one another: Miriam burns some potatoes, while Paul burns a loaf of bread; Paul prays for his father to be killed at the pit, while Miriam prays not to love Paul Morel;[35] more disturbingly, Walter tells Gertrude that he will make her 'tremble at the sound of my footstep' (*SL* 49), while Paul proudly tells his mother that the girls at Jordan's 'quake at my footstep' (*SL* 346). Paul may despise his father's behaviour, but in spite of this he finds himself involuntarily repeating some features of it. We might compare his cruel behaviour towards Miriam with his father's physical cruelty to his mother. The novel is full of images of repetition and return. Like 'the donkeys that plodded wearily in a circle, round a gin' (*SL* 9) on the first page of the novel, characters find themselves repeating the words and actions of their family members, caught up in destructive patterns of behaviour which seem to be outside their control. Clara ultimately returns to Baxter, and Paul walks back towards Nottingham, 'His fists ... shut, his mouth set fast' (*SL* 464).

The manner of narration of *Sons and Lovers* and its perspectival complexities reveal almost as much about Lawrence's early life as the rich social detail it contains and its painstakingly transformed and shaped analysis of his family life and the relationships of his youth. The narrator acts as a cultural guide to the working-class habits, rituals and language of Bestwood, but in places his grasp of mining detail falters and when describing working-class ways he adopts by turns a slightly sardonic and condescending tone and an idealising discourse which sees the working man as simple and wholesome. Yet the shifting perspective and ambiguity which might have been weaknesses in another novel are the main strengths of *Sons and Lovers*. By foregrounding Paul's conflicted relationship to the working and middle classes, Lawrence was bringing to the reader's attention matters which were implicit in his own relationship to his materials. The uncertainties and ambivalences of the text articulate Lawrence's own subject positioning as a scholarship boy living in a working-class community but acculturated to a middle-class outlook. The elaborately structured repetitions reveal the influence on him of European realist writers, and of his mentors. Taken together, these aspects of the novel show that Lawrence was not the straightforward working-class author whom Hueffer thought he had discovered but rather a prodigiously well-read and decidedly literary author *from* the working class.

Notes

1 Ford Madox Hueffer changed his name to Ford Madox Ford in 1919.

2 Lawrence's name appears on his birth certificate as David Herbert Richards Lawrence.

3 Cf. Chambers (1935: 169) and Ford (1937: 77–78). Jessie recalled how, on this occasion, 'Lawrence told me that Hueffer was very fond of this flat and said he felt a sense of satisfaction every time he entered it. / 'I can't say I should', said Lawrence critically'. Ford, taking the suggestion from Jessie, recalled Lawrence being critical of his flat, and himself defending it.

4 See Ford (1937: 76).

5 See Ford (1937: 80).

6 La Ac 2/7/5 (University of Nottingham).

7 La Ac 2/7/9 (University of Nottingham).

8 See Nehls (1957: 29); Worthen (1991: 39).

9 The firm's offices were located at 50 Lime Street.

10 See Ada Lawrence and Gelder (1931: 22).

11 George Eliot, *Scenes of Clerical Life*, stereotyped edition (Edinburgh and London: William Blackwood and Sons, n.d.).

12 See *STH* 223–226.

13 Thomas Carlyle, *Past and Present* (London: Chapman and Hall, 1896), pp. 181, 199, 235.

14 See Grice (2022: 68).

15 See *STH* 226–227 and 140.

16 The so-called Burns Novel fragments are printed in *LAH* 201–211.

17 La Ac 2/8/6/1 (University of Nottingham).

18 *English Review*, Vol. 1, No. 1 (December 1908), pp. 162–163.

19 Lawrence incorporates references to the death of the poet Swinburne in April 1909, to his unfinished poem 'A Life History in Harmonies and Discords', and to the first Christmas of his niece Margaret King – daughter of his older sister Emily – who was born in February 1909.

20 The notebook is Roberts E320.1 (University of Nottingham). It includes 'A Beloved', 'The Punisher', an epistolary sequence of three poems entitled 'An Epistle from Thelma', 'An Epistle from Arthur' and 'Epilogue from Thelma', 'Sickness', 'A Day in November' and Lawrence's unfinished experimental autobiographical poem 'A Life History in Harmonies and Discords'.

21 See Worthen (1991: 43).

22 See *PM* 145-160.

23 See *SL* xxv.

24 Some of Jessie's annotations challenged his fictional depiction of their interactions. For example, she wrote her own alternative account of Miriam Leivers's response to a letter she receives from the 21-year-old Paul in which he calls her a nun. See *SL* 557, explanatory note 293:15.

25 See *1L* 380 (3 April 1912).

26 See *SL* 88–89.

27 See *SL* 112.

28 Bestwood is a mining village in its own right; it is located approximately eight kilometres to the east of Eastwood.

29 See *SL* 51.

30 See *SL* 108–111.

31 See *SL* 345.

32 See Holderness (1982: 146–147).

33 See *SL* 78.

34 See *SL* 297.

35 Cf. *SL* 176 and 245; 85 and 208.

2

Lawrence and Anti-Suffragist Feminism

Lawrence once told Jessie Chambers 'I think a man puts everything he is into a book – a real book' (Chambers 1935: 82). *Sons and Lovers* absorbed Lawrence's early life to such an extent that its publication in May 1913 seemed a watershed moment for him and his writing. On 19 May, he told Edward Garnett 'It's the end of my youthful period' (*1L* 551). The final revision of the novel between early August and November 1912 had been hard work, since the circumstances of Lawrence's life changed so dramatically between March and July 1912 that he must have felt he was looking at Paul Morel across a ravine. In one sense this was helpful because it enabled him to understand the tragedy of Paul's life with a new clarity that came from having escaped the emotional impasse of his earlier self. But returning to that earlier self and analysing its failures when he really wanted to be moving on, leaving all the tragedy behind and writing a novel about 'Love Triumphant' (*1L* 490), proved difficult. The prospect of returning to the novel one more time caused him to tell Edward Garnett 'I *loathe* Paul Morel' (*1L* 427).

The event which consigned the autobiographical material of *Sons and Lovers* to the past was, of course, Lawrence's meeting with Frieda Weekley in March 1912. It is perhaps inevitable that an event which transformed the emotional life of the author should also transform the focus of his fiction. Lawrence's first three novels all concern male characters and their failure to establish stable relationships with women. In *The White Peacock*, Cyril Beardsall is a bystander in life unable to take the initiative in his relationship with Emily Saxton, while George Saxton is spurned by Lettie Beardsall and embraces a lesser marriage to his cousin Meg which is no more than a dreary compensation. In *The Trespasser*, Siegmund MacNair momentarily escapes his unsatisfactory home life with his wife and children, but when he is forced to leave his music student, Helena Verden, after their intense week together on the Isle of Wight, he finds himself unable to readjust and he commits suicide. And in *Sons and Lovers*, Paul Morel – Lawrence's most autobiographical creation – fails to integrate love and desire, recoiling from sex

The Life of the Author: D. H. Lawrence, First Edition. Andrew Harrison.

with Miriam Leivers when she gives herself to him as a form of self-sacrifice, and finding his desire for Clara Dawes a disembodied thing which leads only to solipsism and despair.

Hilary Simpson has traced Lawrence's engagement with the 'dreaming woman' trope in this early fiction: 'the Pre-Raphaelite woman, with her loose romantic clothes and unbound hair and air of *taedium vitae*', who 'represented a radical challenge both to the innocent young lady of Edwardian convention and to the stereotype of the mannish suffragette' (Simpson 1982: 46). In *The White Peacock*, the gamekeeper Annable's tale of his failed marriage to Lady Chrystabel sets the tone for that novel's examination of the thwarted relationship between Lettie and George, and the stunted one between Cyril and Emily Saxton. Annable had gone to Cambridge, but left on the death of his father to take up a post as a curate in Leicestershire. Lady Chrystabel, the cousin of the Rector, initially seemed to him 'very fine and frank and unconventional'. They read together and discussed ideas, but her romantic interest in him was modelled purely on her reading. After they married, her passion for him soon abated and she took to drawing 'Greek statues' of him. She refused to have children and (in his phrase) 'began to affect Burne-Jones—or Waterhouse—it was Waterhouse—she was a lot like one of his women—"Lady of Shalott", I believe' (*WP* 150). He escaped from the marriage and travelled abroad, and after a time she wrote his obituary and remarried. Simpson notes that Lettie too is 'capable of sexual arousal but draws back from its implications' (Simpson 1982: 52): she flirts with George but then retreats into a socially advantageous marriage to Leslie Tempest. Cyril complains of Emily being 'like Burne-Jones' damsels' (*WP* 69), obsessing over shadows rather than fleshly realities. In *The Trespasser*, Helena is described as belonging to 'that class of "Dreaming Women", with whom passion exhausts itself at the mouth' (*T* 64). And Miriam Leivers, in *Sons and Lovers*, seems to Paul as if she is 'in some dreamy tale, a maiden in bondage, her spirit dreaming in a land far away and magical' (*SL* 176). Paul thinks of her as a nun, with an 'eternal maidenhood about her' (*SL* 323); he even writes to her when she is 21 and tells her 'You are a nun—you are a nun', a statement which 'went into her heart ... like a mortal wound' (*SL* 293).

The relationships in the fiction reflect, in different ways, the emotional bonds which Lawrence had formed up to March 1912 with Jessie Chambers, Alice Dax, Louie Burrows and Helen Corke. Too little is known of his short-lived courtship with Agnes Holt in Croydon to trace *her* presence in the fiction, but that relationship and others not in the biographical record must have contributed too. Lawrence grew up around strong women who challenged conventional gender norms in different ways and with different degrees of political commitment. His mother was a member of the Co-Operative Women's Guild in Eastwood. Alice Dax was a member of the National Union of Women's Suffrage Societies, and together with Sallie Hopkin 'was involved with the suffragists' (Hilton 1993: 8), attending large meetings in Nottingham and discussing the issues in Eastwood, but also bringing her political convictions into her daily life in ways that Eastwood found challenging and offensive, cultivating plainness in dress and house decoration, and being 'uncluttered in thought and action, to the point of harshness' (Nehls 1957: 135). Jessie Chambers, on the other hand, whilst bravely standing up to her brothers and resenting her lot in life, reaching out for ideas and opportunities through reading and education, was not politically active in her youth and early adulthood. Helen Corke, who met Jessie through Lawrence and fell in love with her, also had little interest in suffragism, though she shared Jessie's reaction against the traditional roles women were forced to adopt, in her case struggling to understand her own sexuality but feeling sure that marriage and motherhood were not for her. Louie Burrows was more politically-minded; Lawrence wrote to her from Croydon in March 1909 to describe a mob's angry reaction to two suffragette speakers who addressed them during campaigning for a by-election, and in June 1911, when they were engaged to one another, he invited Louie to join him there on a suffragette procession.[1] The following month he sent her a copy of Olive Schreiner's seminal feminist text, *Woman and Labour*, which was published earlier that year.[2] As Annalise Grice has noted, Violet Hunt, whom Lawrence held in high regard as an author and important early supporter of his writing, was 'an active suffragist and founding member of the Women Writers' Suffrage League', and he 'added aspects of Hunt's personality to the character of Lettie in his February–April 1910 rewrite [of *The White Peacock*]' (Grice 2022: 98).

The position of women in a changing world, and the changing practical and ethical grounds on which relationships were based, had preoccupied Lawrence since his earliest childhood. One of the things which comes through most clearly in May Chambers's account of the young Lawrence is his persistent questioning of his mother's sure sense of right and wrong in this sphere. In particular, she remembered him questioning the fuss his mother made when his brother Ernest lay all afternoon on the sofa with his fiancée on a rainy day during one of their visits to Eastwood: 'They just lay and talked softly. Perhaps they went to sleep, I don't know. What if they did? I think it's silly to make such a fuss, or any fuss at all' (Nehls 1959: 569). Lawrence would have been around 14 years old at the time. He also seems to have questioned why his mother was so upset when she learned that Ernest bought his fiancée expensive boots: 'But I don't think it matters, she's his sweetheart' (Nehls 1959: 559). More generally, May shows how Lawrence had to negotiate being made to feel that it was wrong, or somehow abnormal, for him to prefer spending time with girls rather than playing sports with other boys.

Jessie Chambers records how Lawrence broached the subject of sexual ethics with her during her first visit to Croydon in November 1909. On this occasion she stayed with him in his rented lodgings in Colworth Road, much to her mother's consternation. On the first night of her stay he told Jessie that he did not have enough money to marry, despite the fact that he found it 'hard to bear the stress of life alone'. He said: 'I think I shall ask some girl if she will give me ... that ... without marriage. Do you think a girl would?' Jessie answered that she did not know, but felt that the 'kind of girl who would' he 'wouldn't like'. When asked if she thought it would be wrong, she answered: 'No, I wouldn't think it wrong. But all the girls I know would' (Chambers 1935: 167). The following month, when he deliberately re-established his relationship with Jessie on a sexual basis he was evidently testing out her ability to overstep traditional values. Her willingness to give him sex outside marriage but only as a form of self-sacrifice seems to have underscored for him their fundamental incompatibility. Louie Burrows would not have made any such sacrifice, and Lawrence had to be careful to avoid even alluding in his letters to his sexual feelings for her, and his sexual frustration, for fear that her parents may read them. He seems to have been attracted to Alice Dax and Helen Corke precisely because he sensed their capacity, in different ways, to seek fulfilment by challenging and even subverting traditional relationships and values. Alice's commitment to her husband, however, and Helen's resistance to entering into a sexual relationship with a man in part because of the loss of autonomy it augured, only added to the frustration Lawrence felt. That feeling was worked through in the fiction in a manner not always sensitive to the causes of the resistance in the female characters.

Frieda Weekley was, however, a different woman altogether from his earlier soul mates, confidants and partners. She entered Lawrence's life at a moment when he had cut ties with his past and was looking to establish a new future for himself outside England. The two-year period following the death of Lawrence's mother on 9 December 1910 saw a series of major upheavals in his life. At the time of her death, he was an elementary school teacher in Croydon newly engaged to Louie Burrows, a headmistress of a Church of England school in Ratcliffe-on-the Wreake in Leicestershire who had grown up in a strict Anglican family. Louie was just the sort of woman Lawrence's mother would have wanted him to marry, and his strong desire to reassure his mother of the security of his future life must have influenced his impulsive proposal to her on 3 December, just days before his mother's death, on a train journey they took together from Leicester to Quorn. Lawrence's writing still had to be fitted around his main career in the classroom. In addition to the prize-winning story 'A Prelude' which had been printed (under Jessie Chambers's name)[3] in the *Nottinghamshire Guardian* in December 1907, he had published only two sequences of poems and one short story, 'Goose Fair', all in the *English Review* with the support of Ford Madox Hueffer. He was, however, on the verge of making a breakthrough as a promising young author. He had received an advance copy of his first novel, *The White Peacock*, which would be published by Heinemann in January 1911, written a second entitled 'The Saga of Siegmund', which Hueffer had sent to Heinemann, and even begun work on a third ('Paul Morel'). In February 1911, he informed his publisher (on Hueffer's advice) that he did not wish to publish 'The Saga of Siegmund', but to meet the terms of his two-novel contract he could offer them his new novel instead. He worked conscientiously on 'Paul Morel', keeping Louie informed of his progress because their plans to marry rested on Lawrence earning the money he thought it would accrue.

Signs of strain in their engagement, brought on by the differences in their values, became clear in the summer and autumn of 1911, as Lawrence turned to Alice Dax and Helen Corke for the kind of intellectual stimulation and romantic involvement which the more conservative Louie could not provide. As had happened in late autumn 1901, when a bout of pneumonia forced him to leave his employment as a clerk at J. H. Haywood, serious illness changed the course of his life, putting an end both to his career as a teacher and his engagement to Louie. On the weekend of 18–19 November 1911, Lawrence visited Edward Garnett at the Cearne, and on the way home to Croydon he caught a chill which soon developed into pneumonia. He was nursed through the crisis by his sister Ada. In mid-December, shortly after he was able to sit up again in bed, he received a letter from Garnett informing him that 'The Saga of Siegmund' could be published by Duckworth, the firm his mentor worked for as a reader. For the first time he was able to consider leaving teaching and taking his chances as a full-time professional author. Lawrence revised the novel with Garnett's guidance during the month he spent convalescing in Bournemouth (from 6 January to 3 February 1912). He then returned to Eastwood, where he lived at the home of his elder sister Emily King, her husband Sam King and daughter Margaret; Lawrence's father and Ada had gone to live with Emily following the breaking up of the family's house in Lynn Croft. On 4 February, he wrote to Louie to break off their engagement, and on 28 February he resigned from his teaching post on health grounds.

The next step was crucial since Lawrence could not go on living with his family in Eastwood in the packed house in Queens Square. In early March, he arranged to speak with his former Professor of Modern Languages, Ernest Weekley, at Weekley's home in the Nottingham suburb of Mapperley, since he wanted to visit relations on his mother's side of the family in Germany and wondered about securing a temporary lectureship there. Professor Weekley was out when he called, but his German wife Frieda was at home with their three children (two daughters and a son). The next half an hour changed the course of Lawrence's life. His brief conversation with Frieda Weekley convinced Lawrence that he had found the woman of a lifetime and somebody with whom he could create and share his new life as an author. He seems to have opened up to her to a quite extraordinary degree. He 'fiercely denounced' women, telling Frieda that he had 'finished with his attempts at knowing' them. Her response was simply to laugh at him. They spoke about Oedipus, 'and understanding leaped through our words'

(Lawrence 1934: 22). As John Turner has noted: 'It is impossible to say exactly what Frieda knew of Freud in 1912, or what she said to Lawrence; but discussion of the Oedipus complex must have raised the question of infantile sexuality' (Turner 2020: 58). Lawrence had long felt that his extremely close relationship with his mother was in some sense abnormal and had affected his capacity to form lasting relationships with other women; talking about it now with this forthright, receptive and fearless woman would have seemed like a miraculous cutting through of emotional issues which his bonds with Jessie Chambers, Helen Corke and Alice Dax, and his engagement to Louie Burrows, had only deepened and exacerbated.

We know nothing at all about the subsequent conversation which ensued over lunch when Ernest Weekley returned, but afterwards Lawrence never seriously considered applying for lectureships in Germany. Back in Eastwood he wrote to Frieda, telling her that she was 'the most wonderful woman in all England' (*1L* 376). Her indifference to the social and moral structures of her life in the English Midlands was obvious to him from the outset: the next time they met he told her that she was 'quite unaware' of her husband (Lawrence 1934: 22). Her startling insouciance led him to tell Jessie Chambers that it would do her good to meet Mrs Weekley.[4] Jessie's brooding resentment at her lot in life, her doting commitment to Lawrence and sensitivity and attentiveness to changes in his mood and attitude, and what her brother David described as her 'uncompromising sense of rightness',[5] formed a stark contrast to Frieda's heedless drive for self-realisation and her impulse simply to laugh at Lawrence's bitterness and frustration about women. Lawrence soon fell in love with Frieda. They met whenever they could in the ensuing weeks, going together to see a performance of Shaw's *Man and Superman* at the Theatre Royal in Nottingham, spending a day with Garnett at the Cearne, and using the cottage of May Chambers and her husband Will Holbrook in Moorgreen as a safe venue away from Lawrence's family when she came to Eastwood.

Frieda and her two sisters (Johanna, or 'Nusch', and Else) had grown up in a German social and intellectual context whose values were a world apart from those of Lawrence's upbringing in Eastwood, and even from the comparative liberalism of Willie and Sallie Hopkin, Alice Dax, and his teacher friends in Croydon. Their father, Friedrich, was a civil engineer in Metz with a reserve commission in the army; he had injured his right hand in the Franco-Prussian War, and his gambling and womanising (he had fathered an illegitimate child) had reduced the circumstances of his family and damaged his marriage. The Von Richthofen family was, however, very well connected in German political and military circles. As John Worthen has noted, Friedrich and his wife Anna 'while far from rich, preferred to be seen as aristocrats rather than as the gentry they really were' (Worthen 1991: 374). Their daughters were certainly not expected to work.

Johanna, the youngest sister, married an army officer when she was 18; Frieda met Ernest Weekley when she was 19 and married when she was 20. The eldest sister, Else, went to University, studying under the political economist Max Weber at Heidelberg; she earned her doctorate in 1901 and worked for a brief time as a labour inspector in Karlsruhe, marrying in 1902 (at the age of 28) the Professor and economic theorist Edgar Jaffe.

The marriages of all three sisters soon foundered. After just five years, Else started living apart from her husband for extended periods, having extra-marital affairs and even having a child by one of her lovers; she and Edgar Jaffe never divorced and he accepted her illegitimate child and raised it alongside the three children they had together. Johanna remained married for 23 years, but she had separated from her husband (Max von Schreibershofen) long before their divorce. Frieda had married Ernest Weekley in Freiburg on 29 August 1899. Initially, marriage seemed to offer her 'the solidity of family life, an intimate circle, an ideal to strive after' in contrast to her early life with her parents, which 'had been such a scattered thing' (Tedlock 1961: 70). Born into a humble middle-class family, Weekley, who was an etymologist, had worked as a school teacher to earn money to study for an external degree at the University of London before winning a scholarship to Trinity College, Cambridge. He had spent a year at the Sorbonne before taking up a lectureship at Freiburg between May and November 1897. He secured his Chair at Nottingham in 1898. The book that would make his academic reputation, *The Romance of Words*, was close to being published at the time that Lawrence met Frieda. He was liked and respected by both colleagues and students. Yet, for Frieda, the flip side of appreciating having him 'at the back of her days, solid and firm' was her feeling of detachment from the routines of English middle-class life, and the restlessness it created in her: 'that curious sensation that she must run, run away' (Tedlock 1961: 75). She too had had affairs to escape the boredom of her deeply bourgeois life in Nottingham. In 1905, she had an affair with the Nottingham lace manufacturer William Enfield Dowson, who was a friend of the Weekley family and godfather of her daughter Barbara ('Barby'). In 1907–1908 she had an affair with the Austrian psychoanalyst Otto Gross, the husband of her sister Else's school friend Frieda Schloffer. Gross was already involved with Else, who gave birth to an illegitimate son by him in December 1907; Else named the child Peter, possibly after Wolfgang Peter, the son Gross had had with his wife earlier the same year. And Frieda also had an affair with the German painter and anarchist Ernst Frick, who moved in the same circles and was first introduced to her by Frieda Gross, who was at that time having an extra-marital relationship with him.

Affairs, then, were not unusual in the German high society circles the sisters moved in, but there was a major difference between such intrigues and the short-lived but transformative relationship Frieda established with Otto Gross.

Gross, the son of an eminent criminologist, had initially trained in psychiatry and neurology and shared his father's Social Darwinist belief in the need to root out deviant and degenerate elements from an advanced society. However, his interest in the personal testimony of psychoanalysis patients changed his outlook and led him to rebel not only against his father but also against his intellectual mentors, Freud and Jung. John Turner notes that Gross 'came to see psychoanalysis as a highly mediated form of patriarchal authority, with the analyst's interpretations overruling the voice of the patient and acting as a repressing agent' (Turner et al. 1990: 142). In opposition to such repression, his creed was 'Nichts verdrängen!' ('Repress nothing!'). It was his firm belief that the individual could only overcome neurosis through sexual immorality, so that open relationships and free love became paths to liberating oneself from the sick society of the past, and the life of the Philistine, and embracing a timeless and clean future. Gross effectively reversed his father's outlook by transforming himself into the deviant and degenerate type, which he now constructed as the natural aristocrat.

Frieda had met and fallen in love with Gross in Munich in the spring of 1907, during one of her annual visits to Germany to see family and friends; they had spent a week together in Munich, and then met for a further week in Holland, after which he accompanied her on the boat trip back to England before returning to Germany. Thereafter, their relationship was conducted via correspondence. In his letters to Frieda, which she kept all her life, Gross celebrated her as 'the woman that I dream of for future generations ... the only human being who *already*, *today*, has remained free from the code of chastity, from Christianity, from democracy and all that accumulated filth—*remained free through her own strength*' (Turner et al. 1990: 165). For a time in 1908 he encouraged Frieda to join him in Germany and give up her life in Nottingham, and what he termed the 'suffocating *littleness* that slowly settles over everything in that place, with *all* its grey cold *life*' (Turner et al. 1990: 167). During their final hours together on board the boat to England, Frieda apparently told Gross 'I go away only in order to return' (Turner et al. 1990: 168), but his polygamous and anarchic lifestyle, and his addiction to morphine, which would eventually contribute to his early death in 1920, made a long-term relationship with him impossible. Frieda soon realised that he 'lived for his vision. The everyday life he ignored. On visions alone you can't live' (Tedlock 1961: 90). But the vision he offered her of a free life and a new society, and the value he placed in her as an exceptional woman with the power to liberate men from their repressions and melancholy, stayed with Frieda and underscored her dissatisfaction with the life she led as a middle-class wife and mother. In Frieda's own words, she felt she had been 'living like a somnambulist', and Gross's 'undigested theories' awakened her to the consciousness of her 'own proper self' (Lawrence 1934: 21). When Frieda first met Lawrence and spoke with him about Oedipus, she did so with the knowledge of psychoanalytic theory which she would have picked up from Gross. She may have detected in Lawrence the same capacity to courageously overcome Oedipal issues that she had seen in Gross and warmed to him as a young man who needed her help to free himself from the damage they had caused.

On 3 May 1912, Lawrence and Frieda travelled together to Germany, Frieda to attend celebrations to commemorate her father's 50 years jubilee for his service in the army, Lawrence ostensibly to visit Karl and Hannah Krenkow, relations of Fritz Krenkow, the husband of his maternal aunt Ada. They went first to Metz, a heavily fortified city then part of the German Empire in the Imperial Alsace-Lorraine territory; Frieda stayed with her family, while Lawrence lodged in a rather conservative family hotel, meeting her whenever she was able to get away. Frieda immediately informed her mother and sister Else about Lawrence, and her mother was introduced to him. At this stage, they could have had no idea that Lawrence was anything other than Frieda's latest love interest; they would have discussed with her how she could manage an affair with him while retaining the security of her marriage. Lawrence was powerless to act, forced into what he termed 'subterfuge, lying, dirt, fear' (*1L* 393). Frieda had drawn back from leaving Weekley for Otto Gross, and her initial response to Lawrence's attempts to 'make her commit herself finally' was to keep an escape route free: as she later put it, 'He forced the responsibility of himself on to her; she did not want to take it' (Tedlock 1961: 92–93).

The litmus test for her feelings was her willingness to tell her husband about Lawrence. Lawrence had pressed Frieda to tell Weekley about their relationship before they left England, but she had delayed doing so at the last moment because she was afraid of his reaction, informing him instead about the two earlier affairs she had had with Otto Gross and Ernst Frick. Weekley admitted to Frieda that following her disclosure he had been 'insane for ten days' (Worthen 1991: 395). Lawrence wrote a letter to Weekley and urged Frieda to send it. In it he clearly stated 'I love your wife and she loves me': 'I feel as if my effort of life was all for her. Cannot we all forgive something? It is not too much to ask. Certainly if there is any real wrong being done I am doing it, but I think there is not' (*1L* 392). Unfortunately, during one of their secretive meetings in the city, they trespassed into a military area and were questioned by military authorities. Their names and addresses were taken, and they were forced to appeal to Frieda's father for help. Friedrich von Richthofen soon realised that they were having an affair and was appalled that his daughter could be acting so recklessly by attaching herself to a penniless young author (she was six years older than Lawrence). Lawrence, who was suspected of spying, was forced to leave Metz. He took the train to Trier, 80 miles away. Before he left, however, he and Frieda seem to have discussed a way forward. She agreed to tell Weekley everything, and Lawrence's letter was duly sent, either from Metz or Trier. They spent a little time together in Trier, and then Lawrence travelled to Waldbröl in the Rhineland to visit his relations. He was there from 11 to 24 May, when he travelled to Munich to rejoin Frieda. They stayed for a week in Beuerberg, enjoying a kind of honeymoon, before travelling on to Icking, moving into the flat of Professor Alfred Weber, Max Weber's younger brother and the lover of Frieda's sister Else, who had a house in the next village, Wolfratshausen.

The tensions of this period, as well as the excitement of escaping and making a new life with Frieda, can be gauged in the short story 'Once—', which Lawrence wrote between June and September 1912. The Lawrence figure in this story is a middle-class man who is having an affair with a beautiful thirty-one-year-old German aristocrat named Anita. Lawrence used this name for Frieda in two pieces of travel writing he produced in August 1912,[6] but here Anita is a representation of her sister Johanna. Like Johanna, Anita is married to a dashing but disgraced army officer with whom she has a son and a daughter, but for some time she has had affairs to relieve her boredom. We first see her entering the hotel room she shares with the narrator wearing 'a transparent lacy chemise, that was slipping over her shoulder, high boots, upon one of which her string-coloured stocking had fallen, and ... an enormous hat' (*LAH* 153). The narrator, who reacts by donning his own hat and gloves and standing naked before her, causing her to go off into 'a fit of laughter' (*LAH* 154), is evidently unsure of his own place in her life. In the course of the story, he asks her whether she has loved the men with whom she has had affairs and is told 'I loved them—but I have put them all in my pocket' (*LAH* 153). When he suggests that the affairs 'meant more to the men than they have to you' (*LAH* 156), she gives him a deeply erotic account of a fleeting experience she once had in Dresden with a young German aristocrat and army captain. She had been visiting the city to spend time with another man, but he was unable to get away from his wife; she almost ran into the young captain when coming down to breakfast in her hotel. The young man finds her taking tea later that day and arranges to visit her in her room in the evening, after he has attended a Court ball. When he comes to her room he showers her in red and pink roses and they spend the night making love. She recalls the many beautiful things he said to her. He is gone before she wakes up, leaving his dancing card with a note asking her to meet him in the afternoon, but she leaves, taking the morning express train back to Berlin. The complexity of the story resides in the narrator's response to Anita's narrative. On the one hand, he is clearly deeply drawn to her beauty, haughtiness and shamelessness. On the other hand, he wonders whether he 'too were going into Anita's pocket' (*LAH* 153), and he burns with rage that she should 'love a man for the way he unbuckled his belt': 'She made me tired. One could never be on firm ground with her. Always, one was slipping and plunging on uncertainty' (*LAH* 159).

The period in Icking felt like a new beginning for both Lawrence and Frieda, but 'making history' (*1L* 390) (as Edward Garnett had told them they were doing) was a painful process. Here they suffered the first terrible fallout from Frieda's decision to leave her husband and children. Weekley's strong reaction when he finally heard that Frieda was having another affair, and then read the letter from Lawrence, was deepened by his concern for their children and the threat to his career and reputation that the ensuing scandal might create. As well as the upset caused by letters they received from Ernest, Frieda suffered greatly from the loss of her children. Her longing for them soon came to seem to Lawrence like an act of betrayal towards him and the new life they were building together. Yet Frieda too had cause to bemoan her new partner's residual attachment to his earlier life. Lawrence's work on 'Paul Morel' meant that he was forced to re-live his early life and to work through the grief over his mother which Frieda saw herself and her love as helping him to overcome. At some point during his revision of the novel, Frieda read a poem entitled 'My Love, My Mother', which Lawrence had written shortly after his mother's death and which Louie Burrows had copied into one of his College notebooks in April 1911. One stanza ran: 'You sweet love, my mother / Twice you have blooded me, / Once with your blood at birth-time / Once with your misery. / And twice you have washed me clean, / Twice-wonderful things to see' (*Poems* 1448). Frieda wrote 'I hate it' and 'Good God' alongside the poem, and added other marginalia and a frank concluding commentary: 'Misery, a sad old woman's misery you have chosen, you poor man, and you cling to it with all your power. I have tried I have fought, I have nearly killed myself in the battle to get you into contact with myself and other people' (*Poems* 1774).

Yet despite all the struggle and conflict and suffering they were establishing a firm basis for their relationship by recognising one another's needs and vulnerabilities. One striking event from early September 1912 demonstrates this with real clarity. In early August, they decided – on Else's advice – to move to Italy. Else, whom Lawrence described as 'a person who arranges other folk's affairs' (*1L* 530), apparently brushed aside Lawrence's concerns about money by saying 'Ach money! Money will come' (*MN* 237). They travelled as cheaply as they could, going on foot and by train from southern Germany into northern Italy, where they settled in the small village of Gargnano on Lake Garda. They set off on 5 August and four days later they arrived in the Zillertal, in the Austrian Tyrol. They stayed here for two and a half weeks, meeting up with Edward Garnett's son David (known as 'Bunny'), who was training as a botanist at the Royal College of Science, and his friend Harold Hobson, an engineer, who accompanied them on their onward journey on foot across the Alps. They spent a night sleeping in a hay hut near Ginzling and had a night in the Dominicus-Hütte before crossing the

Pfitscherjoch Pass. They stayed the night of 28 August in a hotel ten kilometres from Sterzing. Early the next morning, Garnett and Hobson left them to catch a train from the town; Lawrence and Frieda arrived in Sterzing later the same day. Here they rested for a few days, before setting off on 1 September for Meran en route to Bozen (modern-day Bolzano), which meant crossing the Jaufen Pass. It should have been an easier walk than the one that took them over the Pfitscherjoch, but unfortunately they took the wrong path and, exhausted, were forced to spend the night in the Sterzinger Jaufen-Haus.

At some point on their trek, Frieda, who was tired and angry at Lawrence, admitted to having slept with Hobson in a hay hut close to the Dominicus-Hütte. It may have happened while Lawrence went with Bunny to look at some alpine flowers. Details of Lawrence's reaction to Frieda's revelation are provided in the second part of his unfinished novel, *Mr Noon*. Here, Johanna Keighley (Frieda) tells Gilbert Noon (Lawrence): 'Stanley [i.e. Hobson] had me the night before last ... He had me in the hay-hut—he told me he wanted me so badly'. We are informed that Gilbert 'did not know what to feel, or if he felt anything at all. It was such a complete and unexpected statement that it had not really any meaning for him'. He walks on for some time, but then turns to her and says 'Never mind, my love ... Never mind. Never mind. We do things we don't know we're doing ... And they don't signify. They don't signify really, do they? They don't really mean anything, do they? I love you—and so what does it matter!' Johanna agrees 'a little testily': 'She felt rather caught-out by his passionate spiritual forgiveness: put in a falser position than ever' (*MN* 276–277).

The fictional incident is believable since Frieda had admitted to a similar lapse while she was in Metz and Lawrence in Waldbröl. On this occasion, deeply upset by desperate letters she and her parents had received from Weekley, and a stark and ominous letter she had received from his sister Maude, Frieda took solace in a brief affair with an old friend, the army officer Udo von Henning. Lawrence had responded to news of it by telling her: 'If you want Henning, or anybody, have him. But I don't want anybody till I see you. But all natures aren't alike. But I don't believe even *you* are your best, when you are using Henning as a dose of morphia – he's not much else to you'. He admitted, however, that he too had 'had many a one' (*1L* 404). Lawrence was perhaps thinking of Alice Dax, and of his feelings for Helen Corke whilst he was still engaged to Louie Burrows. The image that Lawrence reached for – of casual sexual relations as doses of morphia to numb the pain of living at fever pitch – shows the extent to which Otto Gross (the morphine addict) was a powerful and haunting presence in this early phase of their relationship: Lawrence alludes to him as a touchstone for what it might be like to live openly and cleanly, without the usual bourgeois moral constraints.

On the face of it, Lawrence's calm, reasoned and understanding reaction to Frieda's infidelity on these two occasions is remarkable. Lawrence had cut himself free from so much of his past, and in travelling with Frieda to Germany he had taken a leap of faith, with only an inviolable belief in his writing and in the strength of his love for Frieda to sustain him. His major concern was that Frieda should commit to him in the face of all the upset this would cause, the ongoing separation from her children, and the loss of the comfortably middle-class, if stifling, life she had made for herself in Nottingham. We might have expected him to react to her casual infidelities, then, with a degree of anxiety created by his own insecurity, or even with outrage at her insensitivity to his feelings and disregard for their relationship. But Lawrence was attracted to Frieda precisely because of the largesse of her nature. In the letter which he had written to Ernest Weekley to explain the situation, he said that Frieda was 'afraid of being stunted and not allowed to grow': 'All women in their natures are like giantesses. They will break through everything and go on with their own lives ... Mrs Weekley must live largely and abundantly. It is her nature.' (*1L* 392).

D. H. Lawrence and Frieda Lawrence in Santa Fe, New Mexico, 1922. University of Nottingham, Manuscripts and Special Collections, La Wb 3.

Lawrence's suggestion that Frieda's need to 'live largely and abundantly' outweighed any moral responsibility she had to her husband and children cannot have seemed very satisfactory to Weekley. Yet Lawrence's belief in a woman's need to realise herself in the face of all the pressures placed upon her to conform to her roles as sister, daughter, wife and mother was something that he had come to believe in quite passionately by early May 1912. A year later, as he waited for *Sons and Lovers* to be published and while he was working on his fourth novel (at that stage entitled 'The Sisters'), he told Edward Garnett: 'I can only write what I feel pretty strongly about: and that, at present, is the relations between men and women. After all, it is *the* problem of today, the establishment of a new relation, or the re-adjustment of the old one, between men and women' (*1L* 546). In Frieda and her sisters, he discovered what Otto Gross had earlier seen in them: a detachment from the values of chastity and patriarchy which in turn liberated him from his residual commitment to the values he had grown up with. As an elementary school teacher, he had had to pay lip service to such values, just as he had been forced to do while attending Chapel for his mother's sake. Once he had resigned from his job and travelled to Germany, he could wash off what he termed the hopelessness of England, 'the oldness and grubbiness and despair' (*1L* 459). He told his old teaching colleague Arthur McLeod that 'Nietzsche said the Germans are the great receptive, female nation' (*1L* 545). Between December 1910 and September 1912, Lawrence had effectively realised through his writing and then through his contact with Frieda and her sisters a Nietzschean transvaluation of all the values of his childhood, youth and early manhood.

This naturally had a profound impact on Lawrence's writing. After *Sons and Lovers* he initially struggled to find a new direction for his fiction. He started but then abandoned three novels: a fictionalisation of the life of Robert Burns, 'Elsa Culverwell' and 'The Insurrection of Miss Houghton' (later completely rewritten as *The Lost Girl*).[7] The last two, in particular, concentrated closely on female experience. In the surviving fragment of 'Elsa Culverwell', the eponymous heroine opens her first-person narrative with the striking assertion: 'My mother made a failure of her life. I am making a success of mine' (*LG* 343). Lawrence was increasingly preoccupied with exploring the situation of the powerful, emancipated modern woman and her attempts to find fulfilment in a society where men hold all the power. This is particularly striking in two prose works he produced in the six months between January and June 1913. Another Elsa figure, young Elsa Laskell in a short story entitled 'The Overtone', sits listening to older women discussing the suffrage, while sensing the unhappiness that exists in the marriage between her middle-aged hosts, Will and Edith Renshaw. At the end of the story, Elsa asserts her right to a fulfilment that her hostess never attained: 'I won't be cheated by my man. When between my still hands I weave silk out of the air, like a cocoon, he shall not take it to pelt me with. He shall draw it forth and weave it up.

For I want to finger the sunshine I have drawn through my body, stroke it, and have joy of the fabric' (*SM* 15). And in the short story 'New Eve and Old Adam', an independent newly-wed woman (Paula Moest) feels oppressed and tired by her conventional husband, who sees her as the flesh of *his* flesh, having no separate existence of her own. She stands up for, and asserts, her independence from him:

> "Well, you have your own independence," he said.
> "Ha," she laughed. "You needn't tell me that. It would take more than you to rob me of my independence." (*LAH* 168)

The story ends with a stalemate, as the couple are separated, with Paula complaining that her husband's 'idea' of a woman is that 'she is an expansion, no, a *rib* of yourself, without any existence of her own. That I am a being by myself is more than you can grasp' (*LAH* 182).

Lawrence is feeling his way in these short stories towards a vision of the modern woman as the pivot from which wider social change will come. In mid-May 1913, when Edward Garnett expressed reservations about the early version of 'The Sisters', Lawrence declared that it had enabled him to 'theorise myself out, and to depict Frieda's God Almightiness in all its glory'. He told Garnett that he would change this early (and now lost) draft from the first person into the third, and 'make it into art' (*1L* 550). By calling his novel 'The Sisters' Lawrence was from the outset emphasising his concern with depicting the revolutionary potential of women like Frieda, Johanna and Else. In *Sons and Lovers*, the discontentment of his female characters was placed in the contemporary English context of the suffrage and of various specific movements for female emancipation. The Co-Operative Women's Guild and the Women's Social and Political Union are both referenced in the novel.[8] There is even a thinly-veiled reference to Margaret Bondfield, the radical suffragist and founding President (in 1905) of the 'Adult Suffrage Society'; Clara Dawes attends a talk by 'Margaret Bonford' (*SL* 270), and Paul Morel enters the meeting too for a few minutes, while he waits for his train home from Nottingham. In 'The Overtone', Lawrence alludes to the call for a 'State-endowment of mothers' (*SM* 5). Yet, these political movements agitating for the female vote, equal working conditions, and state recognition of women's vital role as mothers are treated rather dismissively by Lawrence. They are shown to act as a consolatory focus for unsatisfied women whose only *real* hope for fulfilment rests with attaining the freedom to realise their own needs and desires either within or outside a relationship. There is an underlying implication in the fiction that political action might even distract women from the pressing and difficult task of demanding their right to emotional fulfilment.

Contact with Frieda and her sisters now enabled Lawrence to understand and articulate this insight. In the 'Study of Thomas Hardy', which he wrote between September and December 1914, at a crucial stage in the evolution of 'The Sisters' into *The Rainbow*, he praises the courage of the suffragettes, but suggests that their energies should be directed not at modifying existing laws, but at changing the broader structures of a society which does not allow women the individual liberty to express their true natures:

> The women suffragists, who are certainly the bravest, and, in the old sense, most heroic party amongst us, even they are content to fight the old battles on the old ground, to fight an old system of self-preservation to obtain a more advanced system of preservation. The vote is only a means, they admit. A means to what?—a means to making better laws, laws which shall protect the unprotected girl from a vicious male, which shall protect the sweated woman-labourer from the unscrupulous greed of the capitalist, which shall protect the interest of woman in the State. And surely this is worthy and admirable.
>
> Yet it is like protecting the well-being of a cabbage in the cabbage-patch, while the cabbage is rotting at the heart for lack of power to run out into blossom. Could you make any law in any land, empowering the poppy to flower? You might make a law refusing it liberty to bloom. But that is another thing. (*STH* 14)

This, of course, leads us into a complex and politically controversial area of reflection on the so-called 'Woman Question'. We could view his argument as dismissive of the actual material plight of women. We might think here of the silence of *Sons and Lovers* in the way it deals with Susan, one of the factory girls at Jordan's, who is forced to leave her work because she becomes pregnant outside marriage.[9] What happens to *her* after she leaves Jordan's? We never learn. At Paul Morel's instigation her place is taken by Clara Dawes, who is liberated at a stroke from the sweated labour of lace-making at home with her mother in the 'mean little street' (*SL* 301) on Bluebell Hill.

Lawrence's interest in female emancipation did not rest with women's struggle for accommodation within the existing financial and legal structures of society, but rather with their psychological battle to realise themselves and to throw off the mental constraints imposed upon them from without. This is the origin of a famous statement which he made in a letter of 23 December 1912 to Sallie Hopkin: 'I shall do my work for women, better than the suffrage' (*1L* 490). By showing young women with the courage to demand emotional freedom and satisfaction, and depicting their subversive power to sweep the old world aside and create a new and cleaner, more visionary space for self-realisation, he attempted to exceed what he saw as the rather limited objectives of suffragism. The 'germ' of 'The Sisters' – as Lawrence described it in April 1914 – was 'woman becoming individual, self-responsible, taking her own initiative' (*2L* 165). The revolutionary women whom Lawrence imagined (Elsa Laskell, Paula Moest and Ursula Brangwen) demand a kind of fulfilment in their lives and relationships different in kind not only from an older generation of women but also from their peers. They are *not* conventional heroines in the classic sense: they are not likeable and rational and docile, but headstrong and sexually self-aware. Lawrence set himself the task of trying to understand their position, making his readership see how it might feel for them to be restrained within the old world while reaching out for a new one.

The second title that Lawrence chose for 'The Sisters' – 'The Wedding Ring' – shows that he was particularly concerned with the problems posed to female freedom by marriage. In 'The Overtone', Edith Renshaw's wedding ring is a symbol of her husband's ownership of her;[10] in 'New Eve and Old Adam', Paula Moest symbolically removes her golden ring and spins it on a flower stalk, 'spinning it as if she would spurn it' (*LAH* 162). *The Rainbow* is a novel full of symbolic thresholds (doorways, gothic arches, leaning sheaves of corn, and the rainbow itself); it asks how the fixed circular completion of the wedding ring might suppress or facilitate the kinds of spiritual and emotional striving and transgression articulated in the other, more transient and incomplete symbols.

Available evidence suggests that Lawrence began with the third generation in *The Rainbow* and only later excavated the historical layers in the first two generations that underwrite Ursula Brangwen's experiences. Details in the married life of Will and Anna Brangwen in the second generation, and Ursula's experiences growing up in Cossethay (based on the village of Cossall), becoming a pupil-teacher and going to University College Nottingham, draw closely on the lives of Louie Burrows and her parents.[11] Yet Lawrence transforms these experiences by incorporating the German context which informed the book so closely in its earliest form. Ursula's rebelliousness and her difference from her peers come from the Polish and German blood that runs down the maternal line of her family. Her grandmother in the first generation, Lydia Lensky, has a Polish father and German mother; together with her first husband, the doctor Paul Lensky, Lydia is a Polish 'patriot and émancipée' (*R* 49) who participates in the rebellion against Russian rule in her mother country. Afterwards Lydia and Paul go into exile in London. Her dissident impulses are passed down to Anna, the daughter she has with Paul shortly before his untimely death. Lydia then marries Tom Brangwen, the gentleman farmer who lives at Marsh Farm, located between Ilkeston and Cossethay, but her rebelliousness is transmitted to Ursula, Anna's first born, who as a child growing up in the English Midlands sees herself as a Polish princess in exile, conceiving of her difference in terms of the familiar split which Gross articulated between the democratic Philistines and law followers and the aristocratic law breakers and creators of a new world. Lawrence took the details of Lydia's background from Frieda's paternal grandmother, who was Polish. Frieda's experiences clearly inform the emotional lives of all three generations of Brangwen women, from the sense of strangeness which Lydia feels in England – 'She felt the English people as a potent, cold, slightly hostile host amongst whom she walked isolated' (*R* 50) – to Anna's rebellion against her husband Will's patriarchal religious mindset, and on to Ursula's rejection of marriage. Foreignness is a force for positive change in the novel: it overturns static tradition and emotional impasse through the subversive potential of difference and an inability to see, and/or a refusal to accept, the moral imperatives and forms of male power ingrained in English social and religious life.

The blurb which Lawrence wrote for the novel, and which Methuen printed on the spine of the dust jacket, clearly emphasises Ursula's position as a modern heroine occupying a central place in the novel:

> This story, by one of the most remarkable of the younger school of novelists, contains a history of the Brangwen character through its developing crises of love, religion, and social passion. It ends with Ursula, the leading-shoot of the restless, fearless family, waiting at the advance-post of our time to blaze a path into the future. (Sagar 1980: plate 1)

The language here echoes the language of warfare current when the novel was published in September 1915. An 'advance-post' is the exploratory frontline of an army, sent out to check that the way is clear before being joined by reinforcements. Ursula strikes out as a woman into unknown territory, ahead of her time and in advance of the apparently emancipated women whom she meets along the way. Like Frieda in the letters from Otto Gross, Ursula is a woman with the revolutionary potential to 'blaze a path into the future'. The earliest form of the novel clearly celebrated the radical nature of the Von Richthofen daughters, and to accentuate their importance to the novel at its inception – and to express his love and gratitude to Frieda's elder sister for her help in facilitating his relationship with Frieda – Lawrence asked on 31 May 1915 that it be dedicated in Gothic script 'Zu Else' (*2L* 349). The wartime context meant that he had to be satisfied with an English dedication 'To Else'.

In *The Rainbow*, fearlessness or courage is a crucial feature of Ursula Brangwen's nature; it is the one quality that she tells Anton Skrebensky is more important than intelligence.[12] She shares with her Brangwen siblings and predecessors a restless, anti-authoritarian desire for self-realisation which is felt in her subversive and sensual approach to religion:

> The Brangwens shrank from applying their religion to their own immediate actions. They wanted the sense of the eternal and immortal, not a list of rules for everyday conduct. Therefore they were badly-behaved children, head-strong and arrogant, though their feelings were generous ... It was the vulgar mind which would allow nothing extra-human, nothing beyond itself to exist. (*R* 255)

Ursula is remarkably liberated in her openness to her own feelings. She responds to Anton's possessive courtship of her by appearing to conform to her submissive role, but she does not try to hide the intensity and violence of her feelings towards him. She undermines his vocation as a soldier and refuses his demand for the kind of support and submission he craves in a woman.

Her development towards individuality and self-responsibility entails not simply the rejection of Anton and the conventional married life he offers her in colonial India, but also the ultimate rejection of certain female role models she encounters at school and work. The first of these is her class-mistress, Winifred Inger. Miss Inger is in some respects the stereotypical emancipated woman, educated at Newnham College, Cambridge in the sciences and moving in intellectual and advanced circles.[13] We are told that she is 'interested in the Women's Movement' (*R* 318) and she tells Ursula stories of the subjection of women and the wrong-doings of men, reflecting her dissatisfaction with her society: 'Miss Inger was telling Ursula of a friend, how she had died in childbirth, and what she had suffered: then she told of a prostitute, and of some of her experiences with men' (*R* 315). The nature of Ursula's attraction to Miss Inger reflects her emotional and intellectual development outside Cossethay and the experiences of her mother. She grasps at a new outlet for her emotions and momentarily revels in the intellectual and physical closeness she feels to her teacher.

The exact nature of this relationship is complex: 'lesbian' seems too prescriptive a term for it, though of course a powerful sexual attraction forms a central part of it. Lawrence is ahead of his time in breaking down these conventional – and often censorious – ways of categorising relationships. In describing Ursula's admiration for Winifred, and her sensual attraction to the body and proud posture of her teacher, Lawrence may have drawn on things he had heard through Frieda about Katherine Mansfield's experiences.[14] Yet the exploration of desire as an untrammelled and subversive force leading to self-realisation or to greater self-awareness is grounded very much in the German context to the novel and the experiences of Frieda and her sisters. In the copy of *The Rainbow* which Lawrence gave to his younger sister Ada, he made several significant changes to the text of the novel.

In particular, he changed the title of this chapter in Ursula's life from 'Shame' to the German word 'Schwarm' (meaning 'crush') (Kinkead-Weekes and Worthen 2000: 14). Ursula has a youthful crush on her teacher, but she swiftly comes to realise that the trappings of Winifred's liberation mask a deeper emotional acceptance of the status quo. She senses something disturbing and unsatisfactory in Winifred's world: 'It was a strange world the girl was swept into, like a chaos, like the end of the world' (*R* 318). Winifred ends up marrying Ursula's Uncle Tom, a colliery owner in Yorkshire whose grotesque immersion in industry and mechanisation appeals to some 'ugly' (*R* 319) element in Winifred's nature. Later we learn that she has had a child by him. Ursula moves beyond, and forcibly represses, this episode in her life, which she comes to regard with a degree of 'shame'. Winifred is the first false light in Ursula's life.

Yet illicit encounters offer the characters in the novel a glimpse of some other possibility in life. When Tom Brangwen sleeps with a prostitute at the age of 19, it comes as a 'shock' to him: 'He did not know what to feel' (*R* 20). His disillusionment reinforces his 'innate desire to find in a woman the embodiment of all his inarticulate, powerful religious impulses' (*R* 21). After his subsequent encounter with the married lady in Matlock, he is alerted to the possibility of a strange world of glamour and excitement outside Cossethay and Ilkeston. Likewise, after Will's brief flirtation with Jennie the warehouse girl he returns to Anna, and their new-found strangeness to one another initiates a new phase of intimacy in their marriage.[15] For Ursula, the experience with Miss Inger causes her to fight against the constraining circumstances of home, as we realise in a comical interaction with her mother:

> Ursula would try to insist, in her own home, on the right of women to take equal place with men in the field of action and work.
>
> "Ay," said the mother, "there's a good crop of stockings lying ripe for mending. Let that be your field of action."
>
> Ursula disliked mending stockings, and this retort maddened her. (*R* 329)

Soon Ursula goes out into the 'Man's World' of work as a teacher at St Philip's School on Brinsley Street. This is the first real test of her courage, and her first serious experience of disillusionment, as she is brutalised by the need to discipline the children and patronised by the overbearing Headteacher, Mr Harby. In this setting she meets the other female role model in her life, Maggie Schofield. We are immediately made aware that Ursula does not share Maggie's political commitment to the women's movement: 'Maggie was a great suffragette, trusting in the vote. To Ursula the vote was never a reality. She had within her the strange, passionate knowledge of religion and living far transcending the limits of the automatic system that contained the vote' (*R* 377). As Anne Fernihough observes, Ursula 'refuses to be constrained by the carapace of an ideology' (Fernihough 2013: 121).[16] Yet she and Maggie are inseparable for a time, and Ursula is quite open to encountering the feminist voices with which her friend is so preoccupied: 'She and Maggie went to all kinds of places together, to big suffrage meetings in Nottingham, to concerts, to theatres, to exhibitions of pictures ... And it was a great joy, finding, discovering ... they talked and read Shelley or Browning or some work about "Woman and Labour"' (*R* 378). Again, though, the temporary kinship breaks down because of a discordance Ursula perceives between the outward emancipation of her friend and an inner submission to the terms of her society. Maggie's mood of sadness and subjection reflects her conventional feeling that a woman must avoid the lustful desires of men and grasp the rare signs of love when they show themselves. She seems committed to marriage and a stable domestic life in spite of her outward dissatisfaction with a woman's lot:

> They talked of love and marriage, and the position of woman in marriage. Maggie said that love was the flower of life, and blossomed unexpectedly and without law, and must be plucked where it was found, and enjoyed for the brief hour of its duration.
>
> To Ursula this was unsatisfactory. (*R* 382)

Marriage, of course, is the one thing that Ursula cannot finally accept, neither with Anthony Schofield (Maggie's brother) nor with Anton, in spite of her engagement to him, and her interest in playing the role of his partner during their trips to London, Paris and Oxford, and despite the two rings he buys for her (one of them an actual wedding ring).[17]

Anton comes back to Ursula, after a two-year break, during her period at college, where she is studying for an honours degree in Botany. For some time he compensates her for the growing sense of disillusionment she feels at college education. She is appalled by the commercial aspect of the college; it does not satisfy her desire to find some religious significance in knowledge. The gothic building in which she studies is a sham. Finally, she casts off both Anton and college, this latest manifestation of female 'emancipation'. She fails her exam and she tells Anton: 'I don't think I want to be married ... I mean never' (*R* 432). His devastation is total, until (that is) he marries the Colonel's daughter. Ursula is left pregnant. She is in the same situation as Susan in *Sons and Lovers*: she is a 'lost girl', without a partner and without work. Yet the ending to the novel attempts to show us that Ursula has fought her way to a kind of freedom that none of the women in her family, nor Winifred and Maggie, ever managed to achieve. She takes the path of the emancipated modern woman, through work and education, but she refuses to marry Anton and become his wife, choosing instead to cherish the religious vision of a world where things are different, and where men and women can throw off the forms of life they inhabit and come to realise themselves fully: 'She fought and fought and fought all through her illness to be free of him and his world, to put it aside, to put it aside, into its place' (*R* 456).

Ursula's miscarriage neatly removes her from the material consequences of her sexual liberation. She recuperates at home in Beldover: 'As she grew better, she sat to watch a new creation. As she sat at her window, she saw the people go by in the street below, colliers, women, children, walking each in the husk of an old fruition, but visible through the husk, the swelling and the heaving contour of the new germination' (*R* 457–458). What might have been seen – in another novel – as a tragic ending (the miscarriage; the failure at college; the return to her parental home) is presented here as a triumphant vision of self-realisation. Where Paul Morel's sense of being cut free from his past at the end of *Sons and Lovers* combines tragedy and self-affirmation, Ursula's alienation from home and society is the only positive conclusion that Lawrence can imagine for his heroine in the world she inhabits. Ursula defiantly declares: 'I have no father nor mother nor lover, I have no allocated place in the world of things, I do not belong to Beldover nor to Nottingham nor to England nor to this world, they none of them exist, I am trammelled and entangled in them, but they are all unreal. I must break out of it, like a nut from its shell which is an unreality' (*R* 456). This is presented as an alternative ending to the female *Bildungsroman*: a tale *not* of rebellion followed by social integration through marriage (Winifred's plot), nor of a sad but principled isolation (Maggie's plot), but of a courageous refusal to accept the conventional roles allotted to a young woman, and a keeping alive of the religious impulse to find something more eternal and meaningful in life: 'She saw in the rainbow the earth's new architecture, the old, brittle corruption of houses and factories swept away, the world built up in a living fabric of Truth, fitting to the overarching heaven' (*R* 459).

Notes

1 See *1L* 123 (28 March 1909) and 277 (14 June 1911).
2 See *1L* 288 (16 July 1911).
3 Lawrence entered three stories in different categories for the Christmas competition, so he was forced to submit them under different names. 'A Prelude' was entered under Jessie's name (using the nom de plume 'Rosalind'); 'The White Stocking' was submitted under a nom de plume for Louie Burrows; and 'Ruby-Glass' (an early version of 'A Fragment of Stained Glass') was sent in under the pen name 'Herbert Richards'. See *LAH* xlvii fn. 110.
4 See Delavenay (1969: 707).
5 La Av 3/2/8 (University of Nottingham).
6 See 'A Chapel Among the Mountains' and 'A Hay-Hut Among the Mountains', *TI* 27–35, 36–42.

7 For the 'Burns Novel' fragments, see *LAH* 200–211; for 'Elsa Culverwell', see *LG* 342–358.

8 See *SL* 69 and 274.

9 See *SL* 305.

10 See *SM* 7.

11 On 29 January 1914, Lawrence admitted to Edward Garnett that his central character (at that stage named Ella Brangwen) was incoherent because he was 'trying to graft on to the character of Louie the character, more or less, of Frieda' (*2L* 142).

12 See *R* 270.

13 The women's college was founded in 1871.

14 Lawrence and Frieda first met Mansfield and her partner John Middleton Murry in June 1913.

15 See *R* 218.

16 Fernihough compares Ursula Brangwen to Dora Marsden's concept of the 'Freewoman' as outlined in her contributions to the magazine of that title which she founded in 1911 (and which later became the *New Freewoman* and then the *Egoist*). Fernihough writes that the distinction Marsden makes between the freewoman and the bondwoman 'is a feminised version of Nietzsche's distinction between the *Übermensch*, who creates his own values, and the common herd'. For the freewoman, 'the vote is an irrelevance, a chimera' (Fernihough 2013: 11).

17 See *R* 420.

3

Lawrence, the Great War and Protest

The summer of 1914 was full of hope and anticipation. In mid-June, Lawrence and Frieda travelled to London from Heidelberg (where they had been staying for a few days with Alfred Weber). They had spent eight months living in Fiascherino in northwest Italy, on the Golfo della Spezia, and they only intended to be in England for a short time before returning to Italy. Lawrence had just completed 'The Wedding Ring', the third version of *The Rainbow*. They stayed in south Kensington at the home of Gordon Campbell, a barrister whom they had met through Katherine Mansfield and her partner John Middleton Murry. In late April, Frieda's divorce from Ernest Weekley had been made absolute, so on 13 July they married at Kensington registry office.

Lawrence now felt more accepted by London literary society, and he was able to move in literary circles on his own terms, free from what he termed the 'Hueffer-Pound faction', which he felt had been inclined to lead him round 'as one of their show-dogs' (*2L* 132–133). He saw old acquaintances, but he had also acquired a new set of friends and contacts in London, including the author and reviewer Catherine Jackson (later Carswell) and two people with a strong interest in psychoanalysis, Barbara Low and her brother-in-law David Eder.[1] He met too the American poet Amy Lowell, and Richard Aldington and Hilda Doolittle (known as H.D.). Back in the winter of 1912, Lawrence had contributed a poem to Edward Marsh's very successful anthology *Georgian Poetry 1911–1912*, and through Marsh he had met Lady Cynthia Asquith. In late November 1913, Marsh had arranged for several of the contributors to his anthology to visit Lawrence in Italy. At the end of June, Lawrence had lunch with the poet Rupert Brooke, who had also contributed to Marsh's book.

On 30 June, Lawrence, wishing to place his new novel, made a decisive move and struck out for himself as a professional author. The literary agent J. B. Pinker had approached him on behalf of Methuen with the offer of a lucrative three-novel contract, promising him £300 per book. Duckworth had paid Lawrence

The Life of the Author: D. H. Lawrence, First Edition. Andrew Harrison.

just £100 for *Sons and Lovers*. Edward Garnett, who had helped him to publish *The Trespasser, Love Poems and Others* and *Sons and Lovers* with Duckworth, had criticised the drafts he had seen of the new novel, which made the offer of going with a more commercial publisher all the more attractive. In early June, Lawrence had responded to Garnett's criticism that the novel was 'shaky' and the psychology of the characters 'wrong' by firmly defending it, telling his mentor that the latest developments in his thinking about character necessitated 'a different attitude in you' (*2L* 182–183). Lawrence met Duckworth and asked whether he could match Methuen's offer; he replied in a peremptory manner that he could not, so Lawrence gave the book to Methuen. The deal gave him a £150 advance on delivery of the manuscript, and £150 on publication of the book. This was a sum of money which secured his immediate future with Frieda. He offered his first book of short stories to Duckworth as an acknowledgement of Garnett's support for his writing.[2] He was also commissioned to write a short book on Thomas Hardy for the publishing firm Nisbet and Company. Marsh bought him a set of Hardy's works as a wedding present. The future seemed laid out before him.

On 31 July, Lawrence left Frieda in London and went on a walking tour of the Lake District with three men: A. P. Lewis (an engineer whom he had got to know in Fiascherino), S. S. Koteliansky (known as 'Kot', a Ukrainian translator working at the London Law Bureau, with whom he would have a lifelong friendship) and William K. Horne (one of Kot's colleagues). They walked in Westmorland and Lawrence was in good spirits. He later recounted how, during a storm, they 'shouted songs, and I imitated music hall turns, whilst the other men crouched under the wall and I pranked in the rain on the turf in the gorse, and Kotilianski [*sic*] groaned Hebrew music – Ranani Sadekim Badanoi'.

The merriment was cut short by the declaration of war on 4 August. The holiday ended abruptly, and when Lawrence arrived in Barrow-in-Furness to visit the home of Lewis he was confronted with the reality of the situation. At the train station, he saw reservists being sent off by their loved ones. The engineering firm which employed Lewis, Vickers Maxim, recalled its workers because it needed to increase the manufacture of armaments as part of the national war effort. Lawrence saw 'the great notices on Vickers' gateways – and the thousands of men streaming over the bridge' (*2L* 268).

On 10 August, shortly after his return to London, Methuen sent back to him the manuscript of his novel. In response to the outbreak of war, they were delaying the publication of any new books for six months, but they also took the opportunity to supply a few criticisms of the novel's sexual outspokenness. The majority of Lawrence's advance had already been spent, so he was immediately plunged into financial difficulty.[3] He and Frieda were unable to get back to Italy, where they could have lived cheaply; Frieda was effectively trapped in England as an enemy alien. Fortunately, the novelist, playwright and critic Gilbert Cannan and his wife Mary had a friend who owned a cottage close to their own home near Chesham, Buckinghamshire, which could be rented cheaply. They moved around 15 August.

Shortly before he left London, Lawrence wrote an article entitled 'With the Guns' for the *Manchester Guardian*. In it, he reflected on his experiences at Barrow and predicted what the war might be like for those men who were leaving on the trains. In the autumn of 1913, he had witnessed German military manoeuvres in the Isar valley in Bavaria, and in his article he described the awe-inspiring spectacle of flares and searchlights illuminating the countryside, and seeing large guns firing shells at distant targets: 'This was the glamour and the glory of the war: blue sky overhead and living green country all around, but we, amid it all, a part in some iron insensate will, our flesh and blood, our soul and intelligence shed away, and all that remained of us a cold, metallic adherence to an iron machine' (*TI* 82). The piece, which was published on 18 August, ended with the memorable sentences: 'It is so unnatural as to be unthinkable. Yet we must think of it' (*TI* 84).

The declaration affected Lawrence very deeply. Naturally, the fact that he and Frieda had family and friends in Germany, a number of whom served in the government or the army, brought the reality home to them on both sides of the conflict. Yet for Lawrence the war was more devastating still. In January 1915, he would declare that it 'finished' him: 'it was the spear through the side of all sorrows and hopes' (*2L* 268). John Worthen has suggested that the war shook Lawrence's 'very belief in English civilisation', destroying his faith in progress and his 'self-assurance that what he wrote addressed the deepest needs of his society' (Worthen 2005: 150–151). Since meeting Frieda and breaking free from his earlier emotional ties and teaching career his vocation as an author had been premised upon changing the outlook and lives of his English readers, alerting them to new possibilities for emotional fulfilment. Early in 1913, he told Edward Garnett: 'I think, do you know, I have inside me a sort of answer to the *want* of today: to the real, deep want of the English people, not to just what they fancy they want' (*1L* 511). Elsewhere he expressed a desire to 'bludgeon them into realising their own selves' (*1L* 424) and said that he wrote 'because I want folk – English folk – to alter, and have more sense' (*1L* 544). The outbreak of war came at a moment when Lawrence was tentatively exploring this sense of vocation in his writing.

Lawrence had begun by articulating his beliefs in letters to sympathetic friends. In June 1912, he told his former teaching colleague Arthur McLeod that he was 'in love – and my God, it's the greatest thing that can happen to a man'. He instructed McLeod to 'find a woman you can fall in love with. *Do* it. *Let* yourself fall in love, if you haven't done so already'. He stated: 'Nowadays, men haven't the courage and the strength to love. You must *know* that you're committing slow suicide' (*1L* 418). The phrase 'slow suicide' is used in *Sons and Lovers*: Gertrude Morel tells Paul that she wishes he 'could meet some *good* woman who would *make* you happy', and when he dismisses this by suggesting that he is the same as her in making the best out of battle and suffering, she feels 'as if her heart would break for him', since he had 'that poignant carelessness about himself, his own suffering, his own life, which is a form of slow suicide' (*SL* 299–300). The incident shows Lawrence analysing Paul's failure to love as emerging out of his acceptance of what Frieda had termed 'a sad old woman's misery' (*Poems* 1774). In January 1913, he told the artist Ernest Collings, one of his earliest acolytes: 'My great religion is a belief in the blood, the flesh, as being wiser than the intellect' (*1L* 503). Mark Kinkead-Weekes suggests that the first version of 'The Sisters' may have explored this as part of its 'theorising' (*R* xxi). The wisdom of the body was certainly something that Lawrence foregrounded as he revised the novel and emphasised Ursula Brangwen's honesty in prioritising her bodily feelings over the abstract patriarchal strictures of religion and education which threaten to silence and marginalise her. The body's wisdom was also emphasised in the significant revisions which Lawrence made to his short stories to prepare them for publication by Duckworth.[4]

Lawrence was intensely aware of the difficulties involved in embodying his worldview in his writing in a manner which would engage and challenge his readers without being too insistently authorial, and without preaching. He did not want to subdue his art to a metaphysic.[5] *Sons and Lovers* had been written over a period of two and a half years, and in that time Lawrence had gone from identifying with Paul Morel and his mother to critiquing the mother's emotional hold over her son and the son's own failure to break free from her influence. The shifts of focus during the composition of the novel contributed to its multi-perspectival ambiguity. Perhaps for this very reason, Lawrence and Frieda 'fought over' its meaning. In January 1913, Lawrence wrote a seven-page Foreword to the novel which he sent to Garnett. By the time he had finished the novel, Lawrence had come to view it as 'the tragedy of thousands of young men in England' (*1L* 476). The Foreword describes how unsatisfied mothers turn to their sons for the emotional fulfilment that is lacking in their marriages, which then prevents the sons from establishing satisfying relationships with their lovers and wives, thus creating a vicious cycle of dissatisfaction and damage. One can understand the personal investment of both Lawrence and Frieda in this argument, since Frieda saw herself as having helped Lawrence get over the damage that came from his own close bond with his mother, while Lawrence continued to react with a mixture of sympathy and impatience, even anger, to Frieda's yearning for her children. Yet the biblical language of the Foreword is quite obfuscating, and its connection with the novel is not immediately obvious. Lawrence swiftly disowned it; he told Garnett that he wanted to '*write* a Foreword, not to have one printed ... I am fearfully satisfied with myself as it is, and I would die of shame if that Foreword were printed' (*1L* 510).

Work on his fourth novel had begun in March 1913, and in its earliest form it sought to represent the 'God Almightiness' (*1L* 550) of Frieda and her sisters. Lawrence admitted that the first version was too theoretical, but also 'flippant and often vulgar and jeering' (*2L* 165). As he re-wrote 'The Sisters', transforming it into 'The Wedding Ring' and then *The Rainbow*, the novel drew on and reflected issues closest to his own experience as a man and author, most notably the repressive nature of English life and the transformative potential of contact with foreignness, and with a powerful woman who refuses to acknowledge tradition or patriarchal authority. There was always the danger, therefore, that the authorial perspective which had dominated in the theoretical first version would obtrude in the later versions too. In the final revisions he made to the novel between March and August 1915, Lawrence would try to achieve a greater sense of balance in his depiction of the conflict between Will and Anna Brangwen in the second generation, to ensure (in Mark Kinkead-Weekes's words) that 'their partial failure to achieve the marriage of opposites is attributed as firmly to her as to him' (*R* xxxviii). In doing so, he sought to remove his own authorial judgement from the novel, though in contrast his opposition to the war found its way into it through his increasingly critical depiction of Anton Skrebensky as a soldier in the Royal Engineers.[6]

Once Lawrence and Frieda were settled in the cottage in Buckinghamshire, he began writing the book on Thomas Hardy. This was to have been a 15,000-word introduction to Hardy's writing, combining biography and critical analysis, and on delivery of the manuscript the publisher offered a £15 advance on royalties. However, as Lawrence wrote and revised it between September and December 1914, it soon became obvious that he had strayed beyond the generic series requirements. Lawrence's primary interest in Hardy lay in the relation between the author's metaphysic and his writing. Lawrence reads Hardy's fiction as focusing almost obsessively on the strong, anti-social and amoral passions of his characters, and especially of his female characters, who are linked to the wildness of Egdon Heath. Lawrence shows how Hardy the bourgeois moralist punishes these characters, demonising them or enveloping them in tragedy. The tension he detects in Hardy's fiction between self-realisation and social morality provides the pretext for a series of digressions into contemporary contexts. In Chapter II, he addresses the suffrage, suggesting (as we have seen) that rather than seeking enfranchisement within a 'very, very clumsy and mechanical' (*STH* 14) political structure which prevents self-realisation, the energies of the suffragettes should be directed against the entire social system of which it is a part.

Lawrence then turns his attention to the war. The widespread enthusiasm for joining up is accounted for as a mass reaction against the stultifying safety of the State: 'No wonder there is a war. No wonder there is a great waste and squandering of life. Anything, anything to prove that we are not altogether sealed in our own self-preservation as dying chrysalides' (*STH* 15–16). Lawrence discusses the war not as a matter of politics and international relations, nor as a moral issue, but as a psychological reality: soldiers are said to embrace war at an unconscious level, in a desperate and self-destructive response to a society which preserves the self while preventing fulfilment. In his view, for those enlisting, danger, pain and suffering have become the only means of asserting their humanity and realising the value of life. Lawrence effectively reverses the terms of the moral discourse in war propaganda, seeing the soldiers as motivated not by conscious moral values and a defence of the State, but by unconscious forces and a reaction against it.

The 'Study of Thomas Hardy' was Lawrence's first fully-developed attempt at what he would later term his 'pollyanalytics': the 'pseudo-philosophy' in which he sought to 'abstract some definite conclusions' from his 'experiences as a writer and as a man' (*PFU* 65). It became an unwieldy 50,000-word treatise. Lawrence told Amy Lowell that it was 'supposed to be on Thomas Hardy', but was 'in reality a sort of Confessions of my Heart' (*2L* 235). It remained unpublished during Lawrence's lifetime. Kinkead-Weekes has argued that it helped Lawrence to articulate his dualistic approach to character at a crucial stage in the composition of *The Rainbow*, and so facilitated his work on the final draft between November 1914 and March 1915.[7] Like the Foreword to *Sons and Lovers*, however, it also revealed Lawrence's failure to find an appropriate form or language with which to address his English readership. Part of the problem in the first months of the war was that he could not know whom he was speaking for or to. At times in the 'Study of Thomas Hardy', he uses the plural pronouns 'we' and 'our', speaking for his English readership, while elsewhere he is more impersonal and theoretical, developing his own line of argument using religious language and what he would term 'philosophicalish' (*2L* 292) logic and terminology. As the 'Study' progresses, he sometimes appears to have forgotten his readership altogether and follows instead some intensely personal train of thought.

The collective sense of purpose that Lawrence asserts in the early parts of the 'Study' was soon lost as he began to realise the difference between his own thoughts on the war and the different camps into which his friends and fellow authors fell. Some of them had government posts or connections which meant that they must reflect State views on the conflict. Edward Marsh, for instance, was Private Secretary to Winston Churchill, First Lord of the Admiralty, and Cynthia Asquith was daughter-in-law of the Prime Minister, H. H. Asquith. On the outbreak of war, Ford Madox Hueffer worked for the War Propaganda Bureau under C. F. G. Masterman; in 1915, he published two books of propaganda, *When Blood is Their Argument: An Analysis of Prussian Culture*, which was produced with the help of Richard Aldington, and *Between St Dennis and St George: A Sketch of Three Civilizations*. Murry, who moved with Katherine Mansfield to a cottage close to the Lawrences, joined up but then thought better of it and managed to get a medical exemption, later taking up sedentary work in the War Office.

By contrast, Lawrence's other neighbour Gilbert Cannan was a conscientious objector, as was the artist Mark Gertler, a regular visitor to Cannan's windmill home. Cannan introduced Lawrence to Lady Ottoline Morrell, who would in turn put him in contact with her friend and sometime lover, the philosopher Bertrand Russell, who was a prominent pacifist. Edward Garnett, who had sympathised with the Boers in the Boer War, would come out against the war; in 1915, he served in the first British ambulance unit in Italy, and in 1918 he would publish a volume of anti-war satires entitled *Papa's War and Other Stories*. Yet Lawrence would express irritation at Garnett's decision to entitle his volume of short stories *The Prussian Officer* prior to its publication by Duckworth on 26 November 1914; shortly after the declaration of war Garnett changed the title of the story 'Honour and Arms' to 'The Prussian Officer' and named the entire collection after it in order to cash in on its topicality and the propaganda value of its depiction of sadism in the German army.[8]

Lawrence's anti-war views enabled him to live comfortably enough alongside conscientious objectors and pacifist friends, and he shared with some of them fantasies of escape from war-time England and even, in due course, practical plans to protest against the war. Yet he was never himself a pacifist. For him, conflict and war were inescapable aspects of the psyche, existing as necessary complements to the equally strong drive to union and constructive action. For Lawrence, the war was deplorable not on the absolute moral grounds that to kill is wrong, but because a death drive which emerged out of a collective reaction against the empty values of self-preservation enforced by Western societies was being dressed up in the cant of patriotism and religious virtue.

We can assess the complexity of Lawrence's early attitude to the war by considering his reaction to the special November 1914 'War Number' of the Chicago journal *Poetry*, and the war poem which he wrote in response to it. Lawrence seems to have established contact with this journal, and its editor Harriet Monroe, through Ezra Pound. A sequence of poems by Lawrence was published in the January 1914 number, for which he received the princely sum of £20;[9] he sent further poems to Monroe on 8 May, several of which would appear in the December 1914 number, for which he received a further £8.[10] Monroe informed Lawrence about the planned 'War Number' in late September, and she also told him about the associated competition which the journal was running to find the best war or peace poem based on the current conflict, for which the prize was $100.[11]

On 17 November, the 'War Number' arrived in Buckinghamshire. It contained 16 poems. There were contributions by two of Lawrence's new contacts: Amy Lowell's 'The Bombardment' and Richard Aldington's 'War Yawp'. Monroe had received 738 entries for the competition, and the winning poem was 'The Metal Checks' by Louise Driscoll, which opened the number. Lawrence read the poems straight away and wrote to Monroe later the same day. He told her that it put him 'into such a rage – how dare Amy talk about Bohemian glass and stalks of flame?': 'I hate, and hate, and hate the glib irreverence of some of your contributors – Aldington with his "do you know what it's all about, brother Jonathan, we don't?" It is obvious he doesn't. And your nasty, obscene, vulgar in the last degree – 'Hero' – John Russell McCarthy – may God tread him out – why did you put him in? You shouldn't'. Lawrence said he liked 'the woman who wrote 'Metal Checks' – her idea, her attitude', but he found her poetry 'pretty bad'. 'The Camp Follower' by Maxwell Bodenheim he considered 'common' and 'ugly ugly': 'something for the nasty people of this world to batten on'. He concluded: 'Your people have such little pressure: their safety valve goes off at the high scream when the pressure is still so low. Have you no people with any force in them. Aldington almost shows most – if he weren't so lamentably imitating Hueffer' (*2L* 232).

Hueffer's poem 'In October 1914' (better known as 'Antwerp') had been published in the magazine *The Outlook* on 24 October and had become a cause célèbre.[12] It focused on Belgian citizens' heroic resistance to the German forces advancing into France, expressing incredulity at their actions and commemorating the tragedy of the Belgian refugees and their children hopelessly waiting at St Pancras Station for the arrival of their husbands, lovers and fathers. The poem's haunting quality had been created in part by the use of unanswered and unanswerable questions: 'In the name of God how could they do it?', 'And what in the world did they bear it for?', 'And what in the world did they dare it for?' It drew analogies between the fighting in Belgium and earlier conflicts, from the Punic Wars to the Battles of Minden and Waterloo. Aldington's 'War Yawp' is an address not to Belgium, but to America ('England's cheeky kid brother'), and it draws analogies between the latest European war and battles in the American Civil War ('Bull Run, Gettysburg, Fredericksburg'), using the device of the unanswered question ('D'you know what it's all about?') and invoking ancient Greek myth ('Leucothea and Thetis'), but only in order to reassure the reader that the 'rock-citadel of the artists' will win out, as it always does, 'Against all the wars of the world'.[13] Lawrence clearly considered the poem derivative.

What Lawrence took against in some of the other poems – their glib irreverence and vulgarity – he seems to have instinctively associated with the distance of the Americans from the scene of the conflict. In adopting this stance, he directly contradicts the argument of Alice Corbin Henderson in a short discursive piece on 'Poetry and War' printed after the poems, which identifies a 'lack of conviction' in Hardy, Kipling, Bridges and Masefield in contrast to the Americans' 'genuine revolt against war' and their 'spirit of protest'.[14] The next day Lawrence wrote to Amy Lowell, explaining that he was cross with her for writing 'The Bombardment' and aestheticizing the scene of battle because 'The war-atmosphere has blackened here – it is soaking in, and getting more like part of our daily life, and therefore much grimmer' (*2L* 234). The stress naturally falls on 'here' and 'our': Lawrence is making a distinction between the Americans, for whom the war is a distant event which one must adopt an attitude towards, and the Europeans, who are hopelessly immersed in the war atmosphere and choked by it. Lawrence's response to the poems seems to imply that the conviction whose absence Henderson laments in the English poets is won through a failure to fully grasp the complex psychological reality of the war.

The validity of this point becomes obvious if we consider the poem that Lawrence considered 'nasty, obscene, vulgar in the last degree': 'The Hero' by John Russell McCarthy. This was a poem whose violent detail 'endangered the issue with the censor' (Monroe 1938: 342). It describes a group of German soldiers entering a house occupied by a husband and wife, their three daughters and the family dog. The soldiers cut the man's throat, tie up the woman and force her to watch while they rape the three girls, and then kill them all and lead the dog away as a mascot. The subject matter is conventionally shocking in the way that it draws on allied propaganda describing German atrocities in Belgium. It is structured in a manner that shifts between the different perspectives of the combatants. It starts out mimicking the jaunty tones of the marauding German 'corporal, nameless' and his 'little troop / Of nameless men'. The corporal's officer-class voice presents the violence as a mere lark, while stern parenthetical interjections at the end of each stanza drive home the irony in a heavy-handed fashion. The second part adopts the perspective of the fleeing allied soldiers whose retreat is checked by a corporal whose heroic raising of the flag rouses the loyalty of his soldiers, who return to the battle and vanquish the enemy. In contrast to his German counterpart, he is 'A nameless corporal, now to be named forever'. The final stanza presents the corporal as a divinely-ordained figure commemorated in bronze on a granite plinth: 'Was he not chosen of God?' The moral of the poem is 'Men can do worse than follow a flag'. It combines a voyeuristic involvement in war-time violence with a conventional religious stance, invoking a prurient fascination with sadism and violation only to reinstate the reader's moral complacency at the finish.[15]

Lawrence had recently read and admired George Bernard Shaw's essay 'Common Sense About the War', which was published on 14 November as a 32-page *Supplement to the New Statesman*.[16] Shaw debunked the moral cant spoken about the war, exposing the hypocrisy of English attacks on Prussian Junkerism and militarism and suggesting that politicians might have done more to avoid war with Germany. He proposed that 'the heroic remedy for this tragic misunderstanding is that both armies should shoot their officers and go home to gather in their harvests in the villages and make a revolution in the towns'. Shaw claimed to speak with an 'Irish capacity for criticizing England with something of the detachment of a foreigner, and perhaps with a certain slightly malicious taste for taking the conceit out of her' (Shaw 1914: 3). As I have indicated, when Lawrence revised *The*

Rainbow between November 1914 and March 1915 he added detail to his depiction of Anton Skrebensky's role as a soldier. At this time, and during final revisions between March and August 1915, he underscored the link between Skrebensky's violently possessive attitude to Ursula Brangwen and his role as an unthinking agent of empire in South Africa and India. In September 1916, Lawrence would express sympathy for the British Consular agent and Irish patriot Roger Casement, who was executed for high treason in August 1916, and he would hope, when the war was over, to 'shove a stiletto into the stout heart of Britannia' (*2L* 656). For the moment, though, he told Harriet Monroe: 'It is the business of the artist to follow it [i.e. the war] home to the heart of the individual fighters – not to talk in armies and nations and numbers – but to track it home – home – their war – and it's at the bottom of almost every Englishman's heart – the war – the desire of war – the *will* to war – and at the bottom of every German's' (*2L* 232–233).

With this intention in mind, he immediately wrote his own war poem and sent it to Monroe. It was entitled 'Ecce Homo' ('Behold the man!': Pontius Pilate's words on seeing the scourged Christ). The first manuscript page of the poem has been lost, but enough survives for us to assess how it writes back to the other war poems.[17] Its speaker is a common allied soldier immersed in conflict at the Front and speaking directly to us in a desperately confessional mode which reveals his confusion and trauma. The poem describes him killing two soldiers: one is shot, while the other is bayoneted. Yet the speaker is certainly no 'hero': he has no animosity towards the enemy and he is grotesquely fulfilled by the deathly consummation of conflict in spite of himself. Lawrence makes reference to the failure of the speaker's ideal of love as a way of accounting for the fulfilment he seeks in desecration and death: 'And I had dreamed of love, of love, of love, / And a woman glad of me, and I of her/ And my body glad as the bell of a flower, /And hers a flowerbell swinging'. The women in his life have turned into 'Harpies, Erinnies ... Eumenides' (*Poems* 1516), classical deities revenging themselves on men, clapping their hands at the hurt, defilement and destruction to which men are subjected. The soldier wearily reflects that the Germans he kills are not his enemy, and since he cannot kill the estranged women who seem to will his destruction, suicide is the only honourable act.

We might pause here to consider the purpose of 'Ecce Homo' as a war poem. It does not carry conviction in the same sense as the poems sent on to Lawrence by Harriet Monroe. It is not a protest poem in any obvious sense, and it certainly is not a call to arms. Instead, its central effect is to create a soldierly voice which speaks for all of us in its immersive failure to grasp the forces which compel it. The loose, free-verse form seems calculated to offset the kind of careful formal control brought to bear in the poem by McCarthy. The poem confronts us with a confused and confusing interior monologue wholly devoid of any consoling external perspective. We are thoroughly implicated in the destructive involution of thought and deed enacted in the poem's syntax.

Harriet Monroe did not accept 'Ecce Homo' for *Poetry*, though she copied out several sections from it and may have considered doing so. Lawrence also sent a copy to J. C. Squire, literary editor of the *New Statesman*, since it had just published Shaw's essay and seemed to Lawrence 'the only place where a bit of dignity remains' (*2L* 236). What Squire made of it we do not know, but he did not publish it. Between 17 November 1914, when the poem was written, and May 1915, when it was first published in a heavily revised form under the title 'Eloi, Eloi, Lama Sabachthani?' in an Imagist number of the *Egoist*, edited by Aldington, Lawrence's vision of the war changed, as the analysis of the war-time psyche in the 'Study of Thomas Hardy' gave way to the darker vision of his latest philosophical essay, 'The Crown' (written between March and October 1915). The sense of individuals throwing away their lives as the only form of self-realisation available to them in a society premised upon self-preservation was displaced by a feeling that people actually enjoy and revel in the deathliness. If 'Ecce Homo' showed us Man as he actually is (tortured by his desire for deathly consummation), then 'Eloi, Eloi, Lama Sabachthani?' presents us with a bleak world in which God has wholly forsaken us. Christ's words on the cross ('O God, O God, why have you forsaken me?'), from Mark xv. 34, quoting Psalm 22, are used to drive home the loss of reverence for life in the blood-lust of the battlefields. A comparison of the act of bayoneting the enemy soldier in 'Ecce Homo' with the eighth stanza of 'Eloi, Eloi' reveals Lawrence's introduction of the shocking central conceit in the poem. 'Ecce Homo' describes the coupling of the soldier with his victim-double in the act of bayoneting:

> And when I ran across to the trenches
> And saw his face with blue eyes, startled, frightened, agonized,
> And I knew he wanted it, he wanted it
> Like a fierce magnet he drew my bayonet
> Like a spent shaft it sank to its rest
>
> (*Poems* 1515)

This becomes altogether more explicit and sinister in the revised version:

> So when I run at length thither across
> To the trenches, I see again a face with blue eyes,
> A blenched face, fixed and agonised,
> Waiting.—And I knew he wanted it.
> Like a bride he took my bayonet, wanting it,
> Like a virgin the blade of my bayonet, wanting it,
> And it sank to rest from me in him,
> And I, the lover, am consummate,
> And he is the bride, I have sown him with the seed
> And planted and fertilised him.
>
> (*Poems* 1518)

The revised version seems calculated to shock readers with a sense of the specific satisfaction and relief which violent destruction can bring. Lawrence's purpose is to jolt his readers out of their moralising complacency and make them feel and recognise in themselves the capacity for obscene satisfaction in atrocity which he invokes.

If Lawrence had found Lowell's aestheticizing of the war in 'The Bombardment' irreverent, Lowell considered 'Eloi, Eloi' the indecent product of a damaging personal obsession. She wrote: 'for pure, farfetched indecency [it] beats anything I have ever seen ... He loses his eye about things; sometimes I think his condition is almost pathological, and that he has a sort of erotic mania' (Tedlock 1952: 411). To write at high pressure, and with full force, meant to expose as well as to critique the violent irrationalism of the self.

Lawrence's response to war-time England was deeply conflicted. Part of him wanted to retreat into fantasy. Over Christmas and the New Year of 1914–1915 Lawrence and Frieda, Murry and Katherine Mansfield, and Gilbert and Mary Cannan, together with Gertler and Kot and Gordon Campbell, had parties in which they sang songs and improvised little plays. There was a manic quality to their exuberance which only masked their collective unhappiness with the war. In the course of the celebrations, Lawrence conceived his 'Rananim' idea. Taking its name from Kot's chanting in Hebrew of Psalm 33 ('Rejoice in the Lord, O ye righteous') in the Lake District, the 'island scheme' as it came to be known was a fantasy that Lawrence conceived to establish a small colony with friends, 'built up on the real decency which is in each member of the Community' (*2L* 259). Lawrence intended at one stage to include Ottoline Morrell in his plans, even thinking that her Oxfordshire home, Garsington Manor, which she and her husband Philip had purchased in March 1913 and would take possession of in May 1915, might serve as its venue. Gilbert Cannan, who wrote about an island retreat from war in his book of fantastical fables *Windmills*, which he published in April 1915 and dedicated to Lawrence, was almost certainly in on the fantasy at its inception.[18] Mansfield and Murry seem to have considered it as a genuine possibility, but ultimately decided it was not for them. For Gertler and Kot, it was little more than a flight of fancy. The scheme opened up an imaginative world which was a welcome distraction for Lawrence from the reality of the war and his poverty.

In January 1915, desperate to leave their dark and damp house, Lawrence and Frieda accepted Viola Meynell's offer to move into her cottage in Greatham, Pulborough, Sussex. Here the other aspect of Lawrence's relation to the war made itself felt: the part of him that wanted to speak out against the war and take direct action. In early March 1915, Bertrand Russell invited Lawrence to spend a weekend with him in Cambridge. The two men later planned to deliver anti-war lectures together in London in the autumn, but their views on the war were always very different; the plans ended with recriminations and enmity when Lawrence took against Russell's outline of his own contribution as being too critical of the existing State and insufficiently constructive, and Russell went from admiring Lawrence's psychological insight to suspecting him of political naivety as he emphasised first the necessity of wholesale nationalisation and then the need to reject democracy and install a dictator.

As Lawrence's views on the war darkened, so feelings of depression, frustration and anger surfaced more frequently in his letters. Writing was always his outlet for grasping these feelings and gaining relief from them. Sometimes it was a simple matter of releasing intense emotions in his letters, turning feelings of powerlessness and humiliation into statements of disgust which allowed him for a moment to feel himself outside, and above, the mass of men. He also sought relief by articulating his own view of the conflict, and of soldiers' deathly motivations, in letters, philosophical writings and fiction as a means of offsetting and undermining official discourses of heroism and patriotism. Lawrence became more autocratic, and his thought more systematic and inflexible, as the war dragged on. He did not shy away from upsetting those close to him who were directly affected by the war, and who naturally had very different views of soldiers and their motivations.

On 19 June 1915, Cynthia Asquith came to visit Lawrence in Greatham with her husband Herbert (or 'Beb') Asquith. Beb, who was a barrister in peace-time, was a serving officer in the Royal Artillery. He had been fighting in Flanders and had a lucky escape when a piece of shrapnel grazed his lip and broke several of his teeth. He had returned to England for a dental operation and was recuperating. Lawrence was convinced that Beb was so immersed in the fighting and death at the Front that they had become his only reality. He told Ottoline Morrell: 'He is home slightly wounded – three teeth knocked out. But he is well. Only all his soul is left at the war. The war is the only reality to him. All this here is unreal, this England: only the trenches are Life to him. Cynthia is very unhappy – he is not even aware of her existence. He is spell-bound by the fighting line. He ought to die. It all seemed horrid, like hypnotism' (*2L* 359–360). Beb would recall walking with Lawrence on the beach at Littlehampton. Lawrence plunged straight into the topic of war, 'a subject which seemed to devour him with a curious alternation of hatred and fascination' (Asquith 1937: 242). He discussed the war 'not at all from the point of view of strategy or tactics, the movement of nations or men in the mass, but entirely from the angle of the individual soldier'. He told Beb that the war was the sum total of all the individual soldiers' 'will to destroy' (Asquith 1937: 243). Beb responded that 'delight in the mere act of destruction ... though it might often be seen in grown-up iconoclasts, was not at all typical of soldiers'. Lawrence, however, watched Beb unthinkingly throwing stones at a bottle he had spotted bobbling about in the waves, and gave him 'a humorous but baleful glance', taking this as a confirmation of soldiers' underlying will to destroy. Beb said 'it was in vain that I protested that I had no passion for the destruction even of a medicine bottle' (Asquith 1937: 244).

Lawrence's view of soldiers and their unconscious attraction to conflict and destruction for its own sake is explored in the 1915 version of his short story 'England, My England'.[19] The cottage which Viola Meynell had invited Lawrence and Frieda to live in was situated on the Meynell family estate. Viola's parents, Wilfrid and Alice Meynell, had a house there, and they gave cottages to each of their three daughters, Monica, Madeline and Viola. Madeline was given a cottage half a mile from the main farmhouse. She and her husband Perceval Lucas had three daughters. The eldest, Sylvia, had hurt her leg in the summer of 1913, while her father was away in Italy; she fell on a sickle which a visitor had left lying in the garden, and it had left her with a limp. Perceval enlisted in September 1914. Lawrence met Madeline and her daughters, and in June 1915 he wrote his story, which draws closely on details of the Meynell family, and especially of what he knew about Madeline and Perceval Lucas. Lawrence used the details to create a fable showing how a lack of fulfilment in civilian life might drive a soldier to find emotional compensation in the exhilaration of death at the Front.

Through his depiction of Evelyn Daughtry Lawrence undermines the popular image of the soldier out at the Front to defend his wife, family and country. The opening to the story situates Evelyn in the midst of all the things which propaganda saw as formative. He dreams of his idyllic English cottage, with his wife and children around him. Yet conflict infiltrates the sanctity of his home: he hears the 'conflict of authority, echoed even in the children!' (*EmyE* 219), and in their opposition to one another he and his wife, Winifred, 'never put down their weapons for a day'. Thc image of England and the family as full of 'peace and sunshine and loveliness' (*EmyE* 220) is treated with caustic irony by Lawrence: in this account, they are almost indistinguishable from the Western Front.

The action of the story begins to unfold when Evelyn unknowingly inflicts a serious injury on his eldest daughter. He leaves a sharp old iron (or scythe) lying in the garden. The daughter cuts her knee on it, and the ensuing blood poisoning renders her lame. The implication seems to be that the conflict at home represents a kind of warfare in which Evelyn is already engaged before he is called upon to enlist. When War is declared, then, 'a shiver went over his soul' (*EmyE* 223). Something within him finally connects with the world of men and action: 'There, in the absolute peace of his sloping garden, hidden deep in trees between the rolling of the heath, he was aware of the positive activity of destruction, the seethe of friction, the waves of destruction seething to meet, the armies moving forward to fight. And this carried his soul along with it' (*EmyE* 224).

Enlisting, he enters a purposive mode of life after years of refusing to accept employment. The newly-conscious Evelyn is, however, under no illusions concerning his role as a soldier, as we are told in this rather shocking account of his response to Winifred's celebration of him as a hero figure:

> She [Winifred] tried to tell him he was one of the saviours of mankind. He listened to these things; they were very gratifying to his self-esteem. But he knew it was all cant. He was out to kill and destroy; he did not even want to be an angel of salvation. Some chaps might feel that way. He couldn't; that was all. All he could feel was that at best it was a case of kill or be killed. As for the saviour of mankind: well, a German was as much mankind as an Englishman. What are the odds? We're all out to kill, so don't let us call it anything else. (*EmyE* 226)

The absolute clarity of his thinking at this point alerts us to the irony of the title, 'England, My England'. Lawrence alludes in a subversive manner to a famous patriotic poem of 1900 by W. E. Henley, celebrating England as a colonial power during the Second Boer War of 1899–1902. That poem opened: 'What have I done for you, / England, my England? / What is there I would not do, / England, my own?' (Henley 1907: 253). Evelyn, in contrast to the speaker of Henley's poem, has no commitment at all to his country. Yet, there is also a troubling sense in which as readers we are implicated in his desire for death, forced to connect with him even as we recognise his nihilism, lack of volition and emptiness.

For the majority of the story, we can feel very little for the character of Evelyn. In tracing his drift towards deathly consummation, the story is inventive in its employment of adjectives suggestive of detachment and blankness: he is aloof, silent, neutral, cold, unnatural, frightful, detached, reserved, abstracted, incommutable, impervious, nihilistic, off-hand, negligent and nullified. Being drafted as a private into the Artillery, he leaves the unreal conflicts of home and marital disquiet for the more real conflict in France: 'Then he was really engaged. He hated it, and yet he was fulfilling himself. He hated it violently, and yet it gave him the only real satisfaction he could have in life now. Deeply and satisfactorily it fulfilled him, this warring on men. This work of destruction alone satisfied his deepest desire' (*EmyE* 226).

At the end of the story, Evelyn, hearing two German shells land nearby, feels himself on the brink of consummation: 'his blood became still to receive it' (*EmyE* 228). The third hits its target. As Evelyn regains consciousness and lucidity he becomes fully aware of his mutilated body: he thinks of his wife and children, but can find no connection with them, even now. In the clarity of the aftermath he shoots three Germans as they come to check the bodies on the ground. Lawrence's handling of the battlefield scenes is at once fascinating and slightly loose and melodramatic. He uses the term 'machine-guns' inaccurately (connecting it with rifle fire) and the deaths of the Germans are almost comic in their hideousness. One soldier pitches forward and collapses, writhing; the second has his neck broken by a bullet; and the third has 'a bullet through its brain'. Yet, the extremely black comedy has its point, for Evelyn's final smile implicates and troubles the reader, just as it troubles the German soldier who finally stabs him to death and mutilates his face:

> The German cut and mutilated the face of the dead man as if he must obliterate it. He slashed it across, as if it must not be a face any more; it must be removed. For he could not bear the clear, abstract look of the other's face, its almost ghoulish, slight smile, faint but so terrible in its suggestion, that the German was mad, and ran up the road when he found himself alone. (*EmyE* 232)

In the end, Evelyn's self-realisation in the one direction of deathliness and destruction is so complete that his smile provokes an act of desecration. His effacement is a symbolic realisation of his lack of being throughout the story.

Interestingly, Lawrence makes it clear that the German does not run mad in the aftermath of the graphic violence because of the horrors involved in the act of killing, but because of the implications of the smile he has felt compelled to remove. This enigmatic slight smile leaves a final question mark hanging over Evelyn, and over our relation to him as readers. Is it a final gesture of self-satisfaction for a man who finds his only realisation in imminent death at the Front? Is it a nihilistic smile, expressing his absence of feeling for all that we might deem formative and valuable (family, work, ambition, a sense of individual and collective purpose, a belief in the preciousness of life itself)? Or is it merely an act of defiance, with Evelyn jeering at the enemy and assuring him that the worst he can do holds no fear for *him*? It is, of course, all of these things and more. Lawrence dismantles the idea of the heroic soldierly self as constituted by traditional ideas of nationhood and the family. In this story, the modern self emerges as a troubled psychological entity lacking any stable moral values, and committed instead to the violence and self-destruction of its own unconscious desires.

Lawrence characteristically picked up on details in the lives of Madeline and Perceval Lucas, and their family, and saw them as symptomatic of a deeper cultural malaise. The accident that befell young Sylvia becomes eerily proleptic in the story, foreshadowing Evelyn's maiming at the Front. There is a powerful unspoken sense in the story that the maiming of Evelyn's daughter is so painful to him because it exposes his own hidden craving for death and destruction. The story would have been terribly hurtful to the Meynell family when it was written in June 1915. Later events would make it even more so. On 22 June, Perceval Lucas was commissioned in the Infantry. He died in France on 6 July 1916. The story was first published in the *English Review* in October 1915. When Catherine Carswell informed Lawrence about Perceval's death, he said he wished it 'at the bottom of the sea, before ever it had been printed'. His further comments, however, show that he valued the psychological truth he was committed to tracing in his writing over any upset it might cause to those whose lives he fictionalised: 'Lucas was, somehow, a spiritual coward. But who isn't? I ought never to have gone to live at Greatham. Perhaps Madeleine [*sic*] won't be hurt by that wretched story – that is all that matters. If it was a true story, it shouldn't really damage' (*2L* 635).

Lawrence and Frieda left Greatham at the end of July 1915. They spent a few days in Littlehampton before settling into their new home in the Vale of Health, Hampstead. Moving from Sussex to London felt like going from 'the wilderness ... back into the world to fight' (*2L* 374). In early September, Lawrence and Murry decided to set up a small fortnightly journal, which they called *The Signature*, primarily as a vehicle to publish in instalments Lawrence's anti-war essay 'The Crown'. They sent out leaflets seeking subscriptions. On 30 September 1915, *The Rainbow* was finally published by Methuen.

On 31 May, Lawrence had confidently asserted 'We shall have peace by the time this book is published' (*2L* 349). As he ruefully admitted in 1924, 'I'm afraid I set my rainbow in the sky too soon, before, instead of after the deluge' (*IR* 77). The defiantly optimistic final lines of the novel now seemed wholly misplaced. *The Signature* failed to secure sufficient subscriptions; only three numbers were published (on 4 and 18 October, and 1 November) before the money ran out, meaning that only three of the six parts of 'The Crown' were published in 1915. Lawrence and Murry had hired a room in London at 12 Fisher Street, Southampton Row, to meet subscribers on a fortnightly basis in order to discuss the war, but just one meeting took place (on 11 October); the second meeting on 24 October only went ahead because they did not have sufficient time to cancel it.

An early anonymous review of *The Rainbow* in the *Standard* was promising: it called Lawrence 'a realist to the point of brutality' and said that the novel 'may cause offence and be condemned', but it also acknowledged that it was 'an important piece of work' (Draper 1970: 89–90). Catherine Carswell was as supportive as she could be in the *Glasgow Herald*, stating that the novel was 'so very rich in emotional beauty and in the distilled essence of profoundly passionate and individual thinking about human life', but even she had to concede that its depiction of modern life as 'mad and sick and sad because it does not know how to love' was 'merciless, almost gloating' and would be 'strongly offensive to most readers' (Draper 1970: 100–101). She lost her job at the newspaper for her failure to condemn it outright. Other reviewers did not hold back. Robert Lynd in the *Daily News* called the novel 'a monotonous wilderness of phallicism' (Draper 1970: 92). James Douglas in the *Star* referred to its 'morbidly perverted ingenuity of style', arguing that the artist has a moral responsibility to his readers and his society, a 'duty of reverence', and an 'elementary obligation of restraint and selective conscience': 'The wind of war is sweeping over our life, and it is demolishing many of the noisome pestilences of peace. A thing like *The Rainbow* has no right to exist in the wind of war' (Draper 1970: 93–95). In the *Sphere*, Clement Shorter suggested that the novel was more objectionable than the novels of Émile Zola: 'There is no form of viciousness, of suggestiveness, that is not reflected in these pages' (Draper 1970: 96–97).

Douglas and Shorter hardly addressed the plot and structure of the novel at all; instead they took issue with Lawrence's entire vision of human life and vocation as an author. Lawrence had explored the conflicted relationship between the individual and modern society, and the search for new forms of religious experience in and through the body. In the process, he had challenged traditional English social ideals, showing how the patriarchal values that Ursula encounters through religion and in the workplace as a teacher, and the commercial values that she feels underpin her studies at college, might check her drive for emotional fulfilment. He had depicted Anton Skrebensky as a soldier who had unthinkingly accepted all the beliefs in traditional gender norms, colonialism and hierarchy that threaten Ursula's sense of self. He had asked his reader to imagine how different life might be if these things were challenged and seen for what they are. The things that meant most to Lawrence were publicly condemned. Shorter dismissed Lawrence's 'artist impulses' as those of 'a mind that has decadent tendencies', while Douglas stated that 'The artist is not his own law-giver'. For Lynd, the book was 'not true, either in its representation or in its propaganda' (Draper 1970: 91, 94, 97). The reviews alerted the authorities to the novel, and a magistrate's warrant was issued for the suppression of *The Rainbow*, resulting in the police visiting the Methuen offices on 3 and 5 November to seize unsold copies of the novel. At a trial on 13 November, it was successfully prosecuted under the 1857 Obscene Publications Act and all unsold copies and unbound sheets were ordered to be destroyed.

This had a devastating effect on Lawrence. Almost a decade later he reflected that people were 'robbing me of my freedom then' (Nehls 1958: 415). The destruction of his novel was terrible, but just as bad was the publicity the trial generated, since this made publishers wary of him and his writing. His freedom of expression and his capacity to earn a living as a professional author were taken away from him. In mid-October, he had discussed escaping to America, and in early November he and Frieda had even obtained passports, but the fallout from the prosecution prevented them from travelling. He declared that it was the end of his writing for England, and henceforward he would find an audience for his work in America.[20] Planning for a new life there would become another fantasy to sustain Lawrence in the coming months. In late November, he spoke to a man who owned a place near Fort Myers in Florida where he thought he and a few friends might 'gain a new footing in a freer place' (*2L* 449), and he asked a new contact, the composer Philip Heseltine, to enquire whether Frederick Delius might be prepared to let them have use of a small estate he owned which was also located in Florida, 'nearer to Jacksonville' (*2L* 450), but it was said to be too derelict for human habitation. In early December, he discussed the possibility of sailing from Glasgow to the West Indies, with the idea of travelling on from there to America.[21]

Other plans and schemes helped him feel he was striking back at the authorities. Philip Morrell, who was a Liberal MP, asked to meet Lawrence in Westminster to arrange to ask questions in the House of Commons about the prosecution of *The Rainbow*. On 18 November, the Home Secretary, Sir John Simon, confirmed that the police had acted 'in pursuance of their ordinary duty' (Nehls 1957: 333) and did not need Home Office authorisation; Lawrence was not given the opportunity to reply to the charge made against his work because the publishing firm, Methuen, was the defendant and not the author. In response to a further written question from Morrell seeking clarification on why proceedings were taken for the suppression of the novel 'without any notice being given to the author', on 1 December the Home Secretary confirmed that the police and magistrate had acted perfectly legally: 'the provisions of the law were strictly complied with' (Nehls 1957: 334, 335). In the meantime, Lawrence was exploring the possibility of getting the novel published in Paris, with the help of Prince Antoine Bibesco, a Romanian diplomat.[22] Lawrence sought legal advice from Donald Carswell (Catherine's husband, who was a barrister) about whether reprinting the book would infringe Methuen's rights.[23] Carswell suggested that Lawrence might have a sound basis for bringing a case for libel against James Douglas and Clement Shorter. When pressed by Philip Morrell, the Home Secretary had conceded that it might be possible to put another copy of *The Rainbow* into the hands of the authorities in order to induce a second prosecution in which Lawrence might defend his book, and this seemed a possibility for a time too.[24]

The thought of leaving the country and going to America with the passports he and Frieda had acquired still appealed, and with this in mind on 11 December he went to a recruiting station in Battersea Town Hall to attest and acquire a medical exemption, but after waiting in the queue for two hours he decided against it. This meant that he must stay in England. The next best thing to moving abroad was to live somewhere as far from London and officialdom as possible, so Murry arranged for him to live rent free in a house in Cornwall owned by the novelist J. D. Beresford.

On 21 December 1915, Lawrence left Hampstead. He spent Christmas with his sister Ada in Ripley. Then, he and Frieda travelled to Beresford's house in Porthcothan, near Padstow. They arrived there on 30 December. Lawrence embraced the remoteness of Cornwall and set about convincing himself and others that it was a Celtic homeland in which he could establish a new life away from the war-time England he despised. He started to write another (now lost) philosophical essay entitled 'Goats and Compasses'. In February, he planned with Heseltine – who stayed with him in Porthcothan – a project they called 'The Rainbow Books and Music' with a view to publishing *The Rainbow* and other controversial or non-commercial works of literature and music by private subscription. Heseltine printed and sent out flyers, but once more the scheme foundered for lack of interest.

D. H. Lawrence's cottage at Higher Tregerthen, near Zennor, Cornwall. The 'tower room' of the larger cottage next door, initially lived in by Katherine Mansfield and John Middleton Murry, is on the left-hand side. University of Nottingham, Manuscripts and Special Collections, La R 4/6/15.

At the end of February 1916, Lawrence and Frieda moved from Porthcothan further down the coast to Higher Tregerthen, near the isolated village of Zennor, six miles north of Penzance, where they eventually settled in a small cottage close to a farm, with rocks at the back of it and a view in front over fields to the farm and then the sea. Lawrence invited Katherine Mansfield and Murry to join them by taking the slightly larger cottage next door, creating a small and intimate community. They came in early April, but the experiment was a disaster and they moved out in mid-June. Katherine was unable to work in such close proximity to the Lawrences, while Lawrence was extremely productive. Around 19 April he started work on his next novel, *Women in Love*, which drew on the later material from 'The Wedding Ring' which he had removed in January 1915 to produce *The Rainbow*. Lawrence worked intensively on the novel until late June. He produced the first draft of around 120,000 words in just two months. On 24 June, general conscription came into effect, and in the following week he had to travel to Bodmin to undergo a medical examination for military service, after which he was granted a complete exemption. In mid-July, he began typing the novel, making additions and changes to it as he progressed, moving into the cottage vacated by Murry and Mansfield. He hated the typing and abandoned it in mid-October, when J. B. Pinker arranged to have a professional typist complete it. In preparation for this, Lawrence wrote out again and revised some 65,000 words between 13 and 31 October. He told Pinker that he would later add a 'sort of epilogue' (*2L* 669) to it. He made revisions to the typescript between 6 and 20 November.[25]

The 1916 version of *Women in Love* – first published in 1998 as *The First 'Women in Love'* – contains Lawrence's most pointed and thoroughgoing critique of the war atmosphere in England. Lawrence said that it contained 'the results in one's soul of the war' (*3L* 143). It was written in a spirit of opposition to the English State and out of a feeling that an entire phase of civilisation was collapsing. Within weeks of starting it, Lawrence declared that it was 'beyond all hope of ever being published' and he was writing to 'the unseen witnesses' (*2L* 602). He may have begun by writing the Prologue, which he later decided to remove from the novel, in which he dealt with the breakdown of Rupert Birkin's relationship with Hermione Roddice, and described Birkin's physical attraction to men and especially to Gerald Crich. At the trial of *The Rainbow*, the prosecution had drawn particular attention to the chapter entitled 'Shame', which dealt with Ursula's physical attraction to her teacher Winifred Inger, so addressing same-sex desire again in his new novel could be expected to invite rejection from publishers. Yet the novel's atmosphere in its first chapter is also very different from anything in *The Rainbow*, and Lawrence knew it was likely to cause offence and disgust. The writing is imbued with a sense of world-weariness and cynicism. The dialogue and action show how the outer forms of life have become meaningless and empty, leaving individuals subject to feelings of frustration and despair.

In the opening conversations between Ursula and Gudrun Brangwen in their parents' home in Beldover, and in the local churchyard, where they watch the wedding procession for Laura Crich and Theobald Lupton, they express profound scepticism about marriage. 'I'm getting bored' declares Gudrun: 'Things don't seem to materialise with me, I find. There's so much that just withers in the bud' (*FWL* 4; cf. *WL* 8).[26] Yet when she sees Gerald Crich, the bride's brother, her interest is 'piqued': 'she experienced a keen paroxysm, a transport, as if she had made some incredible discovery, known to nobody else on earth. A strange transport took possession of her, all her veins were in a paroxysm of violent sensation' (*FWL* 10; cf. *WL* 15). On the surface, characters such as Gudrun, Gerald and Hermione Roddice appear very assured: Gudrun is an artist, Gerald an industrialist (the heir to his father's coal mines) and Hermione a wealthy patron of the arts. Yet each has secret vulnerabilities. We are told, for instance, that Hermione 'always felt vulnerable, vulnerable', her problem being 'a lack of confidence, she had no natural sufficiency, there was a terrible void, a lack, a deficiency of being within her' (*FWL* 12; cf. *WL* 16–17). Their vulnerabilities cause them to react adversely to apparently innocuous situations: they experience uncontrollable violent emotions, and sometimes they are driven to act these out in sadistic or murderous ways.

As Lawrence worked away at the novel, well over half a million British and French soldiers were either killed or wounded at the Battle of the Somme.[27] Heavy ammunition was being deployed on an unprecedented scale, and new kinds of industrial-scale warfare were entering the fray (chlorine gas had first been used by the Germans at the Second Battle of Ypres in 1915). The English people whom Lawrence felt that he could change in 1913 now seemed unreachable. On 19 February 1916, Lawrence told Bertrand Russell: 'One must be an outlaw these days, not a teacher or preacher. One must retire out of the herd and then fire bombs into it' (*2L* 546). Lawrence described the novel as 'purely destructive, not like the *Rainbow*, destructive-consummating' (*3L* 143). The violence of Ursula's actions in the earlier novel, as she rejected Anton, formed the prelude to her vision of a new kind of life at the end of the novel. By contrast, the characters in *Women in Love* are caught up in acts of violence which have no creative consequence. As in trench warfare, they are bogged down by violence. Lawrence told Catherine Carswell in November 1916: 'The book frightens me: it is so end-of-the-world' (*3L* 25). In October 1916, he briefly considered entitling it 'Dies Irae', a Latin phrase from a thirteenth-century hymn, meaning 'Day of Wrath'. If the biblical significance of *The Rainbow* suggested hope after the deluge, this novel would concern itself with last things: with Judgement Day.

Although *The First 'Women in Love'* is not a war novel in the ordinary sense of that term because it does not directly describe the Great War as an event in its fictional world, Lawrence said that 'the bitterness of the war may be taken for granted in the characters' (*WL* 485). It is full of indirect references to soldiers and military conflict. The conversation between the intellectuals who gather at Breadalby, Hermione's country house, barely conceals a feeling of hidden violence and hatred: 'The talk went on like a rattle of small artillery, always slightly sententious, with a sententiousness that was only emphasised by the continual crackling of a witticism, the continual spatter of verbal jest' (*FWL* 73; cf. *WL* 84). In Innsbruck, Gudrun Brangwen shares with the artist Loerke a fantasy about a weapon so effective that it destroys the world, and she imagines a state of the world in which conflict is endemic and unavoidable:

> They never mentioned the future, except Gudrun laughed out some mocking dream of the destruction of the world by a ridiculous catastrophe of man's invention: a man invented such a perfect explosive that it blew the earth in bits among the stars, or that the world became so perfect that by unanimous consent it committed suicide, because it had come to pass that any step taken by any man was an infringement of the rights of some other man. (*FWL* 418; cf. *WL* 453)

When at the end of Chapter VIII Birkin tells Ursula that he loves her, he says that 'if we go wrong—I shall know—ich habe es nicht gewollt' (*FWL* 294); his words, meaning 'I did not want it', echo those of Kaiser Wilhelm II, who declared on 31 July 1915, the first anniversary of the outbreak of the war, 'Ich habe den Krieg nicht gewollt' ('I did not want the war').[28] Birkin repeats the phrase again when he grieves over the dead body of Gerald: 'I didn't want it, really' (*FWL* 437; cf. *WL* 479). We are invited to think of Gerald's personal tragedy in terms of the wider conflict and world-tragedy of the Great War.

Women in Love constantly embodies the feelings and experiences of the war without attempting to make sense of them. Perhaps this lends the novel a greater sense of power to disturb. Lawrence holds a mirror up to his society, showing how the war spirit has infiltrated every corner of English life and is not something that can be contained on the battlefields. The uncanny feeling we sometimes get when reading it comes from the sense that characters are doing or saying things involuntarily which signify on some unconscious and global level. Take, for instance, the deathly scene at Gerald's annual water-party when his youngest sister, Winifred, alerts him to the fact that another sister, Diana, has fallen into the water. She is drowned, grasping the body of the young doctor who jumps in to save her. But Winifred's cries are more than simply expressive in the text:

> And then again came the child's high, screaming voice, with a note of weeping and impatience in it now:
>
> "*Di—Oh Di—Oh Di—Di—!*"
>
> It was a terrible sound, coming through the obscure air of the evening. (*FWL* 166; cf. *WL* 179)

Here, as elsewhere, the Crich family's tragic propensities give Gudrun that feeling of wonder and terror that Lawrence himself felt in his novel: Winifred's '*Di—Oh Di—Oh Di—Di—!*' is also '*Die—Oh Die—Oh Die—Die!*'

We should recall that Gerald had played with a rifle in his youth and killed his own brother.

> "You know he shot his brother?" said Ursula.
>
> "Shot his brother!" cried Gudrun, looking up aghast.
>
> "Didn't you know? I thought you were sure to. He and his brother were playing together with a gun. He said to his brother, 'Look down the gun', and it was loaded, and blew the top of his head off.—Isn't it a horrible story?"

It is Ursula who diagnoses the apparent 'accident' as actually a symptom of a hidden, repressed desire for violence and death in Gerald's unconscious. 'Perhaps', she says, 'there *was* an unconscious will behind it ... This playing at killing has some primitive *desire* for killing in it, don't you think?' (*FWL* 40–41; cf. *WL* 48–49). When Lawrence revised the text, he changed Gudrun's aghast reaction to ambivalent fascination: she frowns 'as if in disapprobation' (*WL* 49), the implication being that she is to be counted among those who are fascinated – or even aroused – by killing.

Throughout the novel, we see people giving vent to a primitive desire to attack others. We might think here of the scene at the water-party when Gudrun suddenly deals Gerald a blow on the face with the back of her hand,[29] or Pussum's similarly impulsive violence towards one of the London bohemians:

> "Not afwaid of blood!" exclaimed a young man with a thick, pale, jeering face, who had just come to the table and was drinking whisky.
>
> The Pussum turned on him a sulky look of dislike, low and ugly.
>
> "Aren't you really afraid of blud?" the other persisted, a sneer all over his face.
>
> "No, I'm not," she retorted.
>
> "Why, have you ever seen blood, except in a dentist's spittoon?" jeered the young man.
>
> "I wasn't speaking to you," she replied rather superbly.
>
> "You can answer me, can't you?" he said.
>
> For reply, she suddenly jabbed a knife across his thick, pale hand. He started up with a vulgar curse. (*FWL* 60; cf. *WL* 70)

Like the intellectuals at Breadalby, the bohemians who gather around Julius Halliday in London profess a pacifist interest in freedom of expression, yet the very manner of their talk reveals the violence of their inner lives. In the Café Impérial, 'tipsy, and malicious' (*FWL* 350; cf. *WL* 382), they mock one of Birkin's letters to Halliday, offering advice on his strained relationship with Pussum. Their mockery soon modulates from sarcasm into a genuine feeling of hatred for Birkin: 'I think it's awful cheek to write like that', says Pussum (*FWL* 352; cf. *WL* 384). Birkin's letter reads like parts of 'The Crown', and here Lawrence shows society people treating it with contempt. What hope is there for changing their attitudes and behaviour? The novel sees none; it concentrates instead on diagnosing their states of disintegration.

One could list many instances when violence breaks to the surface in *The First 'Women in Love'*: Hermione Roddice, for instance, attacks Birkin with a paperweight, and Gerald Crich forces his terrified Arab mare to stand before a passing train and hits his young sister Winifred's rabbit (which is named Bismarck after

Otto von Bismarck, the late 'Iron Chancellor' of the German Empire). Lawrence had always been fascinated by conflict, both psychological and physical. We might think of Baxter Dawes pushing Thomas Jordan over in *Sons and Lovers* and attacking Paul Morel at Daybrook Station, or of Ursula brutally caning her pupil Williams in *The Rainbow*.[30] Yet, in *The First 'Women in Love'*, the violence is inexplicable and indiscriminate, and people are attracted to the spectacle of violence and suffering even when they are the victims of it. Towards the end of the novel, Gerald throws his love-rival Loerke to one side and attacks Gudrun. He starts to strangle her. His motivation is fairly obvious, since Loerke has essentially taken Gudrun from him, yet Gerald's feelings as he attacks her – and Gudrun's response to the attack – are more troubling:

> He took the throat of Gudrun between his hands, that were hard and indomitably powerful. And her throat was beautifully, so beautifully soft. Save that, within, he could feel the hard frame of her life. And this he crushed, this he could crush. What bliss! Oh what bliss, at last, what satisfaction, at last. The pure bliss of satisfaction filled his soul. He was watching the unconsciousness come into her swollen face, watching her eyes roll back. How ugly she was! What a fulfilment, what a satisfaction! How good this was, oh how good it was, what a god-given gratification, at last! He was unconscious of her fighting and struggling. That struggling was her reciprocal lustful passion in this embrace, the more violent it became, the greater the frenzy of delight, till the zenith was reached, the crisis, the struggle was overborne, her movement became softer, appeased. (*FWL* 436; cf. *WL* 471–472)

The attack is narrated in terms of a sexual encounter: both Gerald and Gudrun feel bliss, satisfaction, fulfilment, gratification and lustful passion, and the feelings are 'reciprocal'. We are shown here a kind of erotic desire which is openly sadistic and sado-masochistic. They revel in the violence; it gives them a kind of sensual fulfilment.

It is against this overwhelming lust for death and violence that Birkin and Ursula commit themselves to salvaging some genuine feeling for one another. They feel compelled to leave the sick society that surrounds them, resigning from their jobs and flitting between places, leading a nomadic life, and the novel shows that it is a painful process, entailing a break from all known ties. Ursula has done it once before, of course, when she renounced family and friends and country at the end of *The Rainbow*,[31] but for Birkin it is a more bitter and unresolved experience. Is it even possible for those living through violent times to escape the general atmosphere? Birkin tells Ursula that all activity is twofold: it is either for production or corruption. He says that 'some people belong almost altogether' to the 'Flux of Corruption' (*FWL* 159). His own physical sickness in the novel suggests that he cannot completely escape the cultural disintegration going on around him.

How are we to understand Birkin and his endless preaching about a new kind of love? Is he the answer to a cultural malaise, or is he merely another symptom of it? The novel is perhaps more compelling in its analysis of what is wrong with society than in its description of the kind of love that can be salvaged from it. It was Lawrence, after all, who called it 'purely destructive'. Birkin himself has recourse to the most apocalyptic fantasy of all in the novel. When he and Ursula speak by the side of Willey Water, he states that it is a 'really beautiful thought' (*FWL* 113; cf. *WL* 127) to imagine everybody in the world destroyed and the world empty of people: 'Humanity is like the ichthyosauri, a creation gone wrong, become enormous instead of becoming wonderful and lovely' (*FWL* 114; cf. *WL* 128). We have travelled a long way – culturally, historically, imaginatively – from Ursula's hope-filled bedroom at the conclusion of *The Rainbow* to the freezing Austrian Tyrol and Birkin's torn heart beside the dead body of Gerald. The novel ends with the merest glimmer of hope as he strives to say 'All is not lost, because many are lost.—I am not afraid or ashamed to die and be dead' (*FWL* 443).

Such writing could never be published during the war. It is offensive not only in its depiction of violence as a sexual thrill, but also in its broader picture of a nation overcome by the passion for death and destruction. This was not what a country at war wanted to hear about itself. Lawrence anticipated the publishers' response to it, telling J. B. Pinker he would 'hate it and nobody will publish it' (*2L* 669). Pinker had to offer the novel first to Methuen, since – despite their failure to defend *The Rainbow* – Lawrence was still under contract to produce three novels for them. They kept it for a month before rejecting it and cancelling the contract.[32] Duckworth, Constable and Secker were then approached in turn and they too rejected it. Constable commissioned two reviews of it; one openly stated that 'the present would be a most unfavourable time for the publication of the book in its present form' because of 'the writer's expressions of antipathy to England and the forms of English civilisation', and the novel's 'destructive philosophy' and '"detached" attitudes toward the events of the present day' (*FWL* xxxvii).

Typescripts of the novel circulated among Lawrence's friends. At some point, Lawrence explored the possibility of dedicating it to somebody with sufficient social status to stand up for it against the censors, but his approach to Lady Cynthia Asquith apparently went unheeded. He could not approach Lady Ottoline Morrell (to whom he had recently dedicated his poetry collection

Amores) because he was anxious, with good cause, of the offence she might take at his having drawn upon her for some features of the appearance and attitude of Hermione Roddice.[33] When Cynthia Asquith finally read the novel, in March 1918, she found it 'rather nightmarish': in her diary she wrote, 'It is interesting—painfully so, and full of extraordinary bits of stark writing, but what is it all about and *why*? It seems a *misapplication* of such a wealth of strenuous analysing and writing. Surely he is delirious—a man whose temperature is 103?—or do I know nothing about human beings?' It seemed to her 'unpleasant' and 'morbid to a degree', and she admitted that she did not know '*what* to think about it' (Asquith 1968: 424). Even a sympathetic reader like Catherine Carswell, who had stood up for *The Rainbow*, found it a difficult novel. It made a 'painful but powerful impression' on her; she said that she 'resented the infliction of an almost physical suffering and malaise by what purported to be a novel' (Carswell 1932: 79–80). This was precisely the effect Lawrence wished the novel to have. In his writings about the war, he had gone from addressing his readers as fellow witnesses to the coming catastrophe, to articulating his beliefs about the motivation of soldiers in a 'Confessio Fidei' (*2L* 243), to producing a poem and short story intended to counteract the moralising glibness of allied war commentators and war propaganda, to finally creating a psychological critique of England in 1916 which he hoped would force people to recognise the obscene and grotesque bullying, violence and deathliness which he saw everywhere. In the process, he had transformed himself from a promising emerging novelist of ideas with a felt vocation to change his English readership into a disreputable anti-establishment figure: a belligerent outsider who refused to be silenced and sought to attack English values and attitudes in any way he could.

Notes

1 Lawrence also met the psychoanalyst Ernest Jones in 1914.
2 See *2L* 190 (1 July 1914): 'Mr Duckworth did not see his way to make the same offer Methuen made, so he will accept a book of short stories in place of the novel'.
3 Lawrence was encouraged to apply to the Royal Literary Fund for money to support himself, which resulted in a payment of £50 in October 1914. See *2L* 225 (21 October 1914). Friends and literary contacts, including Edward Marsh and the playwright and translator Alfred Sutro, also sent him money.
4 Compare, for instance, the attitude of Elizabeth Bates to her husband's dead body in the endings to the early versions of 'Odour of Chrysanthemums' printed in *PO*

203–205 and *VicG* 77–99 and 103–121 with her response to it in the version published in the Duckworth volume in November 1914 (*PO* 181–199).

5 See *1L* 544 (23 April 1913).

6 See *R* xxxvii, xliii.

7 See *R* xxxii–xxxvi.

8 On 5 December 1914, Lawrence wrote to J. B. Pinker: 'Garnett was a devil to call my book of stories *The Prussian Officer* – what Prussian Officer?' (*2L* 241).

9 See *2L* 138 (21 January 1914).

10 See *2L* 232 (17 November 1914).

11 See *2L* 219 (1 October 1914).

12 Ford Madox Hueffer, 'In October 1914', *The Outlook* (24 October 1914), pp. 523–524.

13 Richard Aldington, 'War Yawp', *Poetry*, Vol. V, No. II (November 1914), pp. 78–81.

14 Alice Corbin Henderson, 'Poetry and War', *Poetry*, Vol. V, No. II (November 1914), pp. 82–83.

15 John Russell McCarthy, 'The Hero', *Poetry*, Vol. V, No. II (November 1914), pp. 57–59: pp. 57, 59.

16 See *2L* 236 (19 November 1914).

17 The surviving parts of the poems are transcribed in *Poems* 1515–1516.

18 For a fuller discussion of Cannan, Lawrence and 'Rananim', see Harrison 2018a.

19 'England, My England' was extensively revised prior to its publication in *England, My England and Other Stories* in October 1922. The shorter 1915 version discussed here is available in *EmyE* 219–232 and in D. H. Lawrence, *Selected Stories*, ed. Sue Wilson (London: Penguin, 2007), pp. 165–180.

20 See *2L* 429 (6 November 1915).

21 See *2L* 462 (3 December 1915).

22 See *2L* 453 (26 November 1915).

23 See *2L* 456 (29 November 1915).

24 See Nehls (1957: 335).

25 See *FWL* xxviii–xxxi.

26 My analysis refers to *The First 'Women in Love'* because I am concerned with the 1916 context of the novel, but where possible I have also provided corresponding page references to the later and better-known version of the text.

27 Peter Hart estimates that there were 419, 654 British casualties (of whom around 131,000 were killed) and 204,253 French soldiers either dead or wounded. See Hart (2005: 528).

28 See *FWL* 494–495 n. 294:16.

29 See *FWL* 157; cf. *WL* 170.

30 See *SL* 393, 409–411; *R* 370.

31 See *R* 456.

32 See *3L* 58 (20 December 1916).

33 For Ottoline Morrell's response to reading the novel, see Morrell (1974: 128–129). Her husband, Philip Morrell, briefly threatened to bring a case for libel. Philip Heseltine was also angered by his depiction as Julius Halliday, and he threatened Lawrence with legal action, in response to which Martin Secker asked for alterations in his English edition of the novel.

4

Writing Against the Middle Class: Lawrence, the Literary Marketplace and Censorship

The transformation of Lawrence's sense of vocation as an author between the publication of *Sons and Lovers* in May 1913 and the completion of *The First 'Women in Love'* in November 1916 is so striking that it requires one to step back from the biographical narrative for a time in order to reflect on crucial aspects of his early writing which came to a head during the Great War. In this chapter, I will consider Lawrence's anti-establishment views and outspokenness from the start of his career, and trace his conflicted relationship to the literary marketplace up to the winter of 1916, to show how the author who wished to work on behalf of his English readership changed into the belligerent outsider who saw himself as aiming destructive blows against the English middle class. In the next chapter, I will discuss Lawrence's distinctive and challenging conceptualizations of the body, sex and desire, and his troubling engagement with discourses around sexuality in his war-time writings, as a means of identifying both progressive and reactionary qualities in his thinking on these subjects.

In mid-July 1928, Lawrence wrote a short autobiographical note for Philippe Soupault, the literary director of the French publishing house Kra. In it he summed up his war experiences as follows: 'In England during the period of the war—pretty well isolated. In 1915 *The Rainbow* was suppressed for immorality—and the sense of detachment from the bourgeois world, the world which controls press, publication and all, became almost complete. He had no interest in it, no desire to be at one with it. Anyhow the suppression of *The Rainbow* had proved it impossible. Henceforth he put away any idea of "success", of succeeding with the British bourgeois public, and stayed apart' (*LEA* 114).

The Life of the Author: D. H. Lawrence, First Edition. Andrew Harrison.

Up to late June 1914, Lawrence's first literary mentors (Ford Madox Hueffer and Edward Garnett) helped him to place his work with publishers, and – in Garnett's case – also edited his work to make it acceptable to publishers and the powerful circulating libraries. In the autumn of 1909, when Hueffer first introduced Lawrence to literary London and he moved among 'all the Swells', he could feel that he was being accepted as one of them. He told Louie Burrows in November 1909: 'Aren't the folks kind to me: it is really wonderful' (*1L* 145). In the first flush of his excitement at 'London's opulence' he exclaimed to Jessie Chambers 'I'll make two thousand a year!' (Chambers 1935: 168). Yet he soon grew suspicious that he was being condescended to as a writer from the working class; Hueffer's labelling of him as a 'genius', being repeated by him and taken up by others, seemed calculated to 'console' Lawrence 'for not having their own incomparable advantages' (*LEA* 179). He came to see himself as an outsider who needed to be carefully managed, and mentored, in order to fit in, or conform, to the literary scene.

Hueffer and Garnett helped Lawrence to establish his career as a professional writer, but both men sought to shape his writing and were critical of the work he produced without their guidance. Hueffer published Lawrence's poetry in the *English Review* and helped him to place *The White Peacock* with Heinemann, but he admitted that the novel, 'with its enormous prolixity of detail', sinned 'against almost every canon of art as I conceive it' (*8L* 2–3). Without fully understanding Lawrence's complex relationship to Eastwood and his working-class roots, he encouraged Lawrence to write about them with the eye for telling material detail and economy of expression of the French realists. In June 1912, Lawrence would tell Walter de la Mare that he 'suffered badly from Hueffer re Flaubert and perfection' (*1L* 417). When Lawrence pursued his own interests after *The White Peacock* by writing *The Trespasser*, Hueffer was unimpressed. He told Lawrence that it was 'a rotten work of genius. It has no construction or form – it is execrably bad art, being all variations on a theme. Also it is erotic – not that I, personally, mind that, but an erotic work *must* be good art, which this is not'. He warned that publishing it would damage Lawrence's reputation 'perhaps permanently' (*1L* 339).

Despite their very different views of fiction and literary form, Lawrence certainly felt the loss of the mentorship of Hueffer and his partner Violet Hunt when they gave up the editorship of the *English Review* in early 1910, and when Hueffer reacted so negatively to *The Trespasser* in September of that year. Lawrence said that Hueffer left him 'to paddle my own canoe. I *very* nearly wrecked it and did for myself. Edward Garnett, like a good angel, fished me out' (*1L* 471). Garnett saw the potential in the novel and helped Lawrence to revise it and publish it with Duckworth. He was initially much more sympathetic than

Hueffer to Lawrence's more erotic writing, and his sympathy also extended to Lawrence's affair with Frieda. Lawrence felt comfortable taking Frieda to see Garnett at the Cearne before they departed together for Germany. He described his new mentor as 'most beautifully free of the world's conventions' (*1L* 362). Garnett had openly opposed state censorship of drama. His own play *The Breaking Point*, about a young woman who falls pregnant by a married man and – torn between love for him and duty to her controlling father – drowns herself, had been accepted for a run at the Haymarket Theatre in London but was declared unfit to be performed on grounds of its indecency.[1] Garnett published it in 1907 with the subtitle 'A Censured Play', and he wrote a Preface in which he stated that by suppressing his play 'the Censor is flagrantly abusing his powers' (Garnett 1907: xi). He appended a proposal for the founding of a 'Society for the Defence of Intellectual Drama' consisting of leading drama critics and others who would advise the censor on issues relating to the suppression of plays. Lawrence recalled Garnett saying to him in the 'early days' that where sexual matters in literature were concerned he would 'welcome a description of the entire act' (*6L* 520). Yet regarding Lawrence's own writing, Garnett's convictions were in conflict with his role as a publisher's reader for Duckworth trying to safeguard the early career of a young author he admired. As such, in the autumn of 1912 Garnett asked Lawrence to tone down 'the most unrespectable lines' (*1L* 462) in his Eastwood dialect poem 'Whether or Not', and took it upon himself to remove several of the more outspoken sexual words and phrases from *Sons and Lovers* when he edited that novel to make it suitable for publication by Duckworth. Although Lawrence was deeply upset by the extensive changes Garnett made to *Sons and Lovers*, he understood the need for them and he dedicated the novel to Garnett.

Lawrence, however, clashed with Garnett when writing his next novel. Garnett openly criticised 'The Sisters' and 'The Wedding Ring' (early versions of *The Rainbow*). Lawrence was upset by some comments which Garnett sent to him in April 1914 because he felt they 'insulted rather the thing I *wanted* to say: not me, nor what I had said, but that which I was trying to say, and had failed in' (*2L* 164). In June 1914, Lawrence responded assertively to Garnett's criticism that the novel was 'shaky' (*2L* 183) and the psychology of the characters wrong. He willingly renounced Garnett's guidance when he placed the novel with Methuen, but while the decision secured him a new level of independence as a professional author, and the promise of more money, it also exposed him to the censors. Neither his new agent, J. B. Pinker, nor Methuen offered sufficient guidance on, or oversight of, textual matters, and when *The Rainbow* was successfully prosecuted under the Obscene Publications Act the publisher offered no resistance and did not seek to defend it.

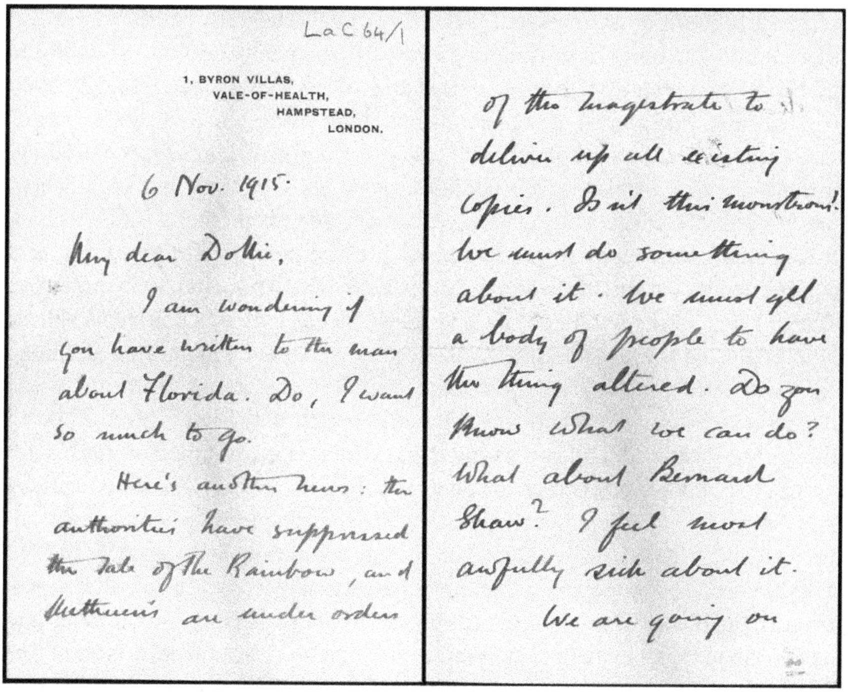

1, BYRON VILLAS,
VALE-OF-HEALTH,
HAMPSTEAD,
LONDON.

6 Nov. 1915.

My dear Dollie,

I am wondering if you have written to the man about Florida. Do, I want so much to go.

Here's another news: the authorities have suppressed the sale of the Rainbow, and Methuens are under orders of the magistrate to deliver up all existing copies. Isn't this monstrous! We must do something about it. We must get a body of people to have the thing altered. Do you know what we can do? What about Bernard Shaw? I feel most awfully sick about it.

We are going on

'Here's another news: the authorities have suppressed the sale of *The Rainbow*'. Letter from D. H. Lawrence to Dollie Radford, 6 November 1915. University of Nottingham, Manuscripts and Special Collections, La C 64.

At the trial, Herbert Muskett, who appeared on behalf of the Commissioner of Police, called the novel 'disgusting, detestable and pernicious': he added that although 'there might not be an obscene word to be found in the book, it was in fact a mass of obscenity of thought, idea, and action, wrapped up in a language which in some quarters might be considered artistic and intellectual'. The judge, Sir John Dickinson, drew attention to the suggestion contained in the chapter title 'Shame', citing it as evidence that the publisher 'could not have read it very intelligently' prior to publication. He said that he had 'never read anything more disgusting'; 'It was appalling to think of the harm that such a book might have done. It was utter filth; nothing else would describe it' (Delavenay 1969: 662–663).

Muskett's reference to an 'obscenity of thought, idea, and action', and his and Dickinson's emphasis on the perniciousness of the novel and the harm it might do, show that their objection was not simply to particular aspects of the novel (such as its depiction of same-sex desire) but to its broader depiction of life, society and moral values. The intensity of their reaction against the book – and their reference to the 'disgust' it created in them – strongly suggests that they were also affected by its manner of narration and use of perspective. Here it is helpful to refer back to Lawrence's late reflections on the trial and his comment that it served to underline his almost complete detachment from 'the bourgeois world'. Lawrence grew up as a scholarship boy; he was from a working-class community but mixed with the children of middle-class parents at Nottingham High School and University College Nottingham. He came to see his mother's values as conventionally middle class: in the late poem 'Red-herring', he described her as 'a superior soul', 'cut out to play a superior rôle / in the god-damn bourgeoisie' (*Poems* 425). On the one hand, he was subject to his mother's bourgeois values, which reflected the strict codes of decency and propriety which inhered among the women in working-class Eastwood, including the strong desire for social distinction and upward mobility. On the other hand, he was perceived as being different in Eastwood, and as a young man he was teased and mocked for his difference (e.g. for his preference for playing with girls, and for his studiousness). Growing up in a conflicted household very much influenced by his mother's values, but being shaped too by a tight-knit mining community with strongly-policed unwritten codes of conduct, made Lawrence especially conscious of, and critical towards, the power of the unspoken. He was driven to question moral codes and explore taboo topics in an open and subversive manner. The outspokenness of *The Rainbow* and *Women in Love* on a range of subjects including (but not limited to) sex and sexuality, morality, patriotism and militarism, and violence, had its roots in his earliest work, so that in retrospect one could argue that he was always on a collision course with the censors. From the very start of his career, Lawrence had addressed issues which were taboo in British culture, and he had systematically critiqued bourgeois values and taken a critical view of the social forms and institutions which underpin them such as marriage, the family and religion.

Illegitimacy is a central theme in several of his Eastwood writings. In its earliest state, the plot of *The White Peacock* concerns a young woman who falls pregnant outside marriage and plans to marry and move to Canada with another man who will raise the child as his own. Lydia Lawrence told her son that she wished he had 'written on another line' (*1L* 49). The poem 'Whether or Not', which Garnett advised Lawrence to tone down, concerned a 25-year-old man, Tim Merfin, who is engaged to be married but gets his 45-year-old landlady pregnant. His fiancée, Lizzie Stainwright, is understandably upset about his indiscretion when she first hears of it through her mother, and she goes to confront the landlady. Yet in a darkly comical twist she makes arrangements to pay the landlady off, agreeing to marry Tim despite (or even because of) his fathering of the child and telling him that if his landlady will part with it they will raise it as their own.[2]

The short story 'The Christening', written in summer 1912, also takes a darkly comic approach to illegitimacy, using a real-life event to criticise the repressive small-mindedness of religious values and community gossip in Eastwood. Lawrence drew on the situation of the Winterbottom family, who lived in Woodbine Cottage on Walker Street and had been neighbours of the Lawrences. In this story, Emma Rowbotham has given birth to a child outside marriage by the 'baker's man' (*PO* 179). Her eldest sister Hilda (a teacher at the British School who has attempted to hold the family together following the death of her mother) is intensely conscious of the stain on the family's reputation, and the gossip and innuendo it has exposed them to in the mining community. A private christening ceremony is organised at their home on a weekday afternoon, after the school day has ended. With the help of a neighbour, Hilda puts on high tea for the visiting clergyman. She walks from work to the baker's shop, where she buys cakes for the occasion. She moves about the village 'like a black swan of mournful, disreputable plumage' (*PO* 172); her walk home from the shop feels like 'a half mile of slow-stepping torture, with shame flushing over her neck' (*PO* 173). The private christening is one of the ways in which she seeks to 'keep up the prestige of her house in spite of blows' (*PO* 176), yet it only serves to expose deep conflicts within it. Emma, who scorns her sister, is sulky and sullen. Her brother Laurie, a collier, rudely interrupts proceedings when he returns home in his pit dirt; he aims cruel jibes at Emma about her situation. Meanwhile, their broken father (a former collier suffering from locomotor ataxy) goes off into a half-crazed sermon of his own, which reveals his sense of despair at the shame his daughter has brought on the family.

Rather than focusing on Emma's transgression, the story critiques the patriarchal authority of both the father and the clergyman. The father dominates his children, who are angry and ashamed but also afraid of him. The control he has exerted over them has left them 'only half-individuals' (*PO* 180). The clergyman, Mr Kendal, is strangely ineffectual: a 'big-boned, thin, ugly man of nervous manner', 'full of vague tenderness' (*PO* 175). Hilda's heart disease symbolises the damage done to her by the home environment. Her siblings' rebellion reveals the persistence of their vital naturalness in opposition to parental control and moral constraints: Laurie Rowbotham inflates and explodes a paper bag in order to interrupt the christening, calling his father a 'Blortin', slaverin' old nag' (*PO* 179), while Emma, feeling 'humbled' and 'dishonored' (*PO* 175), is silent and unresponsive during proceedings, 'stupefied with anger against this emotion let loose on her account' (*PO* 177). We are told that she 'hated' her baby 'when she looked at it, and saw it as a symbol, but when she felt it, her love was like fire in her blood' (*PO* 175). The story reverses traditional moral terms by presenting passion and physical affection as sources of lifefulness and purity which are repressed and distorted by religion.

Lawrence's friend George Neville, who was a year younger than him and became (after Lawrence) only the third child of a collier in Eastwood between 1882 and 1899 to win a scholarship to Nottingham High School,[3] got a girl pregnant in 1906. Lawrence was 'very distressed' by the news. His mother, using the occasion to deliver a timely warning to her youngest son, told him 'how terrible might be the consequences of only five minutes' self-forgetfulness' (Chambers 1935: 126). She would have had in mind the example of Lawrence's brother George, who had married in May 1897 when his girlfriend was three months pregnant. In March 1912, shortly after Lawrence met Frieda, he went to stay with Neville for a week at his home in Bradnop, a village close to the town of Leek in Staffordshire, where Neville had a job as a headteacher. Lawrence learned during his visit that Neville had got another girl pregnant and had married her under duress seven months later, on 4 November 1911; their son was born in January 1912. Neville's wife and child were living with her parents in Stourbridge.

This time Lawrence was much more sanguine about Neville's transgression. The following month he wrote a comical play entitled *The Married Man*, which drew on his friend's unenviable situation. In the play, Billy Brentnall (the Lawrence figure) is visiting his friend Dr George Grainger (Neville). He learns from Grainger that he has married a woman who has given birth to his child; she is living with her mother in Wolverhampton. In the meantime, he has had affairs with several women. He has started a relationship with a 32-year-old woman named Annie Calladine and attracted the attention of a farmer's daughter named Sally Magneer, the sister of his friend Jack Magneer. Grainger has lost his job and is due to leave his lodgings, but he is not sure where he will go or what he will do. The situation comes to a head when Brentnall informs Annie that Grainger is married. Her sister Ada writes a letter to Grainger's wife, Ethel, who turns up to claim him. Yet just when the play seems about to move from farce into tragedy Lawrence has a Frieda figure named Elsa Smith, Brentnall's 'fiancée' (*Plays* 218), act as a *deus ex machina*: Elsa injects a healthy amorality into proceedings, reassuring Ethel that Grainger is 'not a villain if he makes love to other girls', since by loving these two women he has lost none of his love for his wife. Sally Magneer comments that Elsa's liberal view of marriage is 'worse than Mormons' (i.e. worse than their practice of polygamy, or 'plural marriage', during the nineteenth century), but Brentnall says that it is 'better than subterfuge, bestiality, or starvation and sterility' (*Plays* 233). This is the first instance of Lawrence espousing Frieda's amatory values. He even includes the detail that Elsa was driven to see Brentnall by 'Will Hobson' (*Plays* 231) (an allusion to Will Dowson, one of the men with whom Frieda had had an extra-marital affair in Nottingham). The play ends with Grainger agreeing to go with his wife to Brentnall's rooms in London, but his palpable lack of feeling for his wife and child makes him a rueful figure as his landlady hands him the baby.

Lawrence was clearly fascinated by Neville's fathering of a son outside marriage. He used this detail from Neville's life once again in the first part of his unfinished novel *Mr Noon*. During his visit to Neville, Lawrence asked his old friend about his feelings for his wife and for the child. In the play, when Brentnall asks Grainger if he feels any paternal emotion, he replies 'No. Don't talk rot' (*Plays* 194). Lawrence's brother Ernest called Neville 'Teufel' (German: Devil), after Carlyle's *Sartor Resartus: The Life and Opinions of Herr Teufelsdröckh* (1831).

Neville recalled Lawrence once saying to him: 'Teufel, the real knowledge of the world consists of the related experiences of the men and women who have lived in it. To each human being separate experiences, thoughts, and emotions come, and it is a duty which each of us owes to the world, to add our own contributions, just as we know them, whether they be the result of our own experiences or as related to us by others' (Neville 1981: 44). Taboo subjects and experiences which disturb one sufficiently that one is inclined to bury them in the past, or to hide them from oneself and others, were the very things which Lawrence argued should be brought to the surface, articulated and shared for the benefit of a wider humanity.

Lawrence had used a similar argument to encourage Helen Corke to share with others (and not just himself) her experiences with Herbert Macartney, her married violin instructor, who joined her for a short holiday on the Isle of Wight in August 1909. She showed Lawrence some of the writings she produced in which she reflected on the week she spent with Macartney as a way of coming to terms with her feelings after Macartney's subsequent suicide. After he had read 'The Freshwater Diary', Lawrence told her that she should share her experiences more widely because 'human experience is the common property of humanity' (Corke 1962: 171). In February 1920, he would draw out the American expatriate Maurice Magnus's more extreme experiences in the French Foreign Legion during the Great War (including his homosexual experiences), asking about them in order to broaden his own horizons, while also encouraging Magnus to write about them with greater frankness in his memoir.

This commitment to exploring and articulating taboo subjects created problems for Lawrence in the novel form. The gamekeeper Annable, whom Lawrence introduced into *The White Peacock* to act as a foil to the narrator Cyril Beardsall, was the first character he created who voices a strong criticism of middle-class values. Annable has escaped from an unhappy marriage to a titled Lady and is embittered against polite society. He is described as 'a man of one idea:—that all civilisation was the painted fungus of rottenness. He hated any sign of culture' (*WP* 146). His motto is 'Be a good animal, true to your animal instinct' (*WP* 147). Lawrence's friend Alice Dax, who was herself a strong critic of traditional values, told Lawrence that she found Annable 'really coarse' (*1L* 69). After the novel had been accepted for publication by Heinemann he was asked to 'alter a bit in parts' (*1L* 152) to satisfy possible objections from 'the old ladies of Croydon' (*WP* xxvi). In addition to making the requested alterations, he took the opportunity to rewrite the third part of the novel. He told Sydney Pawling, a partner at the publishing firm, that it was 'a new labour of Hercules': 'I think I have removed all the offensive morsels, all the damns, the devils and the sweat. I hope nothing of the kind remains. My own skin is not super-sensitive, so I can hardly judge what will make delicate people dither' (*1L* 158). Lawrence's 'first experience of the objectionable'

(*IR* 76) came when Heinemann required him at a late stage in the novel's production to make further changes to expression in a passage in which Annable reflects on his marriage to Lady Chrystabel. The publisher changed two additional sentences without seeking his permission to do so, each time toning down instances of Annable's rather too direct speech.[4]

Hueffer's strong reaction against *The Trespasser*, which convinced Lawrence that it was 'finally, pornographic' (*1L* 229), may have been occasioned by the way in which its immersive exploration of a married man's despair at the state of his marriage and profound physical feelings for his pupil spoke to Hueffer's estrangement from his wife Elsie Martindale and extra-marital affair with Violet Hunt, which exposed him to gossip and scandal, and which had given rise to suicidal feelings. The taboo nature of Siegmund MacNair's involvement with Helena Verden, and her involvement with him, is reflected in the moody refusal of his wife Beatrice and their eldest daughter Vera to refer directly to Helena, in the silent disapproval of Helena's parents, and in some words spoken to Helena by their landlady on the Isle of Wight, who despite thinking that they are an engaged couple sees the risk to her reputation of their being out alone together late at night.[5] Lawrence foregrounded Siegmund's desperate longing for, and dependence on, Helena; his use of free-indirect discourse forced the reader to inhabit Siegmund's feelings and suicidal ideation in a manner that Hueffer clearly found deeply disturbing. Hueffer would go on associating Lawrence with the feeling the novel engendered in him. He would recall how he found Lawrence 'disturbing enough' when they first met; in the same reminiscence he repeats the point, calling Lawrence 'really disturbing' and admitting 'He remained too disturbing even when I got to know him well' (Ford 1937: 75, 78, 85).

It was the immersive quality of Lawrence's treatment of taboo subjects and feelings which Hueffer found so disconcerting. He said: 'It wasn't that his words were either jaunty or offensive. He uttered them as if they had been not so much assertions as gropings for truth' (Ford 1937: 78–79). The sexual connotation of Hueffer's carefully chosen verb in this sentence is telling. Hueffer used his writing as a controlling medium through which to explore feelings which he could not – or would not – articulate more directly. His own subsequent novel about infidelity and suicide, *The Good Soldier* (1915), employs an unreliable first-person narrator who fails to register, and then refuses to admit to understanding, the adulterous actions of his wife and best friend. The material reasons for their suicides are clear, but their psychological motivation remains slightly mysterious. In contrast, Lawrence came to see the primary function of art as being to directly confront his readers with uncomfortable topics and feelings and experiences as a route to collective self-understanding and to a realignment of their way of thinking. This was what he meant when he stated that he wrote because he wanted 'folk – English folk – to alter, and have more sense' (*1L* 544). He considered the purpose of art as being to address complacency, which he saw as the main bourgeois vice.

Lawrence confronts taboo forms of relationship again in *Sons and Lovers*. This novel traces Paul Morel's affair with Clara Dawes, a married woman who is estranged from her husband, and his relationship with Miriam Leivers, with whom he has sex outside marriage. Among the passages in the novel which Edward Garnett toned down was one dealing with Paul's first sexual experience with Miriam, and two dealing with his encounters with Clara. In the scene with Miriam, Paul thinks that she has 'the most beautiful hips he had ever imagined' (*SL* 333); Garnett changed 'hips' to 'body' and deleted the following remark that Paul 'threw off his things'. In Chapter XII ('Passion'), Paul misses the last tram back from Nottingham after he and Clara go together to the Theatre Royal, and he has to stay with Clara and her mother at the parental home, occupying Clara's room (while Clara sleeps with her mother); Garnett cut a description of Paul trying on a pair of stockings which Clara had left draped over the back of a chair.[6] In the subsequent description of Paul and Clara making love, Garnett cut the material between the left- and right-facing arrows:

> Then he loosed her, and his blood began to run free. Looking at her, he had to bite his lip, and the tears of pain came to his eyes, she was so beautiful, and so desirable. The first kiss on her breast made him pant with fear. < The great dread, the great humility, and the awful desire, were nearly too much. Her breasts were heavy. He held one in each hand, like big fruits in their cups, and he kissed them, fearfully. > He was afraid to look at her. His hands went travelling over her, < soft, > delicate, discriminate, fearful, full of adoration. < Suddenly he saw her knees, and he dropped, kissing them passionately. She quivered. And then again, with his fingers on her sides, she quivered. > (*SL* 383)[7]

At the proof stage, the entire paragraph was removed.[8] In the next chapter, in which Paul and Clara rent a cottage near Theddlethorpe, on the Lincolnshire coast, Garnett removed a reference to Paul kissing Clara's breasts, 'the two white, glistening globes she cradled' (*SL* 401), and replaced it with 'kissed her neck'.

In *The Rainbow*, Lawrence's focus on transgressive sexual acts and on physical desire as an overwhelming power analogous to religious feeling is taken a stage further. This novel contains the full force of Frieda's influence. In Lawrence's retelling of Genesis, women yearn for a world of knowledge and understanding, and their transgressions in the flesh are acts of self-assertion which radically undermine patriarchal authority and Christian family structures. A striking instance of this occurs in the second generation in the novel, in the chapter entitled 'The Child'. Following 'a long bout of hostility', Will and Anna Brangwen seem alienated from one another within their marriage. Anna has 'closed with him': 'For seven years she had been absorbed in wifehood and motherhood'. Will is 'silent and separate': 'Gradually he became indifferent of responsibility. He would do what pleased him, and no more' (*R* 210). He starts going out alone on Saturdays, to watch football and attend the music hall. On one occasion, at the music hall he sits next to 'two girls' (*R* 210), and afterwards goes off with one of them, walking from the streets of Nottingham into the Park area of the city. Here they embrace: 'He was given over altogether to the sensuous knowledge of this woman, and every moment he seemed to be touching absolute beauty, something beyond knowledge' (*R* 214).

Will's behaviour towards the young woman is disturbingly coercive, and she resists his advances, but she agrees to meet him again. He returns by train, arriving at midnight. Although Anna asks him where he has been, she is 'indifferent as to whether he lied or not'. Indeed, she is attracted to his new quality of independence from her: 'So, he was blossoming out into his real self! It piqued her. Very good, let him blossom! She liked a new turn of affairs. He was a strange man come home to her' (*R* 217). Their reconciliation happens at a sensual level, which supplants their earlier co-existence as husband and wife, and as parents:

> He was the sensual male seeking his pleasure, she was the female ready to take hers: but in her own way. A man could turn into a free lance: so then could a woman. She adhered as little as he to the moral world. All that had gone before was nothing to her. She was another woman, under the instance of a strange man. He was a stranger to her, seeking his own ends. Very good. She wanted to see what this stranger would do now, what he was.
>
> She laughed, and kept him at arms' length, whilst apparently ignoring him. She watched him undress as if he were a stranger. Indeed he was a stranger to her.
>
> And she roused him profoundly, violently, even before he touched her. The little creature in Nottingham had but been leading up to this. They abandoned in one motion the moral position, each was seeking gratification pure and simple. (*R* 218)

We are told that afterwards their children 'became mere offspring to them, they lived in the darkness and death of their own sensual activities' (*R* 219).

Such writing emerged out of Lawrence's earlier treatment of the idea of infidelity and illegitimacy as distorting moral categories linked to moribund Christian teachings and patriarchy. In *The Married Man*, Elsa Smith had urged Grainger's wife to recognise that his philandering was not inconsistent with his love for her. In 'The Christening', Lawrence had associated the taboo against illegitimacy with a possessive paternal authority which inflicts on women a sense of shame and dishonour. It is only a short leap from critiquing attitudes to infidelity and illegitimacy in *The Married Man* and 'The Christening' to exploring in *The Rainbow* how infidelity might be an enabling route to self-realisation, and parenthood a mere mechanical function. And Lawrence takes his assault on bourgeois values a stage further in this novel by attacking the religious underpinnings of the family unit. Anna destroys Will's unthinking acceptance of the Christian version of Genesis, and his love of church architecture and biblical symbolism, by insisting that genesis and creation are features of the very female body which religion has sought to police and demonise. When she is pregnant she dances naked in front of her husband 'before her Creator in exemption from the man' (*R* 170).

Critics naturally objected to the way that traditional morality as represented by religious teaching and family feeling is superseded by sensual self-realisation in *The Rainbow*. Robert Lynd complained that Lawrence's characters were 'as lacking in the inhibitions of ordinary civilised life as savages'; James Douglas called them 'creatures who are immeasurably lower than the lowest animal in the Zoo' (Draper 1970: 91, 93). As we have seen, at the trial the prosecution and the judge expressed disgust at the novel; the judge referred to it as 'utter filth' (Delavenay 1969: 663). Yet Lawrence never stopped insisting that self-realisation could only be achieved by confronting taboo feelings and experiences and overcoming the associated feelings of shame.

Two texts will serve to demonstrate his commitment to this. Illegitimacy is once again the subject in his 1919 short story 'The Last Straw' (also known as 'Fanny and Annie'). Its 30-year-old central character, Fanny, returns from her job as a lady's maid to live with her aunt in a fictional version of Eastwood. We are told that 'the doom of home-coming went through her veins like a drug' (*EmyE* 153). She had wanted to marry her cousin Luther, who was 'brilliant and ambitious' (like Lawrence's brother Ernest), with a job in London and knowledge of Latin, French and German, but he had jilted her and died, and her other affairs had come to nothing, so she returns to 'marry her first love, a foundry worker, after having left him dangling' (*EmyE* 154). Harry Goodall, who is two years older than Fanny, is unambitious and she hates his 'peculiar obstinate limitedness', but she has to admit that he is not common or greedy and he has a certain charm because of his 'blondness and sensitiveness and his way of making a woman feel that she was a higher being' (*EmyE* 157). Harry still lives with his parents and siblings, and he has saved less than £20, while in addition to her savings Fanny has inherited £200 from her Aunt Kate. Fanny's aunt feels that she is too good for Harry, while Harry's mother is irritated that her son has been kept dangling and expresses regret that he took her back. The story explores how, underneath Fanny's acquired snobbery, she is still physically attracted to him: 'He was the first man who had ever kissed her. And his kisses, even while she rebelled from them, had lived in her blood and sent roots down into her soul' (*EmyE* 160).

Shortly before they are due to marry, Fanny goes to Morley Chapel to hear Harry sing solos at the Harvest Festival service. Proceedings are interrupted by a local woman named Mrs Nixon, who publicly denounces Harry, calling him 'A scamp as won't take the consequences of what he's done' (*EmyE* 161). Harry explains to Fanny and the Reverend Enderby, 'an odd bachelor soul, emotional, ugly, but very gentle' (*EmyE* 162), that his accuser is charging him with having got her youngest daughter Annie pregnant. Harry does not deny that it is possible, but says 'It's no more mine than it is some other chap's' (*EmyE* 163). Fanny now has a pretext for calling off her marriage to Harry, but her initial response in the Chapel is not unlike Anna's reaction to Will when he returns from his trip to Nottingham; she views the knowledge of his transgression as a 'sudden surprise' (*EmyE* 163) which offers relief from the routine and habit that she associates with him. She walks with Harry back to the corner of his street and impulsively goes with him into his home. Here she witnesses his family denouncing Mrs Nixon, and she decides to stay with them that night, telling Mrs Goodall 'I'll stop with *you* to-night, Mother' (*EmyE* 166). Harry's indiscretion in going off with Annie Nixon, since it suggests the hidden passion in him which Fanny had earlier experienced through his kisses, tips the balance away from social propriety and snobbishness and in favour of his charm and her physical attraction to him. The story ends with Fanny accepting Harry through his mother, whose passion and power she shares and will presumably usurp.

In Lawrence's final novel, *Lady Chatterley's Lover*, the upper-middle-class Connie Chatterley also has to overcome snobbishness in order to realise her passional connection with the gamekeeper Oliver Mellors. Their relationship entails a confrontation with taboo on two levels. In attempting to arrive at a shared understanding of their sexual experiences, they have to establish a language for their bodily feelings which exists outside his defensive regional speech, the deadening language of literature, and the divisively supercilious language of the upper classes. Mellors teaches Connie new meanings for the proscribed words 'cunt' and 'fuck' which cleanse them of their dirty associations and make them poetic terms identifying intangible shared feelings. On another level, Connie learns to overcome the shame associated with anal intercourse. Her sexual experiences with Mellors transcend their culture, since passion is 'The same thing, a thousand years ago: ten thousand years ago! The same on the Greek vases—everywhere! The refinements of passion, the extravagances of sensuality!':

> In this short summer night she learnt so much. She would have thought a woman would have died of shame. Instead of which, the shame died. Shame, which is fear: the deep organic shame, the old, old physical fear which crouches in the bodily roots of us, and can only be chased away by the sensual fire, at last it was roused up and routed by the phallic hunt of the man, and she came to the very heart of the jungle of herself. (*LCL* 247)

The realignment of Connie's outlook here from the superficial values of her bohemian upbringing and the repressive values of her class and her country to the transcendent imperative for the realisation of her physical desires is reflected in the enforced realignment of the reader's perspective. We are made to see the perverseness of a society in which her husband could suggest that she gets pregnant by another man simply in order to get an heir, or in which Connie can feel the need to pretend that the father of her unborn baby is Duncan Forbes, a man of her own class, to placate her husband's prejudices. As we share Connie's journey to confronting taboo and overcoming shame, we too come to see civilised society as insane.

In the poem 'Immoral man', from the collection *Pansies* (1929), Lawrence writes that 'The deep instincts, when left alone, are quite moral' (*Poems* 459). It is only the mental life and the craving for collective affirmation and social superiority which introduce the spectre of immorality as a means of looking down on and regulating others. Herd morality is, in this view, characterised by bigotry, hypocrisy and a cowardly fear of life. The problem, as Lawrence sees it, is to avoid both the craven-hearted mindlessness of middle-class conformism and the deliberate dirty-mindedness of the non-conformist. As he puts it in 'Worm either way', 'If you live along with all the other people / and are just like them, and conform, and are nice / you're just a worm—', but equally 'if you live with all the other people / and you don't like them and won't be like them and won't conform / then you're just the worm that has turned, / in either case, a worm'. The non-conformist says 'Look at me, I am *not* respectable, / I do all the things the bourgeois daren't do, / I booze and fornicate and use foul language and despise your honest man.—' (*Poems* 375). Although in the wake of the Chatterley Trial, Lawrence was lauded by some as a non-conformist and became an icon for forms of sexual liberation he would have abhorred, it is perhaps more fruitful to view him as a lifelong critic of bourgeois moral standards who sought to critique the accepted forms of life and to suggest (rather than to actively advocate) alternative possibilities for fulfilment. Today, the central ambition of his writing to expose repressive social norms and censoriousness, and to explore and embrace taboo feelings as a route to self-realisation, speaks more meaningfully to attempts to redress social prejudice. While Lawrence's views sometimes reflected the homophobia and racism of his day, his writing was always attuned to exposing and critically examining sources of cultural power and celebrating difference in oneself and others.[9] In the following chapters, I will address his conflicted attitudes to homosexuality, nation and race. In the final part of this chapter, I want to discuss his treatment of same-sex desire in his fiction as a prominent feature of his radicalism.

As we have seen, Lawrence's exposure to, and acceptance of, Frieda's sexual ethics in 1912 transformed his writing in different genres as he found ways to incorporate into his plays and fiction a critique of repressive English attitudes to relationships. His treatment of illegitimacy, infidelity and non-normative forms of sex as positive routes to self-realisation was part of a far-reaching critique in his work of the sacredness of the traditional Christian family unit. The conflicts within Lawrence's own nuclear family, and particularly in his parents' marriage, cast a long shadow over his life and thought. Although he could, in a particular mood, express nostalgia for aspects of his early life in Eastwood,[10] he had little sentimental attachment to his upbringing in the family. When his sister Ada and his father left the family's Lynn Croft house after the death of his mother, Lawrence was asked whether he wanted anything from it. He said: 'No, there is nothing I want – saving the woman, and, if you like, the black vases, which will always remind me of home: not, God knows, that one wants too much to be reminded thereof' (*1L* 233). The only former possessions of his mother that he retained were a pair of brass candlesticks.[11] He told Ada that she was now his 'one, *real* relative in the world: only you' (*1L* 231). He would fall out with his brother George (who had disapproved of his relationship with a married woman) and he was aware of fundamental differences from his other sister, Emily. When Emily and her daughter Margaret ('Peg') visited him in Gsteig bei Gstaad, Switzerland, in August to September 1928, he confided to Enid Hilton: 'I am not really "our Bert". Come to that, I never was. And the gulf between their outlook and mine is yawning, horribly obvious to me' (*6L* 535).

His detachment from sentimental views of the family was accompanied by a critical attitude to marriage. In *The White Peacock*, the disillusioned George Saxton says: 'Marriage is more of a duel than a duet. One party wins and takes the other captive, slave, servant' (*WP* 301). Lawrence once described his parents' marriage as 'one carnal, bloody fight' (*1L* 190). The primary motive behind his engagement to Louie Burrows in December 1910 was arguably to reassure his mother of the security of his future life as she lay on her deathbed. Although he married Frieda, and strongly believed in the value of lifelong commitment to a relationship, he did not rigidly believe in monogamy. His concept of marriage was flexible enough to accommodate infidelities on both sides. He never had children of his own, but he was convinced by the emotional fallout from his close relationship with his mother of the damage that doting parents could cause to their offspring. He resented Frieda's longing for her three children by Ernest Weekley as a form of betrayal. He developed close bonds with at least three men during his lifetime (Alan Chambers, John Middleton Murry and William Henry Hocking) which find their way into his fiction. His writing frequently shows individuals trying to discover forms of relationship outside, or in addition to, marriage which answer to the full range of their emotional needs.

Explorations of same-sex desire in Lawrence must be understood in this context as part of his ongoing attempt to trace his characters' reaching out for that which will satisfy and fulfil them. In *The White Peacock*, heteronormative relationships are conflictual or purely pragmatic and mundane. Cyril Beardsall's parents live apart, and his father dies a lonely death in his lodgings. Cyril's relationship with Emily Saxton is never formalised. After George Saxton is spurned by Lettie Beardsall, she marries Leslie Tempest based purely on his social position while George marries his cousin Meg and becomes an unfulfilled alcoholic. Annable's marriage to Lady Chrystabel founders due to their different values, and he escapes from it; he leaves his second wife and their children to fend for themselves. Towards the end of the novel, we learn that Emily has chosen to marry the 'fresh, winsome' Tom Renshaw, a former soldier who works on his father's farm and 'did not dream of questioning or analysing anything'; she tells Cyril that she has chosen Tom because he is 'wonderfully sagacious—and so gentle', unlike the 'restless' and 'urgent' (*WP* 308) Cyril, who pretends to be wounded by finding her engaged but clearly has no genuine desire himself for marriage. The only relationship which seems truly fulfilling is the intimate friendship between Cyril and George. In the chapter 'A Poem of Friendship', they swim together in a pond, and afterwards George rubs Cyril dry with a towel 'as if I were a child, or rather, a woman he loved and did not fear':

> I left myself quite limply in his hands, and, to get a better grip of me, he put his arm round me and pressed me against him, and the sweetness of the touch of our naked bodies one against the other was superb. It satisfied in some measure the vague, indecipherable yearning of my soul; and it was the same with him. When he had rubbed me all warm, he let me go, and we looked at each other with eyes of still laughter, and our love was perfect for a moment, more perfect than any love I have known since, either for man or woman. (*WP* 222–223).

The relationship between Cyril and George draws closely on Lawrence's friendship with Jessie Chambers's eldest brother, Alan. A similar scene in *Aaron's Rod*, in which Rawdon Lilly rubs the ailing Aaron Sisson's lower body with oil in order to revive him, transposes the feelings shared between Lawrence and Alan Chambers onto the feelings Lawrence invested in, or projected onto, his friendship with Murry.[12]

Siegmund MacNair's marriage and family life in *The Trespasser* are sources of despair and alienation. He had married Beatrice at the age of 17, but their lack of shared values has made home life a dreary responsibility and forced him to put all his feeling into music and his career as a violinist. As Helena tells him, 'marriage has been a tight corner you couldn't get out of to go to anybody' (*T* 124). Although he feels a bond with his youngest daughter Gwen, the other children (two daughters and a son) treat him with suspicion, and in the case of the eldest two, Vera and Frank, actively side with their mother and show little or no sympathy for him. He summarises his domestic life in terms of his messy suburban home: 'a broken, coarse comb, a child crying because her hair was tugged, a wife who had let the hair go till now, when she had got into a temper to see the job through; and then the teddy-bear, pathetically cocking a black worsted nose, and lifting absurd arms to him' (*T* 51).

Siegmund naturally gravitates towards the pupil whom he is teaching to play violin in order to address the emotional absences in his life, but the musical harmony he seeks with her is tinged with disharmony and dissonance. His encounter with a 'sort of Doppelgänger' (*T* 115), Hampson, a fellow musician, when on the Isle of Wight gives readers an outside understanding of Siegmund's predicament not otherwise afforded them. Although Hampson did not marry, he also seems to have escaped a long-term relationship and is yearning for 'intensity' in life: 'a vivid soul-experience'. He describes Siegmund as 'one whose flame goes nearly out, when the stimulant is lacking' (*T* 111). Hampson acts as a tragic chorus, telling Siegmund that the 'best sort of women ... aim at suppressing the gross and animal in us' (*T* 112). Siegmund's tragedy is that he fails to find a lasting relationship which speaks to and nourishes the simultaneously sensuous and spiritual feeling he puts into his music. Before he hangs himself, his wife Beatrice is trying to force him to honour his engagement at the Comedy Theatre purely in order to earn money to support the family. The social form into which his feelings must be channelled is a poor parody of the Wagnerian oneness he seeks with the world and with a partner.

Sons and Lovers is also full of conflictual or unsatisfactory heteronormative relationships. Gertrude Morel turns to two of her sons, William and Paul, for the fulfilment lacking in her marriage, and this in turn makes them emotionally dependent on her and unable to establish satisfactory relationships with women. William becomes engaged to a woman whom he thinks will satisfy his mother's ambition that he should enter the middle class, but their incompatibility and his disdain for her soon become clear, while Paul fails to integrate love and desire in his relationships with Miriam Leivers and Clara Dawes. Once again, the most fulfilling relationship is that which develops between two men: Paul and Baxter Dawes. As the estranged husband of Clara, Baxter clashes with Paul and the two men fight at Daybrook Station, but their subsequent rapprochement is charged with repressed feeling. Lawrence even uses this word when he describes Paul's reaction to Dawes when he visits him at the fever hospital in Sheffield: 'The strong emotion that Dawes aroused in him, repressed, made him shiver' (*SL* 426). Baxter is in some ways a double for Walter Morel, and Paul's sympathy for him and scheme to reunite him with Clara seem to enact his unconscious wish for a reconciliation with his father and desire to heal the rift between his parents.

In *The Rainbow*, Ursula Brangwen first experiences heteronormative courtship as a pressure to conform and surrender her integrity; in this, it is analogous to her experience of other patriarchal institutions in the text such as religion and education. Her lover, Anton Skrebensky, is an extremely conventional soldier who contributes to realising Britain's colonial ambitions in South Africa and India, and he views the teenage Ursula as a strange and desirable object to be claimed and made over into his own world. When he dances with Ursula at her Uncle Fred's wedding party, we are told that 'He appropriated her': 'He held her very close, so that she could feel his body, the weight of him sinking, settling upon her, overcoming her life and energy, making her inert along with him, she felt his hands pressing behind her, upon her' (*R* 297). Ursula's experience of her parents' marriage hardly offers a positive model for equal conjugal relations: her mother, Anna, has had to fight her father, the significantly named Will, each step of the way to assert her own rights as a woman within the relationship, attacking his patriarchal view of religion and forcing him to recognise and respond to the reality of her body and its desiring and procreative aspects. The novel ultimately traces Ursula's refusal to conform to Anton's desire, as she decides not to marry and then miscarries his child.

Ursula's brief schoolgirl relationship with her teacher Winifred Inger shows her reaching out for a relationship based on mutual desire and respect and not on the male need for dominance and ownership. Miss Inger's position as the masculinised modern woman with suffragette sympathies in rebellion against male control speaks to Ursula's sense of her own difference. Ursula's yearning to possess the qualities which the teacher embodies becomes clear when the conventional contract between teacher and pupil is broken during a swimming lesson:

> Ursula, trembling, hardly able to contain herself, pulled off her clothes, put on her tight bathing suit, and opened the door of her cabin. Two girls were in the water. The mistress had not appeared. She waited. A door opened, Miss Inger came out, dressed in a rust-red tunic like a Greek girl's, tied round the waist, and a red silk handkerchief round her head. How lovely she looked. Her knees were so white and strong and proud, she was firm-bodied as Diana. She walked simply to the side of the bath, and with a negligent movement, flung herself in. For a moment Ursula watched the white, smooth, strong shoulders and the easy arms swimming. Then she too dived into the water.

> Now, ah now she was swimming in the same water with her dear mistress. The girl moved her limbs voluptuously, and swam by herself, deliciously, yet with a craving of unsatisfaction. She wanted to touch the other, to touch her, to feel her. (*R* 313)

The passage is closely focalised through Ursula, and the breathless nature of her crush on her teacher is clear in the ebb and flow of the sentences, matching the flow of the water and fluctuations in her gaze. Ursula sees in Miss Inger the masculine qualities of strength, firmness and warmth which she also longs to possess. In Anton, these qualities had been coercive, or imposed on Ursula, whereas here they are things which she must pursue. The Christian teachings which confuse her by offering stark and polarising accounts of desire in the flesh and spirit are displaced here by the classical reference to her teacher as Diana. Miss Inger's difference is suggested by the tunic she wears, 'like a Greek girl's', hinting at her sapphic nature. Ursula's yearning is both physical and spiritual: the modulation between 'touch her' and 'feel her' shows that physical contact and the inner life coalesce in Ursula's fluid desire. The slippage of meaning in the repeated word 'mistress' also shows how power in this scene moves from being institutional and hierarchical to a matter of inner strength.

When Sir John Dickinson wondered how Methuen could have failed to register the suggestion contained in the title of this chapter in the novel ('Shame'), he implied that Lawrence was depicting Ursula's feelings for Miss Inger as inherently shameful. Lawrence, however, was drawing his reader's attention to the shame that Ursula feels once she realises the illusory nature of her childish infatuation. When Winifred Inger capitulates and accepts life as a wife and mother, Ursula is left disillusioned and deprived again of a relationship through which she can realise her complex passions. This episode is very self-contained in the novel, and it would therefore be easy to understate its significance for her emotional development, but by showing Ursula that the qualities she craves in life, and the integrity she seeks, are to be discovered in herself and not in the outer world, it is arguably an essential stage in her self-realisation, paving the way for her rejection of Anton.

If the prosecution of *The Rainbow* made Lawrence aware of his almost complete 'sense of detachment from the bourgeois world', it only intensified his attack on bourgeois structures and modes of feeling. In the abandoned 'Prologue' to *Women in Love*, Lawrence explored Rupert Birkin's loss of belief in his work as a school inspector. Birkin reasons that if 'education is nothing but the process of building up, gradually, a complete unit of consciousness' and 'each unit of consciousness is the living unit of that great social, religious, philosophic idea towards which mankind, like an organism seeking its final form, is laboriously growing', then when society is going through a 'process of decay and decomposition' (*WL* 495) education becomes meaningless. Birkin comes 'to a knowledge of the essential futility of all attempt at social unanimity in constructiveness' (*WL* 496). His sense that society is in a state of disintegration is reflected too in his failure to discover a fulfilling form of emotional relationship. Although he has established a bond with Hermione Roddice, we are told that 'he did not desire her. But he wanted to force himself to love her and to desire her'. She too does not want him, but 'with all her soul, she *wanted* to want him' (*WL* 497). Although Birkin is 'more at home with a woman than with a man, yet it was for men that he felt the hot, flushing, roused attraction which a man is supposed to feel for the other sex' (*WL* 501). Lawrence traces the feelings of shame, and the willed suppression of his desire, created in Birkin by internalised social pressures. Yet he also insists on Birkin's honesty in confronting and seeking to understand his emotional needs: 'He wanted to cast out these desires, he wanted not to know them. Yet a man can no more slay a living desire in him, than he can prevent his body from feeling heat and cold' (*WL* 504).

When Lawrence decided to remove the 'Prologue' from the novel, he started it instead with an opening chapter in which Ursula and Gudrun Brangwen discuss and dismantle the traditional concept of marriage. Gudrun asks her sister whether she wants to get married, suggesting that it might put a woman in 'a better position' or be an experience 'one needs'; Ursula responds that it might put one in a better position, but it is more likely to be 'the end of experience' (*WL* 7). They go together to the church at Willey Green to see people arrive for the wedding of Theobald Lupton and Laura Crich, but the social form of the occasion is broken when the groom arrives after the bride and then impulsively chases her inside. Rupert Birkin, the best man, is accidentally late too. This is the first indication that marriage has ceased to be a meaningful religious and social form. Later in the novel, when Birkin goes to propose to Ursula she is out, and his interactions with her father Will show the utter mismatch between the older man's belief in social propriety and Birkin's sense of Ursula's right to choose and belief that a marriage is merely an emotional bond which is ended when the requisite feeling is gone. Will does not believe in Birkin's 'new-fangled ways' and 'new-fangled ideas', while Birkin sees his future father-in-law as 'a roomful of old echoes' (*WL* 257). Birkin considers marriage 'in the old sense ... repulsive': it is worse, he says, than '*Egoïsme à deux*' (*WL* 352). Birkin's aim throughout the novel is to re-define terms and to discover more meaningful forms for his committed relationships. 'A pure balance of two single beings' (*WL* 148) is what he seeks in his relationship with Ursula, while with Gerald Crich he wants to swear a 'Blutbrüderschaft', establishing an intimacy akin to that of 'the old German knights', who would make 'a little wound in their arms, and rub each other's blood into the cut' as a symbolic act, swearing 'to be true to each other, of one blood, all their lives' (*WL* 206).

In November 1916, when Lawrence had finished the first version of *Women in Love*, he told J. B. Pinker: 'I don't think this book is likely to be suppressed for *immorality*, like the *Rainbow*' (*3L* 29). The statement reveals Lawrence's awareness that his novel was liable to be rejected by publishers or censored by the authorities for more than simply localised explicit phrases or outspoken passages. He clearly anticipated the objections which publishers would raise to its deeply critical depiction of England in 1916, including his latest and most thoroughgoing attack on bourgeois values and social forms. The response of the reader at Constable shows that it was indeed the broader vision of the book which caused offence; the report objected to 'the writer's expressions of antipathy to England and the forms of English civilisation' (*FWL* xxxvii). Lawrence's writing had started out by addressing taboo subjects in order to bring suppressed aspects of experience into the open. It had questioned and critiqued the cherished bourgeois institutions of marriage and the family as a means of changing entrenched attitudes. The prosecution of *The Rainbow* had underscored Lawrence's alienation from the bourgeois world. *Women in Love* took his critique of bourgeois norms a step further with its satirical attack on their destructive outmodedness and its reaching out for new ideas of selfhood and relationship. It was the first novel Lawrence wrote as an outsider who had retired 'out of the herd' (*2L* 546) and his first novel of ideas, or (to use his own term) his first tentative 'thought-adventure' (*RDP* 214).

Notes

1. See Moran (2015: 52–53).
2. See *Poems* 1642–1649.
3. See Worthen (1991: 84).
4. See *WP* xxxiv–xxxv.
5. See *T* 115.
6. See *SL* 381.
7. See p. 474 of the manuscript in Schorer (1977).
8. John Worthen notes that 'either Garnett had second and still more censorious thoughts, or Duckworth himself [the publisher] intervened' (Worthen 1991a: 23).
9. See the poem 'Minorities in danger', from 'The "Nettles" Notebook': 'Now above all is the time for the minorities of men, / those who are neither bourgeois nor bolshevist, but true to life, / to gather and fortify themselves, in every class, in every country, in every race' (*Poems* 574).
10. See, for instance, the famous letter to Rolf Gardiner of 3 December 1926 in which he refers to the view from the Lawrence house on Walker Street as 'the country of my heart' (*5L* 592), and also the letter to Gertrude Cooper of 23 January 1927 in which he warmly recalls the vesper verse being spoken at Eastwood Congregational Chapel, 'Then off out into the dark, with Dicky Pogmore and the Chambers and all the rest' (*5L* 634).
11. See *2L* 584 (22 March 1916).
12. See *AR* 96: 'He rubbed every speck of the man's lower body—the abdomen, the buttocks, the thighs and knees, down to the feet, rubbed it all warm and glowing with camphorated oil, every bit of it, chafing the toes swiftly, till he was almost exhausted'.

5

Sex, Sexuality and Sexual Identity

Lawrence is often invoked in popular culture as a writer whose chief preoccupation was with sex. This view of Lawrence has been conditioned in part by his final novel, *Lady Chatterley's Lover*, and the furore caused by the Chatterley Trial in October and November 1960, when Penguin Books successfully defended it against charges of obscenity under the amended Obscene Publications Act of 1959. On one level, *Lady Chatterley's Lover* carried forward the attack on bourgeois values which I have traced through Lawrence's early- and middle-period writings. From the beginning of his career Lawrence had focused in strategic ways on subjects such as illegitimacy and same-sex desire to address middle-class prejudice and the pressures brought to bear on people by religion and social institutions which enforce an unthinking subservience to traditional ethics and normative kinds of gender and class identity, establishing strong taboos around difference policed through feelings of disgust, shame and dishonour. I have suggested in the previous chapter that part of Connie Chatterley's learning curve in *Lady Chatterley's Lover* is to overcome her upper-middle-class social conditioning by accepting sexual desire and experience in all its forms (including the taboo form of anal intercourse) as a means to attaining a wholeness of being otherwise denied her. In this novel, Connie's relationship to the physical act of sex is so important because her culture is said on the one hand to have sentimentalised it through cinema and popular romance literature, and on the other denigrated it as a mere mechanical function subservient to so-called 'higher faculties' such as the intellect and spirituality.

In his essay *A Propos of 'Lady Chatterley's Lover'*, Lawrence asserts: 'We are, today, as human beings, evolved and cultured far beyond the taboos which are inherent in our culture' (*LCL* 307). He suggests that reflecting honestly and without shame on our bodies and their feelings and desires will enable us to move beyond taboos and so redress the privileging of the mind over the body and the damaging self-division it creates. The amended Obscene Publications Act allowed

The Life of the Author: D. H. Lawrence, First Edition. Andrew Harrison.

books to be defended against charges of obscenity on the grounds of their literary merit, and this essay was drawn upon in an abbreviated, and inevitably simplified, form to underpin the case for the defence as it was made by the authors and critics brought to the witness stand. Penguin Books won the case by convincing the jury that the descriptions of sex and the use of the four-letter words 'cunt' and 'fuck' were not intended simply to titillate, and so to deprave and corrupt, but were part of a committed, indeed almost puritanical, effort to explore the importance of sex in human relations.

Sex in *Lady Chatterley's Lover* is a complex physical and psychological experience which can either instrumentalise the body and deepen self-alienation in the individual and the estrangement between couples, or else enable individuals to reconnect with their bodies, with their partners, and with the world around them. Cynthia Asquith commented in an interview on Lawrence's intense dislike of the word 'sex': it was, she said, 'a word he detested, "mean, belittling, sordidifying little word", he called it'.[1] In her memoir *"Not I, But the Wind ..."*, Frieda Lawrence expresses views very similar to those of her late husband: 'When people talk about sex, I don't know what they mean – as if sex hopped about by itself like a frog, as if it had no relation to the rest of living, one's growth, one's ripening' (Lawrence 1934: 21). Connie and Mellors have the courage to renounce their controlling and defining mental consciousness through sexual desire and during sex, and this allows them to overcome class prejudice and move on from the damage caused by their past relationships. Sex in their case becomes not an end in itself, but a means to self-realisation.

As Mark Kinkead-Weekes has noted, Lawrence was never concerned with sexual intercourse as an isolated act but with sexual relationship in its broadest sense: in his fiction, 'Sexual activity and consciousness become the vehicle for exploring wider and wider relationships, within people, between them, throughout society, and the connection of man to the universe' (Kinkead-Weekes 1978: 102). When Paul Morel and Clara Dawes have intercourse outdoors in *Sons and Lovers*, they both feel connected to an impersonal will in nature which is 'terrible' and which makes them almost strangers to each other: Clara feels the 'naked hunger and inevitability of his loving her, something strong and blind and ruthless in its primitiveness', and their coming together includes 'the thrust of the manifold grass stems, the cry of the peewit, the wheel of the stars' (*SL* 397–398). As Kinkead-Weekes observes, the language Lawrence used to represent sex and sexual feelings 'insists that sex is a way of talking about something else' (Kinkead-Weekes 1978: 102). Often in Lawrence's writing, then, the emphasis falls not on 'sex' per se but more broadly on our need to accept and be attuned to what he once termed the 'dark continent' (*STH* 202) of the self, comprising the chaos of our unexplored bodily feelings. In the late poem 'The Heart of Man', Lawrence speaks of 'the other universe, of the heart of man / that we know nothing of, that we dare not explore':

a place in whose mysterious interior, 'darker still than Congo or Amazon / flow the heart's rivers of fulness, desire and distress' (*Poems* 522). Lawrence's realignment of 'the heart of man' away from sentimental and spiritual views of idealised love and towards the ebbs and flows of the blood is typical of his attention to sex, desire and love as being linked to an alternative logic of the body which challenges and overturns the logic of the mind.

This alternative logic of the body is foregrounded in several of the short stories from the collection *England, My England and Other Stories*, which was first published in America on 24 October 1922.[2] In 'Hadrian' (otherwise known as 'You Touched Me'), the two Rockley sisters, Matilda and Emmie, live with their elderly and sick father in Pottery House, an imposing but ugly building on the site of the family's now-closed pottery works. The young women have been brought up to see themselves as socially superior to the local population of colliers, so they have become 'old maids' (*EmyE* 92), assuming the role of their dead mother. Matilda is 32 and Emmie 30. Their father, Ted Rockley, has four daughters and we are informed that he has resented living in an exclusively female household. Fifteen years before the opening of the story he went off to London and adopted 'a boy out of a Charity Institution' (*EmyE* 93). The boy, who is named Hadrian, was raised as a member of the family, though the daughters insisted that he address them as 'Cousin Matilda' and 'Cousin Emmie'. Matilda and Emmie were only superficially kind to Hadrian; in private they called him 'sly'. He in turn treated them with 'a certain laconic indifference'. It is clear that the sisters were jealous of their father's tacit understanding of Hadrian, and the men's 'real but unemotional regard for one another'. Matilda and Emmie were also wary of Hadrian coming between them and the £20,000 which they stand to inherit on their father's death. Hadrian was sent to High School, but Matilda's efforts to make him a 'little gentleman' were in vain. At the age of 15 he chose to leave for the colonies and went to Canada under the protection of his former Institution. He worked at an electricity works near Montreal, but when war was declared he signed up and came back to Europe.

As the story opens, the war is over and the father, an habitual drinker, is dying of dropsy and wishes to see Hadrian again. Hadrian is now 21 and he writes to announce that he will visit them during a long period of leave from the army. Matilda and Emmie are 'terribly fluttered' (*EmyE* 94) when they learn of Hadrian's intended visit, and they are wrong-footed when he arrives a day early. Emmie responds to Hadrian with her former feeling of resentment, calling him 'Mannie!' and '*Sly—!*' (*EmyE* 96). Matilda's feelings, however, are more ambivalent. The careful attention she pays to her dress and appearance following his arrival is the first clue that she might have feelings for him which she cannot admit to Emmie or to herself. When she overhears a conversation between Hadrian and her father in which the young man states that he would not live again in England because 'there's too much difference between the men and the employers over here' (*EmyE* 97), she rebounds away from him, retreating into her habitual snobbishness and demeaning him in private conversations with her sister. Emmie is now convinced that he has come back to steal their inheritance, but the father tells Matilda that on his death the house and all the money will pass to her and Emmie equally, and Hadrian (who will not feature in the will) should be given his watch and chain plus £100, and be helped out if he is ever in trouble. The father stipulates that the women should never part with the house.

The story's denouement hinges on an apparently trivial incident which occurs on the second night of Hadrian's stay. Since the father is gravely ill, Emmie persuades him to move to a downstairs bedroom, leaving Hadrian to sleep in the father's vacant room. In the middle of the night, Matilda, who is deeply upset by her father's condition, goes to see him. She twice enquires whether he is asleep, then directly asks him if he is unable to sleep before laying her hand gently on his face and brow. It is only when Hadrian answers her that she realises she is touching Hadrian instead of her father. While Matilda dismisses the incident as a simple mistake and wishes to cut off her hand as if it is an embodiment of sin, Hadrian sees it as a bond between them and asks Ted Rockley whether he would like him to marry Matilda. The father at first seems surprised by the idea, and his facial gestures express mockery and contempt, but he soon comes round to it. He asks Matilda to marry Hadrian, and when she tells him he must be out of his mind and calls the suggestion 'disgraceful' (*EmyE* 102) he threatens to rewrite his will and leave everything to Hadrian unless she does what he tells her. After a period of resistance during which the daughters try to scare Hadrian off, Matilda speaks to Hadrian. He tells her that he only thought of marriage because she put her hand on him. She calls his wish to marry her 'so indecent', but he responds by saying 'How? ... You touched me' (*EmyE* 106). After this exchange with Hadrian, Matilda informs her father that she will accede to his wishes and marry Hadrian, and the ceremony takes place three days later at a registry office. When she returns to Pottery House as Hadrian's wife, her father asks her to kiss him and then to kiss her husband. The story ends with the dying father saying 'That's right! That's right!' (*EmyE* 107).

On a first reading the story might strike one as a study of parental tyranny and the abuse of male power over women. We are told that Ted Rockley 'seemed to have a strange desire, quite unreasonable, for revenge upon the women who had surrounded him for so long, and served him so carefully' (*EmyE* 104). Hadrian's name invites us to see him as a conqueror who claims Matilda against her will. Yet the story forces us to confront the irreducible complexity in the motivations of all its characters. In the case of the two daughters, and especially of Matilda, there are constant hints at the dichotomy between avowed views and beliefs, and underlying feelings. The girls agree, for instance, that they prefer the quietness of their lives now that the pottery factory is closed and they can no longer hear the 'pottery-lasses' shrieking and larking with the men, but we are told that 'whether the two Rockley girls really liked it better, or whether they only imagined they did, is a question' (*EmyE* 92).

At a deeper level, both emotional and bodily, Matilda craves the thing which she abjures. Her error, then, in touching Hadrian instead of her father, seems much more than accidental. Since she goes to Hadrian's bedside in a sleep-like trance, we might understand that it is her body acting according to its own logic without the interference of her mind. By laying her hands on Hadrian in the middle of the night, Matilda initiates a mutual awakening. However, whereas the charity boy is instantly made aware that the compassion she expresses through touch is something that he has been missing and badly desires, Matilda's snobbishness and middle-class disgust at all things sexual cause her to recoil from her actions and this threatens to alienate her still further from her desires. Her father is an emotional pragmatist who acts straightforwardly to address his own emotional needs, firstly by adopting Hadrian and then by ensuring that Hadrian is formally bonded to him as his son-in-law. By forcing Matilda to marry Hadrian, Ted Rockley compels her to confront her own emotional needs and sexual desires. The story shows how Matilda's body urges her to replace compassion for her father with passion for a sexual partner. This substitution, which had until recently seemed so indecent to her, is stressed in the conclusion, when the father asks his daughter to kiss first him and then Hadrian. The father's concluding utterance – 'That's right! That's right!' – underscores the feeling that Matilda's body, by acting of its own accord, has restored the correct order of things.

This redressing of the balance away from mental logic and towards the logic of the body is also enacted in 'The Blind Man'. In this tale, a facially disfigured and blinded soldier, Maurice Pervin, returns home from the war to his wife, Isabel, who is pregnant with their second child (the first having died in infancy). The couple are well off, living in Maurice's 'own place' (*EmyE* 46): a Grange with a farmstead at the back, which they rent out to the Wernhams, who act as farmers. When Isabel is not occupied with farm matters, she reviews books for a Scottish newspaper. Although Maurice seems to adapt well to his blindness, he initially experiences uncontrollable feelings 'worse than depression—a black misery, when his own life was a torture to him, and when his presence was unbearable to his wife' (*EmyE* 47). Maurice and Isabel are evidently a middle-class couple accustomed to living a life where appearances are everything. Isabel, in particular, is shown to evaluate and understand herself and others visually. For this reason, Maurice seems to Isabel 'cancelled' (*EmyE* 56) or nullified by his blindness. However, he gradually begins to discover a new and rich, though ineffable, sense of being and identity through touch, which compensates him for the loss of his former self. Isabel is at once deeply attracted to this tactile mode of being, and afraid of it.

The story associates mental consciousness with mirrors and light, and bodily consciousness with animals and darkness. When Isabel goes to fetch Maurice one stormy night from the stables attached to the farmstead, she finds him attending to the horses; as they leave the building, he asks for her hand, but this time it is not because he needs to be guided by her, but because she is disorientated and needs to be led by him. In the rainy and windswept night, he seems to her like 'a tower of darkness ... as if he rose out of the earth' (*EmyE* 53). Maurice agrees to Isabel inviting her barrister-friend Bertie Reid, a fellow Scot, to visit. She clearly misses her childhood soulmate, and Maurice, who has never previously got on with Bertie, seems to hope that the visit will help to assuage his wife's feeling of being burdened by him as she waits to give birth. Bertie's intellectualism is, however, severely threatened by Maurice's blood-consciousness. In a scene which directly mirrors the earlier encounter between Maurice and Isabel, Bertie is sent by Isabel to retrieve Maurice from one of the farm outhouses. He finds Maurice holding the handle of a turnip-pulper, with a 'half-wild grey cat' (*EmyE* 60) rubbing against his leg. Maurice notes that he does not really know Bertie, but his subsequent attempt to establish a bond with him based on mutual knowledge and understanding relies wholly on touch. First, Maurice asks whether he can touch Bertie, and his hand moves over Bertie's head and face to his shoulders, arm and hand. He then asks Bertie to touch his (Maurice's) eyes and his scar. Bertie has always relied on mental logic to know people; he has held himself back from establishing physical intimacy with others, so being forced to touch Maurice fills him with 'an unreasonable fear, lest the other man should suddenly destroy him' (*EmyE* 62). Maurice is convinced that they have attained mutual understanding through touch and he is curiously elated, but Bertie, in an obvious role reversal, is left 'haggard, with sunken eyes': Bertie is now the one who is nullified, 'like a mollusc whose shell is broken' (*EmyE* 63).

The story demonstrates the dualism which often characterised Lawrence's thinking about the self, but it is explored with a characteristically subtle and complex relativism. Maurice has no control over the 'chaos inside himself' (*EmyE* 54), while Isabel, despite believing herself to be otherwise, is 'really fatally self-determined' (*EmyE* 50). Bertie is more self-aware than Isabel, but just as helpless as Maurice where his inner life is concerned. Although he has built an impressive life for himself as 'a brilliant and successful barrister' and 'a *littérateur* of high repute', he feels himself to be 'neuter, nothing' because of his inability to 'approach women physically' (*EmyE* 58) and his fear of physical contact with, and commitment to, others. Lawrence avoids a straightforward alignment with Maurice's tactile worldview by emphasising his childlike dependency on Isabel, and his exasperation at his powerlessness in both practical and emotional matters. As Bertie says to Isabel, 'I suppose we're all deficient somewhere' (*EmyE* 59). Yet, there is a crucial difference in kind between the deficiency of Maurice and the deficiencies of Isabel and Bertie. While Maurice is honest with himself and others regarding his feelings, Isabel and Bertie, like Matilda and Emmie in 'Hadrian', cultivate and project middle-class sophistication, which prevents them from ever confronting their underlying bodily feelings. When Maurice overhears the first exchange between Isabel and Bertie, we are told that he 'disliked the slight purr of complacency in the Scottish speech. He disliked intensely the glib way in which Isabel spoke of their happiness and nearness. It made him recoil' (*EmyE* 55).

We might understand Maurice forcing Bertie to touch him as both a malicious act of revenge against a man who clearly patronises him and who has temporarily displaced him from his own, very different intimacy with Isabel, and an attempt, however ill-conceived, to force Bertie to address his fear of intimate contact. However, whereas in 'Hadrian' there is an underlying sense that Matilda recognises her own deeply repressed bodily feelings for Hadrian through her enforced marriage to him, and that she can break free from Pottery House and make a new life with him in Canada, 'The Blind Man' ends on a note of mutual incomprehension, with Bertie simply destroyed by being forced to do something from which he shrinks.

In a letter to Katherine Mansfield of 5 December 1918, Lawrence referred to the ending of 'The Blind Man' as 'queer and ironical'. He added that he realised '*how* many people are just rotten at the quick' (*3L* 303). The target of his satire is ambiguous. On the one hand, the ending might be said to demonstrate how trapped both Bertie and Maurice are in their own modes of being. Yet Lawrence's comment that people are 'rotten at the quick' seems to relate more obviously to Bertie's complacency and refusal or inability to confront his own bodily feelings.[3] Lawrence would return to the basic plot structure of 'The Blind Man' in several of his later short stories, showing how excessively cultured and/or complacently middle-class and Westernised characters refuse to confront their bodily desires, so that when they are compelled to do so the experience is destructive for themselves and others, resulting in madness and death. We might think here of 'The Princess' and 'None of That!', in which contact with cultural difference has catastrophic consequences for fatally self-determined female characters whose identities are premised on the repression of bodily desire, or 'The Man Who Loved Islands', in which the central male character wishes to create an island utopia based on a generalised spiritual love but finds his idealism defeated by nature and compromised by his getting a woman pregnant and escaping from her into isolation and insane solipsism.

It is Lawrence's deep pessimism about people's refusal to accept the logic of the body, and their own physical desires, in these stories that adds pathos to his final novel and its exploration of the way Connie Chatterley manages to cast off the complacency of her cultured upper-middle-class upbringing and the emotional inarticulacy of her aristocratic husband, and reconnect with her bodily feelings through sex with her husband's gamekeeper. In 'The Blind Man', Lawrence describes Maurice Pervin's honest confrontation with his bodily feelings as he begins to experience 'sheer immediacy of blood-contact with the substantial world', 'a certain rich positivity, bordering sometimes on rapture':

> The rich suffusion of this state generally kept him happy, reaching its culmination in the consuming passion for his wife. But at times the flow would seem to be checked and thrown back. Then it would beat inside him like a tangled sea, and he was tortured in the shattered chaos of his own blood. He grew to dread this arrest, this throw-back, this chaos inside himself, when he seemed merely at the mercy of his own powerful and conflicting elements. (*EmyE* 54)

Connie experiences a similar confrontation with bodily feeling, but she comes through tortured self-division to self-acceptance and self-realisation in and through the body. The ebbs and flows of the blood are in her case associated not with the darkness of an inner world but with sexual experience and particularly with the unself-conscious nature of feelings during sex, which combine psychological and bodily elements:

> And it seemed she was like the sea, nothing but dark waves rising and heaving, heaving with a great swell, so that slowly her whole darkness was in motion, and she was ocean rolling its dark, dumb mass. Oh, and far down inside her the deeps parted and rolled asunder, in long, far-travelling billows, and ever, at the quick of her, the depths parted and rolled asunder, from the centre of soft plunging, as the plunger went deeper and deeper, touching lower, and she was deeper and deeper and deeper disclosed, and heavier the billows of her rolled away to some shore, uncovering her, and closer and closer plunged the palpable unknown, and further and further rolled the waves of herself away from herself, leaving her, till suddenly, in a soft, shuddering convulsion, the quick of all her plasm was touched, she knew herself touched, the consummation was upon her, and she was gone. She was gone, she was not, and she was born: a woman. (*LCL* 174)

As was the case with Matilda Rockley in 'Hadrian', embracing the logic, wisdom and feelings of the body results in the death of the old Connie and her reawakening through the discovery of a 'right' self. The difference is that we are made to inhabit Connie's perspective as she fully realises this and consciously rejects as a falsehood the dead, safe world of class superiority and its associated complacency.

It is important that we recognise both the forward-thinking and offensive aspects of Lawrence's writing on sex and sexuality. His critique of a culturally imposed mind-body dualism in 'Hadrian' and *Lady Chatterley's Lover*, and his exploration of the leap of logic and courageousness involved in listening to one's bodily feelings and taking them seriously, must be balanced against the conventional versions of womanhood that the female characters ultimately attain. Although there are signs that Matilda's future life with Hadrian in Canada will be more varied and fulfilling on an emotional level than her life to date at Pottery House, she will go from being the daughter serving her father in the role of her dead mother to a wife compensating her orphan-husband for his lack of parental love. Likewise, although Connie escapes a loveless marriage through her relationship with Mellors and makes the conscious decision to fund their future life together on a farm, the realignment of her relationship with the body is presented as a shift from the use of sexual intrigues with men in her husband's circle of friends to compensate for her lack of sexual satisfaction in marriage to a renunciation of class privilege and sexual initiative as a means to greater self-realisation. Connie goes from being a woman tasked by her husband with getting pregnant by an anonymous member of her husband's circle in order to provide him with an heir, to one who willingly surrenders her body to Mellors and integrates mind and body by listening to the promptings of her womb and realising that what she really wants is to create new life with a man she loves.

It may seem strange that a writer who challenged bourgeois habits of thought and critiqued powerful middle-class institutions and forms of authority should have shown female characters with the courage to act on the promptings of their own bodies and to comprehend their desires in the face of social pressures realising themselves physically and emotionally through caring roles and childbirth. *Lady Chatterley's Lover* is not the only novel in which the female protagonist's brave decision to pay heed to her feelings and re-order her life culminates in the recognition that pregnancy is what her body has really craved. Katherine Mansfield, who once described 'child-bearing' as 'the most ignominious of all professions',[4] was particularly angered by a section towards the end of the penultimate chapter of *The Lost Girl* (1920) in which Alvina Houghton feels 'a strange thrilling in her bowels: a sort of trill strangely within her, yet extraneous to her' (*LG* 320) and realises she is pregnant by her husband, Ciccio. Mansfield wrote: 'a TRILL. What does that mean? And why is it so peculiarly offensive for a man? Because it is *not on this plane* that the emotions of others are conveyed to our imagination – It's a kind of sinning against art' (Kimber and Smith 2014: 708). Mansfield took issue with Lawrence's insistence that feelings are physiological phenomena and so can be invoked through descriptions of bodily sensations, but her anger was mainly directed against what she saw as his conventional and demeaning portrayal of Alvina: 'Take her youth – her thriving upon the horse play with the doctors – They might be beasts butting each other – no more. Take the scene when the hero throws her in the kitchen, possesses her & she returns singing to the washing up. It's a *disgrace*. Take the *rotten* rubbishy scene of the woman in labour asking the Italian into the bedroom – All false. All a pack of lies!' (Kimber and Smith 2014: 706–707). Although Lawrence challenged gender norms and seems to have understood sexuality as fluid to the degree that he gave serious and sympathetic attention to the way that men and women desire members of the same and opposite sex at different points in their lives, he often either had recourse to essentialist notions of the 'male' and 'female', and reproduced homophobic discourse when describing same-sex bonds, or struggled to imagine what long-term relationships between same-sex couples might be like.

We must understand his work, of course, in its historical context. While the writing he produced under the influence of Frieda and her sisters between 1912 and 1915 addressed the suffrage by tracing women's struggle for emancipation from patriarchal structures, from the late war years on he turned his attention to the crisis of traditional male selfhood created by the battlefields of the Great War, where physical and psychological injuries exposed vulnerabilities in men which had earlier been ignored or brushed aside.[5] Maurice Pervin's injury in 'The Blind Man' removes the traditional, abstract power he possessed as Isabel's wealthy husband before the war only for him to discover a more tangible sense of power through touch. He becomes a 'tower of darkness' to Isabel: an embodiment of phallic strength. In this case, Lawrence is exploring in a reactionary manner how male power in the pre-war period might be replaced by a more innate male strength discovered through the body. In his writings from around 1917 onwards, Lawrence focuses on the ways in which men can reclaim power on a more authentic basis and how women can find more fulfilling forms of life through new kinds of accommodation within existing social structures.

I have shown in the previous chapter how Lawrence's empathetic engagement with same-sex desire in *The Rainbow* and the 'Prologue' to *Women in Love* can be related to his critique of bourgeois society and its policing of desire within the bounds of heteronormativity. Same-sex desire is depicted here in relation to an almost overpowering pressure to conform. It is significant, however, that in the same way that Lawrence does not use the term 'lesbian' to describe Ursula Brangwen's relationship with Winifred Inger, he does not describe Rupert Birkin's obviously sexual feelings for men's bodies as 'homosexual'. His attitude to these categories, like his attitude to the social gender categories 'masculinity' and 'femininity', was deeply conflicted. In a letter to the American psychoanalyst Trigant Burrow written on Christmas Day 1926, Lawrence complained: 'I who loathe sexuality so deeply am considered a lurid sexuality specialist' (*5L* 611). He was preoccupied with tracing in his fiction characters' ineffable feelings and desires and showing how they challenge bourgeois complacency and dislodge middle-class categories. In contrast, he could be searing in his attitude to collective social projections of categorised sexualities both heterosexual and homosexual.

Some references to homosexuality in Lawrence's letters show him disavowing contemporary religious and legal prejudices. In a letter to Henry Savage of 2 December 1913, he said he 'should like to know why nearly every man that approaches greatness tends to homosexuality, whether he admits it or not' (*2L* 115). On 19 April 1915, he told David Garnett that he had no 'moral disapprobation' regarding homosexuality, and stated: 'I myself never considered Plato very wrong, or Oscar Wilde' (*2L* 320). These statements were made, however, in the context of letters which express stereotypical homophobic views. As John Turner notes, in 1913–1914 'Lawrence conceptualised homosexuality in narcissistic terms as an instinctive desire for self-fulfilment in one's own sex at the expense of the other' (Turner 2020: 86). In the letter to Savage, Lawrence says that the poet Richard Middleton 'loves the *body* of a man better than the body of a woman', and he goes on: 'I believe a man projects his own image on another man, like on a mirror. But from a woman he wants himself re-born, re-constructed. So he can always get satisfaction from a man, but it is the hardest thing in life to get ones soul and body satisfied from a woman, so that one is free from oneself. And one is kept by all tradition and instinct from loving men, or a man – for it means just extinction of all the purposive influences' (*2L* 115).

During 1915, Lawrence's view of heterosexual intercourse as achieving rebirth through a recognition of the partner's difference was complicated as he began to explore the kinds of disintegrative self-enclosure that he detected in people at a time of war. In a letter to Bertrand Russell of 12 February 1915, Lawrence says that a man comes to a woman for the purpose of 'self discovery', and this can bear a certain amount of repetition, but repeating the experience *ad infinitum* is 'sensationalism': 'This is what nearly *all* English people now do. When a man takes a woman, he is *merely* repeating a known reaction upon himself, not seeking a new reaction, a discovery. And this is like self-abuse or masterbation'. He suggests that in a culture where a man typically goes to a woman not for 'discovery or new connection or progression, but only to repeat upon himself a known reaction ... there is always Sodomy' (*2L* 284–285).

A little over two months later, in the letter of 19 April, Lawrence warned David Garnett against entering into a homosexual relationship with his friend Francis Birrell. He told him he was 'foolish ... to say that it doesn't matter either way – the men loving men', calling it 'all wrong', and he asked: 'Why is there this horrible sense of frowstiness, so repulsive, as if it came from deep inward dirt – a sort of sewer – deep in men like [John Maynard] K[eynes] and B[irrell] and D[uncan] G[rant]' (*2L* 320). Lawrence then explained the overwhelming feelings he experienced during his recent visit to Cambridge, when Russell took him to visit the economist John Maynard Keynes in his rooms in King's College. They arrived at midday, and Keynes seemed to be out, but then 'a door opened and K. was there, blinking from sleep, standing in his pyjamas. And as he stood there gradually a knowledge passed into me, which has been like a little madness to me ever since. And it was carried along with the most dreadful sense of repulsiveness – something like carrion – a vulture gives me the same feeling. I begin to feel mad as I think of it – insane' (*2L* 320–321).

While Lawrence claimed not to have thought homosexuality 'very wrong', he reacted against homosexual sex for the same reason that he reacted against certain forms of heterosexual intercourse, on the grounds that he thought it entailed an instrumentalising relation to a partner. He understood same-sex desire as being part of the full range of people's experience of desire, and was attuned to the suffering individuals were likely to experience through social prejudice and the pressure to conform to heteronormativity, but he was oblivious to the practical realities of life for homosexual and bisexual men in a society where homosexuality was a crime. Public schools, universities and the army were relatively self-contained worlds in which same-sex relationships could be pursued more safely than in other environments, but Lawrence responded very negatively to homosexuality in these rigidly hierarchical settings, mainly it seems because of the shame of repression and the imbalances of power that he perceived as being central to the relationships struck up there.

In 'The Prussian Officer' he explores the violent consequences of the repression of homosexual desire in the hierarchical setting of the army. The lieutenant is clearly deeply drawn to his orderly and irritated that this young man, whose allotted role is to serve him, is in an apparently satisfying relationship with a woman. The officer compels the orderly's attention by beating and brutalising him. At one point, the officer tries to find fulfilment through a casual affair with a woman, but this only intensifies his frustration and so exacerbates his sadistic behaviour on his return. In a letter to Edward Garnett sent around 11 November 1912, Lawrence stated that 'soldiers, being herded together, men without women, never being *satisfied* by a woman, as a man never is from a street affair, get their surplus sex and their frustration and dissatisfaction into the blood, and *love* cruelty. It is sex lust fermented makes atrocity' (*1L* 469). In this case, the officer's 'surplus sex' cannot be satisfied in a relationship so it is displaced into cruelty and abuse. Atrocity ensues when the orderly is pushed beyond the limits of endurance and reacts by murdering his tormentor.

Lawrence's reference to carrion and a vulture when he saw Keynes in Cambridge shows that he associated the man who emerged with sleepy eyes from his bed at midday with a scavenging predatoriness. When Lawrence attempted to describe his objection to Keynes, Birrell and Duncan Grant, he had recourse to words associated with predation on dead or decaying things: it made him think of 'black-beetles' (*2L* 321) or of 'a beetle that bites like a scorpion' (*2L* 319). Although Ursula's relationship with her teacher Winifred Inger shows her a different kind of bond to offset the possessive intensity of Anton Skrebensky's attentions during their early courtship, and the shame of doting on an authority figure seems only to be felt by Ursula once they have separated, the language finally associated with Winifred reflects this homophobic discourse. We are told that Ursula 'still adhered to Winifred Inger. But a sort of nausea was coming over her. She loved her mistress. But a heavy, clogged sense of deadness began to gather upon her, from the other woman's contact. And sometimes she thought Winifred was ugly, clayey'.

The sense of 'deadness' transmitted by Winifred Inger shows Ursula that her teacher cannot offer her (as she had first thought) the doorway to another, finer life. Winifred knows that Ursula 'was beginning to reject her. The fine, unquenchable flame of the younger girl would consent no more to mingle with the perverted life of the elder woman' (*R* 319). The pejorative adjective applied to Winifred here is one that Lawrence also used to describe Keynes, Birrell and Grant: he thought of them as representing an England he wished to escape because it was 'too wicked and perverse' (*2L* 319). In *Women in Love*, Loerke's relationship with the 'well built, soft youth' Leitner, his 'young love-companion', is characterised by an imbalance of power akin to that between an officer and an orderly, or a teacher and a pupil. Leitner is described as Loerke's 'penniless dependent'. Shortly after Gudrun Brangwen is introduced to the guests at the Reunionsaal, she dances with Leitner, which creates deep disdain in Loerke. We are told that he feels 'a sardonic, ruthless hatred' for Leitner, which makes the young man 'red in the face and impotent with resentment' (*WL* 411). The homophobic language of predation, deadness and perverseness is extended in the vocabulary associated with Loerke. Lawrence had said that Keynes, Birrell and Grant made him feel a 'horrible sense of frowstiness, so repulsive, as if it came from deep inward dirt – a sort of sewer' (*2L* 320). Rupert Birkin tells Gerald Crich that Loerke is one of those who 'want to explore the sewers, and he's the wizard rat that swims ahead' (*WL* 428).

Lawrence's only significant discussion of homosexuality occurs in passages from the fourth part of his philosophical essay 'The Crown' which were not published in 1915 because of the collapse of *The Signature* and then omitted from the version of the essay published in *Reflections on the Death of a Porcupine* in December 1925. These paragraphs deal with soldiers and homosexuality. Lawrence states: 'everyone knows that a natural activity in the life of a real soldier is drinking, prostitution, and homosexuality' (*RDP* 473). He argues that in an era of 'dissolution, analysis, disintegration', soldiers' sexual desires can develop in two ways. The 'coarse, insensitive' man will go to a woman in a violent or reductive way, either raping her and knowing 'the extreme of reduction, of death', after which 'he becomes almost a carrion creature, feeding on dead organisms, on real corruption', or realising through intercourse with her 'the destruction of some basic self in him, while the complexity and unity of his consciousness remains intact above the reduction', resulting in horror at his own 'mangled, maimed condition'. The more sensitive soldier will respond to his instrumentalising of the woman in sex by feeling revulsion at her. The soldier will then turn to love 'a man who is to a certain degree less developed than himself' and proceed to 'reduce himself to this level': 'He is given up to the flux of reduction, his mouth is upon the mouth of corruption' (*RDP* 472). Lawrence also comments on another 'type' for whom love is abstract and purely mental: 'the extremely conscious men of strong will and traditional social habit' who critique society and speak for the oppressed. These men, whose selves he describes as having become 'purely instrumental', are 'the purest type of disintegrators': 'Like some extreme instrumental insects, they run brittly hither and thither, at their tiny work of breaking down, breaking down blindly and brittly the vast organic mass before them' (*RDP* 473). The teeming insect and beetle images are associated in this case not with predatory homosexuality but with what he considered to be the false love of pacifist liberals whose destructive desires are sublimated into words.

Lawrence is preoccupied here with the ways in which sexual feelings develop and might be expressed in particular, closed environments: on the one hand, in the army, and on the other in what he variously referred to as the 'shell' or 'envelope of nullity' (*RDP* 474) of disintegrative war-time society. He attempts to explain the mechanisms through which people may be driven to abuse, subordinate or instrumentalise sexual partners, or to dissociate altogether from their feelings and desires. The fact that this analysis relates very specifically to Lawrence's broader critique of war-time English society at the time that 'The Crown' was written between March and October 1915 may have been one reason why he chose to omit it from the essay when he published it in full for the first time over a decade later.

Lawrence always emphasised the need for individuals to understand and accept their desires rather than merely acting them out in ways damaging to themselves and others. He described the process of self-reflection and of confronting the skeletons in one's cupboard as 'fun, fun for a life-time' (*LEA* 93). Sexuality, however, was another matter: during the war years, he reacted to certain forms of sexual orientation and behaviour in ways that David Ellis says 'can only be described as hysterical' (Ellis 2015: 56), conceptualising and judging them in line with his theories on social and cultural disintegration. After a particularly uncomfortable stay with Lawrence in February 1915, during which his host presumed to tell him 'about himself' (*2L* 293), E. M. Forster said he liked the Lawrence who 'wrote *The White Peacock*, he doesn't know why', but admitted to disliking 'the deaf impercipient fanatic who has nosed over his own little sexual round until he believes that there is no other path for others to take' (Lago and Furbank 1983: 219). After the war, Lawrence's views were modified as he spent more time with contacts and friends who were openly bisexual or homosexual, such as Norman Douglas, Maurice Magnus, Witter Bynner and Willard Johnson. As we have seen, he eventually came to consider anal intercourse within a heterosexual relationship not as a selfish or sadistic act inflicted upon a partner but as a route to mutual sensual self-realisation.

Throughout his life, Lawrence developed close, sometimes intimate bonds with both men and women which he saw as complementing (not displacing) his marriage to Frieda. It is fitting that we should find it so awkward to describe and categorise these relationships because, as we have seen in the previous chapter, Lawrence himself emphasised the difficulty of describing feelings and non-traditional forms of committed physical and emotional companionship. Neither his deep affection for Rosalind Baynes, which seems to have resulted in his sleeping with her on one occasion in September 1920, nor his long-standing friendship with Dorothy Brett, which issued in a failed attempt at consummation over two nights in March 1926, can easily be categorised using the clumsy, imprecise term 'affair'.

His relationship with the Cornish farmer William Henry Hocking in the spring and summer of 1917 also evades easy categorisation. At a time in his life when he was perhaps more isolated and unhappy than ever before, and when his relationship with Frieda was more than usually conflictual, he seems to have taken solace in helping out the Hocking family, his near-neighbours in Higher Tregerthen, with farm work, as he had done as a young man with the Chambers family. He became close to William Henry, discussing a range of topics important to him at the time, including theosophy, mysticism and perhaps also bisexuality. Something of his feeling for William Henry, and of their discussions, informed Lawrence's account of Rupert Birkin's feelings for Gerald Crich in the 'Prologue' to *Women in Love*. Years later, he invoked it more directly in the 'Nightmare' chapter of *Kangaroo*, where Richard Lovatt Somers helps John Thomas Buryan on Trendrinnan farm, and they talk about 'half-philosophical, mystical' things such as 'the sun, and the moon, the mysterious powers of the moon at night, and the mysterious change in man with the change of seasons, and the mysterious effects of sex on a man' (*K* 236). Lovatt's German wife Harriett, meanwhile, spends 'many lonely days in the cottage' and has 'many a bitter fight' (*K* 237) with her husband. Frieda evidently resented the time Lawrence spent with the Hockings, and especially with William Henry. In a letter of 6 August 1953, she told John Middleton Murry: 'I think the homosexuality in him was a short phase out of misery – I fought him and won – and that he wanted a deeper thing from you' (Tedlock 1961: 328).

William Henry Hocking, *c.*1917. University of Nottingham, Manuscripts and Special Collections, ACC 2444 Box 4 (part).

Frieda had every reason, of course, to insist that Lawrence's feelings for William Henry Hocking were an isolated phase of homosexuality which she helped him to overcome. It is understandable that she should wish to present his feelings in this way. Maurice Magnus made a similarly blunt attempt to categorise Lawrence's desires, interpreting Lawrence's interest in bisexuality and attempt to get Magnus to share his sexual experiences as signs of his own furtive bisexuality. In October 1920, Magnus told Norman Douglas that when he spoke to Lawrence during a brief visit which Lawrence made to Malta that May, Lawrence had 'opened his "heart" (!) to me ... accidentally' and was 'looking for bisexual types for *himself* ... He revels in all that is not just within his reach' (Kinkead-Weekes 1996: 855). Magnus's gossip, like Frieda's neat categorising of Lawrence's feelings, seeks to impose structure on complexity and in doing so runs counter to Lawrence's own exploration of feelings as bodily and psychological phenomena which elude such classification. One way of conceptualising Lawrence's affection for, and desire for intimacy with, Hocking, and his similarly complex and irreducible feelings for Alan Chambers and for Murry himself, is in terms not of a homosexual drive but of the need for male nurturance created in Lawrence by the failure of his relationship with his father in his earliest years.[6]

In July 1917, during the period when Lawrence was spending a great deal of time with William Henry Hocking, he wrote a letter to the American novelist and poet Eunice Tietjens, advisory editor for the journal *Poetry*, in which he set out his views on desire and what she had clearly termed 'abnormal sex':

> There is all the difference in the world between *understanding* the extreme and awful workings of sex, or even fulfilling them, responsibly; and abnormal sex. Abnormal sex comes from the fulfilling of violent or extreme desires, *against the will*. It is not the desires which are wrong, nor the fulfilment, *per se*; but the fixed will in ourselves, which asserts that these things *should not be*, that only a holy love should be. – You see it is impious for us to assert so flatly what *should be*, in face of what *is* ... It is the labouring under the burden of self-repudiation and shame which makes abnormality. And repudiation and shame come from the false doctrines we hold ... Abnormality and insanity comes from the split in the self, the repudiation and the condemning of the desire, and the furtive fulfilment at the same time.

Lawrence makes it clear that seeking to understand one's feelings and acting on them in a responsible way is pious 'no matter *what* the desire', since 'Desire is holy, belonging to the mystic unknown' (*3L* 140–141). It is only when we suppress our desires, feel a sense of shame about them but act on them nonetheless, or act out desires we do not have in line with collective expectations, that sex becomes 'abnormal'.

This formulation seems to me consistent with the evaluative distinction between desire and sexuality in Lawrence's thought, but it raises a number of fascinating questions. How can one understand one's desires without allowing the mind to intercede in the ways in which one acts on them? What might it mean to act responsibly on one's desires? It is obvious that there are no simple answers to such questions. Lawrence's writing, however, addresses them in ways which cause us to reflect in implicit but far-reaching ways on our own values and our relationship to our feelings and desires. Is Matilda Rockley acting responsibly on her own desires when she impulsively decides that she will marry Hadrian, or is she simply choosing financial independence within an unwanted marriage over a self-determined single life in comparative poverty? And how are we to understand Bertie Reid in 'The Blind Man'? Is he 'abnormal' since he is 'ashamed of himself' because 'he could not marry, could not approach women physically'? Or is he piously attending to his feelings, since he understands that he wants to have physical relationships with women but is unable to do so, and he withdraws when they seem to 'encroach on him' because he is 'helplessly and even brutally afraid' (*EmyE* 58). Does the ending to the story, when he shrinks from Maurice Pervin's touch, cruelly expose his 'abnormality' or does it show him understanding his inability to connect physically with the blind man and responding with understandable terror when his 'insane reserve' (*EmyE* 63) is violated? The proper function of biographically inflected criticism is to enrich the experience of reading texts by posing such questions rather than impoverishing it by presuming to answer them.

The tonal ambiguity of these stories forces us to recognise that where feelings are concerned there is always strangeness and uncertainty. The 1926 short story 'In Love' is a suitable text to turn to in order to draw together the different strands of this chapter. This is a satire on heteronormativity which comically exposes romantic behaviour within relationships as a social performance and therefore inauthentic; it shows how the pressure to conform to collective ways of expressing love prevents us from confronting and seeking to comprehend the rich and chaotic feelings involved in desiring someone with whom one wishes to have a committed relationship. The central protagonist in the story, Hester, is 24 years old and engaged to be married to Joe, a former soldier in the Artillery who has given up a business career to become a farmer in Wiltshire, building a wooden bungalow on his 30-acre plot. The opening to the story makes social expectations quite clear: although Hester's 21-year-old sister Henrietta has 'not the faintest intention of jeopardising her peace of mind by accepting any sort of fatal ring', she has to admit to herself that 'it *was* nice to see Hester "getting off", as they say; for Hester was nearly twenty-five, which is serious' (*WWRA* 138). Hester and Joe have known each other since childhood and have always felt comfortable in each other's company. However, since Hester agreed to marry him, his behaviour has changed, and as the story opens she cannot hide her displeasure at the prospect of visiting him for a weekend in their new home.

Hester turns down her sister's offer to accompany her, to 'take the edge off the intimacy' (*WWRA* 139), but the first evening of her visit is a disaster. Joe tells Hester to sit next to him on the sofa, and he puts his arm around her. Hester's disgust and anger at his actions are made clear through free-indirect discourse: 'How ridiculous of him to stroke the back of her neck! How idiotic he was, trying to be lovey-dovey!' (*WWRA* 141). Hester asks him to play the piano, and while he is preoccupied with this, she escapes out of the house, hiding in a willow tree when he comes to find her. She enjoys the comparative freedom of being outside in the soft moonlight. Here she interprets Joe's feelings towards her through his conventional romantic behaviour: 'The very fact of his being in-love with me proves that he doesn't love me. No man that loved a woman could be in-love with her like that' (*WWRA* 142).

When Henrietta unexpectedly calls at the bungalow in a car, accompanied by Joe's brother and another relation, intending to camp nearby, Hester is initially displeased but then lets her into the house, where Joe is clearly angry and brooding over her conduct. Henrietta asks Hester several times why she dodged out of the house, and Hester is finally provoked into admitting that she 'absolutely *can't stand*' (*WWRA* 147) Joe making love to her. Henrietta is quite clear that this means they cannot marry, and she is on the brink of walking out of the bungalow with her sister when Joe admits 'I never was in love with you, that way' (*WWRA* 148).

He only cuddled and sought to 'spoon' with Hester because he thought it was expected of him. It transpires that he had seen her devotion to the romantic films of Rudolph Valentino and deduced that this was how she wanted him to act. But Hester tells Joe that while she has seemed to adore Valentino she 'loathed him *really*'. Hester says that she loathes Joe in the role of Valentino, and he responds by saying that he loathes her 'altogether'. Ironically, this admission of mutual hatred facilitates their reconciliation. At that moment, Joe realises that his acting the male role in love was a pretence and 'a betrayal of their simple intimacy', while she sees 'the honest, patient love for her in his eyes, and the queer, quiet, central desire' (*WWRA* 149). Joe apologises for his actions and Hester tells him she does not mind what he does as long as he loves her '*really*' (*WWRA* 150).

Lawrence initially entitled the short story 'More Modern Love'. As in *Lady Chatterley's Lover*, the first version of which he began writing around the same time, his satirical target is what he termed 'counterfeit emotion' (*LCL* 312), or the kinds of artificial romantic feeling and conduct in the young promulgated by cinema and popular literature. Joe comes to see that Hester's fascination with Valentino as a male romantic lead is only superficial, and that the performance of male passion and strength that is compelling on the screen is absurd and inauthentic in ordinary life.

However, whereas Lawrence's other writings sought to identify authentic forms of male strength realised in and through the body as a means of offsetting such inauthenticity, and inward forms of female responsiveness to that strength, 'In Love' pays very little attention to the genuine feelings of Joe and Hester. There is only the slightest hint that they include the easy intimacy that they shared with one another in childhood, and that a degree of mutual hatred might be mixed in with their 'patient love' for one another. Lawrence referred to 'In Love' as a 'trivial' (*6L* 46) short story. Although it critiques the artificiality of modern courtship, the characters are too conventional and undeveloped for the social critique to go any further. There is no suggestion, for instance, that they will not marry. There is also little sense that the realisation of their true feelings will result in a change in their gender roles: Joe is still the home-maker at the end of the story, and Hester must still look forward to a future in which she is his wife and helpmate cooking at the 'good little range' (*WWRA* 139). The story is instructive because it reveals the fascinating blend of radical and reactionary qualities which makes Lawrence's writing so challenging and provocative, and so fresh. Readers today who are accustomed to cohabitation on equal terms, and to gender-fluid identities and relationships, will register Lawrence's bravery in questioning the values of his contemporary society, but they are likely to be dissatisfied, and perhaps even angered, by the early twentieth-century social assumptions and unequal power structures that are left in place, and even accentuated on different terms, in his writings on sex and sexuality.

Notes

1 Transcription from 'Son and Lover: A Portrait of D. H. Lawrence', The Third Programme, BBC Radio, 8 May 1955. La Av 3/2/1–2 (University of Nottingham).
2 The volume was not published in Britain until January 1924.
3 Bertie Reid may have been based in part on Bertrand Russell, whom Lawrence felt espoused pacifist views while ignoring the violence of his inner life. The story can be understood as satirising what Lawrence saw as Russell's insincerity, and his refusal to admit his true feelings. See *2L* 392 (14 September 1915) and Monk (1996: 428–430).
4 Katherine Mansfield, 'Frau Fischer', in *In a German Pension* (1911). See Mansfield (1999: 18).
5 Lawrence's 'novelettes' (*4L* 122) 'The Fox', 'The Captain's Doll' and 'The Ladybird' – which from 'early on ... were treated by Lawrence as a single volume' (*Fox* xxvii) – also address issues associated with the crisis of masculinity resulting from the war.
6 I address this topic in Chapter 9.

6

Lawrence and Otherness: Discourses of Nation and Race

In the preceding chapters, I have explored Lawrence's subversive engagement with bourgeois values and institutions and shown how his emphasis on the need to take seriously our complex bodily feelings and desires is in the service of his broader concern with wholeness of being. Lawrence was intensely aware of the ways in which modern life compartmentalises our identities, forcing us to project and maintain social personae based on cultural norms and external drivers such as class and occupation, and marginalising more primal aspects of our being related to our place in what he termed the 'circumambient universe' (*STH* 171). He wrote in opposition to popular media which he felt traded off and intensified the self-alienating tendencies of modernity, including photography (with its insistence on a singular way of seeing the world) and cinema (with its reliance on sentimentalism in relation to love, desire and sex).

Lawrence was a strong critic of 'kodak-vision' (*STH* 168) and 'counterfeit emotion' (*LCL* 312) on the grounds that they reinforce collective modes of seeing and encourage superficial expressions of emotion which ultimately inhibit our capacity to reflect on and comprehend our more complex needs and feelings. In *The Rainbow*, Lawrence depicted Ursula Brangwen as a courageous figure who prioritises her right to emotional fulfilment over the many factors in society which seek to regulate her, from her parents and her suitor, Anton Skrebensky, to religion, college and work. Ursula resists these things, but she is finally unable to discover a relationship or mode of life which will answer to her own need for the free expression and realisation of her feelings and desires. In *Women in Love*, Rupert Birkin attempts to define a new kind of committed relationship with Ursula which will allow them to attain self-realisation as individuals as well as partners. This requires them to give up their jobs in education and to pursue a nomadic life free from the repressive structures of a society that has become violent and destructive. Yet the novel focuses on the disintegrative aspects of English society

The Life of the Author: D. H. Lawrence, First Edition. Andrew Harrison.

and the need to escape it rather than offering a tangible sense of the practical forms of life they would need to develop as a viable alternative.

In the post-war period, Lawrence turned his attention to the reconstruction of self and society, seeking to discover ways in which the individual might recover wholeness of being and find the forms of social and religious life conducive to maintaining it. Travel became central to his life and writing. In the pre-war period, his escape to Germany with Frieda, and the periods they spent living in Bavaria and northern Italy, helped him to gain some outside perspective on 'England, the oldness and grubbiness and despair' (*1L* 459). Self-imposed exile facilitated his movement outside the values of his upbringing. After the war he left England as soon as he could, returning to Italy in November 1919 and living in Capri and then Taormina in Sicily. In the winter of 1921 he was invited to New Mexico by Mabel Dodge Sterne, an American patron of the arts with a deep commitment to the cultures of the Native American peoples, a reverence for the pueblos and a desire to preserve these and the reservations against the claims of settlers. She had read the serialisation in the *Dial* of Lawrence's book of travel writing *Sea and Sardinia* (1921) and hoped that he would write about Native Americans in the same way that he had written about the Sardinian peasants.

Lawrence, who had wanted to move to the United States during the war, accepted her invitation, but decided to approach the country on its west coast rather than travelling via New York. He was also keen to visit his American friends Earl and Achsah Brewster, who were staying in Ceylon (modern-day Sri Lanka). After a period of prevarication, he finally left Sicily in February 1922, travelling first to Ceylon and then spending three months in Australia, before moving on to the United States in August. He lived in New Mexico until September 1925, though this three-year period was broken up by two stays in Mexico (living in Chapala and Oaxaca) and a brief return to Europe between December 1923 and March 1924. Itinerancy stimulated Lawrence; it suited the restless and questing nature of his imagination. It also allowed him to seek out different ways of living and to explore different cultures and religious sensibilities as antidotes to what he now understood to be the decadent ruins of Western civilisation.

In the 'Study of Thomas Hardy' and 'The Crown', Lawrence had analysed the forms of self-division that he felt had created the conditions for the Great War, and the kinds of self-enclosure, violence and self-destruction which had to be undergone by individuals caught up in a phase of cultural disintegration. In the early spring of 1917, however, he began to write about the necessity to turn from death and destruction to rebirth and new forms of life. In the essay 'Whistling of Birds', he describes how the harsh winter of 1916–1917 caused the death of many avian species, so that in the fields and under the hedges there were 'the ragged remains of lapwings, starlings, thrushes, redwings'. The 'heavy silence of frost' persisted for 'many weeks' (*RDP* 21). Yet when it broke, on 22 February 1917, the change was instantly heralded by birdsong, which signalled the movement in nature out of the deathliness of winter and into the new world of spring. The essay presents a parable of the way in which humans must accept the impulse to move suddenly from the death and destruction of war to new forms of life: 'We may remain wintry and destructive for a little longer, if we wish it, but the winter is gone out of us, and willy-nilly our hearts sing a little at sunset'. Lawrence makes it clear that the birdsong only alerts us to our own inward impulses, since the call to turn from death to life is 'in us, as well as without us' (*RDP* 22). Being attuned to the otherness of nature enables us to realise the otherness that lies within.

In his essay 'The Reality of Peace', Lawrence uses numerous images to describe the leap of faith which is required in order to embrace new creation. People must 'give up' their 'assurance' and 'conceit of final knowledge', their 'vanity of charted right and wrong', in order to 'give' themselves, 'not to anything that has been, but to the river of peace that bears us' (*RDP* 28–29). The image again suggests that we must recognise our connectedness to a nature which is both outside and within us, healing self-division: the river of peace is also the 'great systole diastole of the universe' which underpins life, and we are 'like the blood that travels' (*RDP* 27). This vision of humankind being driven by impulses towards destruction and creation, like the ebbs and flows of the blood or the changing of the seasons, informed Lawrence's epochal account of history in the school textbook he wrote for Oxford University Press between July 1918 and May 1919 and published in February 1921 under the title *Movements in European History*.

Being attuned to nature, and recognising one's place in it, is for Lawrence a way of being and knowing which entails the renunciation of old forms of certainty and security, and blind faith in the promptings of the blood and its feelings and desires. In his post-war novels *The Lost Girl* and *Mr Noon*, the central protagonists, Alvina Houghton and Gilbert Noon, leave England to find a new life. Both are dissatisfied with their home country and have transgressed its strictly policed moral codes. They are arrested by the otherness of foreign landscapes whose sublime and primitive qualities reflect their own desires and pave the way for the transformation of their lives and relationships. In both cases, we see the contrast between the human landscape they leave behind in England, which Lawrence would later describe as 'hedged-and-fenced', 'enclosed, enclosed, to stifling' (*SM* 97), and the pristine and impersonal, even foreboding, largesse of the mountainous regions they encounter in Italy and Germany.

In *The Lost Girl*, Alvina Houghton marries Francesco (or 'Ciccio') Marasca, a performer in a touring 'Red Indian' show, in a registrar's office in Scarborough before travelling with him to his home in the Abruzzi region of southern Italy. The interminable passage from London to Califano by train, omnibus and on foot is recounted in Chapter XIV of the novel, which is entitled 'The Journey Across', signifying the almost mythical transformation Alvina undergoes as her old self is extinguished and she discovers a new identity with her husband in an 'almost unbearably lovely' (*LG* 315) landscape. In marrying Ciccio, Alvina was aware that she could be embracing 'atavism' in a 'strange, sleep-like submission to his being' (*LG* 288). Yet she experiences it as a terrifying form of liberation. As their train passes through the 'sub-Alps' in southern France, she reflects that 'it all seemed bigger, nobler than England': 'And for the first time she realised what it was to escape from the smallish perfection of England, into the grander imperfection of a great continent' (*LG* 297). She soon realises that she is 'lost to Woodhouse, to Lancaster, to England—all lost' (*LG* 306). When they reach the primitive house owned by Ciccio's maternal uncle Pancrazio, Alvina embraces it, but in the night she wakes and feels frightened. However, rather than seeking to flee from the horror she feels for her surroundings, and also in this moment for Ciccio, she goes to join her husband in his bed: 'She felt his power and his warmth invade her and extinguish her' (*LG* 313). The novel shows how she must accept and even embrace the death of her past self if she is to discover a new self in Califano and in Ciccio's own home in the nearby village of Pescocalascio.

In Chapter XIII of *Mr Noon*, Gilbert Noon has recently travelled from England to Bavaria. It is early spring and he is staying in Munich in a flat belonging to Professor Alfred Kramer. It is a Sunday, and despite the presence of snow, the Professor, who is too restless to work, suggests that they go together into the country, to see a plot of land where he intends to build a 'little wooden house' (*MN* 105). They take a train to Ommerhausen in the foot-hills of the Alps, then walk to the village of Genbach, where they stop to survey the 'great Isar valley' set out beneath them. Gilbert agrees with Professor Kramer that the place is 'beautiful':

> For the first time he saw England from the outside: tiny she seemed, and tight, and so partial. Such a little bit among all the vast rest. Whereas till now she had seemed all-in-all in herself. Now he knew it was not so. Her all-in-allness was a delusion of her natives. Her marvellous truths and standards and ideals were just local, not universal. They were just a piece of local pattern, in what was really a vast, complicated, far-reaching design.

At this moment, Gilbert becomes 'unEnglished': 'His tight and exclusive nationality seemed to break down in his heart'. The impression of absoluteness created by his island home is replaced by the connectedness that he senses in the valley he surveys: 'the sense of an infinite multiplicity of connections' (*MN* 107). The landscape before him is associated with open-mindedness and a moral relativism which he now realises he has long yearned for and which he will soon discover in Johanna Keighley, who possesses the same qualities of beauty and the same vast complications.

These novels show just how committed Lawrence was to the idea that a new direction in life can only be found by leaving behind an old self and discovering a new one in the otherness of nature, and of foreign landscapes and peoples. Yet the process which he traces in these fictions was far more ambivalent, contradictory and unresolved in his own life. In the second part of *Mr Noon,* he was reimagining his early experiences with Frieda in Germany and Italy in 1912–1913, but in doing so he was shaping those experiences and imbuing them with a significance which he certainly did not see at the time. A similar process of re-seeing this period had occurred as he compiled the narrative sequence of poems relating to his early life with Frieda for the collection he entitled *Look! We Have Come Through!* (1917). Most of the poems included in it were first composed in the period, but poems such as 'Coming Awake', 'Spring Morning', 'Song of a Man Who Has Come Through' and 'New Heaven and Earth', all of which celebrate his having discovered a new life through a recognition of, and desire for, the otherness of Frieda and Germany, gained fresh meaning in the light of his new thinking about rebirth in the early spring of 1917.

Alvina Houghton's experiences in Califano draw closely on his and Frieda's stay of just over a week in Picinisco in December 1919, a month after he had left England. Although, like his heroine, Lawrence found the place 'a bit staggeringly primitive' (*3L* 431) and 'very beautiful' (*3L* 432), they soon 'extricated' (*3L* 446) themselves and 'fled' (*3L* 451) to Capri because it 'was too icy – mountainous' (*3L* 438). The savage and wild otherness which fired his imagination, showing Alvina the qualities she desires in Ciccio and discovers in herself, could not long be borne in reality. Here as elsewhere Lawrence's fiction was exploratory in the sense that it allowed him to shape experience and discover potential meaning in it. His theory of otherness is clearly evident in the scene where Alvina, after shopping at the market in Califano, feels 'a strange thrilling in her bowels: a sort of trill strangely within her, yet extraneous to her' (*LG* 320) and realises that she is pregnant. An otherness which is both within and outside her signals new life. This is the kind of passage which polarises readers. Those who find the theory fascinating will excuse any crudeness in its delineation; those like Katherine Mansfield who deplore what she called Lawrence's 'doctrine of mindlessness' will find it 'false ... a fake' (Kimber and Smith 2014: 706, 708).

Lawrence's first exposure to radical otherness outside Europe was far from transformational; in fact, it produced in him a reaction against difference so strong that it caused him to re-think his rejection of England. On 13 March 1922, he and Frieda arrived in Ceylon. Their hosts, the Brewsters, were Buddhists who had moved to Ceylon to study the religion and to learn its sacred language, Pali, so they were well placed to introduce Lawrence to the religion and to Sinhalese customs and culture. The house near Kandy where they were staying, and where they put Lawrence and Frieda up, was named 'Ardnaree' and it was situated 'among a sort of half wild estate – cocoanut palms and cocoa – and jungle trees – almost like the jungle'. It afforded Lawrence an immersive experience of the local flora and fauna: he could 'sit on the verandahs and watch the chipmunks and chameleons and lizards and tropical birds among the trees and bamboos' (*4L* 215). Lawrence's first impression was favourable. He wrote to a friend: 'think I shall love these tropics' (*4L* 214). On 23 March, he attended a Perahera (a religious parade or procession). He wrote with enthusiasm about the spectacle: there were 'flaming torches of cocoanut blazing, and the great elephants in their trappings, about a hundred, and the dancers with tomtoms and bagpipes, and half naked and jewelled, then the Kandyan chiefs in their costumes, and more dancers, and more elephants, and more chiefs, and more dancers, so wild and strange and perfectly fascinating, heaving along by the flames of torches in the hot, still, starry night' (*4L* 215–216). The Prince of Wales (the future King Edward VIII) happened to be visiting Kandy, and Lawrence sat opposite him. Lawrence told friends that the Prince was 'so thin and nervy: all twitchy: and seems worn out and disheartened'.

Two days later, Lawrence was feeling disorientated: he said in a letter that he was still 'not quite sure where I am: sort of look round for myself among all this different world' (*4L* 216). The extreme heat clearly affected his response to Ceylon. He was unable to write; all he could do was work on his translation of Giovanni Verga's novel *Mastro-don Gesualdo*. Writing was not only a financial necessity for Lawrence, but the only way in which he could gain a purchase on his experiences and make them meaningful. By 28 March, he had decided he did not 'care for the east' (*4L* 217). On 30 March, he wrote to Robert Pratt Barlow, a wealthy English contact in Taormina, that he felt the Prince had been 'almost the *butt* of everybody, white and black alike. They all secretly hate him for being a Prince, and make a Princely butt of him – and he knows it. My sympathy was with him' (*4L* 218). He went on to say that being out in Ceylon had made him realise that 'we make a mistake forsaking England and moving out into the periphery of life': 'I really think that the most living clue of life is in us Englishmen in England' (*4L* 219). His attitude became openly hostile and racist for the remainder of his stay. He told his friend Mary Cannan: 'The native life is picturesque – but to tell the truth, rather silly. The east, the bit I've seen, seems silly. I don't like it one bit. I don't like the silly dark people or their swarming billions or their hideous little Buddha temples, like decked up pigsties – nor anything' (*4L* 221). After he left Ceylon on 24 April, bound for Australia, he wrote to Lady Cynthia Asquith: 'I break my heart over England when I am out here. Those natives are *back* of us – in the living sense *lower* than we are' (*4L* 234).

These outbursts must have been occasioned in part by his reaction against the Brewsters' enthusiasm for the country and commitment to its religion and its people. The tone of Lawrence's letters suggests that he was releasing feelings which he was forced to hide, or at least moderate, in the company of his hosts.

The colonialist and racist views he expressed are inexcusable. They are also deeply ironic, given the bitterness of his wartime experiences and the extremely detached and critical relationship to England and British imperialism they created in him. In October 1915, he had told Cynthia Asquith that he was 'English, and my Englishness is my very vision', but this uncharacteristic declaration to the daughter-in-law of the Prime Minister was offered to offset his belief that the actions of England and its allies were an 'ultimate wrong' (*2L* 414). At some level, Lawrence recognised the irony of his assertion that 'the most living clue of life' was to be found among the English in England. He told Cynthia Asquith: 'We are, have been for five centuries, the growing tip. Now we're going to fall. But you don't catch me going back on my whiteness and Englishness and myself. English in the teeth of all the world, even in the teeth of England' (*4L* 234).

Lawrence's subsequent three-month stay in Australia between May and August 1922 created in him a similar reaction against its otherness and a reassertion of his European, and specifically English, identity. Although he expressed a sense of wonder at his brief encounter with the Australian bush in Perth, he experienced the country as a white settler and seems to have had little or no contact with its native peoples. When he moved to Sydney, he lived in Thirroul, a mining settlement south of the city. The bungalow he rented was perched on a hilltop looking out onto the Pacific Ocean, but he seems to have viewed the area as a ramshackle version of the English mining community he knew in his youth. To Lawrence, Australia was little more than an offshoot of the old country: an empty backwater. It was, he said, 'rather wonderful, with its clear sky and air and sense of emptiness', but he would only consider living there permanently if he were 'chucking up the literary sponge' (*4L* 245). He told his mother-in-law that the people were 'so crude in their feelings – and they only want to be up to date in their "conveniences" – electric light and tramways and things like that' (*4L* 249). When he attempted to describe the landscape of the country to Earl Brewster, who was a keen artist, he compared it to the works of the nineteenth-century French painter Pierre Puvis de Chavannes: he said that it needed 'Japanese treatment – or Puvis' (*4L* 265).

Lawrence and Frieda boarded the RMS Tahiti on 10 August for the onward journey from Sydney to San Francisco, stopping at Wellington in New Zealand (15 August), Raratonga (20 August) and Tahiti (22–23 August), and arriving in the United States on 4 September. Wellington was the birthplace of Katherine Mansfield, so he and Frieda sent her a postcard from the city.[1] Raratonga he thought 'a lovely island ... almost as lovely as one expects these South Sea Islands to be' (*4L* 284). When they stopped at Tahiti two days later they were driven around the island, but he found Papeete 'a poor, dull, modernish place' (*4L* 285): 'mostly Chinese, natives in European clothes, and fat'. He told Mary Cannan: 'These are supposed to be the earthly paradises: these South Sea Isles. You can have 'em'. Travel now seemed to him 'a splendid lesson in disillusion' (*4L* 286). It was hardly the most auspicious prelude to his arrival in the United States.

Lawrence and Frieda stayed for five days in San Francisco before travelling to New Mexico. Mabel Dodge Sterne, who was eagerly awaiting their arrival, sent train tickets. They spent three nights in Santa Fe at the home of the poet Witter Bynner before setting out for Taos in Mabel's motorcar, driven by her Native American partner, Tony Lujan. They arrived in Taos on Lawrence's thirty-seventh birthday, 11 September 1922, initially staying with their host on her small settlement close to Taos plaza, which they labelled 'Mabeltown'. They occupied a 'very pretty adobe house' (*5L* 313) just two hundred yards from Mabel's 'big house'; their neighbour was John Collier, the future Commissioner of Indian Affairs. Lawrence was in a similar situation to the one he had encountered in Ceylon: here too he was a guest of honour afforded an accelerated introduction to the native peoples and cultures by hosts who were wholly committed to preserving and celebrating them.

As Judith Ruderman has shown, Lawrence was thoroughly acquainted with the 'Red Indian' through his reading and through popular culture well before his arrival in the United States.[2] As a young man, he had read and loved Fenimore Cooper's Leatherstocking novels and Longfellow's poems 'The Song of Hiawatha' and 'Evangeline'.[3] He referred in his writing to the famed ability of 'Red Indians' to withstand torture.[4] He was aware of the popularity of 'Red Indian' acts in circus performances and of the international vogue for Wild West stage shows featuring Indian braves, such as that run by Buffalo Bill (the stage name of William Frederick Cody).[5] The Natcha-Kee-Tawara troupe in *The Lost Girl* is described as 'strictly a Red Indian troupe' (*LG* 120). He was also aware of the degree to which the Southwest and the spectacle of the 'Indian' had been thoroughly commodified by artists and speculators interested in developing the burgeoning tourist trade in New Mexico; the region attracted not only archaeologists and anthropologists but also wealthy white Americans from other parts of the United States eager to discover a new identity for themselves in the State, partly through contact with the Native Americans. As Ruderman notes, 'Indian culture was ... apprehended for the twin purposes of selling art and luring sightseers' (Ruderman 2014: 91).

Lawrence initially reacted to New Mexico with the same feeling of disorientation and pattern of resistance as in Ceylon. Just a few days after his arrival he was taken out to see the Jicarilla Apaches at Stone Lake, around one hundred miles northwest of Taos. He attended their mid-September harvest festival, the Go-Jii-Ya. He found the landscape 'weird' (*4L* 297) and declared that the Apaches were 'not very *sympatisch*' (*4L* 296). Back in Taos, on 28 September some 'young Indians came down to dance in the studio, with two drums' and they all joined in; it was 'fun: and queer' (*4L* 313). On 29–30 September, he attended the San Geronimo Festival at Taos Pueblo. Mabel clearly envisaged inducting

Lawrence into her close circle of friends and acting as a conduit for his understanding and appreciation of the pueblos and Native American cultures. She wished to show him 'the false, new, external America in the east, and the true, primordial, undiscovered America that was preserved, living, in the Indian blood-stream' (Luhan 1933: 59–60). Lawrence, however, had his own intention in coming to New Mexico. Although he suggested to Mabel that he shared her belief that one must 'bring together the two ends of humanity, our own thin end, and the last dark strand from the previous, pre-white era' (*4L* 111), he told his American publisher Thomas Seltzer: 'What I want in America is a sense of the future, and be damned to the exploited past. I believe in America one can catch up some kind of emotional impetus from the aboriginal Indian and from the aboriginal air and land, that will carry one over this crisis of the world's soul depression, into a new epoch' (*4L* 157).

Lawrence arrived in Taos at a moment of political unrest regarding Indian land rights and the future of the pueblos. The Bursum Bill was passed in the US Senate during September and it was expected to come before the House of Representatives by the end of the year. If passed, it would allow settlers on pueblo land to legitimise their claims to it, despite pueblo land and water rights, which were held by national treaties and aboriginal settlement. Opponents of the Bill raised loud protests against it. Mabel Dodge Sterne pressed Lawrence to write an article expressing opposition to it. The first piece he wrote about his trip to the Apache reservation (a lost composite piece which was eventually broken up into three separate essays) must have been deeply conflicted. In a surviving early fragment which he revised to produce the essays 'Certain Americans and an Englishman' and 'Indians and an Englishman', he compared his arrival in New Mexico to landing on the moon and described the life he saw around him as a 'comic opera': 'And here am I, a lone lorn Englishman, tumbled out of the known world of the British Empire on to this stage: for it persists in seeming like a stage to me, and not like the proper world' (*MM* 191). In a situation where he was forced 'to take sides', he said he felt like a lamb in a circus ring bleating for its lost mother. He described himself reading the Bursum Bill, then looking at articles and summaries for and against it, and feeling he was 'getting mixed up' (*MM* 192). Yet by foregrounding his ignorance and being honest about the barriers to cultural appreciation, Lawrence was this time signalling his desire to get behind his cultural conditioning.

The part of his original article which dealt with the Bill was eventually reworked and became 'Certain Americans and an Englishman'. It was published in the *New York Times Magazine* on 24 December 1922. Here Lawrence addresses the situation regarding pueblo land rights as he understood it. He explains how 'when the United States took over New Mexico in 1848', Congress 'decided to abide by all the conditions established by Spain and old Mexico in this State'; they also 'decreed that to each pueblo belonged the four square leagues of land surrounding the pueblo'.

The problem was that 'the Indian four square leagues' had been 'much of it for centuries occupied by Spanish or Mexican or white settlers' according to 'Spanish grants from governors', 'Mexican grants', and 'forged grants, forged deeds' (*MM* 106–107). Peace had held because the 'Indian' had 'never measured any leagues, but tilled his land around the pueblo itself', and much of the surrounding land was 'just sage desert'. Lawrence blames 'highbrow palefaces' like Mabel Dodge Sterne and John Collier for raising their voices in favour of Indian land rights and so destroying the peace. He imagines them saying: 'Poor Indian, dear Indian! why, all America ought to belong to him'. He describes the Native Americans themselves as being 'afflicted with the lovable malady of laissez-faire', pitched into a political situation where they are the prairie dogs and the Congress is the 'western American airedale' (*MM* 107).

Lawrence lists the main points of the Bill, commenting in satirical parentheses on their implications. If the Bill were passed, then the 'District Court of the United States for the District of New Mexico' would take jurisdiction over all legal matters within the pueblos, including suits of a civil nature and land right issues; those with particular historical land rights of various sorts would be able to legitimise their claims, but even those with no such rights would be able to purchase land at a price set by the Court, and the money would be held by the Secretary of the Interior on behalf of the 'Indians' as compensation. Lawrence states that this would generate a violent land grab which would inevitably result in 'the scattering of the Pueblos'. He laments the fact that the pueblos are already 'slowly disbanding', the children going to 'Indian schools' and being slowly assimilated into modern America. He expresses a wish that they be left intact to 'die a natural death' (*MM* 109). The ideal solution would be, he says, the creation of an 'Indian Commission' to handle land claims in a fair manner on a case-by-case basis. He describes the pueblos as being still 'at the core of American life': 'The Indians keep burning an eternal fire, the sacred fire of the old dark religion'. Lawrence says that the 'great welter of whites' in America is not yet forming a nation, and he predicts that some 'terrible convulsion' will take place among them in the future. It behoves white Americans to 'shelter these ancient centres of life' and try to adjust themselves to 'the Indian outlook, to take up an old dark thread from their vision, and see again as they see, without forgetting we are ourselves': 'For it is a new era we have now got to cross into. And our own electric light won't show us over the gulf. We have to feel our way by the dark thread of the old vision. Before it lapses, let us take it up' (*MM* 110).

Lawrence thought that 'Certain Americans and an Englishman' would be very topical because it would be published just before the Bill was due to come before the House of Representatives. In fact, national outcries against the Bill resulted in Congressional hearings in January and February 1923, which in turn helped to compromise legislation in 1924. Lawrence's refusal to endorse the political cause of Mabel Dodge Sterne and John Collier is wholly characteristic. Yet his sceptical and pragmatic views encode his own colonialist assumptions about race. Despite his attempts to distance himself from the 'highbrow palefaces', he still assumes the right to speak for the Native Americans, takes the coming death of their cultures for granted, and sees the value of the pueblos primarily in relation to the future of 'white' America (without taking any account of the modern nation's heterogeneity). Wayne Templeton has suggested that Lawrence's approach to Native Americans 'is representative of a colonialist sensibility'. Templeton argues that Lawrence generalised and homogenised in his descriptions of Native American peoples, customs and religions because his understanding of them was too textual and he had no knowledge of the different languages spoken in the American Southwest; he also says that Lawrence was 'unable to appreciate the subtleties and complexities of tribal life' (Templeton 1993–1994: 15) and had no appreciation of the importance of land to the identity of Native American peoples, nor of the long history of their resistance to colonialism.

The tension between Lawrence's responsiveness to the otherness of the pueblos and his colonialist assumptions is wholly evident in the other two essays, which he developed out of the original composite essay. 'Indians and an Englishman', which focuses on his experiences among the Apaches at Stone Lake the night before the festival, was published in the *Dial* in February 1923, and 'Taos', which describes his attendance at the San Geronimo Festival, appeared in the same magazine the following month. In the latter essay, Lawrence projects his own cultural background and knowledge onto Taos Pueblo, comparing it to a European monastery of the Middle Ages, since it seems to him 'final' in its representation of a mode of life and it is one of the places in the world which has 'kept the human spirit from disintegration, from going quite dark' (*MM* 125) in times of cultural crisis. Yet he also emphasises the Native Americans' hostility to the attitudes of outsiders. He describes how an American girl who took a photograph without permission had her camera confiscated and was forced to pay a $1 fine to get it back. A local American woman who accompanied Lawrence was denied access to the church on the pueblo because she was not catholic; she accounted for this by telling Lawrence that young children had loudly mocked the saints in the church the day before, saying 'they looked like monkeys'. Lawrence declares that he has 'long passed the stage when I want to crowd up and stare at anyone's spectacle, white man's or dark man's' (*MM* 127), yet his attempt to distinguish himself from the tourist who wants simply to stare at and photograph things is undermined here and elsewhere in his travel essays by his minute attentiveness to spectacles and events.

In 'Indians and an Englishman', he describes the Native Americans as embodying a hostile negation of the white man. Lawrence actually foregrounds his inability to understand the Native Americans on their own terms. If everybody is playing an exaggerated role in New Mexico, 'commerce' being 'a little self-conscious about its own pioneering importance', high-brows 'bent on getting to the bottom of everything and saving the lost soul', Mexicans 'bent on being Mexican and not yet Gringo', then the 'Indian' is simply 'all the things that all the others aren't' (*MM* 113). Yet the end of the essay contains a troubling statement of Lawrence's feeling of connectedness to the Apaches. Listening to the drums and chanting, and to the reciting of an old man, he did not understand a thing, and did not have 'any curiosity to understand', but since 'the soul is as old as the oldest day, and has its own hushed echoes, its own far-off tribal understandings sunk and incorporated', our 'darkest tissues are twisted in this old tribal experience' (*MM* 120). First contact with the 'Red Men' (*MM* 116) was unforgettable for Lawrence because it made him realise his own derivation: 'I was born of no virgin, of no Holy Ghost. Ah no, these old men telling the tribal tale were my fathers' (*MM* 120). While he cannot, therefore, 'cluster at the drum any more', he never wants to 'deny them, or break with them' (*MM* 120). It is difficult not to see in this formulation a self-serving projection onto the Apaches. Lawrence appears to be making sense of the Native Americans in line with his reading about ancient cultures and 'the Red Indian' (*SCAL* 384) well before his arrival in the United States.[6]

Yet, while it is important to bear in mind Templeton's critique of Lawrence's textual colonialist sensibility when approaching an essay like 'Indians and an Englishman', it should not blind us to Lawrence's foregrounding of his own difference in New Mexico. Templeton notes that in his encounters with Native Americans, Lawrence was 'plagued with the problem of unknown and perhaps unknowable otherness' (Templeton 1993–1994: 17). Neil Roberts sees the challenge implicit in this 'problem', since 'not to be able to put aside cultural difference is to be forced to confront it and work imaginatively within it' (Roberts 2004: 79). Roberts draws attention to Lawrence's poem 'The Red Wolf', written in October 1922, as revealing his creative response to cultural difference and the perceived hostility between the Native American and the European outsider. The poem stages a meeting between an old pueblo Native American and the speaker, whom he addresses as '*pale-face*' and '*white one*'. The Native American acknowledges that he and the '*pale-face*' do not '*get on*', and he instructs the speaker to '*go home*', but the speaker, who admits that his '*white God*' has fallen to dust, responds: 'I have no home, old father, / That's why I come'. The Native American states that his people '*take no hungry stray from the pale-face*', but the speaker tells him that he is 'not asked', and when the Indian tries to frighten him by saying that '*The dogs of the dark pueblo / Have long fangs*', he asserts that he has not travelled so far to be frightened by 'a few fangs'. The poem ends with a stand-off and an admission of difference. The Native American in this poem is wrapped in a white sheet and describes himself as '*invisible*', and the speaker calls him 'no names'; conversely, the Native American labels the speaker '*pale-face*' and gives him the name 'red wolf' (*Poems* 352–355). As Roberts notes, the Native American's assertion of his invisibility and the speaker's inability to name him 'obviously suggests an acknowledgement of failure to "see" the Indian', while the delayed revelation that 'The Red Wolf' refers not to an animal, nor to the Native American, but to the speaker himself 'enhances the sense ... of Lawrence's own otherness, both in the eyes of the Indian and absolutely' (Roberts 2004: 80).

The admission of the Native American's invisibility to the European, and Lawrence's foregrounding of his own status as a stray outsider in willing exile from England, cut against the way in which Lawrence was celebrated and lionised in Taos, and pressurised to write 'authentically' about the Native American peoples. Lawrence always resisted being incorporated into cliques, and he expressed irritation and resentment when he felt he was being patronised or taken under another's wing. Tensions soon developed between Lawrence, Frieda and their host. Shortly after his arrival in Taos, Lawrence told Mabel that he 'wanted to write an American novel that would express the life, the spirit, of America', and he suggested that it should be a fictional version of Mabel's life, from the time she 'left New York to come out to New Mexico', taking in her 'renunciation of the sick old world of art and artists, for the pristine valley and the upland Indian lakes' (Luhan 1933: 59). As he had previously done with Helen Corke back in 1910, Lawrence insisted that Mabel should share with him (and so with the world) the full range of her experiences: he wrote a note to her in which he stated that she must 'remember also things you don't want to remember' (Luhan 1933: 72).

Lawrence began work with her on this fiction, but it was swiftly abandoned.[7] The time which Mabel and Lawrence spent together created suspicion and jealousy in Frieda, and this in turn angered Lawrence. Mabel had suggested that Lawrence could move to her ranch in the village of Questa, around twenty miles north of Taos, and he and Frieda camped there with two Danish painters whom they met through Walter Ufer, a German-born artist and prominent figure in the Taos Society of Artists. When Mabel withdrew her offer, Lawrence was so enraged that he rented the adjacent Del Monte Ranch from the Hawk family, who ran a genuine ranch or farm nearby. On 1 December Lawrence and Frieda moved out of Mabeltown. They arranged for the Danish painters, Knud Merrild and Kai Gøtzsche, to live rent-free in the smaller of two cabins on the Ranch; in return, they helped with the upkeep of the cabins and with more strenuous jobs such as felling and chopping trees to use as firewood. 'The Danes' were independent-minded and practical, and they got on well with the Lawrences; they regularly ate together, took walks, and went on horseback to the local hot springs to bathe. The three and a half months they spent living alongside each other was perhaps the nearest Lawrence ever got to realising the ideal community which he had first fantasised about creating during the Great War, over Christmas and New Year 1914–1915.

This period allowed Lawrence to adjust to his new surroundings, both physically and psychologically. Lawrence was putting the finishing touches to his Australian novel *Kangaroo* when he first arrived in Taos, but when this was finished, in mid-October, he began revising the essays on classic American literature which he had first written in the final year of the war, between August 1917 and September 1918. He told his literary agent Robert Mountsier that the changes he was making showed 'the first reaction on me of America itself' (*4L* 343). He removed much of what he termed the 'esotericism' (*4L* 365) from the earlier versions, taking out a whole chapter entitled 'The Two Principles' and incorporating into them a sharper and more satirical voice, exposing what he termed in a new foreword the Americans' revelling in 'subterfuge' and 'double meaning' (*SCAL* 12). When they were finished he felt that the essays were 'much sharper, quicker' (*4L* 342). In Ceylon, he had been unable to write, and the only outlet he had for his ambivalent feelings towards the country and its people was the letters he wrote to friends and contacts in Sicily and England. In New Mexico, he was able to explore and express his ambivalence in the revisions he made to his essays.

The complexities of the biographical record remind us that our attitudes to a place, a landscape and its people do not 'develop' in any straightforward sense. In a certain mood, Lawrence could see the awe-inspiring setting of the Del Monte Ranch as empty and barren and uncreated, but there are signs that he was gaining a new appreciation of the native landscape and wildlife. In this period he wrote several of the poems which he would include in the volume *Birds, Beasts and Flowers* (1923). The poems 'Eagle in New Mexico' and 'The Blue Jay' reflect his deepening connection with New Mexico. In 'Eagle in New Mexico', Lawrence addresses the bird as 'American eagle', the symbol of the United States, but he sees it not as an embodiment of strength and democracy but sinister power. He asks the bird: 'When you pick the red smoky heart from a rabbit or a light-blooded bird / Do you lift it to the sun, as the Aztec priests used to lift red hearts of men?' The speaker of the poem recognises the primal bloodthirstiness of the bird, but asserts that he does not 'yield' to this 'big, jowl-faced eagle', since 'the sun in heaven can be curbed and chastened at last / By the life in the hearts of men' (*Poems* 325–326).

The sense of nature in New Mexico as being hostile and challenging to humans, but also revivifying, is evident too in 'The Blue Jay'. When Lawrence left Mabeltown, his host gave him a French bulldog terrier puppy to look after. Lawrence and Frieda gave it various names; for Lawrence it was Bibbles, Bambino or Bubastis, for Frieda Pips or Pipsey.[8] Merrild records how the blue jay was a regular visitor to the ranch.[9] In the poem it is described as a 'copper-sulphate blue bird'. Lawrence recounts how it would run 'in the snow like a bit of blue metal'. When Lawrence and Bibbles were outside, it called with a 'strident laugh' from the tall pine tree above the cabin. Bibbles would look up 'inquiringly into the pillar of cloud, / With a tinge of misgiving'. The call was like a 'scrape of ridicule'.

The blue jay in the poem is jeering at the speaker and his dog, and seems to turn its back on them, 'as if darkly saying: / *I ignore those folk who look out*' (*Poems* 326–327). There is the same intense awareness as in the early essays on the Native Americans of the invidiousness of looking at things as an outsider, and the same feeling of resistance in the subject being viewed.

In mid-March 1923, Lawrence and Frieda left the Del Monte Ranch and travelled to Mexico City. They stayed in a hotel until 27 April. They spent time there with Witter Bynner and Willard Johnson. Lawrence made various trips out to surrounding cities to see Aztec temples and antiquities, including the Temple of Quetzalcoatl at San Juan Teotihuacán. On 27 April he travelled to Chapala, where he stayed until 9 July. Here he began work on his Mexican novel, *Quetzalcoatl*, later re-titled *The Plumed Serpent*. Having produced 480 pages between 10 May and 27 June, he took a break from work on it. On 9 July, he went with Frieda back to the United States, visiting New York and staying at the home of Thomas and Adele Seltzer in Morris Plains, New Jersey.

Lawrence intended to sail back to Europe with Frieda, but he could not bring himself to leave, so on 18 August she went by herself. Frieda and Lawrence seem to have fallen out shortly before her departure, perhaps over Frieda's commitment to her children back in England and desire to re-establish a relationship with them. Lawrence told John Middleton Murry: 'wrong or not, I can't stomach the chasing of those Weekley children' (*4L* 480). Their separation represented the most serious breach to date in their marriage. Left alone, Lawrence visited his friend Bessie Freeman in Buffalo, going to see Niagara Falls, then he travelled to Los Angeles, via Chicago and Omaha, to be reunited with Merrild and Gøtzsche, who had found employment painting decorative murals in the home of the geologist Harry Johnson. On 25 September, Lawrence and Gøtzsche travelled together down the west coast of Mexico. Lawrence wished to look for a banana farm to occupy; he apparently fantasised about giving up the literary life. The remoteness of the possible locations, and the challenging circumstances of travelling and living there, ultimately convinced him that it was impossible. They ended their journey in a hotel in Guadalajara, where they stayed for a month before travelling to Mexico City and Vera Cruz, from where on 22 November they sailed back to Europe.

We can judge the extent of Lawrence's adjustment to Taos, Questa and Mexico by his reaction to England and the English as his boat docked in Plymouth. In the essay 'On Coming Home', he described the 'deathly sense of stillness' he felt 'returning to England from the west'. While its soft quietness reinforced his sense that here was an 'accomplished civilisation', now it frightened him 'more than the noise of New York or of Mexico City': 'But God save me from such civilisation. God in heaven deliver me' (*RDP* 178–179). Far from eulogising England as the centre of the world, he now looked on the English with disgust, noting how 'at the middle of this amiable and all-tolerant English complacency, there is fear' plus 'the sense of impotence, and a quiver of spite, of subdued malice' (*RDP* 181). Lawrence notes that Englishmen abroad feel no pride in their country, only 'imbecile superiority', so they are often to be seen 'burning with impatience, disgust, and even contempt, of home' (*RDP* 182). He depicts England as a country losing its imperial pride. The essay, which Lawrence wrote for the *Adelphi*, a journal which Murry told him he had set up as a vehicle for publishing Lawrence's work, was rejected on the grounds that it would '*only make enemies*' (*5L* 94).

Lawrence stayed with Frieda in the same house in Hampstead as Catherine Carswell. They travelled to see his sister Ada in Ripley, before going to Paris and then visiting Frieda's mother in Baden-Baden. At some point, Lawrence learned that Frieda had almost been unfaithful to him with Murry during their separation. He reconciled with his wife, but his relationship with Murry, which had been seriously strained since the war years, would from now on be characterised by mistrust, suspicion and open enmity. On 5 March 1924, Lawrence and Frieda sailed back to the United States with a friend, the artist Dorothy Brett. They spent a week in New York before departing for Taos, arriving on 22 March. They initially stayed back in Mabeltown. Mabel had married Tony Lujan a year earlier, on 23 April 1923; she had adopted a phonetic version of his surname and was henceforth known as Mabel Dodge Luhan. Mabel gifted to Frieda the 'Flying Heart Ranch', which she had suggested the Lawrences might occupy during their first period in New Mexico. Lawrence, being averse to charity and indebtedness, gave her the manuscript of *Sons and Lovers* in exchange for it. They would move there on 5 May. Dorothy Brett took up residence in a tiny cabin on the Ranch. In due course, Lawrence would rename it the Kiowa Ranch after a Native American tribe which had once camped on the land on which it was built.

His arrival back in Taos once again coincided with a threat to the pueblos. On Good Friday, 18 April, officials from the Bureau of Indian Affairs held a meeting with the council of Taos Pueblo. They encouraged the council to give up their dances and festivals, and to ensure that their children attended school instead of participating in them, in order to integrate them into mainstream American society. This time Lawrence's response to the interference in pueblo life was less equivocal. In the poem 'O! Americans!' he stresses 'the obligation of the citizens of this country towards the aborigines of their country'. He asserts that 'The American Indian is, basically, a savage', but 'it is *not* a term of reproach', since 'He lingers on from an old, savage world, that still has its treasures of consciousness, its subtle barbaric forms of civilisation' (*Poems* 1564). Lawrence notes that 'the Poles, the Germans, the English, the Italians, the Russians' can be turned into 'hundred-per-cent Americans' because they have chosen to live in the country, but 'the Indian never came. / It was you who came, Americans. / And before you put out the old savage light for ever, hesitate' (*Poems* 1565). Lawrence's brief return to Europe had underscored his hatred of one form of 'civilisation' and its fading empire. This in turn caused him to re-define the 'savage'. After his experiences in Ceylon, he fell back on European civilisation as a desired norm, denigrating the natives by describing them as 'built round a gap, a hollow pit' (*4L* 226), '*back* of us – in the living sense *lower* than we are' (*4L* 234). In his first period in New Mexico, his encounters with Native Americans combined responsiveness to their difference with this same colonialist mindset, which could only construct them in relation to modern America and his own insights and preoccupations. Now he saw the 'savage' as possessing a different form of civilisation and a different mode of life inimical to his own.

What was at stake here was not just a realignment of Lawrence's thinking but a realisation that the different, 'savage' mode of consciousness he had sensed in the pueblos was something he could learn from and be transformed by. He suggested that attempting to embrace their otherness would mean dying to his old self. Yet *realising* what he termed their 'subtle barbaric forms of civilisation' – encountering and appreciating them – might offer him a new way of seeing the world, which would enable him to get behind Christian ideals and associated democratic, materialistic and scientific worldviews which he had long despised and from which he now felt utterly alienated. This hardly resolves the problems inherent in Lawrence's positioning as a privileged white European seeing in the generalised and homogenised Native American other a clue to the transformation of his own consciousness, but it does represent a further stage in what Roberts terms his attempt to 'confront' cultural difference and 'work imaginatively within it' (Roberts 2004: 79).

Lawrence immediately produced his most imaginative accounts of Native American dances and ceremonies, and began to develop a new ecological awareness from his consideration of them. In 'Indians and Entertainment', he contrasts the experience of modern theatre-goers enjoying a play to the Indians' participation in their dances and races. He notes that the ancient Greeks addressed their plays to the gods, while modern plays are addressed to members of the audience, who perch god-like above the action, sitting like pure spirits in judgement on the actors. The audience is 'a little democracy of the ideal consciousness' (*MM* 59); the pleasure it takes in the spiritualised abstraction from reality is akin to that gained from the 'cinematograph', since here 'the individual watching the shadow-spectacle sits a very god, in an orgy of abstraction, actually dissolved into delighted, watchful spirit' (*MM* 60). Lawrence argues that the Native Americans have no such concept of entertainment because they have no concept of a God separate from the flesh. When they sing around the drum, they do so 'without words or vision': 'The experience is generic, non-individual. It is an experience of the human blood-stream, not of the mind or spirit' (*MM* 62).

In the dances, likewise, they are 'not representing something' but '*being* something' (*MM* 65): participants do not perform for the spectators but to 'gather into their souls more and more of the creative fire, the creative energy which shall carry their tribe through the year' (*MM* 68). There is no God, but everything is Godly, and the 'wonder of creation' (*MM* 66) is in everything, from lightning to 'anger in the little eyes of the bear', 'the beautiful shimmer of the moving deer', 'the pine-boughs softly swaying under snow'. Creation arouses, then, all shades of feeling, from tender wistfulness to abject terror: 'The Apache warrior in his war-paint, shrieking the war-cry and cutting the throats of the old women' is just as much a part of the mystery of creation as the companion who brings sustenance in winter, and no distinction can be made between them. There is, Lawrence says, 'no judgment: absolutely no judgment'. The only negative commandments of the Native Americans are that one should not lie or be a coward, and the only positive commandment that one should acknowledge the wonder.

Drawing by D. H. Lawrence, 'The Corn Dance', published alongside 'The Dance of the Sprouting Corn' in *Theatre Arts Monthly*, Vol. VIII, No. 7 (July 1924), p. 449. University of Nottingham, Manuscripts and Special Collections.

Lawrence refers to 'all the rippling of this untellable flood of creation, which, in a narrow sense, we call Nature' (*MM* 67). He says that nature for the Native Americans includes all things, human and non-human, and strength and fruitfulness are the central qualities in it which their dances and ceremonies seek to access. The vision of ecology which follows from this is unsentimental in that humans are part of creation but seek to usurp the powers in nature for the good of the tribe. Everything is based on the relative power or vigour of things. In the essay 'The Dance of the Sprouting Corn', Lawrence discusses the three-day ceremony taking place from the first Monday after Easter, which he witnessed at the Santo Domingo Pueblo in April 1924, as one which realises 'the mystery of germination—not procreation, but *putting forth*, resurrection, life springing within the seed'. The dancers call forth influences from the sky and from the earth: 'man, the knower, brings down the influences, and brings up the influences, with his knowledge: man, so vulnerable, so subject, and yet even in his vulnerability and subjection, a master, commands the invisible influences, and is obeyed' (*MM* 76).

In 'Pan in America', written in May–June 1924, we can see Lawrence reflecting on what he finds so precious in these Native American ceremonies. While pre-Christians had sought to take unto themselves the qualities and energy of the surrounding elements and flora and fauna, the modern human 'insulates himself more and more into mechanism, and repudiates everything but the machine and the contrivance of which he himself is master, God in the machine' (*MM* 160). Lawrence asserts that in America, 'the oldest of all old Pan is still alive' (*MM* 157). When Native Americans stand around a campfire, they are said to implicitly recognise their triumph in drinking up the life of the tree they are burning to create warmth; when they hunt deer, they are said to give an offering to a big pale rock so that it will give them 'some of its radiant-cold stillness and enduring presence' (*MM* 161); and when the deer meat is presented to the tribe, the hunter is 'full of power, bringing the life-stuff' (*MM* 163). Lawrence asks whether it is 'truer to life, to insulate oneself entirely from the influence of the tree's life, and to walk about in an inanimate forest of standing lumber, marketable in St. Louis, Mo', or 'better' to 'turn on the heat at the radiator, glancing at the thermometer and saying: "We're just a bit below the level, in here"' (*MM* 159–160). 'A conquered world', he writes, 'is no good to man': 'We need the universe to live again, so that we can live with it. A conquered universe, a dead Pan, leaves us nothing to live with' (*MM* 162).

The 'Indians', Lawrence says, will kill Pan with their own hands, 'for the sake of a motor-car' (*MM* 164). Yet, for the moment, up at his Ranch, he can feel the aura of the tall tree outside his cabin: 'It gives out life, as I give out life. Our two lives meet and cross one another, unknowingly: the tree's life penetrates my life, and my life, the tree's. We cannot live near one another, as we do, without affecting one another' (*MM* 158). He realises that the 'Pan relationship', which humans once had with all the world, was better than anything we have now, since 'when all is said and done, life itself consists in a live relatedness between man and his universe;—sun, moon, stars, earth, trees, flowers, birds, animals, men, everything—and not in a "conquest" of anything by anything' (*MM* 164).

Lawrence remained profoundly critical of what modern America made of the Native American dances, ceremonies and festivals. In August 1924, Mabel and Tony took him to see the Hopi Snake Dance at Hotevilla in Arizona. Lawrence was ill a few days before they left, and the long journey by car left him exhausted. His initial account of the dance, written during the journey back, satirises the attitudes of the three thousand people who had travelled to see it. Lawrence mimicked their voices: 'Lots of fun! Oh, the wild west is lots of fun: the Land of Enchantment. Like being right inside the circus-ring: lots of sand, and painted savages jabbering, and snakes and all that. Come on, boys! Lots of fun!' (*MM* 187).

Yet, when he began rewriting the essay four days later, he dwelt on the Snake Dance, and the preparatory Antelope Dance the evening before, as embodiments of the participants' animistic religion. The careful anointing of the snakes in preparation for the Snake Dance, the dusting of the twelve snake priests with 'feather-prayer-sticks' (*MM* 89), the carrying of the snakes in their mouths, their release and recapture, and the use of corn meal to cover them before their collective release by two young priests in a rock known as the snake-shrine, achieved the carrying of 'messages and thanks to the dragon-gods who can give and withhold' (*MM* 91). In order to survive, Man, 'small, vulnerable man, the farthest adventurer from the dark heart of the first of suns, into the cosmos of creation', must both submit to the Source and conquer it. Lawrence now commented that despite the crudity and sensationalism of the spectacle, 'which comes chiefly out of the crowd's desire for thrills, one cannot help pausing in reverence before the delicate, anointed bravery of the snake-priests (so-called) with the snakes' (*MM* 92–93).

Templeton, who notes that what Lawrence witnessed at Hotevilla was a rite and not a religious ceremony, says that in comparing the two versions of Lawrence's essay we witness the contrast between 'what Lawrence saw and what he wanted to see, dreary reality and his idealistic recreation of reality' (Templeton 1993–1994: 19). The contrast is not unlike that between Lawrence's brief experience of Picinisco and what he made of it in *The Lost Girl*. Lawrence's travel writing, like his fiction and poetry, provided an opportunity to discover meaning and significance in life events and experiences which might at the time have seemed deeply ambivalent, troubling or banal. Given that Lawrence was confronted in the American Southwest by an 'unknown and perhaps unknowable otherness', it is difficult to see how he could have engaged so closely with the Snake Dance without introducing speculation and error into his account. As Ruderman observes, 'it is instructive that anthropologists today foreground the interpretive, indeed inventive, nature of ethnography rather than its representation of any objective truth', so that 'Lawrence's depictions of fact are no more or less accurate than any other purported chronicle of Indian life' (Ruderman 2014: 104, 110–111). Lawrence openly admitted that he was no ethnologist,[10] and he foregrounded his own status as an outsider encountering the strangeness of peoples whose ways were inimical to his own; if we are inclined to accept as authoritative fact his sympathetic account of the impact the Snake Dance had on him in the second essay, and the ways in which he sought to interpret it, then we do so against the grain of his other writings on the Native Americans, and indeed against the grain of Lawrence's entire body of work as an imaginative writer.

In mid-October 1924, Lawrence travelled back to Mexico to finish *The Plumed Serpent*. He stayed for a little over a fortnight in Mexico City before settling in Oaxaca. In December 1924, he wrote four essays on his experiences in and around Oaxaca, which would eventually be collected in the deceptively titled book of travel writings *Mornings in Mexico* (which combines essays on Mexico and New Mexico). In early February 1925, having finished the novel, he fell gravely ill. He and Frieda moved back to Mexico City, where the doctor in the American Hospital diagnosed him as having tuberculosis. When he was well enough to travel, in late March, they returned to New Mexico. He was admitted back into the United States on a six-month visa. He and Frieda initially stayed with the Hawks at the Del Monte Ranch, but on 6 April they moved back to the Kiowa Ranch. Here Lawrence's health slowly returned. The period between 6 April and 9 September was perhaps the happiest of his life. He would look back to it in later years with a yearning for return. He lived a fulfilling subsistence life at the ranch, irrigating his land and keeping a cow, which he named Susan, for milk and butter, and chickens for eggs and meat.

Here he was finally able to realise that 'live relatedness between man and his universe' (*MM* 164) which he had heralded in 'Pan in America', and he wrote about it in the lively essays which he published in *Reflections on the Death of a Porcupine*. In the title essay, he describes his initial reluctance to shoot porcupines as pests on his land. However, following his discovery of a stray dog with porcupine quills nestled deeply in its muzzle, and his attempt to help it, his attitude to them changed. He shot a porcupine and finished it off with a cedar pole. It made him realise that 'One must kill': 'Wherever man establishes himself, upon the earth, he has to fight for his place, against the lower order of life'. All things are incomparable in their achieved being, but in time and space they must vie for existence in the relatedness of all things.

The Ranch afforded him many instances of this relatedness. The horses ate the grass, alfalfa shoots and dandelions, Susan snatched off 'the tops of the little wild sunflowers as if she were mowing' (*RDP* 354), the chickens ate the beetles, and his cat Timsy caught and toyed with the chipmunks: 'In nature, one creature devours another, and this is an essential part of all existence and of all being' (*RDP* 356). This leads Lawrence to recognise a hierarchy of 'higher and lower' forms, where one's place on the scale is determined by how 'vividly alive' one is. Lawrence places things in order of vividness, with (for instance) the ant being more vividly alive than the pine tree, the dandelion more alive than the green fern, the snake more alive than the butterfly, and the cat more alive than the ostrich. He describes himself as having more vivid life in him than 'the Mexican who drives the wagon for me' (*RDP* 357). Once again, we see here a colonialist mindset obtruding into his account of otherness and ecology through the racist conflation of discourses of race and species. In terms of '*existence*', he says, 'that is, in terms of species, race, or type', one devours or destroys the other, and one 'race of men can subjugate and rule another race', and there is 'no escaping this law' (*RDP* 357–358). Yet he also insists on the irreducible difference of races and species, since in and of themselves they are incomparable and unique. Existence and being are opposite but complementary aspects of life. To achieve vitality, a species, race or type must be 'moving towards a blossoming', and this means establishing 'a pure, *new* relationship with all the cosmos. This is the state of heaven' (*RDP* 361).

In 'Him With His Tail in His Mouth', Lawrence states that what we want is 'life, and life-energy inside us' (*RDP* 310). He looks to the ancient Greeks and says that, like them, he is a pantheist and a pluralist, but where they were concerned with equilibrium, he considers this too mechanical and intellectual: instead he wants 'relationship' (*RDP* 314). While Raphael and G. F. Watts paint and sculpt animals in their own image, the ancients represented 'the living relation between man and his object'. Lawrence gives examples of ancient art in which the relation of humans to the living universe is fully realised, from paintings of bison and reindeer in the caves of Altamira, to the Ajanta frescoes in India, to 'an Assyrian sculpture of a lion, an African fetish-idol of a woman pregnant, an Aztec rattle-snake, an early Greek Apollo, a cave-man's painting of a pre-historic mammoth, on and on' (*RDP* 316). His celebration of this 'ancient art' reveals a characteristic subversion of European aesthetic ideals and an attempt to think outside the usual demarcations of Western and non-Western histories. Lawrence, however, firmly believed that 'All races have one root': 'Many stems from one root: the stems never to commingle or "understand" one another' (*5L* 142). The emphasis on the common root leads him to elide the differences between the ancient art of various countries and cultures and periods, presenting it as a homogeneous phenomenon in contrast to modern European art. Anne Fernihough has shown how the organic vocabulary Lawrence used to describe Indigenous peoples and the related ideas of vital cultures and decadent civilisations were derived from the *völkisch* ideologies central to fascism.[11] Here, as elsewhere, forward-thinking and retrogressive elements coalesce in his worldview: Lawrence's high valuation of pre-modern and non-European modes of being and knowing encodes disturbing colonialist assumptions and has troubling political implications.

Several years later, in December 1928, Lawrence would state: 'I think New Mexico was the greatest experience from the outside world that I have ever had. It certainly changed me for ever. Curious as it may sound, it was New Mexico that liberated me from the present era of civilisation, the great era of material and mechanical development'. Kandy, he said, 'had not touched the great psyche of materialism and idealism which dominated me'; Sicily 'had not shattered the essential Christianity on which my character was established'; Australia was 'a sort of dream or trance'. Only in 'the magnificent fierce morning of New Mexico' did 'a new part of the soul' spring awake, 'and the old world gave way to a new' (*MM* 176). The essay presents as an instant awakening what was in reality a tortuous process of detachment, resistance, projection, and imaginative engagement and fabulation.

Yet nobody who reads the travel writings of this period can doubt that New Mexico did indeed show Lawrence how an older religious understanding of the world preserved the sense of wonder at creation and being-in-the-flesh. It enabled him to glimpse a mode of life that pre-dated the dualisms of the modern world, existing outside the bland prescriptions of science and logic, and the obsession with money and shallow entertainment. He could now declare that he did not believe in evolution, 'being slowly twisted in unbroken continuity through the ages', but in 'what the Aztecs called Suns: that is, Worlds successively created and destroyed' (*MM* 14). He realised the importance of Man's relatedness to a cosmos full of life energies, which we must hold in reverence but also harness and usurp. Without his time in New Mexico, he could never have described the 'business of art' as being 'to reveal the relation between man and his circumambient universe, at the living moment' (*STH* 171), and the role of the novel as being to help individuals 'be alive, to be man alive, to be whole man alive' (*STH* 197). He could not have described with such assurance the nature of the 'old religion' as showing humanity's 'profound attempt ... to harmonise himself with nature, and hold his own and come to flower in the great seething of life' (*SEP* 130). And he would not have emphasised in quite the same way in the last five years of his life our need to 'destroy our false, inorganic connections, especially those related to money, and re-establish the living organic connections, with the cosmos, the sun and earth, with mankind and nation and family' (*A* 149).

Notes

1 See Harrison (2013).
2 See Ruderman (2014: 94–97).
3 See Chambers (1935: 94).
4 See *TI* 212 and *WL* 322.

5 'Buffalo Bill' is mentioned in *Kangaroo*. See *K* 275.

6 During his time in Cornwall during the war, Lawrence had read about pre-Christian cultures in an effort to engage with the area's Celtic 'spirit of place'. In his first attempt at a 'Foreword' to *Studies in Classic American Literature*, written back in September 1920, before he had even set foot on the American continent, he had encouraged young Americans to ignore the modern achievements of European culture and seek inspiration for their 'unrevealed, unknown destiny' from 'the spirit' of their own 'dark, aboriginal continent': 'They must pick up the life-thread where the mysterious Red race let it fall' (*SCAL* 384).

7 Keith Sagar entitled the unfinished fragment 'The Wilful Woman'. See *SM* 199–203.

8 See Merrild (1938: 161).

9 See Merrild (1938: 107).

10 See *MM* 116.

11 See Fernihough (1993: 16–33).

7

Lawrence, 'Leadership' and the Charges of Fascism

In Chapter 6 we saw how Lawrence sought post-war renewal firstly in an imaginative engagement with wild and awe-inspiring landscapes in Europe whose otherness seemed to offer a vital alternative to what he had come to see as the destructive self-enclosure and narrow-mindedness of England and the English, and then outside Europe through a conflicted engagement with different peoples and cultures in Ceylon, Australia, New Mexico and Mexico. While his dislike of Ceylon made itself felt in his use of imperialist and racist language, and he came to disparage Australia as an advanced democratic country with a striking landscape but 'an abyss' or 'dismal, grey terror, underneath' (*4L* 282), his initial sense of alienation from, and resistance to, the landscape and Indigenous peoples of the American Southwest eventually gave way to a transformative appreciation of the otherness of the Native Americans and their religious dances and festivals. Though Lawrence's accounts of the Native American ceremonies are not always accurate, and he is insufficiently attentive to the differences between the various Indigenous cultures he encountered, he developed a new religious awareness through his contact with them which stressed the wonder and mystery of our relatedness to the cosmos. He came to see nature and culture as driven by hierarchies, with humans taking their place in a world where subordination of lower life forms by higher ones is necessary for survival, and where species and races displace one another in cataclysmic cycles of creation and destruction.

The author who had experienced all this, and who lived a fulfilling subsistence life during his final period of residence at the Kiowa Ranch between 6 April and 9 September 1925, is a deeply divisive figure. For some he is a fascinating countercultural individual who in his travels recognised his own cultural conditioning and confronted his beliefs, values and prejudices with honesty and courage, allowing himself to be transformed by contact with different modes of life. For others he is a troubling, isolated man retreating from the political realities of post-war Europe into a primitivist fantasy which only inflected and deepened his

The Life of the Author: D. H. Lawrence, First Edition. Andrew Harrison.

existing imaginative preoccupation with power, natural aristocracy and the need for the toiling many to be led by the exceptional few.

Marxist analyses of Lawrence perceive unresolved contradictions in his position vis-à-vis modernity. In his chapter on Lawrence in *Studies in a Dying Culture* (1938), Christopher Caudwell asserted that in revolutionary times, when faced by a decaying bourgeois culture, one must choose to go either forward or backward. For him, the forward move was towards Communism, uniting with the proletariat to change social relations: the art of the future was for Caudwell a communist art 'more conscious of itself as part of the whole social process' (Caudwell 1938: 55). Conversely, to go back 'to old primitive values, to mythology, racialism, nationalism, hero-worship, and *participation mystique*' was to embrace fascism, and fascist art is 'like the regression of the neurotic to a previous level of adaptation'. Caudwell said that it was 'Lawrence's final tragedy that his solution was ultimately Fascist and not Communist' (Caudwell 1938: 56). He saw Lawrence as possessing a false consciousness. In Caudwell's view, while Lawrence continually attacked bourgeois culture and values, his only solution was a 'return to instinctive living' which echoes the fascist obsession with the mythical primitive past, the only difference being that while the fascists espoused a cult of action and disparaged consciousness and the intellect, Lawrence consciously and intellectually insisted upon the value of instinctive being. Caudwell argued that this exposes the false nature of Lawrence's position, since it is self-contradictory to wish to lead people 'intellectually and consciously *back* from consciousness' (Caudwell 1938: 59): 'bourgeois intellect ... can only be fought with intellect. To deny intellect is to assist the forces of conservatism' (Caudwell 1938: 66). He described Lawrence as subscribing to a form of humanism which was merely an offshoot of bourgeois conservatism, and he suggested that if Lawrence had lived to see the collapse of this branch of humanism in Nazism, he would have recognised that it made 'straw of his philosophy and his teaching' (Caudwell 1938: 72).

More recently, Terry Eagleton has also emphasised the contradictions inherent in Lawrence's reaction to modernity, but he focuses not on primitivism but on individualism. In his view, Lawrence's work dramatises 'a contradiction within the Romantic humanist tradition', which espoused an 'extreme form of individualism' while also emphasising 'the opposing imperatives of impersonality and organic order'. Eagleton says that Lawrence's work rejects 'the atomistic, mechanistic ideologies of industrial capitalism, yet at the same time subsumes the values of the bourgeois liberal tradition: sympathy, intimacy, compassion, the centrality of the "personal"' (Eagleton 1984: 158). Eagleton refers to Lawrence's 'perpetual oscillation between a proud celebration of individual autonomy and a hunger for social integration; Lawrence wants men to be drilled soldiers but *individual* soldiers, desires to "rule" over them but not "bully" them'. He argues that Lawrence attempted to resolve the contradictions in his concept of the individual through the development of his dualistic metaphysic, which stressed the need for 'male' and 'female' principles to be held in creative tension: 'power, consciousness, spirit, activism, individuation' and 'flesh, sensuality, permanence, passivity' (Eagleton 1984: 159).

Eagleton suggests that the Great War signified the collapse of the 'liberal humanist heritage', and hence of the creative tension in Lawrence's dualism. While Lawrence's early novels had made the conflict between male and female their subject, and if anything sided with the female against the male, the war saw his loss of belief in 'benevolistic idealism' and 'personal' values, 'clearing the way for the "dark gods" of discipline, action, hierarchy, individual separateness, mystical impersonality'. Eagleton argues that this makes Lawrence 'a major precursor of fascism', despite the fact that he condemned Mussolini and incisively criticised fascism as 'a spuriously "radical" response to the crisis of capitalism' (Eagleton 1984: 158). While the unresolved conflict between male and female principles in *Women in Love* is said to create an 'ideology of the text', enforcing 'a "progressive" discontinuity with a realist lineage' (Eagleton 1984: 160–161), Eagleton says that 'the hysterical male chauvinism of the post-war novels (*Aaron's Rod*, *Kangaroo*, *The Plumed Serpent*) represents a strident rejection of sexual love for the male cult of power and impersonality' (Eagleton 1984: 159–160).

In a footnote Eagleton quotes Lou Witt's dismissive reflection on fascism in the novella *St. Mawr* (1925) as evidence of Lawrence's own attitude to Italian fascism. The quotation reads: 'Try fascism. Fascism would keep the surface of life intact, and carry on the undermining business all the better'. The passage from which this is taken takes aim at all established political positions, criticising socialism and bolshevism for making 'a mess of the outside of life', before suggesting that fascism makes a mess of the inside: 'this pseudo-handsome ghoul of outward loyalty, inward treachery, in a game of betrayal, betrayal, betrayal' (*SM* 79). By 1976, when *Criticism and Ideology* was first published, Eagleton would have had access to other sources in which Lawrence attacks fascism, including two letters of 8 August 1927 and 4 March 1928, the 'Epilogue' to the Illustrated Edition of *Movements in European History* (written in September 1924, but rejected by Oxford University Press and not published until 1971), and *Sketches of Etruscan Places* (first published posthumously in 1932). In the letters, Lawrence criticises 'the bossiness of Fascist Italy' (*6L* 121) and refers to its 'false power forced against life' as 'very depressing' (*6L* 308). In the Epilogue to *Movements in European History*, Lawrence describes his experience of fascist uprisings in Italy in 1920, when the devaluation of the currency led to widespread strikes and socialist unrest, resulting in 'an anti-socialist movement started by the returned soldiers in the name of Law and Order' (*MEH* 262–263). He recounts an incident in which the Mayor of Fiesole, near Florence, where he was then staying, was woken by the fascists, put against a wall and shot in front of his wife and children. Lawrence decries the socialism of this time as 'pure bullying', driven by 'the hatred of "superiors" or people with money or education or authority' (*MEH* 262), while the killing of the Mayor is put down to 'Fascism and Law and Order. Only another kind of bullying' (*MEH* 263). *Sketches of Etruscan Places* contains a satirical mention of Mussolini. Here Lawrence refers to his arrival in Volterra to see the Etruscan ruins on 10 April 1927, which happened to be the same day on which a new *podestà*, or Fascist-appointed governor, was scheduled to arrive from Florence. Two girls gave him a Roman salute, which he did not return, partly because for him politics 'of all sorts are anathema', but also because the independence of the Etruscans, and their eventual brutal destruction at the hands of the Romans, made the gesture in that place 'unbecoming' (*SEP* 158). Lawrence reflected ironically on the slogans chalked up on the walls: '*Mussolini ha sempre ragione*! *Mussolini is always right*! Some are born infallible, some achieve it, and some have infallibility thrust upon them' (*SEP* 159).

Eagleton writes: 'Lawrence was not a fascist rather perhaps in the same sense that he was not a homosexual. He thought both fascism and homosexuality immoral, but was subconsciously fascinated by both' (Eagleton 1984: 158 fn. 72). Lawrence's views on homosexuality were far more complex than Eagleton allows, but his emphasis on Lawrence's *subconscious* fascination with fascism and his suggestion that it began during the war are more convincing and interesting. Eagleton is correct when he identifies the Great War as the moment when Lawrence began to actively assert his commitment to qualities central to fascist ideology, such as hierarchy, discipline and strong leadership. As I have noted in Chapter 3, in the early summer of 1915 Lawrence and Bertrand Russell planned to deliver a series of anti-war lectures together in London in the autumn. Russell was to lecture on ethics and Lawrence on immortality.[1] Russell sent Lawrence the outline for his proposed lectures, which he called 'Philosophy of Social Reconstruction'. In this document, he proposed to focus on things which had once underpinned social cohesion but were now in need of reconstruction: the State, property, the churches, law and morality, and marriage. His aim was to imagine an organisation of society which enabled fulfilment for individual citizens in all areas of their lives, from relationships and family to work, and in which the need for risk and self-assertion which (like Lawrence) he felt had been frustrated and so turned violent in the war might be accommodated and redirected to creative ends.[2] He wanted to nurture in people 'freedom for impulse of growth and creation, by freedom to love', and he explicitly stated that the remedy to the current situation was 'cooperation, not authority' (Moore 1948: 79).

For Russell, who was a pacifist deeply concerned with existing political forms of opposition to the war, the lectures were a means of working out his own values and thinking through their practical application in dialogue with, for instance, the objectives of existing organisations with which he was involved, such as the Union of Democratic Control. Lawrence felt that Russell was too focused on merely criticising existing aspects of society rather than proposing a credible alternative. He was convinced that the war would 'develop into the last great war between labour and capital' and might ultimately create 'another French Revolution' unless the people could be given 'a higher aim than the triumph of Labour' (*2L* 366). In contrast to the anti-authoritarian, liberal humanist values informing Russell's social critique, Lawrence called for wholesale nationalisation to address the basic needs of the people and then the establishment of a new State based on a unanimous religious commitment to Truth: 'Let the law be established on the sense of truth, & then you can use force. Because the truth is greater than any one of us' (Moore 1948: 87). Lawrence wrote: 'There are 2 conceptions of the State now: 1. Monarchy 2. Democracy. Democracy is the falser' (Moore 1948: 82).

Ray Monk notes that by the summer of 1915 Russell 'had begun to feel that the State ought to cease to exist altogether' (Monk 1996: 420). He proposed a loosening of State control in order to govern without authority; he stressed the need for workers' rights to be advanced through a form of syndicalism. In three surviving letters to Russell of 14, 16 and 19 July 1915, Lawrence implored him to 'drop' his belief in democracy and 'the people': 'It must be a case of Wisdom, or Truth'. He said that there must be 'an aristocracy of people who have wisdom, and there must be a Ruler: a Kaiser: no Presidents and democracies' (*2L* 364). In fact, he saw 'the extant *democracy*' as the 'enemy'. He told Russell that the working man should be allowed to elect the immediate government as it related to his work and district, but not the government of the nation, since this should be managed by 'a body of chosen patricians'. Women should govern equally with men, 'especially all the inner half of life. The whole must culminate in an absolute *Dictator*, and an equivalent *Dictatrix*' (*2L* 365). In response to Russell's objections, he said: 'I don't want tyrants. But I don't believe in democratic control'. He once more stated his belief that society 'must culminate in one real head, as every organic thing must – no foolish republics with foolish presidents, but an elected King, something like Julius Caesar': 'It isn't bosh, but rational sense. The whole thing must be living. Above all there must be no democratic control – that is the worst of all. There must be an elected aristocracy' (*2L* 370–371).

Lawrence and Russell subsequently quarrelled, and despite a brief period of reconciliation fell out of contact with one another. Lawrence relinquished his plan to lecture, while Russell went ahead and delivered his series of lectures at Caxton Hall in Westminster early in 1916; he published them in November 1916 as *Principles of Social Reconstruction*. In the second volume of his autobiography, published in 1968, Russell wrote that in the summer of 1915 he gradually realised that Lawrence 'had no real wish to make the world better, but only to indulge in eloquent soliloquy about how bad it was'. The soliloquies were designed, he said, to 'produce a little faithful band of disciples who could sit in the deserts of New Mexico and feel holy. All this was conveyed to me in the language of a Fascist dictator as what I *must* preach, the "must" having thirteen underlinings'. He commented: 'I was a firm believer in democracy, whereas he had developed the whole philosophy of Fascism before the politicians had thought of it' (Russell 1968: 21). The composer Cecil Gray, with whom Lawrence also quarrelled irreparably during the war years, similarly used his autobiography to settle old scores with Lawrence. In *Musical Chairs* (1948), he suggested that Lawrence 'could easily have become a British Hitler': 'there was in Lawrence also the same dark, passionate, fanatical power, the same capacity for casting spells and captivating the sympathies and imagination of the common people, and especially the under-dog' (Gray 1985: 130).

Lawrence's negative views of democracy and his idea of a new State founded upon strong leadership and the directing of people's outer and inner lives were developed in the post-war essays 'Democracy' and 'Education of the People'. 'Democracy' was written between September and October 1919. In it, Lawrence argues that in an age when materialism is rife, the only purpose of the State is to ensure that the material needs of the average 'Man-in-the-Street' (*RDP* 65) are met. Modern States only serve their citizens in their social roles as personalities performing mechanised functions. In Lawrence's view, modern democracy is governed by the 'principle of the idealised unit, the possessor of property', so that 'all the *isms*' are determined by mechanical laws and represent the 'fall into sheer mechanical materialism': he includes here 'socialism, bolshevism, liberalism, republicanism, communism' (*RDP* 81). He suggests that all the 'ideal drapery' should therefore be stripped from our understanding of 'nations, peoples, states, empires, and *even from Internationalism* and Leagues of Nations'. Governments should be seen as simple 'board meetings of big business men', politics as 'another, extra-large commercial wrangle over buying and selling' (*RDP* 67) and the nation as little more than a company, like a larger version of Selfridges, Krupps or Heidsiecks.[3]

Lawrence writes that what modern collective social forms and movements leave out of account is the individual, with 'Spiritual and Mystical needs'. At the level of their desires and impulses, 'Men are not equal, and never were' (*RDP* 65). While in the past nations may have been meaningful entities when their social forms catered for the spiritual and mystical needs of their people through 'collective self-expression' (*RDP* 66), in the modern world desire and impulse tend to 'fall into mechanical automatism' by being converted into 'fixed aspirations or ideals' (*RDP* 79). He argues that the purpose of education should be to prevent this fall into 'mechanisation or materialism' (*RDP* 81) and to facilitate 'spontaneous creativity' (*RDP* 79) and the coming into being of the 'single, incommutable, and unique' (*RDP* 78) individual. The 'first great purpose of Democracy' should be to ensure that 'each man shall be spontaneously himself—each man himself, each woman herself, without any question of equality or unequality entering in at all' (*RDP* 80).

'Education of the People' was written in its first form by 7 December 1918 and submitted to the *Times Educational Supplement*. In summer 1920, after the paper had rejected it, Lawrence rewrote and extended the essay. In it he attacks idealistic and sentimental approaches to education, which he says are muddled and misguided, creating confusion, resentment and neurosis in the child and serving and perpetuating a society based on cash values, materialism and jealousy, and fear of poverty. He argues that existing school values merely encourage conformity to approved standards of appearance and behaviour, creating the 'perfect citizen' at the expense of the 'perfect individual' (*RDP* 94). He sees parents, and especially mothers, as being complicit in impairing the independence of their children. The mother's desire to personalise the relationship with her baby and infant is said to arouse abnormal development in the sympathetic centres of the child's body at the expense of volitional aspects. While sympathetic and volitional nerve centres in the child should achieve a circuit of creative flow, and a balance between empathy with others and a capacity for independence, the mother's insistence on the personal element creates an excess of empathy and abnormal dependence on her.

Lawrence's answer to this situation is radical and his proposal for changes to parenting and school education effectively constitutes his own scheme for social reconstruction. Mothers should encourage motor skills in their babies and joy in self-expression but avoid the personal element altogether. Babies should be raised by wet nurses who will only attend to their basic physical needs, and young children should be punished when they exhibit signs of over-dependence. School should begin at the age of seven, when children should be taught reading, writing and arithmetic for three hours per day in the morning, with another hour given over to physical and domestic training. At the age of 12, teachers, school masters, school inspectors and parents must choose which children should be educated further. Those not chosen will have their mental education reduced to two hours, with three hours given over to physical and domestic training, to include 'the rudiments of domestic labour', and at the age of 14 they will be apprenticed half-time to a trade for a further two years before entering work 'as artizans' (*RDP* 97). Those chosen will go to secondary school and pursue an extended curriculum including Latin, French and some science. For two years they will study for four hours per day and have one hour for workshops and physical training, and at the age of 14 a further decision will be made, with those who are considered to have reached the limits of their mental education being drafted into an apprenticeship to a 'semi-profession, such as school-teaching, and all forms of clerking' (still spending two hours per day split between reading and workshops or physical training), while the remainder continue their education to 16 before being 'drafted into colleges' to study specialist subjects according to their particular aptitudes. They will continue to spend one hour per day 'devoted to some craft', but will eventually take up professional jobs, becoming 'a doctor, a lawyer, a priest, a professor, and so on' (*RDP* 98).

Lawrence notes that his proposed system of education would 'produce distinct classes of society': 'the great class of workers', 'the clerkly caste' and 'the higher professionals'. The social structure would not be established according to money or heredity, but according to 'the profound life-quality, the very nature of the child' (*RDP* 107). The 'new ideal for society' would be 'not that all men are equal, but that each man is himself' (*RDP* 103). Lawrence states that the system he envisages through this educational reform would be 'primarily religious, and only secondarily practical'; it would be built upon 'the inward worship of the creative life-mystery' and rely upon the educators and professionals who exercise judgement on behalf of the State and the nation to act not merely as 'technical experts' but as 'life-directors' (*RDP* 108). He suggests that his new State would enable people to achieve independence and individuality, replacing materialism with creativity, and jealousy and competition with physical pride and a joy in dexterity and contest. Where modern society is built upon a 'sliding scale of shifted responsibility', in which the man 'flings himself either at the feet of a woman, and makes her his conscience keeper; or at the feet of the public' (*RDP* 162), Lawrence's new State would encourage self-responsibility and proud singleness in men, who would 'go always ahead of their women, in the endless trek across life' (*RDP* 165).

Lawrence would address the same issues in his second psychology book, *Fantasia of the Unconscious* (1922), which takes an even stronger approach to educational reform, arguing that no child should be sent to any public institution before the age of 10,[4] and suggesting that the '*great mass of humanity should never learn to read and write—never*' (*PFU* 118). He again stresses here the need for leaders to encourage proud independence in boys: 'First and foremost establish a rule over them, a proud, harsh, manly rule'. He calls for Americans to establish 'a great league of comrades' throughout the United States, with each 'ten comrades to have a leader, the leading soul among them, to whom they will give life and death obedience': 'Each ten decurions to choose their centurion, and each ten centurions their leaders of a thousand'. The league should exist 'in the name of living freedom, of pledged obedience, and sacred responsibility of command' (*PFU* 119).

Taken out of context, without an understanding of these post-war writings, the three surviving letters to Russell in which Lawrence advanced his ideal of a State run by an elected aristocracy and culminating in one or more dictators might seem to bear out the later views of Russell and Gray that Lawrence 'developed the whole philosophy of Fascism before the politicians had thought of it' and 'could easily have become a British Hitler'. Russell evidently took Lawrence at his word, initially dismissing his ideas as 'bosh' and later construing them as something much more sinister, but I think one must view the letters primarily as failed provocations intended to dislodge Russell's criticism of an existing social system and make him 'allow and acknowledge and be prepared to proceed from the fundamental impulse in all of us towards The Truth' (*2L* 361).

Lawrence the would-be politician is certainly a much less interesting and more blandly disturbing figure than Lawrence the radical thinker and provocateur. His fiction challenges readers to understand the emotional effort involved in freeing oneself from old social ideals and developing collective forms which might accommodate and fulfil the deepest desires and impulses of the individual, but it does so in a manner that encourages them to reflect critically on the consequences of top-down reform for both the individual and society. Eagleton's description of *Aaron's Rod*, *Kangaroo* and *The Plumed Serpent* as 'hysterical' and 'strident' seems to me to reflect received wisdom about these novels. In fact they are far from hysterical, and the stridency of the characters in them is offset by the novels' dialogical structures, which juxtapose different perspectives in a questioning and unresolved manner. As John Worthen notes, 'fiction compelled [Lawrence], as Frieda did, to recognise opposition' (Worthen 2005: 161). The novels carefully explore their male characters' reactions against women, and both the male and female characters' equivocal attraction to charismatic male leader-figures, within the context of specific unstable political climates and of the characters' disillusionment with existing social values and search for new principles of action.

Lawrence began writing *Aaron's Rod* in October 1917 at Mecklenburgh Square in London following his expulsion from Cornwall under the Defence of the Realm Act. He worked on it fitfully during 1918 and in the first half of 1919, resuming work on it in July 1920, setting it aside again at the end of November 1920 before finally finishing a first draft in a burst of creative energy in May to June 1921. In October 1921, having revised the novel, he told Thomas Seltzer that it was the last of his 'serious English novels – the end of *The Rainbow*, *Women in Love* line' (*4L* 92). Comparison to the earlier novels helps one to understand the structure and ambition of *Aaron's Rod*. Where *The Rainbow* had rewritten Genesis, *Aaron's Rod*, as seems fitting for a novel begun following his enforced flight from Cornwall, is full of allusions to the Book of Exodus. T. R. Wright (2000) has traced the many parallels between Aaron Sisson and the biblical Aaron, who is charged by God with helping his brother Moses lead his people out of bondage in Egypt. Aaron's rod in the Bible is a symbol of his divine power: before the Pharoah it transforms into a serpent and swallows up the tricks performed by the Pharoah's magicians, and it is used to bring plagues on Egypt, to turn water to blood, and to bring down upon the country frogs, lice and flies. God decrees that Aaron and his sons are to be consecrated as priests by being anointed with oil. When Aaron's divinity is challenged, God proves it by sending a plague and by challenging all comers to lay down their rods so that the one that blooms claims his favour. Moses ultimately falls out of favour with God because when he is leading the Israelites out of Egypt and they complain of thirst he smites a rock with his rod in order to make water flow from it rather than simply speaking to it as he was directed to do. God affords him a view from Pisgah of the Promised Land, but he dies before the Israelites enter it.

Lawrence's Aaron is a 32-year-old miner's checkweighman and secretary to the Miners Union in Beldover, the town based on Eastwood to which Will and Anna Brangwen move with their children at the end of *The Rainbow*. Aaron has a wife, Lottie, and three daughters, the oldest being eight at the opening of the novel and the youngest just nine months old. Yet he has a curiously neurasthenic detachment from his family, which he abandons on Christmas Eve. He wanders that night to Shottle House, where he meets Jim Bricknell, his sister Julia and their partners Josephine Ford and Robert Cunningham. He stays the night at Bricknell's invitation, but leaves early in the morning and moves to London. He rents a place in Bloomsbury and arranges for his wife to be given a monthly allowance. In order to support himself he plays the flute in an orchestra (his own version of Aaron's rod in the Bible). His former acquaintances see him again at a performance of Verdi's *Aïda*, an opera significantly set in Egypt. In the same box at the opera house is an author named Rawdon Lilly. Lilly has a Norwegian wife, Tanny, who joins them afterwards and goes with them to Bricknell's rooms in Adelphi. Lilly is an enigmatic figure whose relationship with his wife incorporates a good deal of freedom and independence on both sides. His central belief is that men need to stand alone and possess their souls in peace rather than relying on their women for a sense of security and identity.

Lilly has the same dislike of domesticity and politics as Aaron. When Jim Bricknell visits Lilly's cottage in Hampshire, Lilly actively denounces his visitor's love-lorn self-pity. Bricknell punches him and is asked to leave. Staying alone in a flat above Covent Garden while Tanny is visiting her family in Norway, Lilly sees Aaron collapse in the street and rescues him. Aaron has been seduced by Josephine Ford and claims that his health has collapsed as a result of giving in to her advances. When the doctor is unable to cure Aaron, Lilly massages his lower body with oil. This brings sleep and renewed health, but the two men argue soon afterwards and Lilly asks Aaron to leave. Aaron sees out the opera season, then returns to Beldover, but his confrontation with Lottie only reinforces his alienation from his marriage and family, and he escapes again.

This time he travels to Italy, arranging to meet Lilly at the home of Sir William Franks in Novara, but Lilly has decamped when he arrives. Aaron moves to Milan, where he meets two Englishmen, Francis Dekker and Angus Guest, who patronise him for a time, encouraging his flute playing and inviting him to travel with them to Florence. They soon tire of him there, but not before introducing him to a new group of ex-pats. He meets the Marchese Del Torre, otherwise known as Manfredi, and his American wife the Marchesa. They ask him back to their home, where he plays the flute and the Marchesa seems to fall under its spell, making Aaron feel the power returning to him. However, he is robbed in the street on his way home, and he feels that this – like his earlier illness – was brought on by the lowering of his defences. Despite this he returns to the Marchesa and asks her to become his lover. Their assignations hold a certain allure for Aaron, but ultimately they make him realise that what he wants from life is not 'kindness or love' but 'the fight': he writes a note to Sir William Franks in which he says: 'I want the world to hate me, because I can't bear the thought that it might love me' (*AR* 263). He tells the Marchesa that he wants to be friends, not lovers.

In the end he returns to Lilly, whom he has met by chance in the street in Florence. In a café, Lilly tells Aaron and his companions that he no longer believes in the ideal of love, brotherhood, unanimity and benevolence. He says he wants instead 'a sort of slavery': 'People are not *men*: they are insects and instruments, and their destiny is slavery. There are too many for me, and so what I think is ineffectual. But ultimately they will be brought to agree—after sufficient extermination—and then they will elect for themselves a proper and healthy and energetic slavery'. What he means by slavery is the voluntary 'committal of the life-issue of inferior beings to someone higher', though he notes that once the inferior beings have voluntarily given themselves to the higher, their commitment 'must be held fast by genuine power' (i.e. by military power). One of the group in the café, Levison, suggests that Lilly's idea represents 'the preposterous pretentiousness of a megalomaniac'. When he is challenged, Lilly denies that it is his 'gospel' and says that he would 'say the blank opposite with just as much fervour'. He then declares that 'every man is a sacred and holy individual, *never* to be violated', and that the only thing he hates, 'to the verge of madness', is '*bullying*' (*AR* 281–282). The conversation is halted by the explosion of an anarchist bomb, which destroys Aaron's flute.

Aaron and Lilly leave the café together, and at Lilly's instigation Aaron throws the remaining part of his flute into the River Arno. The loss seems to Aaron 'symbolistic': 'the bomb, the smashed flute, the end'. Aaron, thinking of making a new start, decides that he would prefer to commit himself to a man rather than seek social acceptance and money: 'he would rather give in to the little Lilly than to the beastly people of the world' (*AR* 290). In the final chapter, Lilly expresses a wish to leave Europe, since he feels caged in by it. He does not seek love and God and religion but to be himself. When Aaron asks what he should do, Lilly tells him that there are only two dynamic urges in life, love and power. A man wants to be either loved or obeyed. Lilly urges him to develop his 'innermost, integral unique self' (*AR* 295). He implores Aaron never to betray his soul's urges. Lilly says that the era of man as the lover and woman as the beloved is over, and in the reign of power 'woman must submit, but deeply, deeply submit. Not to any foolish fixed authority, not to any foolish and arbitrary will. But to something deep, deeper'. Aaron is profoundly sceptical, but Lilly insists that woman and man too must submit 'to the deep power-soul in the individual man' (*AR* 298). The novel ends with Aaron asking to whom he should submit, and Lilly replying 'Your soul will tell you' (*AR* 299).

Wright locates the central link between the biblical Aaron and Lawrence's character in the trajectory of escape from a moribund land: Aaron Sisson is said to be 'portrayed as escaping slavery to tradition and travelling through the wilderness of alienation towards a promised land of new ideas' (Wright 2000: 140). Wright admits, however, that 'the sheer density of biblical allusion ... threatens to engulf [Lawrence's] characters in contradictory and overdetermined significance'; what Lawrence does with religious language is 'develop it, complicate it, and alter its significance by reinscribing it in new senses and in different contexts' (Wright 2000: 143, 145). The doors in Aaron's house in Beldover admit draughts because 'the settling of the mines under the house made the doors not fit' (*AR* 7), and this sense of things not quite fitting properly becomes a motif in the novel. As Lilly states in Chapter VI ('Talk'): 'World coming to pieces bit by bit' (*AR* 58).

In the immediate post-war world of the novel, the things that once held society together are dissolving: for Aaron, marriage and family are meaningless, Christmas celebrations are a sham, and he no longer believes in his fellow workers. Religious faith, commitment to creating a meaningful life in society and solidarity with others have been replaced by a feeling of simmering unrest and violence. In the first paragraph we are told: 'A man felt the violence of the nightmare released now into the general air' (*AR* 5). The novel is framed by explosions: in the opening chapter, while she is decorating a Christmas tree, Aaron's daughter Millicent throws an old blue bauble that used to belong to her father into the air, and it smashes to pieces on the floor 'with a little splashing explosion' (*AR* 11), and in the penultimate chapter the anarchist's bomb breaks in on Lilly's sermonising with a resounding 'C R A S H !' (*AR* 282). Characters try to shore up their fractured identities in any way they can: Jim Bricknell, who feels he is 'going to pieces' (*AR* 52), craves love and gorges himself on bread in a darkly comical reference to the sacrament; other war veterans, like Captain Herbertson, are unconsciously compelled to re-live their war traumas, offloading tales of their horrific experiences oblivious to the state of depression they create in the listener;[5] older figures, like Sir William Franks and his wife, seek to preserve and perform outmoded identities, pinning medals on their jackets and keeping up a spurious sense of class superiority. Some constantly express their nightmares, while others experience disturbing dreams which emphasise the inescapable divisions in their identities.

The structure of the novel, with its dream-like interiorised narration, unresolved dialogue and snatchy transitions, leaves readers with the same vertiginous feeling of fragmented meaning and incoherence that the characters themselves experience. This is partly a consequence of its tortuous process of composition; Lawrence's interests and preoccupations shifted dramatically between October 1917 and June 1921, and he struggled to discern a way forward with the novel, looking to 'Divine Providence' (*3L* 594) to find new directions for his characters to follow. *Aaron's Rod* ends not with what Eagleton terms 'hysterical male chauvinism' and a 'strident rejection of sexual love for the male cult of power and impersonality', but with receptive scepticism and unrealised possibilities. Lilly's final speech to Aaron is described as an 'harangue' (*AR* 296). Though Aaron seems poised to turn again to Lilly, relying on him as he had done at a similar 'Low-water Mark' back in London, he remains sceptical of Lilly's ideas and of what it might mean to renounce having a goal in life and attend instead to the urges of one's own soul. Earlier in the novel, Sir William Franks says of Lilly: 'Never was such a man for crossing frontiers. Wonderful person, to be able to do it' (*AR* 137). Lilly, who is so hard to pin down, is planning to move to Naples for the winter, and beginning to think of leaving Europe altogether. In a novel in which people have lost any vital collective sense of belief or purpose, only the individual self and its urges matter; Aaron must understand the urges of his own soul, which will tell him to whom he must submit, if indeed he *does* wish to submit to what Lilly calls 'the heroic soul in a greater man' (*AR* 299).

I have suggested that the unresolved and puzzling qualities of *Aaron's Rod* can be ascribed to its over-determined use of biblical allusion and its dialogical structure, both of which are underwritten and compounded by the abrupt transitions in its structure. Lawrence frequently expressed frustration at being unable to advance the novel, suggesting at one stage that if all else failed he could 'jump him picaresque' (*3L* 602). It is helpful to view Aaron Sisson as a picaresque outlaw figure experiencing adventures and interacting with quasi-comical characters in his flight from place to place. Like Don Quixote, Aaron is gullible, hapless and prone to mistaking fantasies for realities.

Rawdon Lilly and his wife Tanny are obvious avatars for Lawrence and Frieda, but as was the case with Rupert Birkin in *Women in Love*, Lawrence uses Lilly not only to express his own dissatisfaction with the state of society and to suggest alternatives, but also to satirise and critique the autocratic and messianic qualities he recognised in himself. Lilly preaches the need for men to possess their own souls in isolation, knowing that they are alone: 'Eternally alone. And choosing to be alone' (*AR* 246). Aaron notes Lilly's self-sufficient qualities during the time when Lilly cares for him in the flat above Covent Garden. However, when Lilly criticises Jim Bricknell for needing a woman to love and accompany him, Tanny tells Lilly not to be spiteful: '*You* see that you have a woman always there, to hold *your* hand' (*AR* 81). Lilly seems to believe in his difference from others and to covet the role of the charismatic leader. We are told that 'he had a certain belief in himself as a saviour' (*AR* 73). Tanny, however, belittles him by telling him that he 'shouldn't play at little Jesus' (*AR* 85). Despite Lilly's insistence on male self-possession and his apparently strong self-belief, Aaron tells him: 'Why you're all the time grinding yourself against something inside you. You're never free. You're never content. You never stop chafing' (*AR* 103). Lilly is surprised by Aaron's criticism, but has to concede the point. In such ways we come to see Lilly not as the ideological centre of the novel, but as a 'funny customer' (*AR* 58), a restless figure whom Tanny says will 'always exaggerate' (*AR* 75) and whom Aaron accuses of 'word-splitting' (*AR* 105).

In contrast to *Aaron's Rod*, *Kangaroo* was written in a single, intensely creative period of around six weeks, between early June and 15 July 1922. Here Lawrence explores a political form of social reconstruction similar to that he had set out in his post-war writings. The Lawrence-figure in this novel is Richard Lovatt Somers, an English author who together with his German wife Harriett has arrived in Australia from India, having escaped Europe traumatised by his war-time persecution in England and disillusioned with the political situation in Italy. Following his arrival in Sydney, Somers is befriended by his neighbours Jack and Victoria Callcott, and by their brother-in-law, the Cornishman William James Trewhella (commonly known as 'Jaz'), who is married to Jack's sister. Jack has been a Captain in the war, and he is deeply involved in a secretive political group chiefly composed of ex-soldiers or 'Diggers'. Jack and Victoria invite Somers and Harriett to move in to the house Victoria owns and rents out in Mullumbimby, in the south, a house looking onto the Pacific Ocean which Lawrence modelled on the one which he and Frieda rented in Thirroul (where he wrote the novel).

Soon after their move Jack tells Somers about his dissatisfaction with Australian public life. He fears that with the weakening influence of Empire, Australia is vulnerable to foreign influence and he sees the Labour party and the socialists as selling out their country through their populist commitment to 'the Workers of the World' (*K* 90). He decides to confide in Somers, informing him about the Diggers group and explaining its hierarchical organisation. The group has been in existence for about 18 months. It is organised through clubs and lodges. Each club has a leader, a lieutenant and a secretary, and each lodge is composed of local leaders, lieutenants and secretaries, and has a chosen master, Jack (or lieutenant) and Teller (or secretary). Jack tells Somers that they have 'lodges in all the biggish places' and 'the masters of the lodges of the five states of Australia keep in touch, and they choose five masters who are called the Five, and these five agree among themselves which order they shall stand in' (*K* 93). The masters, Jacks and Tellers are all ranked in order of position. The overall leader is a lawyer named Benjamin Cooley (otherwise known as 'Kangaroo'). The Diggers group is presented as an athletics organisation. Later Jack tells Somers the clubs 'went in for boxing, wrestling, fencing, and knife-throwing, and revolver practice'; 'they had swimming and rowing squads, and rifle-ranges for rifle practice, and they had regular military training' (*K* 184). The military training is organised through squads of 20, each with a sergeant and a corporal. The squads are called 'Maggies', and members have a distinctive badge and wear a broad-brimmed white felt hat with a tuft of white feathers. There are around 1400 squads in the country, and 'more than a hundred clubs in New South Wales, and nearly as many in Victoria' (*K* 185). Somers soon realises that the group aims to bring about 'a sort of revolution and a seizing of political power' (*K* 93); it has 'roused some comment in the press' and Kangaroo is 'supposed to be working himself in as a future Prime Minister, with a party behind him that would make him absolute, a Dictator' (*K* 185).

The plot of the novel is structured around Somers's subsequent interactions with Kangaroo and his political rival, the socialist leader Willie Struthers. Somers is initially flattered by Kangaroo's interest in his writing and desire to involve him in the Diggers organisation. He is seduced by the leader's 'innocent charm' and 'extraordinary winsomeness' (*K* 118). Kangaroo explains that in order to 'remove physical misery as far as possible' and 'keep *order*' it is necessary to exert 'strong, just *power* from above' (*K* 111). He does not believe in education for everyone, but he does want people to lead 'full, substantial lives'. When Somers suggests that what Kangaroo envisages is 'a kind of benevolent tyranny', Kangaroo replies that the power of the leader would be 'so much circumscribed by the constitution I should establish', but he concedes that he *would* be a tyrant, or rather 'a patriarch, or a pope: representing as near as possible the wise, subtle spirit of life' (*K* 112).

Yet Somers also reacts against Kangaroo; he shares Jaz's doubts about his capability as a leader. Although Somers wants to be convinced and carried away, he challenges Kangaroo's belief that love is 'the only inspiration of creative activity' (*K* 133). He explains to Kangaroo his own belief in the 're-entry into us of the great God, who enters us from below, not from above'. He says that the lower self is 'the dark self, the phallic self, if you like'. Kangaroo is nonplussed and dismisses it by saying that he 'was never able to follow mysticism and metaphysics' (*K* 135). Jaz takes Somers to see Willie Struthers, the Socialist leader, at his office in Canberra House in Sydney. Struthers draws Somers out on his experience of the political situation in Italy. Somers says that when he left Europe the socialists seemed to be losing ground everywhere: 'Florence, Siena—hateful! The Fascisti risen up and taking on airs, all just out of a sort of spite' (*K* 194). Struthers's subsequent conversation with Somers is far more transactional than Somers's exchanges with Kangaroo. Struthers states that 'the socialistic and communal ideal is a great ideal, which will be fulfilled when men are ready' (*K* 196). His idea is to 'knock down the middle-class fetish and the middle-class medicine-men' while also building up 'real fellow-feeling between fellow men' (*K* 197). A new passional bond between men is to be the cornerstone of a new democracy. He asks Somers to help his cause in a practical way by editing 'a sincere, *constructive* Socialist paper'. Somers asks for time to think about it, but he is unsure of Struthers's appeal to human love and trust, since he has seen how they 'break down' (*K* 198): 'It all seemed so far from the dark God he wished to serve' (*K* 202).

The novel ends with threats and violent recrimination. Somers (repeating an idea first put to him by Jaz) suggests to Kangaroo that he should help to install Struthers as Prime Minister: 'let him nationalise all industries and resources, and confiscate property above a certain amount: and bring the world round his ears.

Then you step in like a saviour'. Kangaroo is deeply offended and says Somers is like 'a wayward child', '*perverse*' (*K* 207, 208). He tells Somers 'I could have you killed' (*K* 209), and suggests that it would be best for him to leave Australia. The exchange causes Somers to recall his persecution in England during the war years, when he and Harriett were hounded out of Cornwall by the authorities and he was subjected to humiliating medical examinations after the introduction of conscription. Kangaroo's insistence on the power of love makes him 'the mob: the *vengeful* mob'. Struthers is the same, but 'if the old ideal had still a logical leaf to put forth, it was this last leaf of communism'.

All Somers now wishes to do is 'to get clear' (*K* 265). Jaz gets him a ticket to attend a big meeting of Labour in Canberra Hall. The atmosphere at it is charged because the basic wage has been cut and the government is attacking the power of the unions, arresting union leaders for attacks on non-union workers. There are meetings in the morning and the evening. The evening event is 'wild' (*K* 307). Struthers speaks on 'the Solidarity of Labour', attacking 'the profit grabber' and suggesting that there should be 'no unearned incomes' (*K* 308–309). He stresses the need for mateship among the workers of the world, but when he gets to discussing the kinship of Australian wage-earners and workers of other nations, a large group of Diggers, led by Jack Callcott, counts him out. A mass brawl ensues, during which there is gunfire and an explosion. Kangaroo is shot. Somers goes to visit Kangaroo in hospital. He is very sick but continues to insist on the importance of love.[6] During a later visit, Kangaroo tells Somers that it is he who has killed him. He asks Somers to say that he loves him, but Somers says that he cannot. Only after Jack intervenes does he answer in the affirmative to the question 'You love our one and only Kangaroo all right, don't you, Mr Somers?' (*K* 337). Kangaroo dies shortly afterwards, and Somers and Harriett leave Australia bound for San Francisco.

Through Somers, Lawrence explores his equivocal attraction to establishing close bonds with others and developing forms of collective action. The Diggers group is similar in some respects to the 'great league of comrades' which he called upon Americans to establish throughout the United States, but Lawrence's imaginative exploration of it as a political organisation is informed by deep scepticism. Somers is drawn to the impulse in both Kangaroo and Willie Struthers to find a common purpose and make a fresh start, and he is momentarily attracted to the idea of becoming a figurehead for their causes, but his lack of interest in politics and his temperamental resistance to merging himself with others cause him to keep clear and eventually to leave Australia. The novel dwells on the seductive appeal of the leaders through the flattery, friendly repartee and visionary rhetoric of Kangaroo, and the impassioned political discourse of Struthers, but it also shows how Kangaroo's personal appeal to Somers masks an underlying threat that links his movement to the violent actions of the unleashed mob implementing government rule in England during the war, while Struthers's more impersonal appeal is based on hatred of the existing system and a desire to destroy it rather than any more constructive belief in a new State. Somers rejects both options. He realises that his own interest in establishing bonds between men based on ancient religious impulses – 'The mystery of lordship. The mystery of innate, natural, sacred priority. The other mystic relationship between men, which democracy and equality try to deny and obliterate' (*K* 107) – is inimical to both Kangaroo's mateship ideal and Struthers's socialist pragmatism.

In *The Plumed Serpent*, Lawrence imagines a religious revolution of the kind envisaged in very vague terms by Somers. This novel traces the establishment of a religion in Mexico which displaces the Catholic Church and restores the pre-Christian Aztec gods and their associated forms of authority. His central protagonist this time is female. Kate Leslie is a 40-year-old widow with two grown children who has travelled to Mexico with her American cousin, Owen Rhys, and his friend (or partner) Bud Villiers. She is Irish and has links to Cornwall, so like Jaz Trewhella she has within her the Celtic spirit which Lawrence felt acted as an antidote to modernity in both its modern technological sense and its commitment to political democracy and religious conservatism. Kate divorced the father of her two children to marry Joachim Leslie, a recently-deceased agitator for Irish independence whom she comes to see as having needlessly sacrificed himself for his political cause. Kate's age is important, since Lawrence viewed 40 as heralding the change of life.[7] While Owen and Bud enjoy Mexico as a tourist experience, getting a thrill out of the abject spectacle of a bullfight and enjoying the sense of social tension, raucousness and simmering violence in Mexico City even when they feel targeted as American 'gringos', Kate is at once appalled by these things and deeply drawn to the underlying instability of the country because it is so different from the safety and predictability of the life she has known.

At a tea party in Tlacolula hosted by the elderly widow of an English ambassador, we see conservative Americans including a judge and a major complaining about the disorder in Mexico and lamenting the impending inauguration of a 'new Labor President' (*PS* 35), Sócrates Tomás Montes. Also present at the party are General Cipriano Viedma, whom Kate had first met when he assisted her in leaving the bullfight, and an eminent Mexican historian and archaeologist named Ramón Carrasco. Cipriano had known the brother of Joachim Leslie during his time at Oxford. Their hostess has a collection of Aztec objects, including obsidian knives. Kate tells Ramón that she finds Aztec things 'oppressive' and sees 'no hope in them'; he agrees that they '*are* oppressive' but says 'Perhaps the Aztecs never asked for hope' (*PS* 39). He tells her that she is 'very clever' to realise that revolutions in Mexico always culminate in 'killing and death' (*PS* 40).

Soon afterwards Kate reads an article in the English page of a newspaper that tells of ferment in the village of Sayula in Jalisco on the Lake of Sayula (based on

Chapala, where Lawrence wrote the first version of the novel). Local women washing clothes in the lake witness a man of great stature emerging naked from it and stealing some of their husbands' items to cover himself. When he is challenged, he announces that the clothing will be given back to them. He states: 'Your gods are ready to return to you. Quetzalcoatl and Tlaloc, the old gods, are minded to come back to you' (*PS* 57). The article mentions that Ramón Carrasco has a hacienda in the vicinity of Sayula.

Kate is invited to Ramón's house in Tlalpam, where she meets Cipriano again and learns more about the two men. Cipriano tells her that he was sent to England by his late godfather, Bishop Severn, with the idea of his becoming a priest, but he felt alienated from the English forms of religion, and on his return the godfather's hacienda was appropriated and sold during the revolution. Cipriano had never married because he was affected by his promise to his godfather to become a priest. He tells Kate he is 'half a priest and half a soldier' (*PS* 70). Ramón had graduated from Columbia University and is married to a Catholic, Doña Carlota; their two sons, Cyprian and Pedro, are studying in California. Cipriano is a pure Zapotec Indian, while Ramón is 'almost pure Spaniard, but most probably he has the blood of Tlaxcalan Indians in his veins as well' (*PS* 64).

Owen leaves Mexico, but Kate decides to stay. On Cipriano's recommendation, she travels with Bud Villiers by Pullman train and boat to Orilla. On their arrival, a man who wades out to their boat informs Kate that the lake belongs to the old Gods of Mexico and she must offer a tribute to Quetzalcoatl. When Kate asks why the man wants the tribute when it is for Quetzalcoatl, he answers that he is 'Quetzalcoatl's man' (*PS* 91). When she enquires about the Men of Quetzalcoatl, the German manager of the hotel she stays in says that it is 'another try-on of the bolshevists. They thought socialism needed a god, so they're going to fish him out of this lake' (*PS* 102). He informs Kate that they sing songs, but in his view it is 'another dodge for national-socialism, that's all': 'They say Don Ramón Carrasco is at the back of it. Maybe he wants to be the next President—or maybe he's aiming higher, and wants to be the first Mexican Pharoah' (*PS* 103).

One evening shortly after her arrival in Sayula she hears 'a pulse-like thudding of the drum, strangely arresting on the night air'. It reminds Kate of 'the drums and the wild singing of the Red Indians in Arizona and New Mexico', and she instantly feels 'that timeless, primeval passion of the prehistoric races' (*PS* 117). She goes to see what is happening and is given a leaflet with a song of Quetzalcoatl printed on it; the sheet has an emblem on it, 'an eagle within the ring of a serpent that has its tail in its mouth' (*PS* 118). Kate is 'at once attracted and repelled' (*PS* 122) by the spectacle, but she stays to hear a man speak of the return of Quetzalcoatl. They sing the hymn from the sheet. The men dance in circles around the fire, and eventually women are invited in. Kate is drawn into the dance: 'She felt her sex and her womanhood caught up and identified in the slowly revolving ocean of nascent life' (*PS* 131).

It is 10 days before Kate hears from Ramón, but then he asks whether he can bring his wife to see Kate. Doña Carlota is 'an intense, almost exalted Catholic' (*PS* 156) who is utterly opposed to the Men of Quetzalcoatl. When Kate goes to see them at their hacienda in Jamiltepec, she learns the full extent of Ramón's role as leader of the movement, and of the involvement of Cipriano as his general. Ramón oversees the creation by local peons of the ceremonial sarapes and the symbol, which is 'The bird within the sun' (*PS* 171). He writes and prints the hymns of Quetzalcoatl, which are distributed throughout Mexico. Kate witnesses another gathering around the drum, this time with Ramón presiding. He declares: 'I am the Morning and the Evening Star, and lord of the day and the night. By the power that is put in my left hand, and the power that I grasp in my right, I am lord of the two ways' (*PS* 179). The salute of the Men of Quetzalcoatl sees the right hand raised into the air and the left hand lowered to the earth, to signify the coming together of earth and air, the Morning Star and the Evening Star. The next day Cipriano arrives. He tells Kate that he would like to marry her, but Kate says 'I don't think I shall *ever* marry again' (*PS* 187).

Although Ramón wishes to remain free from Mexican politics, the Quetzalcoatl movement becomes so powerful that he is caught up in revolutionary fervour. The new President causes unrest by imposing his socialist principles, and the Church reacts against him, led by a mysterious militia called 'the Knights of Cortés and a certain "black" faction' (*PS* 247). Kate's new landlord is 'a great Fascista' and 'the reactionary Knights of Cortés held him in great esteem' (*PS* 308). The German manager of the hotel in Orilla had correctly suggested that the President's socialist cause would be linked to the revival of the old Aztec gods. Ramón wishes to establish the Quetzalcoatl religion as the only religion in Mexico, and he hopes that other countries will follow suit in re-establishing their own ancient gods so that 'the First Men of every people' can form 'a Natural Aristocracy of the World' (*PS* 248). When the 'Holy Images' (*PS* 262) are thrown out of a church in Mexico City the Catholic Church tries to suppress the Quetzalcoatl movement, but the President prevents a violent crackdown. Ramón, wishing to avoid bloodshed, arranges a meeting with the Bishop of the West, but when he suggests that a truly 'catholic' church could accommodate the old Mexican gods the Bishop refuses to listen. Ramón informs him that he intends to remove the holy images from the church at Sayula, burn them and replace them with the image of Quetzalcoatl.

Things move swiftly from this point on. The holy images are removed and burnt, and the church temporarily closed. During a visit Kate makes to Jamiltepec, the hacienda is attacked by a former employee of Ramón acting in league with his lover in the household. The Knights of Cortés are implicated in the attack. Ramón is stabbed and almost killed, but Kate saves him by firing at one of the assailants. Seven men are killed and others are taken into custody by the army, under the command of Cipriano. Kate is deeply shaken by the experience. She is now lauded as the saviour of Ramón and drawn further into his movement. She comes to see in Cipriano 'the ancient phallic mystery, the ancient god-devil of the male Pan' (*PS* 311). Ramón marries them in his guise as the living Quetzalcoatl. Since Cipriano is the First Man of Huitzilopochtli, the Aztec god of war, Kate becomes 'The bride of Huitzilopochtli' (*PS* 328).

At the re-opening of the church in Sayula, Doña Carlota speaks out against what she sees as the sacrilegious preaching of her husband. She collapses and dies soon afterwards. Ramón's sons, who are alienated from him, decide to return to the United States. Cipriano takes a more active military role in the Quetzalcoatl movement, instilling discipline into the army of men who serve under him. He becomes the living Huitzilopochtli, and he presses Kate to become the goddess Malintzi in their new Mexican pantheon. Cipriano takes charge of a church gathering in Sayula at which the two instigators of the attack on Jamiltepec, the man and his lover, have their necks broken by guards and their bodies are thrown in quick lime. Of the four remaining conspirators, one is saved in the name of Malintzi and the other three are blindfolded and stabbed through the heart by Cipriano.

Kate is initially 'shocked and depressed' (*PS* 387) by the killings. Yet, after a period of reflection, she agrees to become Malintzi. Ramón remarries a young Mexican woman named Teresa. Although Kate initially despises Teresa's subjection to Ramón, thinking of her as the 'harem type' (*PS* 397) engaged in 'self-prostitution' (*PS* 399), and she hates the thought of entering into marriage to Cipriano on the same terms, long passages in which she reflects on the 'grimalkin women' (*PS* 439) of her own age back home, who have developed their own egos only in order to be 'looking for [male] prey that became scarcer and scarcer' (*PS* 438), end in her telling herself that she must not 'recoil against Cipriano and Ramón' (*PS* 439). Kate comes to see that legal marriage to Cipriano will entail a form of self-realisation which far exceeds the purely personal relationships of which she has grown weary. She marries him and moves into his house, the Villa Aragón. A religious coup takes place. Cipriano asserts military control over forces allied to the Church, and President Montes 'declared the old Church illegal in Mexico' (*PS* 420). At the end of the novel, Kate has made plans to return to England to see her children and her mother. Ramón and Cipriano are prepared to let her leave, but they want her to stay. She is forced to admit that she does not want to go away from Cipriano, but she remains deeply conflicted. Her last words to Cipriano are: 'You won't let me go!' (*PS* 444).

The Plumed Serpent is certainly an oppressive and haunting novel. Its power comes in part from the disorientating shifts between different voices and perspectives in the opening chapters, and our increasing closeness to Kate Leslie as she hears (and reads) the hymns and songs of Quetzalcoatl, and the opinions of Ramón and Cipriano, and as she vacillates between disgust at Mexico and the Mexicans, and shock and depression at (and resistance to) the Quetzalcoatl movement, and deep fascination with them. Barbara Mensch refers to Kate's 'sometimes cynical and always independent view' (Mensch 1991: 212). Kate reacts against the bullfight and the crowd's collective enthralment at the spectacle of mutilation and death; she is similarly angered by the sight of a young 'urchin', or 'brat' (*PS* 218), torturing a young bird on the lake by her home in Sayula. She claims at one point to 'loathe the very sound of Quetzalcoatl and Huitzilopochtli': 'Horrible, really, both Ramón and Cipriano. And they want to put it over me, with their high-flown bunk, and their Malintzi' (*PS* 371). At times her disdain for the movement and reluctance to participate in it and to marry Cipriano and become Malintzi call to mind the very different critique of the religion, and of Ramón's role in it, advanced by Doña Carlota and their sons. Yet unlike Doña Carlota, Kate capitulates to Cipriano largely on the strength of her disillusionment with her life in Europe and her growing hatred of Western ideas of the self and political action.

As Neil Roberts notes, 'one reason for the novel's unpopularity is that it seems to enact a narrative coercion on the heroine to act in violation of a conclusion responsibly reached' (Roberts 2004: 159). Lawrence's prose is most troubling when it captures Kate in the process of capitulation. For example, when she first conceives of being married to Cipriano and recognises in him 'the ancient phallic mystery, the ancient god-devil of the male Pan', she realises that he will not woo and sees how 'the power of his blood rose in him, the dark aura steamed from him like a cloud pregnant with power, like thunder, and rose like a whirlwind that rises suddenly in the twilight and raises a great pliant column ... clear between heaven and earth': 'Ah! and what a mystery of prone submission, on her part, this huge erection would imply! Submission absolute, like the earth under the sky' (*PS* 311). The phallic rhetoric here works, in Roberts's phrase, 'to will the direction of the story' (Roberts 2004: 160). After Ramón has married them, and before she agrees to become his legal wife, she reconsiders Cipriano in the light of his killing of the prisoners and feels that his demonic male 'exertion of pure, awful will' is both 'terrible' and 'wonderful'; she questions where woman comes 'in this terrible interchange of will' (*PS* 387). Yet soon her reflection on the need to renounce her old ideas of individuality causes her to set aside her objections and become his wife.

One problem here is that identified by Roberts: while the 'discourse on individuality' is an important aspect of 'Kate's development through the encounter with cultural difference', it 'becomes manipulative' when it is 'conscripted to the insistence that Kate is incomplete specifically without Cipriano' (Roberts 2004: 163). Another problem resides in the manner of Kate's acceptance of him. Rather late in the novel we are told of her upbringing in 'a proud old family' which had instilled in her a belief in 'the English, Germanic idea of the *intrinsic* superiority of the hereditary aristocrat'. Kate's belief that she is an individual set apart from others, which causes her to resist the Mexican belief in 'blood-unison' – '*Blood is one blood. We are all of one blood-stream*' (*PS* 416) – and refuse assimilation into the Quetzalcoatl movement, ironically also works to overcome her objection to the atrocities Cipriano commits. She can clearly see herself as part of the 'Natural Aristocracy of the World' which

Ramón hopes to establish. She tells herself that Cipriano is 'of the gods, and so am I. Why should I judge him!': 'What do I care if he kills people?' (*PS* 394).

These moments of capitulation are so disconcerting precisely because we closely inhabit the modes of thought which lead up to them, and we know that Kate still retains her powerful individuality and capacity to detach herself from Cipriano and Mexico. The novel is haunting because of the complexities and contradictions in its characters, and the ethical issues it poses but does not seek to resolve. Ramón is at once the urbane intellectual who abhors politics and bullying, is committed to fostering a new iteration of an older religious sensibility in his countrymen, and accommodates to some degree the differences of Carlota and his sons, *and* the messianic zealot who oversees the creation of the Quetzalcoatl movement and its displacement of Catholicism at a national level on his sheer force of will. The Oxford-educated Cipriano is suavely attentive to Kate when he encounters her as a foreign stranger leaving the bullfight in the opening chapter, faithful to the memory of his beloved godfather to the point where he has steadfastly refused to marry, and yet the 'power of his blood' commands submission in Kate, and he is capable of executing prisoners in a quasi-sacrificial manner in the guise of the living Huitzilopochtli. In his role as a General serving the government, Cipriano hunts down and kills nameless hundreds of bandits and revolutionaries; while this does not detract from the horror we rightly feel at his killing of the three prisoners who sought to murder Ramón, it might just cause us to reflect on the continuities and differences between his actions as a General and as the living Huitzilopochtli.

Willard Johnson and D. H. Lawrence at the Pyramid of the Sun at Teotihuacán, Mexico, 3 April 1923. University of Nottingham, Manuscripts and Special Collections, La Wb 1/26.

Abdulla Al-Dabbagh refers to Ramón and Cipriano, and even Kate herself, as fascists, and suggests that the novel itself 'fulfils Lawrence's desire to create a fascist movement that is completely to his liking' (Al-Dabbagh 2011: 55). Yet Lawrence's ambition in writing the novel was quite different. As Michael Bell has noted, Lawrence's reading of W. H. Prescott's *The History of the Conquest of Mexico* (1843) would have alerted him to the curious fact that the Aztecs mistook Hernán Cortés, the leader of the Spanish conquistadors, for their returned god Quetzalcoatl, which may have contributed to the ease with which his few hundred soldiers overcame an empire. Bell observes that the 'ancient religion of Mexico was not only perhaps exploited at the time of the conquest, it was then systematically extirpated and replaced by Christianity'; Lawrence felt that 'this whole story of the conquest called out for utopian reversal', and the novel can be read as tracing 'a systematic reversal of the process of the conquest'. While the leadership ideal in *The Plumed Serpent*, then, 'inevitably invites comparison now with the subsequent development of European fascism', Bell suggests that Lawrence's 'utopian concern at the time was directed towards the psychic consequences of an earlier cultural catastrophe brought about by European imperialism' (Bell 1992: 185–186). From the perspectives of Ramón and Cipriano, the Quetzalcoatl movement is a popular uprising for the Mexican peon, conceived in opposition to the Catholic Church and the fascist Knights of Cortés.

The novel is never, however, simply aligned to a single perspective, and in Kate's case her perspective constantly shifts and becomes particularly unstable as she contemplates taking up a role in the Quetzalcoatl religion and spending the rest of her life with Cipriano. Despite the fact that Lawrence changed the first version of the novel – now known as *Quetzalcoatl* – to remove Kate's determination to leave Mexico,[8] she never unequivocally decides to stay. Towards the end of the novel she tells herself that she does not '*altogether want*' Ramón and Cipriano: '*I want myself to myself*' (*PS* 443). Although *The Plumed Serpent* explores how the reinvention of an ancient religion might captivate the people through ritual and symbolism, and how power can be consolidated through executions, it is far more than a simple fascist fantasy because it foregrounds disillusionment with both socialist and fascist politics, and like *Aaron's Rod* and *Kangaroo*, it subjects its central charismatic leader-figures to criticism, suggesting the fatuity of any movement that relies for its authority on an assertion of will. Kate recognises the 'steady, urgent, efficient *will* which had to be exerted all the time. Everything was kept going by a heavy exertion of will. If once the will of the master broke, everything would break, and ruin would overtake the place almost at once' (*PS* 406). In 'Blessed Are the Powerful', one of the essays Lawrence wrote at the Kiowa Ranch in the summer of 1925 for inclusion in *Reflections on the Death of a Porcupine*, he stated: 'A will-to-power seems to work out as bullying. And bullying is something despicable and detestable' (*RDP* 321). If the author's subconscious attraction to male power and authority is evident in Kate's capitulation to Cipriano's phallic strength and her acceptance of the brutal executions as of little consequence, Lawrence the conscious artist never simply endorses these things: the novel's structure forces us to see and understand them in relation to Kate's uncertainties, her tiredness with 'home', and the omnipresence of political instability, violence and death in Mexico that forms the backdrop to the novel from the opening bullfight on.

In an engaging re-evaluation of Lawrence and fascism, Nidesh Lawtoo argues that the value of what he terms Lawrence's 'political novels' resides in the diagnostic insight they offer into the individual's drive to renounce individuality in favour of the 'affective contagion' (Lawtoo 2020: 289, 300) of mass movements. Lawtoo argues that 'by dramatising the mimetic *pathos* that flows from authoritarian leaders to crowds and back, Lawrence's political novels urge contemporary readers to reflect critically *on* – and thus *contra* [to] – (new) fascist pathologies that have recently returned to cast a shadow on the Western Demos' (Lawtoo 2020: 289). Lawtoo draws particular attention to Lawrence's interest in crowd psychology. He detects an 'escalating progression' in Lawrence's engagement with the masses, from a 'critique of the mass-spirit for "the horror" it generated during the Great War' in *Aaron's Rod*, to 'a more ambivalent differentiation between a condemnation of the "mob's" lack of direction and a more positive evaluation of leaders who provide the "mass" with a direction in *Kangaroo*', to 'an active promotion of a type of authoritarian politics ... in *The Plumed Serpent*' (Lawtoo 2020: 303). Yet Lawrence's depiction of Kate Leslie's resistance to the Quetzalcoatl religion, as well as her attraction to it and her willingness and desire at times to renounce her old identity and become a part of it, are said to reveal his 'affective understanding of fascist power'. Lawtoo describes Lawrence as 'an acute diagnostician of the power of leaders' (Lawtoo 2020: 304) who is particularly alert to the ritualistic 'non-verbal forms of mimetic communication mobilised by aspirational fascist leaders' (Lawtoo 2020: 305).

Bertrand Russell described Lawrence as 'a sensitive would-be despot who got angry with the world because it would not instantly obey' (Russell 1968: 23). Lawtoo's essay suggests that if the author had autocratic tendencies and at times grew impatient with those who would not immediately accede to his ideas, his fiction looked at things from the other perspective, analysing the tactics used by leaders to encourage assent and the processes through which the individual either accepts or resists the call of the would-be despot or dictator. What Lawtoo identifies in *The Plumed Serpent* is its open-ended, relativistic structure, which at once involves readers in Kate's attraction to the Quetzalcoatl movement and allows them to reflect critically on it through her persistent scepticism as a female

European outsider. It is no coincidence that the essays in which Lawrence espoused the importance of relativism to the novel form were written in the summer of 1925, after Lawrence had finished rewriting *The Plumed Serpent*, and during that final period he spent living at the Kiowa Ranch. In 'Morality and the Novel', he writes: 'The novel is the highest complex of subtle interrelatedness that man has discovered. Everything is true in its own time, place, circumstance, and untrue outside of its own place, time, circumstance' (*STH* 172). Bell refers to the 'consciously speculative relativity' that replaced the 'relational ontology' (Bell 1992: 149) of *The Rainbow* and *Women in Love*. In *Aaron's Rod*, Rawdon Lilly can argue with equal conviction for an authoritarian State led by a superior being which exterminates insubordinates and for the 'blank opposite' (*AR* 282), the sacred inviolability of the individual and a hatred of bullying. Aaron is drawn to Lilly but retains the capacity to criticise him. In *Kangaroo*, Somers – who is attracted by turns to both Benjamin Cooley and Willie Struthers, but ultimately commits to neither – reflects that 'everything is relative': 'even relativity is only relative. Relative to the absolute' (*K* 280). And we leave the deeply conflicted Kate Leslie at that moment of decision and suspense. The impulse in the novels to question, probe and critique is at the opposite extreme to the letters Lawrence wrote to Bertrand Russell in the summer of 1915, and his suggestion that 'one must proclaim "the Truth" to the multitude' (Russell 1968: 21).

The novels are risk-taking thought-adventures rather than dogmatic works of political propaganda. They pose serious questions: What might it mean to be an individual in the modern world? How can one be an individual and still have relationships? What seismic changes in public life might facilitate self-realisation on both an individual and a collective level? And what consequences might these changes have on a national and global scale? These were questions that had occupied Lawrence since the end of the war, and particularly since he left England for Italy in November 1919. His experiences in New Mexico had allowed him to glimpse forms of religious expression in which he perceived a breaking down of the modern boundaries between self and community, God and nature. Yet despite the deep satisfaction and fulfilment he discovered in his last period living with Frieda at the Kiowa Ranch, and the sense of interrelatedness to all things that he wrote about in *Reflections on the Death of a Porcupine*, he must have realised that what lay ahead on his return to Europe was a yet more stark confrontation with all those old values and attitudes that he had criticised before he left Sicily for Ceylon, and which in the intervening years he had sought to leave behind, both literally, through contact with other cultures, and imaginatively, through the exploration in his fiction of new political and religious possibilities.

Notes

1 See *2L* 359 (20 June 1915).
2 The outline of 'Philosophy of Social Reconstruction' and Lawrence's comments on it are transcribed in Moore (1948: 77–96).
3 See *RDP* 68.
4 See *PFU* 114.
5 See *AR* 112–118.
6 See *K* 325.
7 See *6L* 36–37 (14–15 April 1927).
8 See *Q* 303: 'She didn't want to stay longer at Las Yemas. She felt a certain tenderness for Cipriano, but she almost hated Ramón. Teresa too. But particularly Ramón'.

8

Collaboration and Creativity: Private Publication and Mass-Market Polemics

On 21 September 1925, Lawrence and Frieda sailed out of New York aboard the S. S. Resolute, bound for Southampton. Lawrence consoled himself for the grim prospect of autumnal England with thoughts of settling in the Mediterranean. His ultimate plan in Europe was 'to begin to move south' (*5L* 305) to find the warmer and drier climate which was so necessary for his health. When he had been examined in the American Hospital in Mexico City back in March and diagnosed as suffering from tuberculosis, one doctor had told Frieda to take him back to the ranch in New Mexico, since the dryness of the air and the altitude would aid his recovery. Remission was now the most he could hope for. In private the doctor informed Frieda that Lawrence had only 'A year or two at the most' (Lawrence 1934: 167).

Lawrence's career prospects would also have seemed rather bleak. He had achieved literary success in England before the war, but sales of his works were modest. The prosecution of *The Rainbow* in November 1915, and the adverse publicity it generated, made publishers wary of his work and plunged him into poverty for the remainder of the war years and its immediate aftermath. Thereafter his fortunes had rallied. In his early career he had relied upon the help and support of Ford Madox Hueffer and Edward Garnett, but when he signed the contract with Methuen for *The Rainbow* he acquired J. B. Pinker as his literary agent. He eventually parted company with Pinker in December 1919, partly because of his dissatisfaction with Pinker's lack of interest in placing his work in the United States.[1] In February 1920, with an eye on targeting a transatlantic readership, he asked his American friend Robert Mountsier to act as his agent; Mountsier took up the role in the summer of 1920. In April 1921 Lawrence employed the literary agency Curtis Brown to oversee the placing of his work in England.

Lawrence's first real commercial success came in the United States. Early in his career he had earned very little money from sales of his books in America, but from the spring of 1920, when he made Thomas Seltzer the main publisher of his books there, the situation greatly improved. The first book of his which Seltzer

The Life of the Author: D. H. Lawrence, First Edition. Andrew Harrison.

published was the play *Touch and Go* in June 1920; this was followed in November by *Women in Love*, which was privately published by subscription in an edition of 1250 copies. Seltzer worked hard to publicise Lawrence's work and to maximise sales. He published five books by Lawrence in 1921, three in 1922, and six in 1923.

In July 1922 Seltzer's New York offices were raided by John Sumner, the successor to Anthony Comstock as executive secretary of the New York Society for the Suppression of Vice. Seltzer successfully defended *Women in Love*, and two other books, against charges of obscenity. As a result he issued a trade edition of 3000 copies of *Women in Love* in October 1922, which swiftly sold out, necessitating a second printing in early November. There were further reprintings in December 1922 and March and August 1923. On 17 December 1922, a little over three months after Lawrence's first arrival in the United States, he told Catherine Carswell that the novel was 'going now into 15,000' (*4L* 363). There was even some talk of Seltzer selling the film rights to the novel for in excess of $10,000, though this came to nothing.[2] The timing of the commercial success was perfect, since Lawrence was able to live in the United States solely on his American earnings. As John Worthen notes, between 1922 and 1924 'Lawrence made more regular money than he had ever earned before' (Worthen 1996: 107). Seltzer's belief in Lawrence threw into sharp relief Mountsier's less appreciative response to some of Lawrence's non-fiction and to his more ideas-driven fiction, in consequence of which Lawrence split with him in February 1923.

Unfortunately, Seltzer got embroiled in a further lengthy legal case as a consequence of the fallout from the trial in 1922. Justice John Ford of the New York State Supreme Court, who had been horrified to find his daughter reading a copy of *Women in Love*, reinstituted proceedings against the three books, and while *Women in Love* was exempted from the case Seltzer was indicted for publishing unclean books and a trial by jury was organised. Seltzer was released on bail for $1000.[3] The case was finally settled in 1925 when remaining copies of the other two books were withdrawn from sale and the plates destroyed. The case plunged Seltzer into serious financial difficulties which would soon lead to bankruptcy. Lawrence learned of Seltzer's situation sometime in the spring of 1924. He ultimately lost a lot of money in unpaid royalties as a result of Seltzer's insolvency.

Lawrence had to act decisively in order to protect his future earnings. In January 1924 he asked the New York branch of Curtis Brown to take charge of his work in the United States. Through his agent, he arranged for Knopf to publish the American edition of Maurice Magnus's *Memoirs of the Foreign Legion* (containing his lengthy memoir of the author). In the same month that this volume was published, January 1925, Lawrence decided to place his next book, *St. Mawr*, with Knopf too.[4] During the week he spent in New York in September 1925, prior to his departure, Lawrence met Seltzer and his wife Adele; he described them as 'dangling by a single thread, over the verge of bankruptcy' (*5L* 305–306). He also arranged to meet Alfred and Blanche Knopf at their plush offices on Fifth Avenue. His new publishers seemed 'really sound and reliable' (*5L* 306) and he told Blanche: 'I am glad I know you and Knopf – it feels like having something safe behind me – a feeling I've never had before, in America' (*5L* 303).

Lawrence, however, knew that his future prospects for earnings with Knopf would be nothing like as bright as the few bumper years he had enjoyed with Seltzer. Those years had been unusually remunerative, but they had also offered Lawrence the kind of supportive and collaborative context for his writing which was so important for him. Seltzer believed in Lawrence the man as well as the writer. His efforts to market Lawrence's work extended to publishing the foreword to *Women in Love* as a standalone leaflet advertising the novel, and to including colour illustrations by Lawrence's South African contact Jan Juta in *Sea and Sardinia*, and printing designs on the dust jackets of his books by Lawrence and his friends Knud Merrild, Kai Gøtzsche and Dorothy Brett. In addition to offsetting Lawrence's feelings of isolation and persecution, collaborations of this kind helped him to feel part of a creative community in which his art was appreciated and his ideas taken seriously (even when people were nonplussed by them or when they begged to differ).

While some collaborations (such as 'The Rainbow Books and Music' project with Philip Heseltine, his short-lived involvement with John Middleton Murry in running the journals *The Signature* and the *Adelphi*, and his abortive project to write a fiction based on the early experiences of Mabel Dodge Sterne in New Mexico) failed for practical reasons or because Lawrence was too outspoken, he never stopped seeking them out. Around April 1925 he wrote a poem entitled 'Change of Life' in response to one Mabel sent him about the menopause; 44 lines of it either repeat or closely echo lines from her poem.[5] Perhaps his most important collaboration in this period was his co-authoring of a novel with the Australian nurse and author M. L. (Mollie) Skinner, whom he met during his brief stay in Perth on his first arrival in Australia. Lawrence rewrote Skinner's 'The House of Ellis' between September and November 1923 and it was published as a joint work under the title *The Boy in the Bush* in August 1924. In December 1924, at Skinner's request, he wrote a Preface to her next novel, *Black Swans*, though she took his advice and did not use it.[6] In December 1925 he edited her short story 'The Hand' after she submitted it to the *Adelphi*; it was published in May 1926.[7] The guidance and help he offered to her were repeated in his dealings with the aspiring American author Kyle Crichton, who interviewed Lawrence at the Kiowa Ranch in August 1925.[8] Lawrence kept up a brief but supportive correspondence with Crichton, reading and offering advice on a short story he had written.[9]

We can judge Lawrence's mood in the wake of leaving Seltzer by considering the essay 'Accumulated Mail', which he wrote around 18 April 1925 and sent to the New York branch of Curtis Brown to be forwarded to Knopf for inclusion in a compilation of writings by authors who had published with the company over the 10 years since it had been founded. Here Lawrence describes his recent return to the Kiowa Ranch, where he found a large pile of letters awaiting his attention. Among them was a letter from a woman in Nottingham boasting that she had prevented a young woman she found reading *Sons and Lovers* from finishing the book, which was 'so interesting', but 'cannot be mentioned in polite society' (*RDP* 239–240). Another letter was sent by a man in New York who had clearly read Norman Douglas's pamphlet *D. H. Lawrence and Maurice Magnus: A Plea for Better Manners* and asked Lawrence to explain how he had '*come to be profiting by a work that is not your own*' (*RDP* 240). Following Magnus's suicide in November 1920 Lawrence had agreed to write an introduction to Magnus's account of his war-time experiences to get it into print. Douglas took issue in his pamphlet with Lawrence's portrayal in it of both himself and Magnus; he ascribed what he saw as an unfair attack on Magnus to the petty resentment felt by Lawrence regarding Magnus's failure to repay money Lawrence had lent him. Douglas also accused Lawrence of profiteering from a work that he had no rights to publish, since rights to all Magnus's literary effects passed on his death to Douglas as his appointed literary executor. Lawrence would eventually address all of Douglas's accusations in a letter that was published in the *New Statesman* on 20 February 1926. The letter from the man in New York had begun: '*I am afraid you may consider this letter an impudence*'. Lawrence commented that if the correspondent really *was* afraid, then 'what colossal impertinence to carry on to two sheets, and then post his impudence to me' (*RDP* 240).

In the midst of these pointed reminders of the hostility to him and his work in both England and the United States, there was a letter informing him that eight high school students in Trenton, New Jersey had been asked by their teacher to select 'some known man, whom they accept as a sort of guide' and they had chosen Lawrence; the letter requested that he send them 'a letter of encouragement or of help in the battle of life' (*RDP* 239). In the essay Lawrence states his willingness to respond, but wonders what he could possibly say to them. He imagines replying in the following manner: '*My dear young People: I daren't advise you to do as I do, for it's no fun, writing unpopular books. And I won't advise you, for your own sakes, to do as I say. For in details I'm sure I'm wrong. My dear young people, perhaps I need your encouragement more than you need mine*' (*RDP* 239). Fortunately the actual letter he wrote to them has survived. It is addressed to 'My dear Eight' and Lawrence tells them that they must be 'a bold eight, to choose a name which everybody seems to think himself entitled to throw a little mud at!' He says that he places 'courage – courage to live and know life and accept a true lead, as highest' and continues:

> The machinery of the world goes on without pause, and we have to avail ourselves of the world's complex mechanisms: apparently we have to become part of the machine. But it's only an appearance[.] Because all the

> time the soul can be moving on, into strange places that we have not yet opened up, opening a small trail into the unconscious, finding new lands for the consciousness to dwell in.
>
> New thoughts, new feelings, new experiences[,] they are the real treasure for each generation. – And you know I don't mean just sensationalism and excitement. – And if you choose me, I think it is because you see a glimmer of new hope, hope of a wider world of thought, a deeper world of feeling, and a more intensive world of experience.

He ends the letter by declaring that it gives him 'a certain re-assurance to think of an unknown Eight voluntarily choosing to look my way, and thus to back me up. Because, in a world of hostile criticism, eight good spirits on my side are almost a host'.[10]

Although Lawrence was remarkably courageous and single-minded in standing up for the things he believed in, and prepared to alienate people by speaking his truth, it was also essential for him to feel he had the support and loyalty of a chosen few. Returning to Europe after spending over three and a half years travelling, and almost three of these living either in the United States or Mexico, must have felt like starting out all over again. He had to develop new forms of collaboration to sustain and drive his creativity. The clue to one of these can be found in a project he had taken up in his last six months in New Mexico. In mid-April 1925, around the same time that he wrote 'Accumulated Mail', Lawrence responded positively to an approach from Harold Mason of the Centaur Press in Philadelphia, who asked whether he would like to publish with them a little book of uncollected essays. Mason must have heard about Lawrence through Edward D. McDonald, who was putting together a *Bibliography of the Writings of D. H. Lawrence*, which the Centaur Press would publish in June. Lawrence revised 'The Crown' for inclusion in the new volume but all the other essays (including the title essay) he wrote specifically for it. *Reflections on the Death of a Porcupine* would be published on 7 December 1925 in an edition of 925 copies costing $4 (twice as much as Knopf's edition of *St. Mawr*). He loved the volume, with its brightly coloured marble boards, calling it 'the jolliest-faced of all my books' (*5L* 375).

Lawrence had brought *The Plumed Serpent* back with him to Europe, but he had misgivings about publishing it through his mainstream publishers. It was not just negative reviews that deterred him, but the condescension of reviewers and their refusal to take his ideas seriously. Alyse Gregory's review of *Kangaroo* in the *Dial* in January 1924, for instance, expressed disdain for his two psychology books: 'And really what a comic picture he presents in his new rôle of spiritual leader to mankind: this bearded, fox-eyed, irascible prophet with a thundering Jehovah-complex' (Draper 1970: 219). Back in January 1925, while he was rewriting

The Plumed Serpent in Oaxaca, Lawrence wrote of his 'dread' at the thought of it 'going out into the world' (*5L* 200). In June 1925 he said that it was 'different from my other books: and to me, the one that means most to me' (*5L* 260); he felt that it was his 'most important thing so far' (*5L* 267). In October he told the Knopfs that he still considered it 'my most important novel: never mind the weary public' (*5L* 320). It was published by Secker in January 1926; Knopf's American edition was published in the following month. On 1 February 1926, Lawrence wrote to Mason asking how his 'dear' *Porcupine* was 'disporting himself'. He had ordered Mason a copy of *The Plumed Serpent* but admitted: 'I could weep over *that* book, I do so hate it's being published and going into the tuppenny hands of the tuppenny public' (*5L* 387).

Reflections on the Death of a Porcupine was not his first experience of privately printing an expensive limited edition. In April 1918 he arranged for the London publisher and bookseller Cyril Beaumont to privately publish a volume of poems entitled *Bay*, having previously attempted to interest him in publishing *Women in Love* and the collection of poems 'All of Us'. The publication process was protracted, and when Lawrence finally saw a copy in January 1920 he was furious to find that Beaumont had printed one of the accompanying illustrations by Anne Estelle Rice upside down and left out the dedication to Lady Cynthia Asquith. The experience did not deter Lawrence from future private publication schemes; in fact, in October 1920 he even stated in a letter to Beaumont that he was considering sending on to him another volume of his poems,[11] and, of course, the following month Seltzer published *Women in Love* by private subscription. The publication of his 'dear *Porcupine*' (*5L* 387), however, inaugurated Lawrence's more extensive and enterprising engagement with private publication in the last years of his life. Charles Lahr, who printed the short story *Sun* in the fourth number of his journal *New Coterie* in the autumn of 1926, published it in September 1926 as a standalone volume of 100 copies under his own imprint, 'E. Archer' (his trade name being that of his wife, Esther Archer). In November 1926 Ernest Benn published the short story *Glad Ghosts* in an edition of 500 copies; Lawrence sent several out to friends as Christmas presents.

A year later, on 17 November 1927, a chance meeting with Dikran Kouyoumdjian in the street in Florence (where Lawrence was then living), and a subsequent conversation with Norman Douglas over lunch at the home of Reggie Turner, resulted in a venture that changed Lawrence's literary fortunes and shaped his subsequent writing. In October 1926 Lawrence had begun a short story inspired by his recent visit to England. He had been shocked to witness the nature and extent of the class enmity in his home country, which had culminated in a General Strike. The story developed into a novel addressing the class struggle and reflecting on class prejudice and how it might be overcome through tenderness and a new reverence for the body. The central character, the upper-middle-class Constance Reid, marries an aristocrat, Clifford Chatterley, who is shortly afterwards paralysed from the waist down in the war. Disillusioned by the stuffy aristocratic life she is forced to lead, and encouraged by her husband to 'Have a lover if you have to!' (*FLC* 11), Connie begins a relationship with her husband's gamekeeper, Oliver Parkin. Parkin, like Connie, is unhappily married. When he loses his job as a result of the scandal caused by fighting with the new partner of his vindictive estranged wife, he takes a job at a steelworks in Sheffield, where he becomes Secretary of the Communist League. Connie becomes pregnant by Parkin, but despite her best efforts to overcome his animosity to her as a member of the ruling classes, the ending to the novel matches hope for their possible future together with upset and despair over the many obstacles they will need to overcome.

Lawrence finished the novel in December, but straight away rewrote it, finishing the second version in February 1927. In revising it Lawrence made Parkin a more complex character with a greater capacity and desire to overcome his bitter hatred of the ruling classes. There is a new degree of hope that the sexual bond between Parkin and Connie can enable them to put right the damage caused by their class conditioning and their unhappy marriages. Lawrence began to develop the sex scenes between them, finding a language for the tenderness they discover in and through the body. In this version, Parkin leaves his employment in Sheffield and seems happy to plan for Connie to use her money to set them up on a farm once he has secured a divorce. In writing the two versions, Lawrence's interest had shifted from addressing class prejudice to focusing on sex as something sacred and vitally important not only in the relations between individuals, but in their relatedness to nature and to society. Its purpose was 'to make the sex relation valid and precious, instead of shameful'. Yet he realised that it was 'what the world would call very improper' (*6L* 29), and after a period of reflection he decided to put it away and not to try to publish it.

The meeting with Kouyoumdjian, whom Lawrence had known during the war years, was important because under the pen name Michael Arlen he had published in 1924 the sensational bestselling novel *The Green Hat*, which had been turned into a popular play and a film. Kouyoumdjian had become spectacularly rich as a result. Lawrence reacted to their meeting by jotting down a memorandum note: 'Definitely I hate the whole money-making world, Tom & Dick as well as en gros. But I won't be done by them either' (Worthen 1989: vi). Over lunch the same day, Lawrence spoke with Douglas and his friend, the Florentine printer and bookseller Giuseppe ('Pino') Orioli, about a private publication scheme they had developed: Orioli would arrange for Douglas's books to be printed in Florence in an edition of 700 copies and they would post them out to subscribers at the cost of two guineas per copy. If he followed suit, Lawrence would be able to by-pass Curtis Brown (and so avoid paying them their percentage as his agent); he would need to finance the printing and postage himself, but he would pocket 90% of any profits (the other 10% going to Orioli). Publishing outside the United Kingdom would also mean that he would avoid paying income tax on his profits.

With private publication in mind, Lawrence rewrote *Lady Chatterley's Lover* for a final time between December 1927 and January 1928. In this version, the gamekeeper (now re-named Oliver Mellors) has been educated in a grammar school and has entered the officer class while in the army, but chooses to return to his working-class roots after the war. He is, then, better placed than his earlier incarnations to meet Connie in a middle ground where tenderness displaces prejudice. While class conflict remains omnipresent in the novel, in this version Lawrence holds out a more joyous possibility of Connie and Mellors escaping it. At times they are able to laugh away their differences by running together naked in the rain or by joking about the contrasts in their spoken language. The greater optimism of the plot is matched by the novel's attempt to cleanse the four-letter words of their dirty associations by using them poetically to describe not just an act but the complex feelings associated with it.

In revising the novel for private publication, Lawrence must have realised that the scandal it would create would be the best form of publicity. He arranged with Orioli to print 1000 copies, 500 for England (to be sold at £2 per copy) and 500 for America (priced at $10 per copy). They began sending out copies in July 1928. Demand was such that they eventually doubled the price of copies. When the edition sold out, in autumn 1928 they began selling 200 paper-bound copies for 21 shillings each. Lawrence made over £1000 from this first edition; this was more than he had made from any of his other writings. When pirated copies began to circulate in Europe he travelled to Paris and arranged with the American bookseller Edward Titus to bring out a cheap paperback edition at the cost of 60 francs to undercut the expensive unauthorised versions. The so-called Paris Popular Edition of *Lady Chatterley's Lover* was published in May 1929; Lawrence wrote an introduction to it entitled 'My Skirmish with Jolly Roger', explaining his experience with the pirate publishers. By the end of 1930 over 30,000 copies had been sold.

Lawrence felt that he had 'shot' the novel 'like a bomb against all their false sex and hypocrisy', and he hoped that it would 'let in a bit of fresh air' (*6L* 513). During the process of printing the Florence edition he designed a phoenix emblem, which he printed on the front board. It would become the stamp of authenticity on other books which he arranged to have privately printed. After the success of privately printing *Lady Chatterley's Lover*, Lawrence authorised a number of private publications. He became more assertive in his dealings with publishers to secure the best possible terms, and he began to insist on taking a larger share of the profits accruing from signed limited editions of his works. Worthen calculates that Lawrence's signature appeared on 'at least 2790 copies of various limited and private-press publications between 1926 and 1929' (Worthen 1996: 117). In March

1929, Elkin Mathews published the short story *Rawdon's Roof* in its 'Woburn Books' series, and Lawrence signed all 530 copies. He often also signed more expensive numbered copies of private editions, such as the 200 copies of his translation of A. F. Grazzini's *The Story of Doctor Manente* printed on Japanese vellum which Orioli produced in November 1929 in addition to 1000 ordinary copies.

Private publication could be more collaborative than publishing mainstream volumes with Secker and Knopf. The Black Sun Press, run out of Paris by the wealthy American couple Harry and Caresse Crosby, published editions of Lawrence's *Sun* and *The Escaped Cock*, containing colour illustrations by the author. In his youth Lawrence had copied paintings in watercolour and produced some original watercolour compositions, a practice that he continued when he taught art at Davidson Road School. He became interested in oil painting through Arthur Gair Wilkinson, his neighbour at the Villa Mirenda (the house he rented near Florence). In October 1926 Aldous and Maria Huxley visited Lawrence and gave him some old canvases. Painting had always been a collaborative endeavour, whether it was copying paintings together with friends in his youth to give as presents, producing drawings or paintings for his friends' autograph albums, or producing a still life at the same time as his pupils. Now he took it up seriously with the encouragement of the Huxleys and his neighbours (who lent him an easel). He discussed his work with the painters he knew (Dorothy Brett, Earl Brewster, plus Millicent Beveridge and Mabel Harrison).

In July 1928 he decided to organise an exhibition of his paintings in London at the small gallery owned by Dorothy Warren, whom he had first met back in late 1915 through Ottoline Morrell. Lawrence oversaw the private publication of the Mandrake Press edition of *The Paintings of D. H. Lawrence* to accompany the exhibition. He took great pains to ensure that the colour reproductions were bright and as true to the originals as possible. Five hundred ordinary copies were printed and sold for 10 guineas; 10 special copies on Japanese vellum sold for an exorbitant 50 guineas. These volumes are a testament to the sheer energy Lawrence put into getting his work out in an uncensored and appropriate form despite his deteriorating health. In the case of his poetry collection *Pansies*, two typescripts of which were intercepted, opened and confiscated in the registered mail in January 1929 on the authority of the Home Office, Lawrence only allowed Secker to remove 14 of the poems and to change others once he knew that Charles Lahr would publish an unexpurgated edition. He agreed to write a shorter foreword to Secker's edition, while he produced a self-portrait in red chalk to use as a frontispiece to Lahr's edition and printed in it a longer and more rebarbative introduction.

Private publication became his means of countering censorship and getting his work in an unabridged form into the hands of people in England and America. *Lady Chatterley's Lover* and the unabridged *Pansies* could not have been published by any other means. The volume of his paintings would play a central role in offsetting the censorship of his work. The exhibition at the Warren Gallery opened on 14 June 1929. It was raided by police on 5 July and 13 paintings were removed; Lawrence sought legal advice but decided not to take an appeal to the High Court because if it failed the 13 paintings would be destroyed, so a settlement was reached for the paintings to be returned to Lawrence on the understanding that they would not be exhibited in Britain again. After 5 July the public could only view the full exhibition in the pages of *The Paintings of D. H. Lawrence.*

Back in April 1927, when Lawrence was pessimistic about ever publishing *Lady Chatterley's Lover*, he felt that it was perhaps 'a waste to write any more novels'. He told Nancy Pearn, the person at Curtis Brown's London offices responsible for placing work with magazines and newspapers, that he 'could probably live by little things. I mean in magazines' (*6L* 29). She advised Lawrence not to publish *Lady Chatterley's Lover* because the damage it might do to his reputation could affect his earning potential with magazines. When he informed her a year later of his intention to privately publish the novel, she thought that it might make editors 'tremble' (*LEA* xx). In fact, it had the opposite effect. At the same time that Lawrence was beginning to exploit the full potential of private publication, a new and lucrative mass-market outlet for his writing opened up. From April 1928 onwards, newspapers began to approach Curtis Brown requesting articles from Lawrence. Nancy Pearn was instrumental in guiding Lawrence so that he could capitalise on demand for his journalistic writing.

Lawrence had previously written disparagingly about journalism and especially about newspapers, which he saw as deepening the complacency and conservatism of the British public. He would refer to the 'artificial stock emotion which comes out with the morning papers' (*LEA* 158). On the face of it, his readiness to write for them in the last two years of his life might seem like a case of financial opportunism tinged with hypocrisy, but I think we must see it instead as part of the broad spectrum approach he took to challenging the bourgeois values of his English readership in the final years of his life. By the time of his return to England in September 1925 Lawrence realised just how difficult it was to truly change attitudes which were deeply ingrained. Shocking people only promised to reinforce their prejudice while creating problems for the author. In 'Education of the People' Lawrence had written: 'the *bourgeois* is not worth my while, I can't demean myself to *épater* him, and I am much too sensitive to my own isolation to want to draw his attention' (*RDP* 151). In *The Plumed Serpent*, when Kate Leslie's guide informs her that the Mexican murals she intensely dislikes are intentionally 'ugly' because 'capitalism is ugly, and Mammon is ugly', she reflects that they seem to exist 'only to *épater le bourgeois.* And Kate was weary of *épatisme*, just as much as of the bourgeoisie. She wasn't interested in *épatant le bourgeois.* The *épateurs* were as boring as the bourgeois, two halves of one dreariness' (*PS* 52). Lawrence saw himself as an outsider suggesting different possibilities for life and different values rather than an insider seeking simply to shock the middle classes. In the case of *Lady Chatterley's Lover*, the alternatives he explored were so outspoken that he had to circumvent mainstream publishers; likewise his paintings, which he produced in part to address what he saw as the castrated sensibilities of the British, could only be privately published, though the exhibition at the Warren Gallery was open to the general public. Otherwise, Lawrence preferred to address as wide a public as possible, simultaneously publishing what he thought of as expurgated texts through his mainstream English and American publishers and unexpurgated texts in privately printed editions. Writing for newspapers allowed him to take on the bourgeois public on their own ground.

Lawrence liked newspaper editors to suggest topics which he could address in his own way, though sometimes he simply produced articles and relied on Nancy Pearn to place them for him. He was able to write short articles very quickly, and some could be placed in both English and American newspapers and magazines with little or no revision.[12] In April 1928, Arthur Olley, Literary Editor of the *Evening News*, invited Lawrence to contribute articles to the newspaper. Olley asked Nancy Pearn to grant him exclusivity for a short period, during which he published five articles by Lawrence. The first of these was 'When She Asks "Why?"' ('The "Jeune Fille" Wants to Know'), which was accepted and published on 8 May (it appeared in the *Virginia Quarterly Review* in January 1929). Lawrence's article invites the reader to reflect on the grounds for the censorship of literary works by humorously identifying the unabashed inquisitiveness of the 'jeune fille' whom elderly male censors claimed to be protecting. Lawrence structures the article around an imagined conversation between himself and a 22-year-old woman whose 'fierce questions', 'shameless language' (*LEA* 71) and hatred of evasions leave him speechless. The young woman asks why her father buries his head in the sand and wishes to protect her from impropriety. When Lawrence concedes that 'it's a sort of funk', the young woman says '*Exactly*! ... But what is there to be in a funk about?' (*LEA* 72). Lawrence suggests that the idea of protecting the young woman from being ruined by a wicked world is wrongheaded firstly because she is 'not quite the raw egg she's supposed to be', and secondly because the stern belief in the wickedness of people is nothing more than 'an *idée fixe* of the elderly'. The young see only 'pure hypocrisy' in the 'parental imagination' because they do not wish to be 'shielded' from a wickedness which never materialises. The 'bogey' of wickedness is simply a fiction from which the elderly 'derive a great sense of parental authority, importance and justification' (*LEA* 73).

The other articles by Lawrence which Olley accepted for publication similarly probe and seek to dislodge the abstract ideas and principles which distract people from experiencing the world as it is. In 'Over-Earnest Ladies' ('Insouciance'), published on 12 July 1928 (and in the *Atlantic Monthly* in November 1928), Lawrence describes standing on the balcony of a hotel where he is staying on a hot and stormy afternoon, taking in the landscape and watching 'two mowers mowing with scythes down-hill just near' when an English lady who is staying in the neighbouring room strikes up a conversation with him and moves from everyday pleasantries onto 'Italy, and the Signor Mussolini'. Lawrence is instantly transported from an immersive contemplation of his surroundings 'into the troubled ether of international politics' (*LEA* 95). He admits 'I don't care about right and wrong, politics, fascism, abstract liberty or anything else of the sort', and asks: 'Why do modern people almost invariably ignore the things that are actually present to them?' (*LEA* 96). People are 'so busy caring about fascism or League of Nations or whether France is right, or whether marriage is threatened, that they never know where they are'. Lawrence writes that 'actual living ... is a question mostly of direct contact'. The irony, of course, is that he is attacking here a modern obsession with abstract issues which he felt that newspapers had helped to create. He is asking newspaper readers to recognise how their own preoccupation with national and international issues might hinder their capacity to experience 'direct, sensuous contact' (*LEA* 97) with their surroundings.

Olley asked Lawrence to provide an article on the topic 'Men Must be Master Again'. In his article, entitled 'Master in his Own House', published on 2 August 1928 (and in *Vanity Fair* in November 1928), Lawrence suggests that 'A man must be master in his own house' is one of several 'ready-made phrases' which epitomise 'mass thinking'. Other examples he gives are 'An Englishman's home is his castle. Two servants are better than one. Happy is the bride who has her own little car in her own little garage. It is the duty of a husband to give his wife what she wants. It is the duty of a wife to say "Yes darling!" to her husband' (*LEA* 99). He argues that there is a fundamental difference between 'a mass idea' and 'real individual thinking' (*LEA* 100). Most people are actually indifferent to the content of the ready-made phrases, but indifference is not the same as insouciance because it is tinged with anxiety. Since past generations of men cared about being master in the house, the current generation feels anxious about its own indifference to it, and when provoked men 'start reiterating like parrots such mass ideas' (*LEA* 101). This perpetuates historical ideals which have become meaningless and prevents people from recognising and seeking to articulate their own individual needs and desires.

'—And If Women *Were* Supreme ...' ('Matriarchy'), published on 5 October 1928, opens by addressing male fear of 'the women of today' and of 'man's subordination to woman' (*LEA* 103–104). Lawrence predicts that in the coming matriarchal society children will inherit their mother's name, property will pass from mother to daughter, and in the marriage vows the husband will swear to honour and obey his spouse. Yet rather than bemoaning the coming society he welcomes it. He notes that in contemporary matriarchal societies the men 'look most jaunty and cocky' and the women 'as if they did most of the work' (*LEA* 104). The 'pueblo Indians of the Arizona desert ... still have a sort of matriarchy', yet for the man this is an enabling arrangement, since it leaves him free to concentrate on being 'an active, religious member of the tribe'. The men pass their time mostly 'in the khiva, the great underground religious meeting-house where only the males assemble, where the sacred practices of the tribe are carried on'. At the age of 12 or 13, boys leave their mother and are given into the charge of old men to be 'initiated into manhood'. This seems to be 'the instinctive form that society takes' (*LEA* 105), since in England boys are sent away to school at the same age, and men gather to fulfil their deeper social needs not in khivas but in clubs or pubs. Lawrence suggests that woman should be given 'her full independence, and with it, the full responsibility of her independence', while men should be freed from the subsidiary role they play in the family, since this thwarts their 'deeper social instincts and intuitions' (*LEA* 106).

The final article accepted by Olley was 'Dull London!' ('Why I don't Like Living in London'), which was published on 3 September 1928. It describes the 'deathly sense of *dulness*' (*LEA* 120) which Lawrence feels whenever he returns to London after spending time abroad. He describes the English as 'the *nicest* people in the world', and life in England as being so 'easy' that it is 'as if the whole air were impregnated with chloroform or some other pervasive anaesthetic'. As a young man encountering London 20 years ago he found it 'thrilling': 'the vast and roaring heart of all adventure'. Now that the adventure has been 'crushed out of London', and it is full of traffic, it seems to be 'crushing out life, crushing everything dead' (*LEA* 121). Since he does not 'jazz' and has no job in London, he spends his time there dining with people and endlessly talking when he wants to be silent: 'it is purely facile' (*LEA* 122). He notes that it is 'terrible' to feel this way 'about one's native land' (*LEA* 120), but he only feels hope and life returning when he is seated on the boat-train and hears all the goodbyes.

All five articles published in the *Evening News* demonstrate the lively anti-authoritarian and oppositional qualities of Lawrence's thought. He mocks the self-importance of the censors by invoking the strength and vivaciousness of the 'jeune fille'. Readers might have thought that the author of *Kangaroo* and *The Plumed Serpent* would be preoccupied with world politics, but he expresses resentment at being drawn out of his enjoyment of the scene in front of him in order to consider fascism, 'which is invisible anyhow' (*LEA* 96). Where readers might have assumed that the author of *Aaron's Rod* would bemoan the loss of male power in the home and the rising power of women, he argues that male precedence in the family unit is a meaningless anachronism only invoked by men in moments of irritation because no new male ideal is forthcoming. Even the reason he gives for disliking living in London seems counterintuitive, since he finds all the metropolitan dinner parties and conversations dull and sees more life in his existence overseas, where he admits to spending most of his days 'saying little, or with a bit of chatter and a silence again' (*LEA* 121).

Lawrence told Nancy Pearn that he found it 'really rather amusing to write these little articles' (*6L* 403). In the blurb printed alongside '—And If Women *Were* Supreme ...' ('Matriarchy'), Olley referred to its 'mood of delicate irony of which he is master' (*LEA* 102). Lawrence himself sometimes wondered whether he was 'too much tongue in the cheek'. The 'fun' (*6L* 404) he had in writing the articles came in part from his natural propensity to upset expectations and to cajole and provoke. In a letter of 22 January 1925, Lawrence had told the Italian critic Carlo Linati that he thought an author should be 'in among the crowd, kicking their shins or cheering them on to some mischief or merriment' (*5L* 201). He depicts modern men as riven by their own indifference and their failure to address their deepest needs. Taking a swipe at the cornerstones of bourgeois society was a way to instil a critical attitude in them and to encourage a new kind of liveliness.

Lawrence considered conformity and complacency inimical to self-realisation and ultimately disastrous for both the nation and the individual. If Lawrence was critical of the old 'master in the house' ideal, he was equally scathing about the self-assurance of women. In August or September 1926, during his last visit to England, Lawrence evidently spoke to his sisters about their mother. At the start of his literary career, Austin Harrison, who replaced Ford Madox Hueffer as editor of the *English Review*, wrote to Lydia Lawrence to tell her that her youngest son would be riding in his own carriage by the time he was 40; she had apparently responded by saying 'Ay, if he lives to be forty!' (*LEA* 18). Lawrence was now convinced that his mother had a condescending attitude towards him, and he began to reassess his early life, which entailed criticising his mother's attitudes and their damaging impact on the family, and starting to see his father in a more positive light.[13]

When the *Daily Chronicle* (which was owned by the same company as the *Evening News*) asked him to contribute to a series of articles by famous authors on the topic of 'WHAT WOMEN HAVE TAUGHT ME', Lawrence focused on his mother. In 'Women Always Know Best' ('That Women Know Best'), published on 29 November 1928, he said that as a small boy he wondered 'why God was a man, and not a woman' (*LEA* 83), since it was his mother who established and upheld the difference between right and wrong in the Lawrence household. We have seen in Chapter 2 how the young Lawrence questioned his mother's sure sense of right and wrong, even while he was forced to accept her decrees. In the essay he says that he 'started early to study the only vivid and lively power which is left on earth, the power of earnest women'. He declares that women do not really know right from wrong: he says that even his mother realised this, when she was older. Their 'courage is largely bravado' (*LEA* 84). Lawrence concludes by saying that there is 'no *absolute* right and wrong', only 'a decent working right and wrong'. Women's self-assurance has created only a terrible 'muddle', so 'the things one can unlearn from women are more effective than the things one can learn. How not to be too sure of right and wrong, for example' (*LEA* 85). In 'Women are so Cocksure', probably written in August 1928, he criticised his mother's conviction that 'a man ought not to drink beer' (*LEA* 116), claiming that her 'moral frenzy over it' when he was young had 'made a tragedy out of what was only a nuisance' (*LEA* 117).

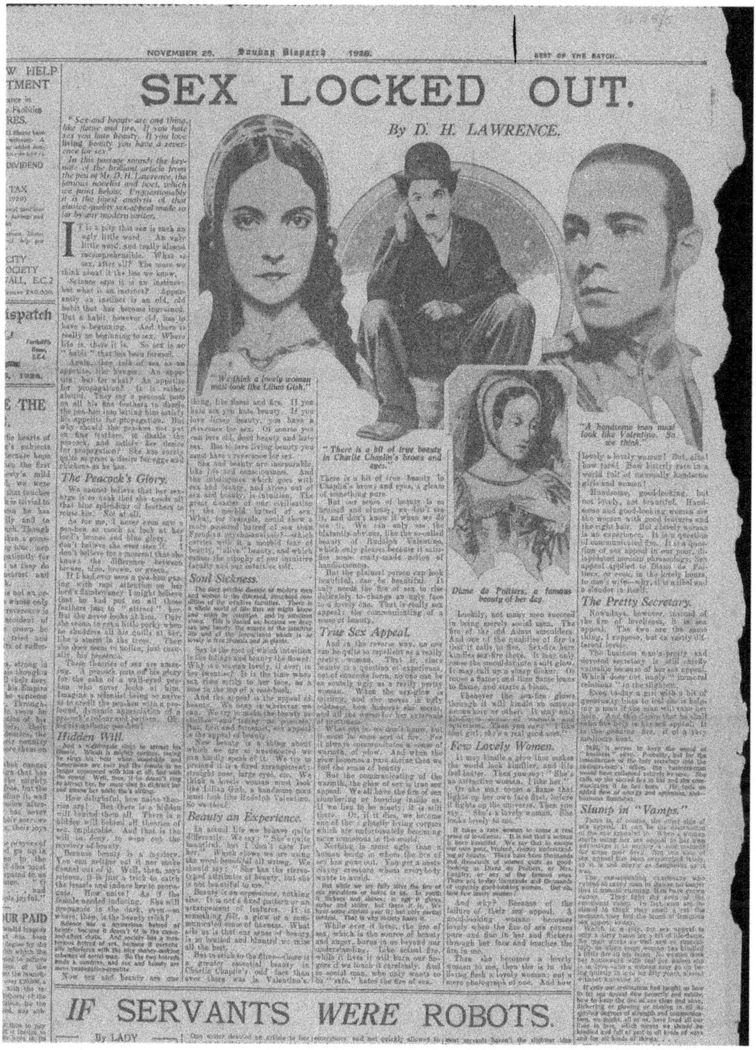

NOVEMBER 25. Sunday Dispatch 1928. BEST OF THE BATCH.

SEX LOCKED OUT.

By D. H. LAWRENCE.

"Sex and beauty are one thing, like flame and fire. If you hate sex you hate beauty. If you love living beauty you have a reverence for sex."

In this passage sounds the keynote of the brilliant article from the pen of Mr. D. H. Lawrence, the famous novelist and poet, which we print below. Unquestionably it is the finest analysis of that elusive quality sex-appeal made so far by any modern writer.

It is a pity that sex is such an ugly little word. An ugly little word, and really almost incomprehensible. What is sex, after all? The more we think about it the less we know.

Science says it is an instinct; but what is an instinct? Apparently an instinct is an old, old habit that has become ingrained. But a habit, however old, has to have a beginning. And there is really no beginning to sex. Where life is, there it is. So sex is no "habit" that has been formed.

Again, they talk of sex as an appetite, like hunger. An appetite; but for what? An appetite for propagation? It is rather absurd. They say a peacock puts on all his fine feathers to dazzle the pea-hen into letting him satisfy his appetite for propagation. But why should the pea-hen not put on fine feathers, to dazzle the peacock, and satisfy her desire for propagation? She has surely quite as great a desire for eggs and chickens as he has.

The Peacock's Glory.

We cannot believe that her sex-urge is so weak that she needs all that blue splendour of feathers to rouse her. Not at all.

As for me, I never even saw a pea-hen so much as look at her lord's bronze and blue glory. I don't believe she ever sees it. I don't believe for a moment that she knows the difference between bronze, blue, brown, or green.

If I had ever seen a pea-hen gazing with rapt attention on her lord's flamboyancy I might believe that he had put on all those feathers just to "attract" her. But she never looks at him. Only she seems to get a little perky when he shudders all his quills at her, like a storm in the trees. Then she does seem to notice, just casually, his presence.

These theories of sex are amazing. A peacock puts on his glory for the sake of a wall-eyed pea-hen who never looks at him. Imagine a scientist being so naive as to credit the pea-hen with a profound, dynamic appreciation of a peacock's colour and pattern. Oh, highly aesthetic pea-hen!

Hidden Will.

How delightful, how naive theories are! But there is a hidden will behind them all. There is a hidden will behind all theories of sex, implacable. And that is the will to deny, to wipe out the mystery of beauty.

Because beauty is a mystery. You can neither eat it nor make flannel out of it. Well, then, says science, it is just a trick to catch the female and induce her to propagate. How naive! As if the female needed inducing. She will propagate in the dark, even—so where, then, is the beauty trick?

Now sex and beauty are one thing, like flame and fire. If you hate sex you hate beauty. If you love living beauty, you have a reverence for sex. Of course you can love old, dead beauty and hate sex. But to love living beauty you must have a reverence for sex.

Sex and beauty are inseparable, like life and consciousness. And the intelligence which goes with sex and beauty, and arises out of sex and beauty, is intuition. The great disaster of our civilisation is the morbid hatred of sex. What, for example, could show a more poisoned hatred of sex than Freudian psycho-analysis?—which carries with it a morbid fear of beauty, "alive" beauty, and which causes the atrophy of our intuitive faculty and our intuitive self.

Soul Sickness.

Sex is the root of which intuition is the foliage and beauty the flower. Why is a woman lovely, if ever, in her twenties? It is the time when sex rises softly to her face, as a rose to the top of a rose-bush.

And the appeal is the appeal of beauty. We deny it wherever we can. We try to make the beauty as shallow and trashy as possible. But, first and foremost, sex appeal is the appeal of beauty.

Now beauty is a thing about which we are so uneducated we can hardly speak of it. We try to pretend it is a fixed arrangement: straight nose, large eyes, etc. We think a lovely woman must look like Lilian Gish, a handsome man must look like Rudolph Valentino. So we think.

Beauty an Experience.

In actual life we behave quite differently. We say: "She's quite beautiful, but I don't care for her." Which shows we are using the word beautiful all wrong. We should say: "She has the stereotyped attributes of beauty, but she is not beautiful to me."

"We think a lovely woman must look like Lilian Gish."

"There is a bit of true beauty in Charlie Chaplin's brows and eyes."

True Sex Appeal.

Diane de Poitiers, a famous beauty of her day.

"A handsome man must look like Valentino. So we think."

Few Lovely Women.

The Pretty Secretary.

Stump in "Vamps."

IF SERVANTS WERE ROBOTS.

By LADY

Article by D. H. Lawrence entitled 'Sex Locked Out', in the *Sunday Dispatch*, 25 November 1928. University of Nottingham, Manuscripts and Special Collections, La N 5/5.

Lawrence suggests in his articles that women are prone to basing their whole lives on ideas and principles which in later life they realise are empty or meaningless. In 'Cocksure Women and Hen-sure Men', which was rejected by the *Evening News* but published in *Forum*, Lawrence argues that the modern woman 'rushes to mad lengths about votes, or welfare, or sports, or business' because she is frightened of 'her own henny self', the 'lovely henny surety, the hen-sureness which is the real bliss of every female'. He suggests that when the ideals she pursues have 'collapsed', she 'realises she has lost her life' (*LEA* 127). Lawrence strove to articulate what he meant by the intuitive, insouciant modes of being which he thought modernity at best ignored and at worst impeded. The 'henny self' is one example. In 'Sex Locked Out' ('Sex Appeal'), which was published in the *Sunday Dispatch* on 25 November 1928 (and in *Vanity Fair* in July 1929 and the New York *Golden Book Magazine* in December 1929), he distinguishes between 'the stereotyped attributes of beauty' which are universally adored in film stars such as Rudolph Valentino or Lilian Gish, and 'true sex appeal' which is more intangible and lasting, but less under our conscious control, consisting of a 'sex-glow' (*LEA* 146) which can make the plainest people beautiful throughout their entire lives.

In an essay now known as 'Give Her a Pattern', written in December 1928 and first published in *Vanity Fair* in May 1929 and then in the *Daily Express* on 19 June, he says that the 'trouble about women' is that they 'must always go on trying to adapt themselves to men's theories of women, as they always have done'. He suggests that men have created various female ideals to which women have conformed, from 'the matron' to the 'fast' woman, the 'chaste and untouched' woman, the 'learned woman', 'the child-wife', the 'noble woman, the pure spouse, the devoted mother'. Since men no longer know what they want a woman to be, they shape their women to the latest ideal and once married hate 'the *type*'. This, he says, is 'the condition of modern marriage'. The modern man is a 'fool' because he 'makes a greater mess of his woman than men have ever made' (*LEA* 164); the modern woman is inclined to be 'hysterical' because 'she doesn't quite know what to be, which pattern to follow, which man's picture of woman to live up to' (*LEA* 162).

Lawrence knew that this depiction of modern women as modelling themselves on men's ideals would irritate and enrage female readers. On 13 June 1929, 'four normal business women' from New York who had read 'Give Her a Pattern' in *Vanity Fair* wrote an open letter to Lawrence taking him to task. They declared that they had 'independent personalities' and 'independent existences completely happy and useful without benefit of masculine thought or influence'. The four women lodged in an all-female hotel on West Thirtieth Street established over a decade earlier by a charitable organisation committed to creating high-quality living quarters for 'self-supporting girls and women with small incomes'. They told Lawrence that they had created a day in mid-June that they designated 'No Man's Sunday', on which they planned 'feminine entertainment, entirely uninfluenced by that bogey: What would the men say?' They informed him that 'women can get along quite nicely, thank you, without borrowing from manhood the virtues and faults peculiar to manhood – because women have their own virtues and faults, woman-made, woman-fostered'. The letter was designed to put right not only Lawrence but 'the persons' he 'might mistakenly have influenced'.[14] Lawrence sent the open letter to the editor of *Vanity Fair*, Frank Crowninshield. He jokingly referred to the authors of the 'open letter' as 'tightly-shut', and he suggested that they were 'still acting under male suggestion – only this time, falling over backwards: – per bacco [Good God!]'.

Sadly, neither the letter nor Lawrence's reaction to it was published in the magazine. The fact that he forwarded it to the editor together with his comments shows how much he valued such cut and thrust exchanges. Back in early 1924, when Lawrence was helping Murry to edit the *Adelphi*, he read a pointedly sexist and misogynistic article by a contributor which Murry published in the April 1924 number. In the piece, which appeared in the regular 'Multum in Parvo' section of the journal under the title 'The Ugliness of Women', the author ('J. H. R.') notes that in his adult life on occasion the most beautiful women had appeared ugly and repellent to him. He ascribed the feeling to 'some terrible, unmentionable evil' in women, traceable to the wickedness of Eve. Lawrence wrote a rejoinder to it in which he suggested that the feeling of repulsion was created not by the woman but by the man's reaction against his own 'nasty lust': 'The hideousness he sees is the reflection of himself, and of the automatic meat-lust with which he approaches another individual'. He suggested that if J. H. R. approached the beautiful woman as a 'human creature', a '*being*' instead of a 'piece of lurid meat', then he would 'have no horrors afterwards' (Harrison 2013a: 15). Murry chose not to publish Lawrence's riposte, perhaps because he feared it might cause offence. The man who emphasised the individual being of beautiful women in order to expose the sexist and misogynistic attitude of a reader of the *Adelphi* enjoyed annoying independent women by insisting their identities were derived from male ideals.

Like Rawdon Lilly near the end of *Aaron's Rod*, Lawrence was capable of advancing different and even contradictory points as the situation demanded. The 'consciously speculative relativity' (Bell 1992: 149) that Michael Bell detects in Lawrence's novels of the early to mid-1920s found its way into these non-fictional writings too. Lawrence was committed to undermining complacency wherever he saw it. Like the short, demotic and direct poems he also wrote in his last years and published in the collections *Pansies* (1929) and *Nettles* (1930), the newspaper articles are 'thoughts which run through the modern mind and body, each having its own separate existence, yet each of them combining with all the others to make up a complete state of mind' (*Poems* 663), and like the poems they were written to address the 'mass thinking' of 'mass-civilisation' (*Poems* 666), to 'get a bit more of my own back' (*6L* 402), and to sting a little too.

In his articles Lawrence frequently took issue with cultural clichés and accepted ideas, adopting ironic and oppositional approaches to topical issues and developing apparently counterintuitive arguments as a means of challenging orthodox opinions. These rhetorical strategies play a central role in the three better-known longer essays Lawrence wrote in 1929. The first two of these, 'Introduction to

These Paintings' and *Pornography and Obscenity*, taken together, offer an extraordinary account of how fear of the body and sex arose and developed in Britain, and its psychological consequences and impact on the arts.

'Introduction to These Paintings' was written between January and March 1929 and first published in June 1929 in *The Paintings of D. H. Lawrence*. In it, Lawrence argues that England has produced so few painters because since the Renaissance its artists and writers have felt a deep horror and revulsion at the body. He traces this horror back to the rapid spread in the sixteenth century of syphilis and other sexual diseases such as gonorrhoea. He suggests that the English were so 'horrified and terrified' by these diseases that 'the pox joke was invented as an evasion, and following that, the great hush! hush! was imposed'. The emergence of euphemisms such as 'pox' and 'clap' (*LEA* 188) is said to reflect a collective desire to avoid confronting uncomfortable feelings. Lawrence asserts that the idea of contracting syphilis through sexual intercourse, and passing it on to one's offspring, affected the 'deep sex imagination' (*LEA* 189), resulting in a fear of the instincts and their suppression. This in turn meant that individuals were 'cut off' from their 'intuitional awareness' of others, 'and from the world' (*LEA* 190). While this affected the whole of Europe, Lawrence suggests that it had a particularly strong impact on the English and the Americans, creating a puritan backlash against the body. In modern people, the 'dread of the instincts' has created 'dread of intuitional awareness'. Lawrence invokes several 'vile proverbs' which have 'been dinned in to us for over two hundred years': 'Beauty is a snare', 'Beauty is but skin-deep', 'Handsome is as handsome does', 'Looks don't count', 'Don't judge by appearances'. He says that these are all false. The death of the intuitional faculty and the appreciation of beauty means that we no longer know how to feel, and our instinct for beautiful objects has deteriorated into a desire for mass-produced crockery and furniture in department stores. The 'crétin ugliness' of the objects for sale is evidence, he says, 'that the modern bourgeois is a crétin' (*LEA* 192). Our alienation from, and denial of, our instincts blocks aesthetic appreciation, since individuals '*cannot* feel anything with the whole imagination' (*LEA* 191).

Lawrence argues that alienation from the intuitive faculties is one reason why England has produced only social portraitists interested in clothing and property, and why English painters have turned with relief to landscapes. 'Hogarth, Reynolds, Gainsborough' are dismissed as 'already bourgeois' (*LEA* 193), while John Singer Sargent, an artist Lawrence particularly disliked,[15] is said to produce pictures that are 'nothing but yards and yards of satin from the most expensive shops, having some pretty head popped on at the top' (*LEA* 193–194). The only English painter of human subjects he credits with having 'intuitional awareness and solid instinctive feeling' is William Blake, and 'there is so little Blake, and even in that little the symbolism is often artificially imposed' (*LEA* 194).

The second half of the essay is given over to a moving account of Paul Cézanne as the one modern artist who attempted to overcome visual cliché and painterly convention in order to depict the phenomenal world through his intuitional faculties. Lawrence says that Cézanne is 'the most interesting figure in modern art', 'not so much because of his achievement, as because of his struggle' (*LEA* 204). Even then, he launches into a bitter attack on modern art critics for their failure to understand Cézanne's battle against cliché, their condescension towards him, and the almost revivalist intensity with which they have celebrated the more self-conscious work of the post-impressionist painters influenced by him. Lawrence expresses special contempt here for Clive Bell's concept of 'Significant Form' in *Art* (1914), and for Roger Fry's book *Cézanne: A Study of his Development* (1927).

Pornography and Obscenity was first published in the July–September 1929 number of Edward Titus's magazine *This Quarter*. It was written in April 1929, shortly after Lawrence arranged for Titus to print the Paris Popular Edition of *Lady Chatterley's Lover*. Following the publicity caused by the police raid on Lawrence's paintings in July, in late August or early September Faber and Faber asked whether he would contribute an essay on censorship to their 'Criterion Miscellany' series. Without telling Lawrence, they invited the Home Secretary responsible for the confiscation of the typescripts of *Pansies* in January, Sir William Joynson-Hicks (now Viscount Brentford), to contribute an essay on the same subject. Lawrence extended *Pornography and Obscenity* from 4000 to 10,000 words. It was published on 14 November as number five in the series; Joynson-Hicks's essay, entitled *Do We Need a Censor?*, was number six.

In his essay, Lawrence argues that the State idea of pornography and obscenity is little more than a subjective judgment advanced by 'the *Vox populi, vox Dei*' (*LEA* 237). Everybody has a mob-self and an individual self. The mob-self unthinkingly labels as obscene any word related to sex and accepts, or even celebrates, the sentimental and suggestive depictions of love in nineteenth-century literature, modern popular fiction and cinema. In a counterintuitive move that he first developed in his journalism, Lawrence writes that 'Boccaccio at his hottest seems to me less pornographical than *Pamela* or *Clarissa Harlowe* or even *Jane Eyre* or a host of modern books or films which pass uncensored ... Wagner's *Tristan and Isolde* seems to me very near to pornography, and so, even, do some quite popular Christian hymns' (*LEA* 240). Lawrence later added J. M. Barrie and John Galsworthy to the list of writers who are 'far more pornographical than the liveliest story in the *Decameron*' (*LEA* 252–253), though he was forced to remove their names at the request of Faber and Faber. He also name-checked Marcel Proust, whom he criticises too in *Lady Chatterley's Lover*; Lawrence included Proust in a list of 'grand perverts' (*6L* 342) he sent to Aldous Huxley in March 1928.[16]

The additions Lawrence made to the essay for Faber offer an account of the pernicious psychological consequences of making sex a 'dirty little secret'.

Lawrence argues that suggestive art and 'rubber-goods shop' pornography 'is an invariable stimulant to the vice of self abuse, onanism, masturbation' (*LEA* 244). While sexual intercourse ('even in the homosexual intercourse') involves 'give and take', introducing a 'new stimulus' to replace a 'native stimulus', masturbation is 'merely exhaustive', deadening the self and creating a 'null effect' (*LEA* 245). In a move which echoes 'When She Asks "Why?"' ('The "Jeune Fille" Wants to Know'), Lawrence charges the Victorians with introducing the dirty little secret and the current older generation with policing it. He suggests that 'perhaps a majority of the young people of today have come out into the open with sex and laid salt on the tail of the dirty little secret', which is 'a very good thing', but he laments the fact that they are 'still entirely under the shadow of the grey elderly ones' (*LEA* 249). Fear of sex is, he argues, 'a condition of idiocy', and a dangerous one at that, since it threatens to 'drive every individual into the masturbation self-enclosure, and keep him there', creating 'a state of general idiocy' (*LEA* 253).

It was, however, in the third long essay of 1929 that Lawrence offered his sharpest and most urgent critique of contemporary attitudes to the body and sex. In 'My Skirmish with Jolly Roger', the introduction to the Paris Popular Edition of *Lady Chatterley's Lover*, he described the actions of the unscrupulous printers who pirated *Lady Chatterley's Lover* in the United States and Europe, and explained his motivation for issuing a cheap paperback edition of the book in order to address their profiteering. In October 1929, apparently with a view to privately publishing it as a separate booklet with the Mandrake Press, Lawrence extended it to four times its original length, producing the essay now known as *A Propos of 'Lady Chatterley's Lover'*. In January 1930 Lawrence decided that he did not want to publish it.[17] The Mandrake Press finally issued it on 24 June 1930, over three months after his death.

This essay sets out the consequences of alienation from the body and sex in far greater detail than *Pornography and Obscenity*. Lawrence describes the recent case of a woman whom he believed had 'masqueraded' as a man, 'Colonel Barker', married an unsuspecting woman in November 1923 and lived undetected for over five years until the deception was uncovered and she was sentenced to nine months in prison for perjury in April 1929. Lawrence comments: 'The situation is monstrous. Yet there are thousands of women today who might be so deceived, and go on being deceived'. He clearly saw the victim's ignorance of sex as having caused the situation, and he ascribed it to a culture in which women 'can't think sexually at all' and are 'morons in this respect'. Then he invokes the case of a 'venerable schoolmaster and clergyman, for years utterly "holy and good": and at the age of sixty-five, tried in the police courts for assaulting little girls'. Lawrence traces the abuse of the little girls back to a society which enforces 'a mealy-mouthed silence about sexual matters' (*LCL* 309).

Central to this essay is another attempt to dislodge the complacency of his readers by subverting accepted forms of logic. Modern society views it as civilised to remain silent about sex and the body, and barbaric and savage to confront and discuss them. Lawrence reverses the terms, showing how an enforced silence about sex and the body leads to cruel deceptions and abuse, to prostitution and conscious forms of lasciviousness, and in the young to a cynicism about the body and sex, and a failure to acknowledge and understand complex feelings in the body which ultimately results in the inability to feel anything except the 'sentimentality' and 'counterfeit feeling' promulgated by 'radio and film', and by 'the current press and literature' (*LCL* 312). He describes modern marriage as being based primarily on superficial modes of love acquired through imitation. He ascribes the high incidence of subsequent separation and divorce resulting from mutual hatred to an inevitable 'organic reaction against counterfeit love' (*LCL* 314). To underscore his reversal of the accepted logic, he clearly states: 'They accuse me of barbarism: I want to drag England down to the level of savages. But it is this crude stupidity, deadness, about sex which I find barbaric and savage' (*LCL* 315).

Lawrence attempts to define a way forward, out of this barbaric ignorance. He stresses how 'all that matters is that men and women shall do what they *really* want to do' (*LCL* 320). What he means here is not that they should satisfy their 'personal, superficial, temporary desires'; they must fulfil 'the inner, impersonal, great desires' that were once addressed by the rituals and ceremonies of the Christian world which Lawrence detects still in the 'Catholic Church, especially in the south' (*LCL* 317). Our deepest sexual instinct is the desire for fidelity, and marriage provides the form to realise this, while the festivals and processions of the Christian calendar put us in touch with the timeless rhythms of nature which we feel in the body: 'Christmas, the Three Kings, Easter, Pentecost, St John's Day, All Saints, All Souls. This is the wheeling of the year, the movement of the sun through solstice and equinox, the coming of the seasons, the going of the seasons' (*LCL* 322–323).

In Lawrence's view, 'the old Church knew best the enduring needs of man, beyond the spasmodic needs of today and yesterday' (*LCL* 322). He argues that unless we realise our deepest needs through this older Christianity, we must fall back on pre-Christian ideas of State control, relying, for instance, on 'priest States' or 'the Soviet State', where 'the State controls every individual direct'. Lawrence invokes 'the great religious States such as early Egypt', which 'may have controlled every individual direct, through priestly surveillance and ritual' (*LCL* 321). This is exactly the form of State control through 'life-directors' (*RDP* 108) that he had proposed in 'Education of the People' and explored in *The Plumed Serpent*, but now to the question 'do we want to go back, or forward, to any of these forms of State control', he answers: 'For my part, I have to say No! every time' (*LCL* 321). In March 1928, Lawrence had admitted to Witter Bynner that 'the leader-cum-follower relationship is a bore'; he suggested that the 'new relationship will be some sort of tenderness, sensitive, between men and men and men and women, and not the one up one down, lead on I follow, ich dien sort of business' (*6L* 321). He was setting out here the new route to fulfilment, and the new way to redress the ills of modern society, that he explored in *Lady Chatterley's Lover*, where Connie's journey is away from her superficial marriage to Clifford Chatterley, and his denigration of the body, obsession with social rank and reputation, and immersion in the abstractions of modern literature and the radio, towards a religious awareness of the life of the body and the flow of the seasons.

In *A Propos of 'Lady Chatterley's Lover'*, Lawrence states that 'marriage is no marriage that is not basically and permanently phallic, and that is not linked up with the sun and the earth, the moon and the fixed stars and the planets, in the rhythm of days, in the rhythm of months, in the rhythm of quarters, of years, of decades and of centuries'. He says that the phallus is 'a column of blood, that fills the valley of blood of a woman', and this is 'the deepest of all communions, as all the religions, *in practice*, know' (*LCL* 324–325). Just as he had earlier discovered the answer to redressing a Western state of alienation resulting from rationalism and science by attending to the clues contained in the Native American dances and ceremonies, and in Aztec beliefs, so now he sought to heal the modern alienation from the body and sex by discovering forms of phallic wisdom in the Bible still present in Catholic rituals but obscured by centuries of preaching and finally lost in Protestantism.

Lawrence's late concerted attempt to come to terms with his own nonconformist upbringing in order to address the damage done to himself and his wider culture by Protestantism was the latest instance of his deliberate shedding of sicknesses. As was the case with his re-evaluation of his mother's bourgeois values after her death, or his loss of belief in progress, England and the authorities during the war, or his attempt to articulate a new conception of the State in the early to mid-1920s, and even his reconceptualising of humans' place in nature during his last months in New Mexico, Lawrence exposed and critiqued forms of power and knowledge so deeply embedded in Western culture that they had become naturalised and even sanctified. To do so exposed him to criticism and ridicule, to prosecution for obscenity, and to persistent interference from the authorities. These things naturally took their toll on him, but at some level he also thrived on opposition. As his late newspaper articles and the essays of 1929 show, in his last years, despite the increasingly debilitating effects of his illness, he was more than ever driven to speak back to power, subverting official forms of discourse and collaborating with so many people, from literary agents and editors, to booksellers, printers and gallery owners, to ensure that his voice was heard and his paintings seen.

Notes

1 See Kinkead-Weekes (1996: 548).
2 See Lacy (1976: 188).
3 See Lacy (1976: 189).
4 See *5L* 193 (10 January 1925).
5 See 'Change of Life' in *Poems* 1568–1572, and Mabel Dodge Luhan's 'Change', which is transcribed in *Poems* 1858–1860.
6 For the 'Preface to *Black Swans*', see *BB* 377–379.
7 See *5L* 351 (12 December 1925).
8 See Nehls (1958: 410–419).
9 See *5L* 288–289 (19 August 1925), 293–294 (31 August 1925) and 307–308 (28 September 1925).
10 John Worthen and Andrew Harrison, 'Further Letters of D. H. Lawrence', *Journal of D. H. Lawrence Studies*, Vol. 5, No. 2 (2019), pp. 8–9.
11 See *3L* 614 (19 October 1920).
12 The titles which Lawrence gave his articles were sometimes altered by editors prior to publication, and some appeared under still different titles in the posthumously published volume *Assorted Articles*; in the following I prioritise the titles under which the articles were first published, but give in brackets the title as it appears in *Assorted Articles* (and in the Cambridge edition of *Late Essays and Articles*).
13 Lawrence invokes the letter from Austin Harrison in the essays 'Return to Bestwood' (probably written in October 1926) and Getting On' (written in early January 1927), in both of which he expresses his more critical attitude to his mother.
14 James T. Boulton, 'Further Letters of D. H. Lawrence', *Journal of D. H. Lawrence Studies*, Vol. 1, No. 3 (2008), pp. 8–9.
15 Frieda's son, Montague ('Monty') Weekley, recalled Lawrence saying to him in the summer of 1926, in a distinctive Midlands accent: 'Sargent, sooch a bad pēynter'. See Nehls (1959: 70).
16 In addition to Proust, Lawrence's list includes St Francis, Michelangelo and Leonardo, Goethe or Kant, Jean-Jacques Rousseau or Louis Quatorze, Byron, Baudelaire and Wilde.
17 See *7L* 633 (30 January 1930).

9

Healing: Lawrence, the Mother-Incest Motive and Wholeness of Being

Most critical accounts of Lawrence's entire oeuvre draw lines through it in relation to perceived phases in his work as a novelist. The early phase is understood to comprise *The White Peacock* (1911), *The Trespasser* (1912) and *Sons and Lovers* (1913); then come the war-time and immediate post-war novels, *The Rainbow* (1915), *Women in Love* (1920), *The Lost Girl* (1920) and the unfinished *Mr Noon*; then the novels of the early to mid-1920s, *Aaron's Rod* (1922), *Kangaroo* (1923) and *The Plumed Serpent* (1926), together, perhaps, with his co-authored novel *The Boy in the Bush* (1924); and lastly *Lady Chatterley's Lover* (1928). Lawrence's non-fiction is usually discussed in relation to these phases. Individual novellas, short stories and poems are, however, sometimes far more difficult to categorise and place because of Lawrence's intensive habits of revision; many texts exist in different forms and some were written and revised over a period of years, so it is not always easy to relate them exclusively to specific periods.

It is understandable that such lines should be drawn, and it is helpful in so far as it enables one to detect shared themes and techniques in each phase. The structure of the present book inevitably reflects conventional taxonomies in Lawrence studies, but my intention has been to question received wisdom and encourage readers to discover patterns in Lawrence's writing not only within specific phases but across his career. In this final chapter, I will address an important subject in Lawrence's life which shaped his imagination and his writing from beginning to end. This subject is his close spiritual bond with his mother as a baby and infant, and the emotional deficits created in him by his overwhelming sense of oneness with her and corresponding hatred of his father. I will begin by discussing Lawrence's understanding of the issues involved and of the mother-incest motive as he read about it in the work of Carl Jung and addressed it in 'Education of the People' and his psychology books, before tracing the legacy of pre-oedipal issues in Lawrence's novels and short fiction, foregrounding his attempts to address psychic wounds and bring about some form of reparation and healing in himself and others.

The Life of the Author: D. H. Lawrence, First Edition. Andrew Harrison.

The conflict between Lawrence's parents, and his mother's dissatisfaction with her marriage, had a profound impact on him in his infancy and youth. Lawrence appears to have intuited his mother's unhappiness well before he could fully understand its cause. As he grew up, he was made to feel that the bond he shared with his mother compensated her for the failure of her marriage. He once told May Chambers that he had to hate his father 'for Mother's sake' (Nehls 1959: 578). He first analysed the bond with his mother in a critical fashion in his 1909 play *A Collier's Friday Night*, in which (as we have seen) stage directions refer to the '*abnormal emotions and proximity*' of the Lawrence-figure, Ernest Lambert, and his mother, to the '*dangerous gentleness*' between them, and to the '*safe reserve of their souls*' being '*broken*' (*Plays* 57, 59). On 3 December 1910, six days before his mother's death from abdominal cancer, Lawrence told a new literary contact that he had been born hating his father because he was 'very bad' before Lawrence was born: 'This has been a kind of bond between me and my mother. We have loved each other, almost with a husband and wife love, as well as filial and maternal. We knew each other by instinct ... It has been rather terrible, and has made me, in some respects, abnormal' (*1L* 190).

Lydia Lawrence, *c*. September 1910. University of Nottingham, Manuscripts and Special Collections, La Phot 1/79.

As I noted in Chapter 2, Frieda seems to have encouraged Lawrence to recognise the Oedipal struggle in his early relationship with his parents, and to analyse it in his fictional portrayal of his early life in *Sons and Lovers*. The psychoanalyst Alfred Booth Kuttner published a review of the novel in 1915, which he expanded into an essay for the *Psychoanalytic Review* in 1916.[1] In the longer essay, Kuttner suggested that the novel contained a remarkably detailed depiction of the Oedipus complex. Yet, as John Turner has explained, there are important differences between Lawrence and Freud: Lawrence is primarily interested in the sexualisation of childhood ('the perverse, premature awakening of sexuality through parental exploitation') rather than childhood sexuality per se, and instead of tracing like Freud the Oedipal 'spiritualisation of an unconscious sexual desire' in the child, a spiritualisation necessitated by 'fear of the father', he shows 'the adolescent sexualisation of an infantile spiritual attachment' (Turner 2020: 57–58). It was the origins and consequences of the premature *spiritual* love for his mother that Lawrence analysed in *Sons and Lovers*.

Frieda noted that when Lawrence wrote about his mother's death in the novel 'he was ill and his grief made me ill too' (Lawrence 1934: 74). This suggests that writing about the loss of his bond with his mother created an abreaction in him, causing him to release emotions which he had not been fully able to express at the time. The understanding he gained from working through these emotions facilitated their partial displacement by the new bond he was forming with Frieda. Lawrence apparently told her: 'If my mother had lived I could never have loved you, she wouldn't have let me go' (Lawrence 1934: 74). Yet Frieda's strong reaction to reading Lawrence's poem 'My Love, My Mother' while he worked on *Sons and Lovers* shows how confronting his powerful feelings for his mother was a painful and *ongoing* process because of the secrecy and shame associated with them. At the end of her annotations on the poem, Frieda wrote: 'you are a sad thing. I know your secret and your despair, I have seen, you are ashamed—I have made you better, that is my reward' (*Poems* 1774).[2] While Frieda wanted to believe that she had cured Lawrence of the emotional consequences of the spiritual bond with his mother, this was clearly wishful thinking, as was Lawrence's related assertion that 'one sheds ones sicknesses in books – repeats and presents again ones emotions, to be master of them' (*2L* 90).

In the summer of 1914, when Lawrence and Frieda were staying at Gordon Campbell's house in south Kensington, John Middleton Murry remembered 'Long queer discussions in the Campbells' little drawing-room, over Oedipus-complexes and incest-motives, for it had been discovered that in *Sons and Lovers* Lawrence had independently arrived at the main conclusions of the psycho-analysts, and the English followers of Freud came to see him' (Murry 1933: 39). Two people we know Lawrence spoke with were Barbara Low and her brother-in-law David Eder. As Turner notes, Barbara Low was 'a school-teacher in Hackney with a growing interest in psychoanalysis', and Eder was 'a doctor who had been actively popularising psychoanalysis since 1911' (Turner 2020: 72–73). Turner discusses how psychoanalysis had become a conflicted discipline by the summer of 1914, since in January 1913 tensions between Freud and Jung had 'erupted into open hostility'. He sets out the three main areas of Jung's thought which differed from Freud as being 'a desexualised view of the libido, an existential view of the causes of neurosis and a creative view of the potential of regression' (Turner 2020: 76). Between 1912 and 1914 Eder responded to the conflicts in psychoanalysis by 'dividing his loyalties more or less evenly' between Freud and Jung; the papers Eder delivered at this time were not 'contributions to psychoanalytic theory but applications or popularisations of it' (Turner 2020: 74–75). Turner is surely right to suggest that Eder's 'unconcern for theoretical writing' would have 'endeared him to Lawrence', who would have been interested to hear about the different views of Freud and Jung and felt 'free to adapt them to creative ends' (Turner 2020: 75–76).

Turner says that Lawrence may have been invited by Eder to hear Jung address the Psycho-Medical Society in London on 24 July 1914, when he delivered a paper entitled 'On Psychological Understanding'.[3] In late November 1918, Lawrence borrowed from his friend S. S. Koteliansky the English version of Jung's *Wandlungen und Symbole der Libido* (1912) translated by Beatrice M. Hinkle and published in 1916 under the title *Psychology of the Unconscious*. Hinkle's lengthy introduction to the volume, which sets out the history of psychoanalysis and the differences between Freud and Jung, contains a whole section on 'The Oedipus Problem'. Hinkle notes how Freud sees in the child 'a definite incest wish towards the mother' which is swiftly repressed due to 'moral reactions' associated with the 'incest barrier' (Jung 1916: xxiv). She notes that if 'development proceeds in an orderly fashion', then when the time comes for the child to make a 'definite object choice' he will 'pass smoothly over from the limitations of the family attachment out into the world and find therein his independent existence'. However, 'if the libido remains fixed on the first chosen object so that the growing individual is unable to tear himself loose from these familial ties, then the incestuous bond is deepened with the developing sexual instinct and its accompanying need of a love object, and the entire future of the young personality endangered' (Jung 1916: xxv).

Turner observes that for Freud adult incestuous desire is caused by past fixation, while for Jung it is caused by regression.[4] Jung speaks of the fear which accompanies 'the longing to go back to the mother, which is opposed to the adaptation to reality'. He notes that the object of this regressive craving is not the *actual* mother but a *fantasised* mother, the 'mother-imago', which takes its power from 'the son's tendency ... to glance backwards to the pampering sweetness of childhood, to that glorious state of irresponsibility and security with which the protecting mother-care once surrounded him'. Such 'retrospective longing' acts, he says, 'like a paralyzing poison upon the energy and enterprise' (Jung 1916: 335).

For Jung, regression can be destructive and infantilising, but it can also free individuals up to discover new forms of cultural activity; the key to them coming through regression rests in the power of symbols revealed in dreams and fantasies, and these symbols – originating in mythology and religion – speak (in Turner's words) to a 'need for sacrifice, creation, rebirth and redemption at crucial moments of their lives' (Turner 2020: 78).

Lawrence subsequently lent *Psychology of the Unconscious* to Katherine Mansfield, telling her: 'Beware of it – this Mother-incest idea can become an obsession. But it seems to me there is this much truth in it: that at certain periods the man has a desire and a tendency to return unto the woman, make her his goal and end, find his justification in her. In this way he casts himself as it were into her womb, and she, the Magna Mater, receives him with gratification. This is a kind of incest' (*3L* 301–302). In Chapter II of *Psychoanalysis and the Unconscious* (1921), Lawrence describes the 'incest motive' as a 'mentally derived' idea logically deduced and damagingly introduced into the 'affective, passional sphere' (*PFU* 14) as a principle of action. A married man who 'finds it impossible to realize himself in marriage' recognises that 'his emotional, even passional, regard for his mother is deeper than it ever could be for a wife'. The situation 'makes him unhappy, for he knows that passional communion is not complete unless it be also sexual'. As he is shut in 'between walls of tortured and increasing passion, he must find some escape or fall down the pit of insanity and death. What is the only possible escape? To seek in the arms of the mother the refuge which offers nowhere else. And so the incest-motive is born. All the labored explanations of the psychoanalysts are unnecessary. The incest motive is a logical deduction of the human reason, which has recourse to this last extremity, to save itself' (*PFU* 13–14). Lawrence writes that at a passional level the incest solution 'rouses the deepest instinctive opposition. And therefore it must be kept secret until this opposition is either worn away or persuaded away. Hence the repression and ultimate disclosure' (*PFU* 14).

The deeply personal nature of his engagement with the incest-motive, and his sensitivity in relation to it, is made clear by the intensity of his falling out with Katherine Mansfield and Robert Mountsier over it. Having sent Mansfield the book by Jung, and shared with her his own ideas on the incest-motive, in January 1920 Lawrence felt outraged by the thought that she had colluded with her husband in rejecting some essays he sent them with a view to publication in the journal Murry was then editing, the *Athenaeum*. Mark Kinkead-Weekes has suggested that one of the essays Lawrence submitted may have been on incest (a version of one of the chapters subsequently included in *Psychoanalysis and the Unconscious*).[5] In February 1923, Lawrence dismissed Mountsier as his agent ostensibly because of the enmity between Mountsier and Thomas Seltzer, but also because he felt that Mountsier did not believe in him and his writing; Mountsier was never forgiven for expressing loathing for the psychology books and dislike of *Aaron's Rod*.[6]

Trying to grasp the emotional consequences of the incest-motive as he revised *Sons and Lovers*, reading about it, and writing about it in his first psychology book offered Lawrence ways of coming to terms with his relationship with his mother. A further aspect of psychic redress consisted in exposing and critiquing in the strongest terms the damage caused in children by excessive mother love. In 'Education of the People' and his second psychology book, *Fantasia of the Unconscious*, Lawrence describes the mother's urge to find conscious emotional reciprocity in the infant as a deadly act which destroys the fragile balance between the positive-sympathetic and negative-volitional nerve centres in the child's body which constitute his soul or unconscious (the life-force in him). In 'Education of the People', Lawrence suggests that the 'proud volitional centres of the lower body, those which maintain a human being integral and distinct', collapse when such reciprocity is demanded from the child, 'so that the whole individual crawls helplessly and parasitically from the sympathetic centres, to establish himself in a permanent life-oneness with another being, usually the mother. And the mother too rejoices in this horrible parasitism of her child, she feels exalted, like God, now she is the host of the parasite' (*RDP* 140). At one point, he moves from this impassioned account into a powerfully embittered reflection on his own experience: 'Would God a she-wolf had suckled me, and stood over me with her paps, and kicked me back into a rocky corner when she'd had enough of me. It might have made a man of me' (*RDP* 133). In *Fantasia of the Unconscious*, he writes that 'to impose *any* ideals upon a child as it grows is almost criminal', since it will mean that the child lives 'terribly and exhaustively from the upper centres', producing a tendency towards 'phthisis and neurasthenia of the heart': 'The great sympathetic centre of the breast becomes exhausted, the lungs, burnt by the over-insistence of one way of life, become diseased, the heart, strained in one mode of dilation, retaliates' (*PFU* 93). He says that such an excess in the sympathetic mode will weaken the child with stress and cause consumption.[7] Among the litany of exhortations at the end of the book is 'Wives, don't love your husbands nor your children nor anybody': 'if your little boy falls down the steps and makes his mouth bleed, nurse and comfort him, but say to yourself, even while you tremble with the shock: "Alone. Alone. Be alone, my soul"' (*PFU* 163–164).

Lawrence's desire to right a wrong by analysing his own early life and deducing from it a general lesson and a way of ameliorating things in the future was only, of course, a form of reparation. In the letter to Mansfield, Lawrence notes how the man's desire and tendency to return to the woman as to the womb is felt 'at certain periods'; the implication here is that it is not something which is overcome through understanding, but a state of the soul which returns. Critics such as Ruderman (1984), Dervin (1984), Storch (1990), Schapiro (1999), Cowan (2002),

Granofsky (2022) and Stoltzfus (2022) have addressed the pre-oedipal deficits, or 'narcissistic wounds' (Dervin 1984: 15), resulting from Lawrence's relationship to his parents, and their consequences. Drawing on the work of Jessica Benjamin, Cowan notes how between 16 and 24 months 'the child must resolve the conflict between the wish to remain in symbiotic union with the mother and the wish for autonomy as a separate individual' (Cowan 2002: 23). Granofsky describes the process of 'separation-individuation' as it is set out in the pioneering work of Margaret S. Mahler: the process takes the child from 'a virtual fusion with its mother to individuality' through 'four overlapping stages, which, in simplified form, may be termed differentiation, practicing, rapprochement, and consolidation'. The 'rapprochement' stage is crucial because it can be viewed as the 'turning point *within* the overall process' when the infant 'realises for the first time that it is not the centre of the universe' (Granofsky 2022: 6). Cowan explains that the child achieves individuation by identifying with the father, who comes to represent freedom, separation and desire.

According to these models of psychological development, Lawrence's failure to idealise his father prolonged the feelings of depression and helplessness associated with the initial stages of separation before rapprochement, and created in him a 'threatened loss of self cohesion' or what Heinz Kohut termed a '*disintegration anxiety*' (Cowan 2002: 20). Several aspects of *Sons and Lovers* are worthy of note here: the young Paul Morel's motiveless crying, which seems to reflect his overwhelming empathy with his mother and the depression and hopelessness he feels in relation to her conflict with his father;[8] his accidental damaging of his sister Annie's doll Arabella, and his subsequent ritual burning of it, which reveals (as Turner suggests) a deep-seated fear of the pain that the damaged doll will cause to his mother, and his absolute inability to tolerate seeing his mother hurt;[9] and the feelings of collapse, dereliction and nothingness Paul experiences following his mother's death.

The feelings arising from infantile emotional deficits are much harder to grasp and understand than the oedipal feelings which have been presented in drama and theorised by the Freudians. Yet, as Granofsky observes, perhaps the pre-eminent concern of Lawrence's 'psychic life' was 'to come to terms with his own complex feelings related to his childhood and its family dynamics' (Granofsky 2022: 15–16). As Dervin notes, for Lawrence 'creativity is more analogous to therapeutic working-through than to catharsis' (Dervin 1984: 10). Presenting the incest-motive and its consequences in his writing, and doing so repeatedly, and compulsively, meant externalising the feelings associated with the disintegration of the self, imposing a degree of order and control by discovering structure and meaning in them. Time and again in Lawrence's fiction, he expresses the attraction to, and fear of, symbiotic merger with maternal figures (in Jung's terms, the mother-imago), and he explores desired forms of intimacy with idealised father-figures (the father-imago) to compensate for the absence of such a figure in his earliest years. In both cases, the desire for merger with these figures is often accompanied by resentment, anxiety and a comparable desire for separation. The need for oneness with the mother is haunted by an unbearable anticipation of the mother being hurt or lost; Turner refers to 'fear of annihilating anxiety', which D. W. Winnicott calls 'unthinkable or archaic anxiety', as 'threatening the existence of the self' (Turner 2020: 59).

We can see how such feelings are worked through if we consider Lawrence's novels. In *The White Peacock*, Cyril Beardsall's father, Frank Beardsall, who abandoned the family eighteen years earlier, is effectively disowned by his son and mother; when Cyril's mother receives a letter from her estranged husband and goes with her son to visit him in his lodgings, they find that he has died and they refuse to admit to others their true relationship with him. We learn that he had lived a secretive life under the pseudonym 'French Carlin', and though he has done well enough financially, his dissolute past (which was partly spent abroad) and his alcoholism have caught up with him. Cyril barely recognises his father when he sees him asleep on a country path close to the Beardsall family home shortly before his death, and he does not mourn his father's passing. In contrast, his bond with another Frank, the gamekeeper Frank Annable, is idealised. Cyril's relationship with Annable is an inverted mirror image of his relationship with his father. He first encounters Annable, as he encountered his estranged father, while out on a walk in the countryside surrounding his home; in this instance, it is Annable who fails to recognise Cyril, his sister Lettie and her fiancé Leslie Tempest (whose family own the land which the gamekeeper polices). Thereafter Cyril actively seeks out Annable, who treats him 'as an affectionate father treats a delicate son' (*WP* 147). Storch describes Annable as 'a father imago who can give pride and independence to the son' (Storch 1990: 63). He combines intelligence with untamed masculinity. He was educated at Cambridge and found work as a curate in Leicestershire, getting married to a Lady, but he became disgruntled by the spiritualised nature of her love for him and ran away. After a period in hiding (during which there were false sightings of him in France and Australia), he took up his current job and, following his wife's death, married a working-class woman with whom he has fathered an unruly brood of children. Cyril is deeply affected when a stone wall collapses on top of Annable and he is killed. While Frank Beardsall is the rejected dissolute and irresponsible father, Frank Annable is the idealised and desired father-imago who haunts Cyril's imagination.

The mother-imago occupies a central position in *The Trespasser*. The novel dwells on Siegmund MacNair's urgent desire for merger and oneness with Helena Verden during their week together on the Isle of Wight. The demands Siegmund makes on Helena are great, requiring her to reciprocate his erotic longing while also adopting an all-encompassing maternal caring role in relation to him. At one point she feels 'sorrowful pity' for him, and kisses him, 'a long, anguished kiss, as if she would fuse her soul into his for ever'. Stunned and half-conscious, 'some other consciousness inside him' tells him that she is 'Eve—Mother!': 'Without touching him, she seemed to be yearning over him like a mother. Her compassion, her benignity, seemed so different from his little Helena. This woman tall and pale, drooping with the strength of her compassion, seemed stable, immortal, not a fragile human being, but a personification of the great motherhood of woman' (*T* 103). When Helena asks Siegmund to imagine what their day of departure will hold, he immediately answers 'Quick curtain' (*T* 87); his refusal to consider their imminent separation shows his almost primal resistance to imagining life without her. Siegmund's desperately strong yearning for Helena is tinged with shame and guilt because of his marriage to Beatrice, whose bourgeois values and emotional pragmatism become clear after his suicide, when she runs a boarding house in the family home where he hanged himself. The novel stages Siegmund's guilt-ridden and death-haunted drive for oneness with the idealised mother-imago against the backdrop of his indifference toward, and disdain for, his wife and the mother of his children.

There is also a mirroring element in *Sons and Lovers*, in which Paul's hatred for his father is set against the strong feelings he develops for Baxter Dawes, the estranged husband of his lover Clara Dawes. Like Walter Morel, Baxter is a working-class man who has been cast off by his more cultured wife and responds by lashing out at others; he starts out as Paul's love-rival and sworn enemy, but after the two men fight Paul seeks Baxter out in a typhus hospital in Sheffield and ultimately facilitates the reconciliation between Baxter and Clara. Lawrence describes the 'strong emotion' that Baxter arouses in Paul as 'repressed' (*SL* 426). In the chapter entitled 'The Release', Paul's guilt-laden feelings for Baxter as father-imago are set alongside his overwhelming feelings for his mother. Paul experiences release partly through the overdose he administers to his mother, which removes the unthinkable spectacle of her suffering, and partly through the bond he forms with Baxter, which enables him to resolve by proxy another psychic ailment through the belated attempt to idealise a father-substitute.

In the autumn of 1914 the American publisher Mitchell Kennerley sent the typescript of Lawrence's next novel, 'The Wedding Ring', to Alfred Booth Kuttner, who was one of his publisher's readers, to gauge Kuttner's opinion of it. Lawrence would subsequently revise this typescript to produce *The Rainbow* and *Women in Love*. Kuttner had read *Sons and Lovers* following its publication in New York on 17 September 1913, but his review of it would not appear in *New Republic* until 10 April 1915. In the report he sent to Kennerley on 10 November 1914, Kuttner said that the plot of 'The Wedding Ring' lacked the 'artistic unity and singleness of purpose' of the earlier novel. Where psychology was concerned, he confessed to 'a certain feeling of monotony and of repetition'. He said that the new novel 'contains simply chunks and chunks of psychological motivation almost literally transferred from "Sons and Lovers"': 'The Brangwens, Skrebensky, Birkin, all take what is practically Paul's attitude towards love and marriage. "And all the while his heart beat tight with pain, a sort of constraint or fear, or an insufficiency ..." (Skrebensky). They all have that same feeling of insufficiency, of failure and of being "half in love with death". They are all minor Pauls' (*R* 483).

Kuttner suggested that the 'Derelict' chapter of *Sons and Lovers*, dealing with Paul's feelings following the death of his mother, was repeated 'almost word for word' in a section of the new typescript. He described Birkin as 'simply an older Paul, more wretched and more pitiless, with consumption to add to the sense of disintegration'. Kuttner said that while the psychology in the earlier novel was 'beautifully and logically motivated', in 'The Wedding Ring' it was 'merely transferred'. He ascribed this to a 'complete breakdown of artistic restraint' in the author, whom he says 'hovers between the artist and the neurotic and often falls a victim to his morbid subjectivism to such an extent that his writing loses artistic validity and becomes merely the expression of a symptom'. On the evidence of this novel and the short story 'Honour and Arms' (an early version of 'The Prussian Officer'), he suggested that Lawrence was 'labouring under terrible sexual morbidities' (*R* 484). It is possible that Kennerley sent Kuttner's report to Lawrence. If he did, it might help to account for the intensity of Lawrence's reaction against Kuttner's 1916 essay on *Sons and Lovers* in the *Psychoanalytic Review*; in a letter to Barbara Low, who sent him the essay, Lawrence said he hated it and he referred to 'complexes' as 'vicious half-statements of the Freudians' (*2L* 655).

In a letter Kuttner wrote to Kennerley shortly after he sent him the report on 'The Wedding Ring', he added: 'It is painful to see such deterioration ... going on in a gifted writer, knowing as I do that it is of neurotic origin'. He suggested that a 'rigorous Freudian analysis would make Mr. Lawrence both a happier man and a greater artist' (*R* 485). In Lawrence's first three novels, the latent psychological content assumes a pattern which one can detect in the narrative. Repetition and mirroring make the latent content available for interpretation. In contrast, Kuttner implies that 'The Wedding Ring' reproduces the feelings associated with the latent content without the pattern or logic which would make it meaningful. He suggests that whereas the artistry of *Sons and Lovers* brought understanding to the neurosis, in 'The Wedding Ring' the neurosis was given free rein.

Since the typescript Kuttner read has not survived it is impossible to properly assess the accuracy of his report. In *The Rainbow*, however, cases of emotional and sexual impasse resulting from the incest-motive must be set against other instances where regression leads to rebirth and renewal in the manner suggested by Jung. In the first generation, Tom Brangwen, the youngest of six children, is 'his mother's favourite' (*R* 16). She sends him away to a Grammar School in Derby when he is twelve years old, hoping that he will become 'clever' and 'a gentleman'

(*R* 17), yet his sensitivity, passionate temperament and inability to 'voluntarily control his attention' (*R* 18) make him a failure academically. He returns to the family farm, Marsh Farm, where on his father's death he lives with his mother and one of his sisters, Effie. He comes to see 'the woman' as 'the anchor and the security' (*R* 20). When he is 23 his mother dies and he carries on living at the farm with his sister. His mother's place is filled by an old maidservant named Tilly, who retains a jealous and proprietary watch over him. Tom lives in a state of regression in the family home, and his only sexual experience is with a prostitute; like Paul Morel, love and desire seem mutually exclusive in his relations with the opposite sex. Yet he experiences an inner transformation when he meets a young married woman in a hotel in Matlock and goes off into the woods with her. Over dinner that evening he meets her husband, a refined foreign gentleman who talks with him, 'chiefly of horses' (*R* 25). The man captivates Tom, who clearly sees in him a gentlemanly sophistication, graciousness and worldliness that he wishes to possess for himself. We are told that 'the girl and the foreigner ... had set fire to the homestead of his nature, and he would be burned out of cover' (*R* 26). The symbol here suggests how exposure to otherness forces Tom out of a protected, known existence which stymies him. He is now prepared to recognise a Polish woman, Lydia Lensky, as the partner who can bring about his renewal. When Lydia first comes to Marsh Farm to ask for butter, she knocks at the front door rather than coming like others around the back of the property, and when he opens the door to her she comes in without being invited. The symbolism of doorways and breached thresholds echoes down the generations in the novel as a harbinger of change. Tom courts and marries Lydia, and although her otherness sometimes brings feelings of incipient disintegration linked to the loss of old maternal certainties, he realises too his desire for her difference and attains a form of wholeness with and through her.

Tom and Lydia create in their relationship what she terms 'a third thing' (*R* 163): their love enables them to leave their old selves behind in a Nietzschean self-transcendence of the sort that Lawrence felt he had achieved with Frieda. Will and Anna in the next generation experience mutual transformation but the third thing eludes them, and for Ursula and Anton Skrebensky in the third generation there is merely a conflict of wills in their mutually exclusive struggle for self-realisation on spiritual and social levels. When Anna refuses to fulfil the maternal role for Will, he regresses into an immersive love for religion and church architecture, with their symbolism of nurturance and rebirth. She negates his regressive spiritual cravings by asserting her right to fulfilment in the flesh through sex and childbirth, and by claiming the domestic space as her own province. Feeling his whole conception of religion challenged, Will burns his Adam and Eve carving. Regression in his case does not lead to new forms of self-realisation; he retreats into his woodwork and the upkeep of the church next door to their home. The pattern of conflict and ultimate female victory is intensified in the next generation, where Ursula's early reaction against her needy father's aggressive appropriation of her is repeated in her relationship with Anton Skrebensky, a child-like man who, like Will, regressively immerses himself in safe abstractions (in his case, the army and service to the nation). Ursula first challenges the grounds of Anton's belief in army and nation, then negates and nullifies him through sex.

In *Women in Love*, the characters all seem to be trapped in violent processes of disintegration and they are overwhelmed by incestuous feelings. The symbolism here is of fruitless labour pains and the desperate struggle of the infant to escape the womb. In the abandoned 'Prologue', Rupert Birkin has to face the inescapable 'entanglement' of his feelings: 'How can a man *create* his own feelings? He cannot. It is only in his power to suppress them, to bind them in the chain of the will' (*WL* 502). In 'Water-Party', Birkin tells Ursula that he wants 'love that is like sleep', because one must die from the old life and be 'delivered over like a naked infant from the womb'. To 'give utterance' to his new conception of love, Birkin must 'break a way through the walls of the prison, as the infant in labour strives through the walls of the womb. There is no new movement now, without the breaking through of the old body, deliberately, in knowledge, in the struggle to get out' (*WL* 186). Yet the draw to the mother is still very strong. In 'Fetish', Birkin tells Gerald Crich that a West African statuette displayed in Julius Halliday's London flat depicting a woman in the pains of labour is 'art' because it 'conveys a whole truth'; Gerald tells him that he likes the wrong things, 'things against yourself' (*WL* 79).

Birkin does not have consumption in *Women in Love*, but he does fall ill and the causes of his illness seem to be psychosomatic. The mysterious scene in the chapter 'Moony', in which Ursula watches him throwing stones at the reflection of the moon on a mill pond, railing against Cybele (the Phrygian goddess of fruitfulness, worshipped as the Great Mother) and Syria Dea (otherwise known as Astarte, a goddess associated with the moon and representing the female principle), suggests an unspoken, and perhaps unspeakable, recognition of his own mother-incest feelings.[10] In August 1917, Lawrence told David Eder that he would like them to talk together about 'the lunar myth – the lunar trinity – father – mother – son, with the son as consort of the mother, the *magna* Mater' (*3L* 150), since he thought the whole of Eder's psychoanalysis rested on it. The novel traces Birkin's attempt to overcome mother-incest feelings, while Gerald succumbs to them. In 'Excurse', Birkin rejects Ursula's 'emotional intimacy' as akin to Hermione Roddice's 'spiritual intimacy': 'Fusion, fusion, this horrible fusion of two beings, which every woman, and most men insisted on, was it not nauseous and horrible anyhow, whether it was a fusion of the spirit or of the emotional body? Hermione saw herself as the perfect Idea, to which all men must come: and Ursula was the perfect Womb, the bath of birth, to which all men must come! And both were horrible. Why could they not remain individuals, limited by their own limits?' (*WL* 309). Later, after he and Ursula achieve mystical sexual union in Sherwood Forest, he senses the life flowing through him in a circuit and we are told 'he was as if born out of the cramp of a womb' (*WL* 311). Compare this to 'Death and Love', in which Gerald Crich goes directly from his father's graveside to the Brangwen family home and sleeps with Gudrun, plunging 'deeper into her enveloping soft warmth' and 'the miraculous, soft effluence of her breast suffused over him, over his seared, damaged brain, like a healing lymph, like a soft, soothing flow of life itself, perfect as if he were bathed in the womb again' (*WL* 344): it is like 'a sleep of fecundity within the womb' (*WL* 345).

Women in Love is a crisis novel, not only because it contains 'the bitterness of the war' (*WL* 485), exploring the violent disintegration of its characters, but because powerful incestuous feelings affect and threaten to engulf Birkin and Gerald. Lawrence's writing about the damaging effects of excessive mother-love in 'Education of the People' and his psychology books underscored the greater degree of understanding of the emotional consequences of his relationship with his parents he gleaned during the war years and in its immediate aftermath. Incestuous feelings are present in Lawrence's subsequent novels, but with the possible exception of *Aaron's Rod* they are more contained and more fully integrated into their plots and thematic structure.

In *The Lost Girl*, Lawrence contrasts the two men in Alvina Houghton's life: Dr Mitchell, to whom she becomes engaged, and Ciccio Marasca, with whom she runs away and gets married. Dr Mitchell has all the trappings of male power through his profession and income, and he tries to bully Alvina into marrying him, but when she resists him, he cries out 'like a child': 'Love me! Love me! Love me!' (*LG* 268). She senses 'the hysterical little boy under the great, authoritative man' (*LG* 271). As Ruderman notes, Alvina is threatened by 'a mother-child dependency that stifles growth' (Ruderman 1984: 45). She has already felt the coercive power of two mother-figures, her governess Miss Frost and Miss Pinnegar, the manageress of her father's ill-fated cotton goods business, and she does not wish to perform the same maternal role for the man she marries. Ciccio offers her a way out. He tells Alvina that his parents are dead, and when she suggests that he has 'for a mother' Madame Rochard (otherwise known by her stage name Kishwégin), the leader of the Natcha-Kee-Tawara troupe, he asks her whether a man needs 'two mothers': 'My mother is dead, see!' He informs Alvina that 'A Frenchman is a little man when he's seven years old—and if his mother comes, he is a little baby boy when he's seventy' (*LG* 139). The implication is that Ciccio himself has no such mother fixation.

In *Mr Noon*, when Johanna Keighley has a brief sexual affair with 'her old friend Rudolf von Daumling' (*MN* 139), the narrator implies that it is a more noble deed for her to 'give to a poor self-mistrustful Rudolf substantial proof of his own virility' rather than 'to give him the baby's dummy-teat of ideal sympathy and a kind breast' (*MN* 140). Addressing his implied female reader in a comical mode, he notes: 'The sterner sex either sucks away at its dummy with such perfect innocent complacency, or else howls with such perfectly pitiful abandon after the lost dummy, that I won't really address the darling any more' (*MN* 141). In order to be reborn through Johanna, Gilbert Noon must 'fight with the matrix of the old era, a bitter struggle to the death with the old, warm, well-known mother of our days': 'Fight the old, enclosing mother of our days—fight her to the death—and defeat her—and then we shall burst out into a new earth, delicious' (*MN* 290).

Aaron's Rod opens in this spirit, with Aaron Sisson running away from the smothering life of domesticity with his wife and daughters, but Rawdon Lilly's ideal that individuals should recognise and embrace their essential aloneness proves difficult to attain for the male characters in the novel. Jim Bricknell, an ex-cavalry officer whom we first see in his family home at Christmas, 'beside himself, in a sort of hysterics' (*AR* 33), complains that 'If only somebody loved me I should be all right. I'm going to pieces'. Rawdon Lilly asks him whether he 'would like to be wrapped in swaddling bands and laid at the breast', to which he replies 'Yes' (*AR* 52). Bricknell is divorced from his French wife, with whom he has two children, and he is engaged to be married to Josephine Ford and in a casual relationship with a third woman named Lois, but he moves between them because of a desperate infantile need to be loved. He is rebuked by Rawdon Lilly and told to stiffen his backbone: 'You shouldn't want to abandon yourself. You shouldn't want to fling yourself all loose into a woman's lap. You should stand by yourself and learn to *be* by yourself' (*AR* 81).

Lawrence's subsequent novels explore collective forms of male-led political and religious life which he felt might be the key on a social level to addressing the mother-incest motive in the individual. In *Kangaroo*, Somers wants a committed bond with a 'mate' to complement his marriage to Harriett, but although he is drawn at various points to Jack Callcott, Kangaroo and Willie Struthers, he ultimately refuses to commit himself to their ideas and schemes for social renewal through the establishment of new forms of love between men. In *The Plumed Serpent*, the strong bond between Ramón Carrasco and Cipriano Viedma underwrites a revival of the Mexican gods which promises to address the psychic needs of the people. The novel suggests that marriage of the old sort, in which the wife assumes spiritual control over her husband, children and the home, will be supplanted by beneficent male control as Ramón's wife Doña Carlota dies and is replaced by the less assertive, more pliant Teresa, and Cipriano marries Kate Leslie and incorporates her into their new Mexican pantheon as Malintzi.

Yet in the last four years of his life Lawrence was still very much preoccupied with the damaging effects of mother-love. His late fiction brings a renewed sense of analytical understanding to the topic which reflects his critical re-evaluation of his mother and her attitude to himself and his father and siblings. In the essay

'Return to Bestwood', which concerns Lawrence's last visit to England in the autumn of 1926, Lawrence writes: 'Oh my dear and virtuous mother, who believed in a Utopia of goodness, so that your own people were never quite good enough for you—not even the spoiled delicate boy, myself!—oh my dear and virtuous mother, behold the indigestion we have inherited, from the cake of perfect goodness you baked too often! Nothing was good enough! We must all rise into the upper classes! Upper! Upper! Upper!' (*LEA* 18). In his late essays, journalistic articles, fiction and poetry we can trace his attempt to 'unlearn' (*LEA* 85) the values she had inculcated in him and his siblings, and to expose the damage he now felt they had caused.

Several of his late short stories explore the harm caused to children by dissatisfied mothers. 'The Rocking-Horse Winner' concerns a son who desperately seeks to satisfy his mother's desire for more money by finding the luck she tells him his father lacks, but his preoccupation with secretive and shameful incestuous feelings becomes so powerful that it kills him. Two other stories, 'Mother and Daughter' and 'The Lovely Lady', show young women acting to break mothers' emotional hold over their lives. 'The Lovely Lady', written in February to March 1927, explicitly works through Lawrence's newly awakened feelings of animosity towards his mother. Its plot re-works the central premise of *Sons and Lovers*, but where that novel had stressed the tragic dimensions of the mother's unhappiness with her lot in life and the inadvertent transmission of her dissatisfaction to her sons, 'The Lovely Lady' focuses on the mother's malign agency, egotism and disdain for her children. The eponymous lady is Pauline Attenborough, a preternaturally young-looking 72-year-old woman who lives with her 32-year-old son Robert and her niece Cecilia. She appears to be 'a wonderfully unaged woman, of perfect *chic*', but the narrator informs us in the second paragraph that 'agelessness is a question rather of strength and subtlety of will than anything else' (*WWRA* 244). Pauline's youthful appearances are maintained partly by a rigorous regime of sunbathing and partly by her domination of Robert and Cecilia, who rely on her financial support and are treated as worthless nonentities. We are told that Robert's older brother Henry, whom Pauline doted upon, died 20 years ago at the age of 22. Henry had chosen to marry an actress whom his mother despised and the mother's resistance to their impending marriage had caused psychic conflict in him, resulting in his death. As Cecilia says to Robert, 'I suppose he was just torn in two between the girl he wanted to marry, and your mother, and he died to get out of it' (*WWRA* 258).

The story sets up, then, a familiar autobiographical scenario: the mother's cherished elder son is killed by internal conflict originating in his mother's dissatisfaction, and the younger son's inner life is stymied by the same family dynamics. In 'The Lovely Lady', however, the niece acts to overcome the psychic damage done to Robert, freeing him from his mother's control. When Pauline Attenborough sunbathes alone, she is free to express her true feelings in an unguarded way. Cecilia overhears her cruel reflections on herself and Robert because they carry up a rain-pipe to the roof of the stables where she too is sunbathing. The voice is implicitly linked to a radio transmission, since her thoughts are 'broadcasting themselves' on a 'wave-length' (*WWRA* 254) which Cecilia intercepts. Learning what her aunt really thinks of them brings Cecilia to an awareness of their invidious position in the house and convinces her to act. She waits several days until she hears her aunt's voice again, then speaks to her down the rain-pipe in the guise of her dead son, warning her to take her will off Robert. The incident has a devastating effect on Pauline Attenborough, who ages overnight and is transmuted into her true guise as a spiteful, witch-like fairy-tale mother-figure. Cecilia forces Robert to realise his strong feelings for her, and Pauline's revelation that Robert is the offspring of a Jesuit priest with whom she had had a short affair makes marriage possible because they are no longer cousins.

In the late poem 'Healing', Lawrence's speaker states that he is ill because of 'wounds to the soul, to the deep emotional self', which 'only time can help / and patience, and a certain difficult repentance' involving 'realisation of a life's mistake, and the freeing oneself / from the endless repetition of the mistake / which mankind at large has chosen to sanctify' (*Poems* 534). 'The Lovely Lady' is clearly a story which gestures towards just such a freeing of the self from the mistake of capitulating to sanctified maternal love. Ben Stoltzfus has recently shown how the shorter fiction Lawrence wrote in the last six years of his life had a broadly holistic purpose, seeking to address wounds and conflicts in the self inflicted in childhood and deepened by the self-alienating aspects of modernity. He describes Lawrence's characters as 'striving to adapt as best they can to a life that has been shaped by parents, culture, and history' (Stoltzfus 2022: 8). In the remainder of this chapter I will show how Lawrence's final novel, *Lady Chatterley's Lover*, encodes his awareness of the self-divisions in his own identity and explores the 'wounds to the soul', including his pre-oedipal deficits and mother-incest feelings, that he had worked through so movingly in his writing, in a late attempt to imagine a form of restitution and achieved wholeness.

In 1955, Frieda told the Lawrence biographer and critic Harry T. Moore: 'The terrible thing about Lady C. is that L. identified himself with both Clifford and Mellors; that took courage, that made me shiver, when I read it as he wrote it' (Tedlock 1961: 352). Lawrence apparently read the first version of the novel aloud to Frieda as he wrote it, working outdoors in the countryside surrounding the Villa Mirenda. There is an obvious reason why Frieda would have been impressed by Lawrence's courage in identifying himself with both Sir Clifford Chatterley and the gamekeeper (Oliver Parkin, later Oliver Mellors), and why this courage might have caused her to shiver. When Lawrence began work on the first version of the novel in September 1926 his relationship with Frieda had entered a new phase. Lawrence's physical health was deeply problematic. In March 1925 he had been diagnosed with tuberculosis. By the autumn of 1926 he had suffered tubercular haemorrhages, and he had been ill with other conditions including malaria and bronchitis. If his poor health did not make him impotent, it would certainly have seriously affected his sex drive. He was aware that Frieda had begun an affair with the Italian cavalry officer Angelo Ravagli, the husband of the woman whose house they rented in Spotorno between November 1925 and April 1926. This affair, possibly begun between late February and early March 1926, became an understood fact between Lawrence and Frieda, though they chose not to discuss it. Reading the novel to Frieda would have been Lawrence's way of communicating his awareness of their situation and his appreciation of her need for (and right to) sexual fulfilment outside their marriage.

Clifford Chatterley is the impotent and cuckolded man who spends his time 'reading, writing, painting' (*FLC* 8); the gamekeeper is a working-class man who has retreated from modern life into the comparative isolation of life in the woods on the Wragby estate, where he rails against industrial modernity. Between them, these two characters encapsulate crucial aspects of Lawrence's own situation as he worked on the novel. As he rewrote it in the three different versions he brought the gamekeeper closer to his own social experience, transforming him from a working-class man with communist beliefs into a figure from the working class with a cricketer for a father and conflicted class sympathies, and finally into a grammar school educated man who has moved in middle-class circles in the army and who abjures politics and is equally sceptical about the motives of both miners and mine owners. In the following analysis I will refer to the third version of the novel.

It is important at the outset to recognise that Lawrence began *Lady Chatterley's Lover* as a means of addressing the class conflict he witnessed during his final visit to Eastwood in September 1926, when he saw for himself the animosity between workers and the ruling classes in the aftermath of a General Strike. Although the gamekeeper is given greater social mobility in the third version of the novel, he is initially reluctant to enter into an affair with his employer's wife (the ironically named Constance, or Connie, Chatterley) partly on class grounds, but also because (like Lawrence's earlier gamekeeper, Frank Annable) he has been damaged by an overly spiritual early relationship and by his brutalising marriage to a sensual woman whom he turned to in reaction against the earlier bond. The novel explores the degree to which physical desire can enable deeply class-conscious individuals like Mellors and Connie to transcend class prejudice, and it holds out some hope that Mellors might be healed by his relationship with Connie and the 'third thing' (the phallic consciousness) they co-create through sex and tenderness. On one level, the novel obviously enacts through our closeness to Connie's experience the joyous religious reconnection with the body and the cosmos which Lawrence saw as a pre-condition for self-realisation. Lawrence's late journalistic articles and longer essays, which I analysed in the last chapter, offer a lens through which to understand the ambition of the novel in this respect. I want to suggest here that on another, more implicit level, it allowed Lawrence to explore conflicting facets of his own experience and identity in an attempt at self-healing through recognition and repentance.

Health in Lawrence's writing entails a balancing of body and mind, so healing is both a bodily and psychic process his characters undergo. Lawrence's ill health left an indelible trace in the novel. His lungs had been weakened by two bouts of pneumonia, and he had almost died of the Spanish flu in the winter of 1918. Towards the end of his life he would go through periods when coughing became a real problem for him, meaning that he passed sleepless nights. Since tuberculosis was incurable, and the most he could hope for were periods of remission, it is understandable that he preferred to ascribe his coughing to bronchial problems. Mellors's ill health is foregrounded in an early exchange with Connie:

> He looked at her with his keen blue eyes. He seemed kindly, but distant. But at least he was sane, sane and wholesome, if even he looked thin and ill. A cough troubled him.
>
> "You have a cough!" she said.
>
> "Nothing—a cold! The last pneumonia left me with a cough—but it's nothing." (*LCL* 112–113)

This exchange can be placed alongside the description of Clifford's sleeplessness, which is revealed shortly afterwards:

> But his dread was the nights when he could not sleep. Then it was awful indeed, when annihilation pressed in on him on every side. Then it was ghastly, to exist without having any life: lifeless, in the night, to exist. (*LCL* 140)

The strange, altered syntax of that last sentence is typical of the slippery language of the novel more generally: it always seems to be switching perspectives, moving from an earnest expression of something, to a detached and ironic stance. It is as if the narrator engages with, but then distances himself from, the suffering of Clifford, which is ascribed in a curiously non-specific manner to his war experiences.

During one of the moments early in the novel when we get closest to Clifford (before he isolates himself more and more in Wragby Hall), we witness his nostalgia for the Wragby estate and all it stands for:

> "I consider this is really the heart of England," said Clifford to Connie, as he sat there in the dim February sunshine.
>
> "Do you!" she said, seating herself in her blue knitted dress on a stump by the path.
>
> "I do! This is the old England, the heart of it: and I intend to keep it intact."
>
> "Oh yes!" said Connie. But as she said it, she heard the eleven-o'clock blower at Stacks Gate colliery. Clifford was too used to the sound to notice.
>
> "I want this wood perfect—untouched. I want *nobody* to trespass in it," said Clifford.
>
> There was a certain pathos. The wood still had some of the mystery of wild old England. But Sir Geoffrey's cuttings during the war had given it a blow. How still the trees were, with their crinkly innumerable twigs against the sky, and their grey, hoary, obstinate trunks rising from the brown bracken. How safely the birds flitted among them! And once there had been deer, and archers: and monks padding along on asses. The place remembered, still remembered. (*LCL* 42–43)

We might feel here that Clifford's nostalgia for 'the old England' is being satirised. Connie hardly pays any attention to what he is saying. She registers the sound of the blower at Clifford's nearby colliery in a manner that suggests how blind he has become to the fact that his family has been instrumental in blighting the very landscape he eulogises. Clifford's desire to preserve Wragby wood is on the one hand deeply ironic, and on the other horribly class-based and elitist, having to do less with preserving living history than asserting ownership of it by eradicating trespassers.

Yet, in a manner replicated elsewhere in the novel, the narrator qualifies Connie's critical view of Clifford by conceding that 'There *was* a certain pathos' (italics added). In fact, Mellors's own (rather more bitter) meditation in Chapter X on the threat posed to the 'seclusion' of Wragby wood by the 'evil electric lights' (*LCL* 119) of the colliery and the miners' houses significantly echoes Clifford's call for its preservation. The narrator's own recourse to the 'mystery of wild old England' anticipates an essay Lawrence would write in September 1929 for the *Architectural Review* entitled 'Nottingham and the Mining Countryside'. Here, Lawrence expresses intense nostalgia for the countryside of his youth, and for an imagined version of 'old England':

> To me it seemed, and still seems, an extremely beautiful countryside, just between the red sandstone and the oak-trees of Nottingham, and the cold limestone, the ash-trees, the stone fences of Derbyshire. To me, as a child and young man, it was still the old England of the forest and agricultural past; there were no motor-cars, the mines were, in a sense, an accident in the landscape, and Robin Hood and his merry men were not very far away. (*LEA* 287)

Although in *Lady Chatterley's Lover*, the narrator's romanticised view of the past is distinguished from Clifford's self-indulgent nostalgia through the estranging effects of satire and irony, the admission that the woods do indeed possess a sense of pathos perhaps hints at an authorial kind of sympathy for Clifford that cuts against the critical, and even cruelly dismissive, perspective of Connie. It is, after all, *sympathy* which the novel asks us to feel as readers in opposition to the divisiveness of class, not disgust or condemnation.[11]

Only when we move beyond the satirical surface trappings of the novel and attune ourselves to its underlying relativism can we see the importance of Frieda's insight that Lawrence identified with both Mellors and Clifford. When Clifford receives the letter from Connie in which she admits that she is in love with another man, we are told that Clifford was not '*inwardly* surprised' to receive it: 'Inwardly, he had known for a long time she was leaving him. But he had absolutely refused any outward admission of it. Therefore, outwardly, it came as the most terrible blow and shock to him'. Lawrence's own *modus vivendi* with Frieda to acknowledge her relationship with Ravagli but not to address it directly is clearly relevant to the description of Clifford's response to having things confirmed. Where we might at first see judgement, we can now detect underlying empathy. The perspective of the narration shifts from a detached analysis of Clifford's response to the use of the inclusive plural pronoun: 'And that is how we are. By strength of will we cut off our inner intuitive knowledge from our admitted consciousness. This causes a state of dread, or apprehension, which makes the blow ten times worse when it does fall' (*LCL* 288).

Clifford's reaction to the news that Connie is leaving him is related to 'male hysteria' (*LCL* 289), which Ivy Bolton has previously encountered through her nursing of soldiers. She seeks to release his self-pity by performing surprise and upset at the situation in a grotesque display of counterfeit emotion. Yet Clifford's reaction to having 'the order of life broken up' (*LCL* 294) is to yearn for maternal love and oneness in a manner wholly reminiscent of Jim Bricknell in *Aaron's Rod*. Clifford becomes 'like a hysterical child' (*LCL* 288) with his nurse: 'he clung to her like a child, wetting the bib of her starched white apron, and the bosom of her pale-blue cotton dress, with his tears. He had let himself go altogether, at last' (*LCL* 290). From this point on, he relates to Ivy Bolton 'in a relaxation of Madonna-worship. It was sheer relaxation on his part, letting go all his manhood, and sinking back to a childish position that was really perverse. And then he would put his hand into her bosom and feel her breasts, and kiss them in exaltation, the exaltation of perversity, of being a child when he was a man'. Ivy Bolton is 'the Magna Mater, full of power and potency, having the great blond child-man under her will and her stroke entirely' (*LCL* 291).

The language of judgement here shows exactly how the shedding of sicknesses works in *Lady Chatterley's Lover*: emotions which the author has experienced are repeated and presented in a manner that asserts mastery over them. However, though the novel might seem to set up sharply contrasting sets of characters and outlooks, and to affirm and condemn them in stark terms, below the surface authorial sympathies typically complicate the picture. Just as Clifford's nostalgia contains a kind of pathos that the narrator detects in spite of Connie's emphasis on his class-based possessiveness and moral obtuseness, so Clifford's desperate regression as a means of restoring order and defending against the threatened disintegration of the self is pathetic in both senses of the term.

Events that occurred several months after the first copies of *Lady Chatterley's Lover* were posted to subscribers in July 1928 suggest the grounds for authorial self-recognition in Clifford's regression as a defensive response to the loss of Connie. Between 16 October and 17 November 1928, Lawrence and Frieda stayed with Richard Aldington, his partner Dorothy Yorke (known as Arabella Yorke) and Brigit Patmore on the island of Port Cros in the south of France. Lawrence had a miserable time there since his health was so poor that he was unable to join his friends on their bathing excursions. There was also a good deal of tension and unhappiness because Aldington told Arabella that he intended to leave her, and he began an affair with Brigit Patmore. While they were on the island Aldington fetched from the post office letters for Frieda which had been sent to her by Angelo Ravagli. He naturally kept these from Lawrence, but on one occasion a letter fell out of Aldington's trouser pocket when he went to bathe and Lawrence read it.[12] Lawrence opened up to Brigit about his feelings. He told her: 'you think you have something in your life which makes up for everything and then you find you haven't got it ... Two years ago I found this out' (Patmore 1968: 138). He was referring, of course, to his loss of Frieda's love in light of her relationship with Ravagli. One of his last acts on the island was to respond to a letter he received out of the blue from David Chambers (the youngest brother of Jessie), who was now a Lecturer in Adult Education at University College Nottingham. His uncharacteristically nostalgic reply shows Lawrence turning to the certainties of the past as an antidote to the upset of the present. He wrote: 'whatever else I am, I am somewhere still the same Bert who rushed with such joy to the Haggs' (*6L* 618). Just two and a half months earlier, on 31 August 1928, reacting to the difference in values with his siblings that had been driven home to him by his sister Emily's visit to see him in Switzerland, he had noted: 'I am not really "our Bert". Come to that, I never was' (*6L* 535). It was the present upset that created his yearning for that former self. In the poem 'Piano', nostalgia is presented as a painful betrayal of the adult self, which entails a loss of manhood: 'The glamour / Of childish days is upon me, my manhood is cast / Down in the flood of remembrance, I weep like a child for the past' (*Poems* 108). The 'child-man' Clifford seems a far more vulnerable and sympathetic figure in light of that recognition in Lawrence.

Lawrence may not have been aware when he began the first version of *Lady Chatterley's Lover* that the connection between the working class and the upper-middle class which he sought to establish was also a connection between two aspects of his own identity. The healing of the rift between the classes in the third version entails not only the coming together of Connie and Mellors, but also a renewed feeling of self-integration within Mellors himself (who speaks both the dialect and received pronunciation, and until he meets Connie is forced to oscillate between one and the other). Can the couple come together, and can Mellors feel comfortable with someone, combining both received pronunciation and dialect? At the narrative level, this attempted act of self-integration on Mellors's part is replicated in Lawrence's desire to express himself through the figures of both Clifford and Mellors.

Lawrence, of course, possessed two languages: the language of Mellors and Clifford. The few direct exchanges which occur between them might be viewed as staging a dialogue between the different personae of the author himself. One such moment strikes me as particularly significant. In Chapter XVII, Clifford writes to Connie in Venice and tells her about events back at Wragby, including Mellors's victimisation at the hands of his estranged wife, Bertha Coutts. Clifford recounts his interaction with Mellors, even reproducing Mellors's own voice in his narrative:

> "I asked him if he thought he would be able to attend to his duty in the wood, and he said he did not think he had neglected it. I told him it was a nuisance to have the woman trespassing: to which he replied that he had no power to arrest her. Then I hinted at the scandal, and its unpleasant

> course. 'Ay,' he said. 'Folks should do their own fuckin', then they wouldn't want to listen to a lot of clatfart about another man's.'
>
> "He said it with some bitterness, and no doubt it contains the real germ of truth. The mode of putting it, however, is neither delicate nor respectful. I hinted as much, and then I heard the tin can rattle again. 'It's not for a man i' the shapes you're in, Sir Clifford, to twit me for havin' a cod atween my legs.'
>
> "These things, said indiscriminately to all and sundry, of course do not help him at all, and the rector, and Linley, and Burroughs all think it would be as well if the man left the place. (*LCL* 268)

Here it is Clifford who brings the language of the two men together in his letter, and he does not simply parody or mimic Mellors's voice: he observes that 'no doubt it contains the real germ of truth'. Clifford even reproduces in this letter to his wife Mellors's insensitive jibe about his own impotence. Connie is appalled after reading the letter by Clifford's 'lack of sympathy in any direction' (*LCL* 269), yet this moment arguably entails the kind of comic engagement with Mellors and his language which Connie herself engages in earlier in the novel, in Chapter XII.[13] It is Mellors himself who is shown to be lacking in sympathy for (and sensitivity towards) Clifford here.

The desire in Lawrence to integrate two selves, and two voices, is expressed in one of his poems from the collection *Pansies*, written shortly after the final version of *Lady Chatterley's Lover*. In 'Red-herring', the speaker remembers his divided upbringing and views his current sophistication as simply a false screen hiding his true desire to reconnect with his father's working-class identity, bringing the two sides of his personality (and his two kinds of spoken English) together:

> My father was a working man
>   and a collier was he,
> at six in the morning they turned him down
>   and they turned him up for tea.
>
> My mother was a superior soul
>   a superior soul was she,
> cut out to play a superior rôle
>   in the god-damn bourgeoisie.
>
> We children were the in-betweens
>   little non-descripts were we,
> indoors we called each other *you*,
>   outside, it was *tha* and *thee*.

But time has fled, our parents are dead
    we've risen in the world all three;
but still we are in-betweens, we tread
    between the devil and the deep cold sea.

O I am a member of the bourgeoisie
    and a servant-maid brings me my tea—
But I'm always longing for someone to say:
    'ark 'ere, lad! atween thee an' me

they're a' a b–d lot o' —s,
    an' I reckon it's nowt but right
we should start an' kick their —ses for 'em
    an' tell 'em to —.

(*Poems* 424–425)

The jaunty, comic aspect of the poem cannot entirely mask the deeply poignant desire it expresses for a father-figure who will restore a lost sense of wholeness to a speaker whose life has been lived in the shadow of his mother. 'Red-herring' makes clear the intensity of Lawrence's delayed mourning for his father, who had died several years earlier (on 10 September 1924). The desire for the plain-spoken working man to step in and speak back to the upper-middle-class author, upsetting the order and complacency of the polite bourgeois world he has come to inhabit, is staged in Clifford's letter to Connie, as Lawrence brings together the two aspects of his own identity: Clifford and Mellors, the satirical modern writer who has no option but to live with his physical injuries and psychic ailments, and the displaced working-class man afflicted with illness who chooses to be an outsider, speaks his mind, and is forced to suffer the consequences.

Notes

1 The review is reproduced in Draper (1970: 76–80); a transcribed and annotated version of the longer essay is included as an appendix in Worthen and Harrison (2005: 263–292).

2 John Worthen thinks it likely that Frieda's comments on 'My Love, My Mother' were written in May to June 1912, but he concedes that they might have been added 'as late as June 1913' (i.e. the month after the publication of *Sons and Lovers*). See Worthen (1991: 412).

3 See Turner (2020: 79).

4 See Turner (2020: 78).

5 See Kinkead-Weekes (1996: 561).

6 See *4L* 57 (30 July 1921) and 375–376 (3 February 1923).

7 See *PFU* 98.

8 See *SL* 64.

9 See *SL* 82–83 and Turner (2020: 59).

10 See *WL* 246.

11 See *LCL* 101: 'And here lies the vast importance of the novel, properly handled. It can inform and lead into new places the flow of our sympathetic consciousness, and it can lead our sympathy away in recoil from things gone dead'.

12 See Harrison (2016: 372).

13 See *LCL* 177–178.

Afterword

Throughout this book, I have attempted to show how engaging with the biographical record and appreciating the contexts of Lawrence's life at any given moment enriches our understanding of his writing. For example, recognising Lawrence's complex relationship to Eastwood and working-class experience can help one to make sense of his ambivalent depiction of miners, unsure handling of mining details, and the way he problematises Paul Morel's relationship to the working class in *Sons and Lovers*. Knowing something about the early years of Lawrence's relationship with Frieda Weekley, and his adjustment to (and acceptance of) her worldview and that of her sisters Johanna and Else, enables one to detect the empathy in his depiction of Ursula Brangwen in *The Rainbow* as the 'leading-shoot' of her 'restless, fearless family' (Sagar 1980: plate 1). Taking account of Lawrence's strong response to the Great War following his marriage to Frieda in July 1914, and his feeling that it represented the collapse of a whole phase of civilisation, can help one to understand his otherwise mystifying analysis of the violent, disintegrative impulses and actions of the speaker in the poem 'Eloi, Eloi, Lama Sabachthani?', and the characters in the 1915 version of the short story 'England, My England' and the first, 1916 version of *Women in Love*.

A close and attentive responsiveness to issues implicit in Lawrence's relationship with other cultures and peoples, with friends and contacts, and with family, allows one to perceive patterns in his writing in different genres on both formal and thematic levels. His conflicted response to cultural otherness during his travels outside Europe between 1922 and 1925, and his desire to find new forms of religious experience and ways of understanding history and ecology, can be traced through the essays he wrote about Native Americans during his time living in the United States. His war-time letters to Bertrand Russell and post-war ideas about democracy, education and the need for top-down reform of the State provide a means of understanding his depiction of his protagonists' attraction to leader figures, and corresponding resistance to co-option into their ideas and political and

The Life of the Author: D. H. Lawrence, First Edition. Andrew Harrison.

religious movements, in *Aaron's Rod*, *Kangaroo* and *The Plumed Serpent*. Lawrence's need for collaboration with sympathetic friends and contacts is evident across his writing career from beginning to end; it informed his energetic engagement with private publication and journalism in the last years of his life. The oppositional polemics he developed in the articles he wrote for newspapers and magazines, responding in challenging ways to the topics fed to him by editors and finding ways to expose and undermine the complacency of readers, can be seen to have shaped his longer and better-known essays of 1929 on painting and on pornography and obscenity. Finally, recognising the lifelong impact on him of the conflict between his parents, and the importance of his subsequent reading about, and reflections on, mother-love, child development, and the mother-incest motive, can alert one to deep structures in his fiction reflecting unresolved issues with attachment. An appreciation of the ways in which his fiction worked through what he termed 'wounds to the soul' (*Poems* 534) facilitates understanding of *Lady Chatterley's Lover* as a novel whose form encapsulates acceptance and understanding of all facets of the self in an attempt to achieve wholeness of being.

At its best, biographically-inflected criticism provides fresh perspectives and compelling angles of approach which illuminate particular facets of texts. It also foregrounds unresolved (and maybe unresolvable) intricacies in the life and writing rather than providing clear-cut evaluations based on the critic's own theoretical and/or ideological investments. I have attempted to show, for instance, that Lawrence's relationship to Eastwood during his youth and early adulthood was variously influenced by his mother's aspirational values, the scholarships he won to attend Nottingham High School and University College Nottingham, and his intellectual movement outside the religious and intellectual conditions of his upbringing and education. His interest in socialism and the empathy he could feel for the working classes were tinged with detachment, condescension and even snobbery. Although he presents working-class life in part through a middle-class lens in *Sons and Lovers*, his natural propensity was always to write *against* the middle class and to critique bourgeois attitudes. Lawrence's responses to sexuality, race and cultural difference were equally conflicted. He declared that he had no moral objection to homosexuality, and he understood sexuality as a fluid concept and explored in sympathetic terms the pressure to conform to heteronormativity and the courage involved in acknowledging and acting on same-sex desire, but he was deeply critical of what he perceived to be the imbalanced power dynamics within same-sex relationships in schools, universities and the army, and he sometimes expressed deeply homophobic views. Although the war deepened his anti-establishment opinions and his critical relationship to England and Empire, his early experiences outside Europe led him to express racist, nationalist and colonialist views. He was in many ways transformed by his contact with the peoples and cultures of the American Southwest, but the extent of his understanding of these cultures is open to question. Lawrence's political views were also complex. His early engagement with socialism was more theoretical than practical. Although he expressed hatred of the bullying insentience of fascism as he experienced it in Italy, he did not believe in modern democracy and for a time felt that strong State control and the directing of people's inner and outer lives by one or more dictators, or 'life-directors' (*RDP* 108), was the way forward in the post-war period.

The richness of the biographical record in Lawrence's case keeps the critic honest by enforcing an acknowledgement of such complexities, contradictions and paradoxes. Lawrence took great imaginative risks, deliberately addressing topics which he knew his readers would find uncomfortable or troubling, and he developed strategies of approach to the literary marketplace to avoid or circumvent censorship, and forms of writing to challenge his readers to think and live differently. He confronted and expressed the full range of his own feelings and ideas; his fiction was a means to explore, test out and so understand them. The prevalence of ambivalent endings in his novels shows that the understanding he gleaned from fictional exploration, and the insights he offered his readers, were always relative and provisional. My aim in this book has been to emphasise the illumination that a biographical approach to Lawrence's texts can provide, while also paying heed to the irreducible complexities that make his writing so challenging, surprising, revealing, moving, disturbing, infuriating and offensive.

Bibliography

Biographical Sources

Aldington, R. (1950). *Portrait of a Genius, But ....* London: Heinemann.

Alpers, A. (1982). *The Life of Katherine Mansfield.* Oxford: Oxford UP.

Asquith, C. (1952). *Remember and Be Glad.* London: Barrie.

Asquith, C. (1968). *Diaries 1915-18.* London: Hutchinson and Co.

Asquith, H. (1937). *Moments of Memory: Recollections and Impressions.* London: Hutchinson and Co.

Bachrach, A. J. (2006). *D. H. Lawrence in New Mexico: "The Time is Different There".* Albuquerque: U of New Mexico P.

Bailey, S. and Nottingham, C. (2013). *Heartlands: A Guide to D. H. Lawrence's Midland Roots.* Kibworth Beauchamp: Matador.

Barr, Barbara (1959). "I Look Back", *The Twentieth Century* (March): 254–261.

Beauman, N. (1987). *Cynthia Asquith.* London: Hamish Hamilton.

Becket, F. (2002). *The Complete Critical Guide to D. H. Lawrence.* London: Routledge.

Bedford, S. (1974). *Aldous Huxley: A Biography.* London: Chatto and Windus.

Booth, H. J. (2002). D. H. Lawrence and Male Homosexual Desire. *The Review of English Studies, New Series* 53 (2): 86–107.

Boulton, J. T. (2000). D. H. Lawrence's *Pansies* and the State, 1929. *The Journal of the D. H. Lawrence Society* 5–16.

Boulton, J. T. (2001). *D. H. Lawrence, Philip Heseltine and Three Unpublished Letters.* Birmingham: Institute for Advanced Research in Arts and Social Sciences.

Brett, D. (1974). *Lawrence and Brett: A Friendship.* [1933]. New Edition, with Introduction, Prologue and Epilogue by John Manchester. Santa Fe, NM: The Sunstone Press.

Brewster, E. and Brewster, A. (1934). *D. H. Lawrence: Reminiscences and Correspondence.* London: Martin Secker.

The Life of the Author: D. H. Lawrence, First Edition. Andrew Harrison.

Burgess, A. (1985). *Flame into Being: The Life and Work of D. H. Lawrence*. London: Heinemann.

Bynner, W. (1953). *Journey with Genius: Recollections and Reflections Concerning the D. H. Lawrences*. London: Peter Nevill.

Byrne, J. (1995). *A Genius for Living: A Biography of Frieda Lawrence*. London: Bloomsbury.

Carswell, C. (1932). *The Savage Pilgrimage: A Narrative of D. H. Lawrence*. London: Chatto and Windus.

Chambers, J. [pseud. E.T.] (1935). *D. H. Lawrence: A Personal Record*. London: Jonathan Cape.

Chambers, J. D. (1972). Memories of D. H. Lawrence. *Renaissance and Modern Studies* XVI: 5–17.

Corke, H. (1933). *Neutral Ground: A Chronicle*. London: Arthur Barker.

Corke, H. (1962). Portrait of D. H. Lawrence, 1909–1910. *The Texas Quarterly* V (Spring): 168–177.

Corke, H. (1965). *D. H. Lawrence: The Croydon Years*, intro. Warren Roberts. Austin: U of Texas P.

Corke, H. (1975). *In Our Infancy: An Autobiography, Part I, 1882–1912*. Cambridge: Cambridge UP.

Daly, M. (1994). D. H. Lawrence and Labour in the Great War. *The Modern Language Review* 89 (1): 19–38.

Daly, M. (1994a). D. H. Lawrence and the 1912 Miners' Strike. *English Studies* 75 (2): 133–145.

Darroch, R. (1981). *D. H. Lawrence in Australia*. Melbourne: Macmillan.

Davis, J. (1989). *D. H. Lawrence at Thirroul*. Sydney: William Collins.

Delany, P. (1978). *D. H. Lawrence's Nightmare: The Writer and His Circle in the Years of the Great War*. New York: Basic Books.

Delavenay, E. (1969). *D. H. Lawrence: L'Homme et la Genèse de son Oeuvre. Les Années de Formation: 1885–1919*. Paris: Librairie C. Klincksieck, 2 volumes. Published in English as Delavenay, Emile (1972). *D. H. Lawrence: The Man and His Work, The Formative Years, 1885–1919*, trans. Katharine M. Delavenay. London: Heinemann.

Diment, G. (2011). *A Russian Jew of Bloomsbury: The Life and Times of Samuel Koteliansky*. Montreal: McGill-Queen's UP.

Doyle, C. (1989). *Richard Aldington: A Biography*. Carbondale: Southern Illinois UP.

Draper, R. P. (ed.) (1970). *D. H. Lawrence: The Critical Heritage*. London: Routledge and Kegan Paul.

Ellis, D. (1996). D. H. Lawrence and the Female Body. *Essays in Criticism* 46 (2): 136–152.

Ellis, D. (1998). *D. H. Lawrence: Dying Game, 1922–1930*. Cambridge: Cambridge UP.

Ellis, D. (2006). The Last Days of D. H. Lawrence: Four New Letters. *JDHLS* 1 (1): 139–147.

Ellis, D. (2008). *Death and the Author: How D. H. Lawrence Died, and Was Remembered*. New York: Oxford UP.

Ellis, D. (2017). Snobbery and D. H. Lawrence. *Essays in Criticism* 67 (4): 392–409.

Ellmann, R. (1982). *James Joyce*, 2e. Oxford: Oxford UP.

Feinstein, E. (1993). *Lawrence's Women: The Intimate Life of D. H. Lawrence*. London: Harper Collins.

Ford, M. (1937). *Portraits from Life*. Boston: Houghton Mifflin Co.

Gates, N. T. (ed.) (1992). *Richard Aldington: An Autobiography in Letters*. Pennsylvania State UP: University Park, PA.

Gertler, M. (1965). *Selected Letters* (ed. N. Carrington). London: Rupert Hart-Davis.

Gray, C. (1985). *Musical Chairs, or Between Two Stools*. [1948]. London: Home and Van Thal.

Green, M. (1974). *The von Richthofen Sisters: The Triumphant and the Tragic Modes of Love. Else and Frieda von Richthofen, Otto Gross, Max Weber, and D. H. Lawrence in the Years 1870–1970*. New York: Basic Books.

Hardy, G. and Harris, N. (1985). *A D. H. Lawrence Album*. Ashbourne: Moorland Publishing.

Harrison, A. (2013). The Lawrences, Katherine Mansfield and the 'Ricordi' Postcard. *Katherine Mansfield Studies* 5: 149–153.

Harrison, Andrew (2013a). "Meat-Lust", *Times Literary Supplement* (29 March): 15.

Harrison, A. (2016). *The Life of D. H. Lawrence: A Critical Biography*. Chichester: Wiley-Blackwell.

Harrison, A. (2018). D. H. Lawrence, Rananim and Gilbert Cannan's *Windmills*. *The Review of English Studies, New Series* 69 (292): 953–966.

Hassall, C. (1959). *Edward Marsh, Patron of Arts: A Biography*. London: Longman.

Healey, C. and Cushman, K. (ed.) (1985). *The Letters of D. H. Lawrence and Amy Lowell, 1914–1925*. Santa Barbara, CA: Black Sparrow Press.

Hignett, S. (1984). *Brett: From Bloomsbury to New Mexico, A Biography*. London: Hodder and Stoughton.

Hilton, E. H. (1993). *More Than One Life: A Nottinghamshire Childhood with D. H. Lawrence*. Stroud: Alan Sutton.

Hunt, V. (1926). *The Flurried Years*. London: Hurst and Blackett.

Huxley, A. (ed.) (1932). *The Letters of D. H. Lawrence*. London: Heinemann.

Huxley, J. (1986). *Leaves of the Tulip Tree: Autobiography*. London: John Murray.

Jefferson, G. (1982). *Edward Garnett: A Life in Literature*. London: Jonathan Cape.

Kader, N. M. (1977). *William Edward Hopkin*. Eastwood: Privately printed.

Kaplan, S. J. (2010). *Circulating Genius: John Middleton Murry, Katherine Mansfield and D. H. Lawrence*. Edinburgh: Edinburgh UP.

Kinkead-Weekes, M. (1989). *A Day in the 'Strife' of D. H. Lawrence: Some Problems of Biography*. Nottingham: University of Nottingham, Byron Foundation Lecture.

Kinkead-Weekes, M. (1996). *D. H. Lawrence: Triumph to Exile, 1912–1922.* Cambridge: Cambridge UP.

Kinkead-Weekes, M. (2004–2005). A Biographer Looks at *Mr Noon. The Journal of the D. H. Lawrence Society* 32–50.

Kinkead-Weekes, M. and Worthen, J. (2000). More about *The Rainbow. DHLR* 29 (3): 7–17.

Lacy, G. M. (ed.) (1976). *Letters to Thomas and Adele Seltzer.* Santa Barbara, CA: Black Sparrow Press.

Lago, M. and Furbank, P. N. (ed.) (1983). *Selected Letters of E. M. Forster*, vol. I. London: Collins.

Lawrence, A. and Gelder, G. S. (1931). *Young Lorenzo: Early Life of D. H. Lawrence.* Florence: G. Orioli.

Lawrence, F. (1934). *"Not I, But the Wind ..."* Santa Fe, NM: The Rydal Press.

Levy, M. (ed.) (1964). *Paintings of D. H. Lawrence.* New York: Viking Press.

Lucas, R. (1973). *Frieda Lawrence: The Story of Frieda von Richthofen and D. H. Lawrence.* London: Heinemann.

Luhan, M. D. (1933). *Lorenzo in Taos.* London: Martin Secker.

MacDougall, S. (2002). *Mark Gertler.* London: John Murray.

Maddox, B. (1994). *The Married Man: A Life of D. H. Lawrence.* London: Sinclair-Stevenson.

Merrild, K. (1938). *A Poet and Two Painters: A Memoir of D. H. Lawrence.* London: George Routledge and Sons.

Meyers, J. (1990). *D. H. Lawrence: A Biography.* London: Macmillan.

Monk, R. (1996). *Bertrand Russell: The Spirit of Solitude.* London: Jonathan Cape.

Monk, R. (1996a). The Tiger and the Machine: D. H. Lawrence and Bertrand Russell. *Philosophy of the Social Sciences* 26 (2): 205–246.

Monroe, H. (1938). *A Poet's Life: Seventy Years in a Changing World.* New York: Macmillan.

Moore, H.T. (1948). *D. H. Lawrence's Letters to Bertrand Russell.* New York: Gotham Book Mart.

Moore, H.T. (1951). *The Life and Works of D. H. Lawrence.* London: George Allen and Unwin.

Moore, H.T. (1954). *The Intelligent Heart: The Story of D. H. Lawrence.* New York: Farrar, Straus and Young.

Moore, H.T. and Roberts, W. (1966). *D. H. Lawrence and His World.* London: Thames and Hudson.

Moore, H.T. (1974). *The Priest of Love: A Life of D. H. Lawrence.* New York: Farrar, Straus and Giroux.

Moore, H.T. and Montague, D. B. (ed.) (1981). *Frieda Lawrence and Her Circle: Letters From, To and About Frieda Lawrence.* Basingstoke: Macmillan.

Morrell, O. (1963). *Ottoline: The Early Memoirs of Lady Ottoline Morrell* (ed. R. Gathorne-Hardy). London: Faber and Faber.

Morrell, O. (1974). *Ottoline at Garsington: Memoirs of Lady Ottoline Morrell, 1915–1918* (ed. R. Gathorne-Hardy). London: Faber and Faber.

Murry, J. M. (1933). *Reminiscences of D. H. Lawrence*. London: Jonathan Cape.

Murry, J. M. (1935). *Between Two Worlds: An Autobiography*. London: Jonathan Cape.

Murry, J. M. (1931). *Son of Woman: The Story of D. H. Lawrence*. London: Jonathan Cape.

Murry, K. M. (1986). *Beloved Quixote: The Unknown Life of John Middleton Murry*. London: Souvenir Press.

Nehls, E. (ed.) (1957). *D. H. Lawrence: A Composite Biography.*, vol. 1. Madison: U of Wisconsin P.

Nehls, E. (ed.) (1958). *D. H. Lawrence: A Composite Biography*, vol. 2. Madison: U of Wisconsin P.

Nehls, E. (ed.) (1959). *D. H. Lawrence: A Composite Biography.*, vol. 3. Madison: U of Wisconsin P.

Neville, G. H. (1981). *A Memoir of D. H. Lawrence (The Betrayal)* (ed. C. Baron). Cambridge: Cambridge UP.

O'Sullivan, V. and Scott, M. (ed.) (1984). *The Collected Letters of Katherine Mansfield*, vol. I. Oxford: Oxford UP.

Owen, R. (2014). *Lady Chatterley's Villa: D. H. Lawrence on the Italian Riviera*. London: Haus Publishing.

Parmenter, R. (1984). *Lawrence in Oaxaca: A Quest for the Novelist in Mexico*. Salt Lake City: Gibbs M. Smith.

Patmore, D. (ed.) (1968). *My Friends When Young: The Memoirs of Brigit Patmore*. London: Heinemann.

Pilditch, J. (2007). *Catherine Carswell: A Biography*. Edinburgh: John Donald.

Pollnitz, C. (1997). 'No Form or Appropriate Ceremony': An Account of D. H. Lawrence's Funeral. *The Journal of the D. H. Lawrence Society* 52–62.

Poplawski, P. (1995). *The Works of D. H. Lawrence: A Chronological Checklist*. Nottingham: D. H. Lawrence Society.

Poplawski, P. (1996). *D. H. Lawrence: A Reference Companion*. Westport, CT: Greenwood Press.

Pound, E. (1971). *The Selected Letters of Ezra Pound* (ed. D. D. Paige). New York: New Directions.

Preston, P. (1994). *A D. H. Lawrence Chronology*. London: Macmillan.

Roberts, W. and Poplawski, P. (ed.) (2001). *A Bibliography of D. H. Lawrence*, 3e. Cambridge: Cambridge UP.

Russell, B. (1968). *The Autobiography of Bertrand Russell*, vol. II (1914–1944). London: George Allen and Unwin.

Sagar, K. (1979). *D. H. Lawrence: A Calendar of his Works*. Manchester: Manchester UP.

Sagar, K. (1980). *The Life of D. H. Lawrence: An Illustrated Biography*. London: Eyre Methuen.

Sagar, K. (ed.) (1982). *A D. H. Lawrence Handbook*. Manchester: Manchester UP.

Sagar, K. (ed.) (1982a). *D. H. Lawrence and New Mexico*. Salt Lake City, UT: G. M. Smith.

Seymour, M. (1992). *Ottoline Morrell: Life on the Grand Scale*. London: Hodder and Stoughton.

Skinner, M. L. (1973). *The Fifth Sparrow: An Autobiography*. London: Angus and Robertson.

Smith, B. (1994). *Peter Warlock: The Life of Philip Heseltine*. Oxford: Oxford UP.

Smith, G. (ed.) (1969). *Letters of Aldous Huxley*. London: Chatto and Windus.

Smith, H. (2017). *The Uncommon Reader: A Life of Edward Garnett*. London: Jonathan Cape.

Spencer, R. (1979). *D. H. Lawrence Country: A Portrait of his Early Life and Background with Illustrations, Maps and Guides*. London: Cecil Woolf.

Squires, M. (2008). *D. H. Lawrence and Frieda: A Portrait of Love and Loyalty*. London: Andre Deutsch.

Squires, M. (2023). *The Limits of Love: The Lives of D. H. Lawrence and Frieda von Richthofen*. Baton Rouge: Louisiana State UP.

Squires, M. and Talbot, L. K. (2002). *Living at the Edge: A Biography of D. H. Lawrence and Frieda von Richthofen*. Madison: U of Wisconsin P.

Stevens, C. J. (1988). *Lawrence at Tregerthen*. Troy, NY: The Whitston Publishing Company.

Storer, R.W. (1985). *Some Aspects of Brinsley Colliery and the Lawrence Connection*. Selston: Privately Printed.

Talbot, L. K. (2012). From Old Germany to New Mexico: An Overview of Frieda Lawrence's Letters. *DHLR* 37 (2): 72–249.

Taylor, J. Clement Phillips (1962). "Boys of the Beauvale Breed", *Eastwood and Kimberley Advertiser* (30 December 1960–17 August 1962).

Tedlock, E.W. (1952). A Forgotten War Poem by D. H. Lawrence. *Modern Language Notes* 67 (6): 410–413.

Tedlock, E.W. (ed.) (1961). *Frieda Lawrence: The Memoirs and Correspondence*. London: Heinemann.

Thornycroft, R. (1991). *Time Which Spaces Us Apart, completed by Chloë Baynes*. Shepton Mallet, Somerset: Privately Printed.

Turner, J. (2002). D. H. Lawrence in the Wilkinson Diaries. *DHLR* 30 (2): 5–63.

Turner, J., Rumpf-Worthen, C., and Jenkins, R. (1990). The Otto Gross–Frieda Weekley Correspondence: Transcribed, Translated, and Annotated. *DHLR* 22 (2): 137–227.

Turner, J. and Worthen, J. (1999). Ideas of Community: Lawrence and 'Rananim'. *D. H. Lawrence Studies* 8: 135–171.

Turner, J. (2010). *Louie: Her Remarkable East Midlands Life, And How the Young D. H. Lawrence Won Her Heart Then Jilted Her*. Loughborough: Reprint, 2010.

Vallero, S. and Ferrari, P. (2012). *The Bay of Lorenzo: D. H. Lawrence at Fiascherino*. La Spezia: Edizioni Cinque Terre.

Vasey, L. and Worthen, J. (1988). *Mr Noon*/Mr Noon. *DHLR* 20 (2): 179–189.

Vogeler, M. S. (2008). *Austin Harrison and the 'English Review'*. Columbia: U of Missouri P.

Waterfield, L. (1961). *Castle in Italy: An Autobiography*. London: John Murray.

West, R. (1930). *Elegy*. New York: Phoenix Book Shop.

Wilson, F. (2021). *Burning Man: The Ascent of D. H. Lawrence*. London: Bloomsbury.

Wolff, G. (1976). *Black Sun: The Brief Transit and Violent Eclipse of Harry Crosby*. New York: Random House.

Worthen, J. (1986). Lawrence and Eastwood. In: *D. H. Lawrence: Centenary Essays* (ed. M. Kalnins), 1–20. Bristol: Bristol Classical Press.

Worthen, J. (1989). *D. H. Lawrence: A Literary Life*. London: Macmillan.

Worthen, J. (1991). *D. H. Lawrence: The Early Years, 1885–1912*. Cambridge: Cambridge UP.

Worthen, J. (1994). D. H. Lawrence and the Society for the Study of Social Questions. *Notes and Queries* 41 (3): 364–366.

Worthen, J. (1995). *Cold Hearts and Coronets: Lawrence, the Weekleys, and the von Richthofens, or, The Right and Romantic versus the Wrong and Repulsive*. Nottingham: D. H. Lawrence Centre Occasional Papers No. 2.

Worthen, J. (1995a). Orts and Slarts: Two Biographical Pieces on D. H. Lawrence. *The Review of English Studies, New Series* 46 (181): 26–40.

Worthen, J. (1996). D. H. Lawrence and the 'Expensive Edition Business'. In: *Modernist Writers and the Marketplace* (ed. I. Willison, W. Gould, and W. Chernaik), 105–123. Basingstoke: Macmillan.

Worthen, J. (2003). The Date of Birth of D. H. Lawrence's Father. *Notes and Queries* 50 (3): 327–328.

Worthen, J. (2005). *D. H. Lawrence: The Life of an Outsider*. London: Allen Lane.

Worthen, J. (2009). 'Over Some Frontiers' at Monte Cassino: Lawrence and Maurice Magnus. In: *Windows to the Sun: D. H. Lawrence's "Thought-Adventures"* (ed. E. Ingersoll and V. Hyde), 50–68. Madison, NJ: Fairleigh Dickinson UP.

Worthen, J. (2012). *Experiments: Lectures on Lawrence*. Nottingham: Critical, Cultural and Communications Press.

Wright, L. E. (1992–1993). D. H. Lawrence, Robert Mountsier and the Journalist Spy Controversy. *The Journal of the D. H. Lawrence Society* 7–20.

Wright, L. E. (2007). *Maurice Magnus: A Biography*. Newcastle: Cambridge Scholars Publishing.

Zytaruk, G. J. (1979). The Collected Letters of Jessie Chambers. In: *DHLR*, 12.

Criticism, Commentary and Other Sources

Adelman, G. (2002). *Reclaiming D. H. Lawrence: Contemporary Writers Speak Out.* Lewisburg, PA: Bucknell UP.

Al-Dabbagh, A. (2011). *D. H. Lawrence: A Study of Literary Fascism.* Oxford: Peter Lang.

Aldington, R. (1927). *D. H. Lawrence; An Indiscretion.* Seattle: University of Washington Chapbooks No. 6.

Alldritt, K. (1971). *The Visual Imagination of D. H. Lawrence.* London: Edward Arnold.

Balbert, P. (1989). *D. H. Lawrence and the Phallic Imagination: Essays on Sexual Identity and Feminist Misreading.* Basingstoke: Macmillan.

Balbert, P. and Marcus, P.L. (ed.) (1985). *D. H. Lawrence: A Centenary Consideration.* Ithaca, NY: Cornell UP.

Bell, M. (1992). *D. H. Lawrence: Language and Being.* Cambridge: Cambridge UP.

Black, M. (1986). *D. H. Lawrence: The Early Fiction. A Commentary.* Basingstoke: Macmillan.

Black, M. (1991). *D. H. Lawrence: The Early Philosophical Works. A Commentary.* Basingstoke: Macmillan.

Black, M. (2001). *Lawrence's England: The Major Fiction, 1913–1920.* Basingstoke: Palgrave Macmillan.

Booth, H. J. (ed.) (2009). *New D. H. Lawrence.* Manchester: Manchester UP.

Britton, D. (1988). *Lady Chatterley: The Making of the Novel.* London: Unwin Hyman.

Brown, C. and Reid, S. (ed.) (2020). *The Edinburgh Companion to D. H. Lawrence and the Arts.* Edinburgh: Edinburgh UP.

Caudwell, C. (1938). *Studies in a Dying Culture.* London: John Lane.

Chaudhuri, A. (2003). *D. H. Lawrence and 'Difference': Postcoloniality and the Poetry of the Present.* Oxford: Clarendon Press.

Clark, L. D. (1980). *The Minoan Distance: The Symbolism of Travel in D. H. Lawrence.* Tucson: U of Arizona P.

Clarke, C. (1969). *River of Dissolution: D. H. Lawrence and English Romanticism.* London: Routledge and Kegan Paul.

Cowan, J. C. (2002). *D. H. Lawrence: Self and Sexuality.* Columbus, OH: Ohio State UP.

Cram, D. and Pollnitz, C. (2001). D. H. Lawrence as Verse Translator. *The Cambridge Quarterly* 30 (2): 133–150.

Cushman, K. (1978). *D. H. Lawrence at Work: The Emergence of the 'Prussian Officer' Stories.* Charlottesville: UP of Virginia.

Cushman, K. and Ingersoll, E. (ed.) (2003). *D. H. Lawrence: New Worlds.* Madison, NJ: Fairleigh Dickinson UP.

Daly, M. (2019). *Lawrence from the Left: Collected Essays on D. H. Lawrence.* London: Critical, Cultural and Communications Press.

Dervin, D. (1984). *A 'Strange Sapience': The Creative Imagination of D. H. Lawrence.* Amherst, MA: U of Massachusetts P.

Donaldson, G. and Kalnins, M. (ed.) (1999). *D. H. Lawrence in Italy and England.* Basingstoke: Macmillan.

Eagleton, T. (1984). *Criticism and Ideology: A Study in Marxist Literary Theory*. [1976]. Fourth Impression. London: Verso.

Eggert, P. and Worthen, J. (ed.) (1996). *Lawrence and Comedy*. Cambridge: Cambridge UP.

Ellis, D. and De Zordo, O. (ed.) (1992). *D. H. Lawrence: Critical Assessments*, vol. 4. Mountfield: Helm Information.

Ellis, D. and Mills, H. (1988). *D. H. Lawrence's Non-Fiction: Art, Thought and Genre.* Cambridge: Cambridge UP.

Ellis, D. (ed.) (2006a). *D. H. Lawrence's 'Women in Love': A Casebook.* New York: Oxford UP.

Ellis, D. (2015). *Love and Sex in D. H. Lawrence*. Clemson, SC: Clemson UP.

Feigel, L. (2022). *Look! We Have Come Through!: Living with D. H. Lawrence*. London: Bloomsbury.

Fernihough, A. (1993). *D. H. Lawrence: Aesthetics and Ideology*. Oxford: Clarendon Press.

Fernihough, A. (ed.) (2001). *The Cambridge Companion to D. H. Lawrence.* Cambridge: Cambridge UP.

Fernihough, A. (2013). *Freewomen and Supermen: Edwardian Radicals and Literary Modernism*. Oxford: Oxford UP.

Ferretter, L. (2013). *The Glyph and the Gramophone: D. H. Lawrence's Religion.* London: Bloomsbury.

Game, D. (2015). *D. H. Lawrence's Australia: Anxiety at the Edge of Empire*. Farnham: Ashgate.

Garnett, E. (1907). *The Breaking Point: A Censured Play*. London: Duckworth.

Gertzman, J. A. (1989). *A Descriptive Bibliography of 'Lady Chatterley's Lover': With Essays Toward a Publishing History of the Novel*. Westport, CT: Greenwood Press.

Gifford, T. (2023). *D. H. Lawrence, Ecofeminism and Nature*. Abingdon: Routledge.

Gilbert, S. M. (1972). *Acts of Attention: The Poems of D. H. Lawrence*. Ithaca, NY: Cornell UP.

Granofsky, R. (2003). *D. H. Lawrence and Survival: Darwinism in the Fiction of the Transitional Period*. Montreal: McGill-Queen's UP.

Granofsky, R. (2022). *D. H. Lawrence and Attachment*. Montreal: McGill-Queen's UP.

Greiff, L. (2001). *D. H. Lawrence: Fifty Years on Film*. Carbondale: Southern Illinois UP.

Grice, A. (2022). *D. H. Lawrence and the Literary Marketplace: The Early Writings.* Edinburgh: Edinburgh UP.

Grice, A. (ed.) (2024). *The Bloomsbury Handbook to D. H. Lawrence*. London: Bloomsbury.

Harris, J. H. (1984). *The Short Fiction of D. H. Lawrence*. New Brunswick, NJ: Rutgers UP.

Harrison, A. (2003). *D. H. Lawrence and Italian Futurism: A Study of Influence.* Amsterdam: Editions Rodopi.

Harrison, A. (2013b). *The White Peacock* and 'The School of Lorna Doone'. *DHLR* 38 (1): 45–56.

Harrison, A. (ed.) (2018a). *D. H. Lawrence in Context.* Cambridge: Cambridge UP.

Hart, P. (2005). *The Somme.* London: Weidenfeld and Nicolson.

Henley, W.E. (1907). *Poems.* 10th impression. London: David Nutt.

Hillier, H. (2008). *Talking Lawrence: Patterns of Eastwood Dialect in the Work of D. H. Lawrence.* Nottingham: Critical, Cultural and Communications Press.

Holderness, G. (1982). *D. H. Lawrence: History, Ideology and Fiction.* Dublin: Gill and Macmillan.

Hyde, G. M. (1981). *D. H. Lawrence and the Art of Translation.* London: Macmillan.

Hyde, G. M. (1990). *D. H. Lawrence.* Basingstoke: Macmillan.

Hyde, H. M. (ed.) (1990). *The Lady Chatterley's Lover Trial.* London: The Bodley Head.

Hyde, V. C. and Ingersoll, E. G. (ed.) (2010). *"Terra Incognita": D. H. Lawrence at the Frontiers.* Madison, NJ: Fairleigh Dickinson UP.

Iida, T. (ed.) (1999). *The Reception of D. H. Lawrence Around the World.* Fukuoka: Kyushu UP.

Ingram, A. (1990). *The Language of D. H. Lawrence.* Basingstoke: Macmillan.

Jansohn, C. and Mehl, D. (ed.) (2007). *The Reception of D. H. Lawrence in Europe.* London: Continuum.

Jenkins, L. M. (2015). *The American Lawrence.* Gainesville: UP of Florida.

Jones, B. (2010). *The Last Poems of D. H. Lawrence: Shaping a Late Style.* Farnham: Ashgate.

Jung, C.G. (1916). *Psychology of the Unconscious.* Trans. Beatrice M. Hinkle. New York: Moffat, Yard and Co.

Kalnins, M. (ed.) (1986). *D. H. Lawrence: Centenary Essays.* Bristol: Bristol Classical Press.

Kearney, M. F. (1998). *Major Short Stories of D. H. Lawrence: A Handbook.* New York: Garland Publishing.

Kimber, G. and Smith, A. (ed.) (2014). *The Poetry and Critical Writings of Katherine Mansfield.* Edinburgh: Edinburgh UP.

Kinkead-Weekes, M. (1968). The Marble and the Statue: The Exploratory Imagination of D. H. Lawrence. In: *Imagined Worlds: Essays on Some English Novels and Novelists in Honour of John Butt* (ed. M. Mack and I. Gregor), 371–418. London: Methuen.

Kinkead-Weekes, M. (1978). Eros and Metaphor: Sexual Relationship in the Fiction of Lawrence. In: *Lawrence and Women* (ed. A. Smith), 101–121. London: Vision Press.

Kohno, T. (ed.) (2004). *The Collected Art Works of D. H. Lawrence.* Tokyo: Sogensha.

Krockel, C. (2011). *War Trauma and English Modernism: T. S. Eliot and D. H. Lawrence.* Basingstoke: Palgrave Macmillan.

Laird, H. A. (1988). *Self and Sequence: The Poetry of D. H. Lawrence*. Charlottesville: UP of Virginia.

Lawtoo, N. (2020). Lawrence *Contra* (New) Fascism. *College Literature* 47 (2): 287–317.

Leavis, F. R. (1955). *D. H. Lawrence: Novelist*. London: Chatto and Windus.

Lewiecki-Wilson, C. (1994). *Writing Against the Family: Gender in Lawrence and Joyce*. Carbondale: Southern Illinois UP.

Malamud, B. (1979). *Dubin's Lives*. London: Chatto and Windus.

Männiste, I. (ed.) (2019). *D. H. Lawrence, Technology, and Modernity*. London: Bloomsbury.

Mansfield, K. (1999). *In a German Pension*. [1911]. London: Penguin.

Mensch, B. (1991). *D. H. Lawrence and the Authoritarian Personality*. Basingstoke: Macmillan.

Michelucci, S. (2002). *Space and Place in the Works of D. H. Lawrence*, trans. Jill Franks. Jefferson, NC: McFarland and Co.

Millett, K. (1970). *Sexual Politics*. New York: Doubleday.

Millett, R.W. (1983). *The Vultures and the Phoenix: A Study of the Mandrake Press Edition of the Paintings of D. H. Lawrence*. Philadelphia: Art Alliance Press.

Milton, C. (1987). *Lawrence and Nietzsche: A Study in Influence*. Aberdeen: Aberdeen UP.

Moran, J. (2015). *The Theatre of D. H. Lawrence: Dramatic Modernist and Theatrical Innovator*. London: Bloomsbury.

Morsia, E. (2020). *The Many Drafts of D. H. Lawrence: Creative Flux, Genetic Dialogism, and the Dilemma of Endings*. London: Bloomsbury.

Nakabayashi, M. (2011). *The Rhetoric of the Unselfconscious in D. H. Lawrence: Verbalising the Non-Verbal in the Lady Chatterley Novels*. Lanham, MD: University Presses of America.

Phelps, J. and Bell, N. (ed.) (2007). *D. H. Lawrence Around the World: South African Perspectives*. Empangeni: Echoing Green Press.

Pollnitz, C. (n.d.). *D. H. Lawrence and the 'Pensée'*. Paris: Carrefour Alyscamps.

Poplawski, P. (1996). *Language, Art and Reality in D. H. Lawrence's 'St. Mawr': A Stylistic Study*. Lewiston, Queenston, Lampeter: Edwin Mellen Press.

Poplawski, P. (ed.) (2001). *Writing the Body in D. H. Lawrence: Essays on Language, Representation, and Sexuality*. Westport, CT: Greenwood Press.

Preston, P. and Hoare, P. (ed.) (1989). *D. H. Lawrence in the Modern World*. Basingstoke: Macmillan.

Preston, P. (2011). *Working with Lawrence: Texts, Places, Contexts*. Nottingham: Critical, Cultural and Communications Press.

Reeve, N. H. (2003). *Reading Late Lawrence*. New York: Palgrave Macmillan.

Reid, S. (2019). *D. H. Lawrence, Music and Modernism*. Basingstoke: Palgrave Macmillan.

Roberts, N. (2004). *D. H. Lawrence, Travel and Cultural Difference*. Basingstoke: Palgrave Macmillan.

Roberts, N. (2016). *'Sons and Lovers': The Biography of a Novel*. Clemson, SC: Clemson UP.

Ruderman, J. (1984). *D. H. Lawrence and the Devouring Mother: The Search for a Patriarchal Ideal of Leadership*. Durham, NC: Duke UP.

Ruderman, J. (2014). *Race and Identity in D. H. Lawrence: Indians, Gypsies, and Jews*. Basingstoke: Palgrave Macmillan.

Sagar, K. (ed.) (2003). *D. H. Lawrence's Paintings*. London: Chaucer Press.

Sagar, K. (2007). *D. H. Lawrence: Poet*. Tirril: Humanities-Ebooks.

Sagar, K. (2011). *Art for Life's Sake: Essays on D. H. Lawrence*. Nottingham: Critical, Cultural and Communications Press.

Salgādo, G. (1982). *A Preface to Lawrence*. London: Longman.

Schapiro, B. A. (1999). *D. H. Lawrence and the Paradoxes of Psychic Life*. Albany: State U of New York P.

Schorer, M. (ed.) (1977). *'Sons and Lovers': A Facsimile of the Manuscript*. Berkeley: U of California P.

Shaw, G. B. (1914). Common Sense About the War. *The New Statesman Special War Supplement* 4 (84).

Simpson, H. (1982). *D. H. Lawrence and Feminism*. London: Croom Helm.

Spilka, M. (1955). *The Love Ethic of D. H. Lawrence*. Bloomington: Indiana UP.

Spilka, M. (1964). Post-Leavis Lawrence Critics. *Modern Language Quarterly* 25 (2): 212–217.

Squires, M. and Jackson, D. (ed.) (1985). *D. H. Lawrence's "Lady": A New Look at 'Lady Chatterley's Lover'*. Athens, GA: U of Georgia P.

Squires, M. and Cushman, K. (ed.) (1990). *The Challenge of D. H. Lawrence*. Madison: U of Wisconsin P.

Sklar, S. (1975). *The Plays of D. H. Lawrence: A Biographical and Critical Study*. London: Vision.

Stewart, J. (1999). *The Vital Art of D. H. Lawrence: Vision and Expression*. Carbondale: Southern Illinois UP.

Stoltzfus, B. (2022). *D. H. Lawrence's Final Fictions: A Lacanian Perspective*. New York: Lexington Books.

Storch, M. (1990). *Sons and Adversaries: Women in William Blake and D. H. Lawrence*. Knoxville: U of Tennessee P.

Templeton, W. (1993–1994). 'Indians and an Englishman': Lawrence in the American Southwest. *DHLR* 25 (1–3): 14–34.

Turner, J. (2020). *D. H. Lawrence and Psychoanalysis*. Abingdon: Routledge.

Wallace, J. (2005). *D. H. Lawrence, Science and the Posthuman*. Basingstoke: Palgrave Macmillan.

Watson, G. (1997). D. H. Lawrence (in *Women in Love*) on the Desire for Difference and 'the Fascism in Us All'. *The Cambridge Quarterly* 26 (2): 140–154.

Widmer, K. (1962). *The Art of Perversity: D. H. Lawrence's Shorter Fictions*. Seattle: U of Washington P.

Williams, L. R. (1993). *Sex in the Head: Visions of Femininity and Film in D. H. Lawrence*. Hemel Hempstead: Harvester Wheatsheaf.

Worthen, J. (1979). *D. H. Lawrence and the Idea of the Novel*. London: Macmillan.

Worthen, J. (1991a). *D. H. Lawrence*. London: Edward Arnold.

Worthen, J. (1999). *The First 'Women in Love'*. *DHLR* 28 (1–2): 5–27.

Worthen, J. and Harrison, A. (ed.) (2005). *D. H. Lawrence's 'Sons and Lovers': A Casebook*. New York: Oxford UP.

Wright, T. R. (2000). *D. H. Lawrence and the Bible*. Cambridge: Cambridge UP.

Index

The Life of the Author: D. H. Lawrence, First Edition. Andrew Harrison.

l

Poetry

Psychology Books

Short Stories